DATE DUE

TOM WATSON

Agrarian Rebel

C. VANN WOODWARD

Copyright 1938 by C. Vann Woodward
First published by The Macmillan Company, 1938

TO MY MOTHER AND FATHER

Contents

© *Pach Bros., N. Y., 1904.*

AT FORTY-EIGHT: HISTORIAN AND PRESIDENTIAL CANDIDATE

AT FIFTY-FOUR: ANTI-CATHOLIC CRUSADER AND STATE BOSS

Preface

AFTER READING THIS BOOK in manuscript, a friend of mine, a man of excellent instincts and sympathies, offered what might have seemed a strange criticism, had I not known his predilections and half anticipated his reaction. "As I look back," he writes, "I feel a little unhappy over having come through those [latter] chapters with so kindly a feeling toward Watson." Believing that Watson, in some phases of his later life, became the embodiment of much that was detestable, my friend felt that his own better instincts had been betrayed into a false alignment of sympathies. Granting the damaging character of certain chapters, were they, after all, "sufficiently damning"? Were not the splendid battles of Watson's early days overshadowed in importance by his later career, and should he not therefore be blamed for certain aspects of Southern society that both my friend and I deplore and condemn? The criticism started an exchange of philosophies, historical and literary, that led to a result somewhat rare in such transactions—an agreement. Only after I had explained my position in some detail, however, was my friend willing to withdraw his criticism and agree with me. In view of this fact we decided that I had best anticipate similar questions among readers of like mind. Readers of another class deserve an explanation. I refer to those whose impressions of Watson were fixed by the last ten or fifteen years of his career. They will likely be puzzled by the first part of the book, just as my friend was troubled by the last—and for much the same reason.

It is usually a truism to say that the life of a man contains paradoxes. To say this of Tom Watson, however, is to make the only broad generalization one can make concerning the man. His life was a paradox. Especially is this true when the two parts of his career, divided by the interval of eight years that began in 1896, are contrasted. One can not arrive at any fair or true judgment of Watson by considering either of these two aspects of his life to the exclusion of the other. When a liberal journal fastens upon Watson the responsibility for "the sinister forces of intolerance, superstition, prejudice, religious jingoism, and mobbism," it is indulging in half-truths as surely as does the veriest demagogue it denounces. The term "Southern demagogue" should be recognized for what it is, a political epithet. It does not contribute anything to our understanding of the men to whom it is applied. I hold no brief for men of this type, nor for Tom Watson in so far as he was representative of them. I do insist upon understanding them clearly. I do not believe it is accurate to blame Watson for the "sinister forces" already mentioned. To do so would be to assign him far too important a rôle, a rôle that belongs to the vastly more impersonal forces of economics and race and historical heritage. To do so, moreover, would be to miss at the same time the deep meaning of his story. He did not produce those forces: he was produced by them. They thwarted at every turn his courageous struggle in the face of them during his early Populist battles, and they led him into the futility and degeneration of his later career. This was what made his life a personal tragedy. Although I have not sought to impose the view upon the reader, I might confess here my private feeling that his story is also in many ways the tragedy of a class, and more especially the tragedy of a section.

To counterbalance various difficulties encountered in writing this book, I have had several advantages, one of which only a biographer can fully appreciate. Miss Georgia Durham Watson has not only permitted but insisted upon my complete freedom in the use of the wide range of manuscripts, photographs, and materials which she has made available to me. Had it not been for her truly rare qualities of intellectual detachment, which are combined with a genuine devotion to her grandfather, this work would have presented problems so difficult that I should never have attempted it. I am deeply grateful to her. In no sense, however, does she stand as sponsor to this work, nor does she share responsibility for any views expressed in it.

I have received valued assistance and counsel from many people. Foremost among these is Professor Howard K. Beale, who has given unsparingly of his time and attention in advising me in the latter stages of the work. For this aid I am especially grateful. I also recall with gratitude the many hours I have spent across a littered desk from Dr. Rupert B. Vance, plundering that storehouse of knowledge about the South. I gladly acknowledge my indebtedness to Professors A. R. Newsome, F. M. Green, W. W. Pierson, H. T. Lefler, W. G. Carleton, M. J. Dauer and J. A. Barnes for their numerous kindnesses, and to Dr. Howard W. Odum for his consistent encouragement and support. Part of the work on this book was made possible by fellowships granted by the General Education Board. Two loyal comrades have given aid and encouragement that has been invaluable—my wife, Glenn MacLeod Woodward, upon whose shoulders fell the heavy burden of typing the manuscript, and Mr. Glenn W. Rainey, who has cheered the work along from the beginning to end.

C. VANN WOODWARD

CHAPTER I

The Heritage

ONE DECEMBER MORNING in 1863 a diminutive, red-headed boy sat astride a large bay mare at the railway station of Thomson, Georgia. Waiting there for his grandfather's mail, he watched a locomotive puff by pulling a string of freight cars filled with Yankee prisoners on their way to Augusta.

"They passed through the town with defiant laughter, with ringing cheers, and with the resounding song of 'John Brown's body lies mouldering in the grave, but his soul is marching on.' "[1] The sight of so many Blue Coats was exciting enough for a boy of seven, but the astonishing thing about these prisoners was their gayety.

Tom Watson was old enough to remember the gay fanfare of patriotism and confident gallantry with which his father and his two uncles had set off to whip the Yankees. Now in December of the third year of war, months after Gettysburg, he felt in place of that old buoyancy and debonair confidence a pervading mood of despondence and melancholy. For him the change was echoed in the songs the people sang, in the plaintive, wailing refrain that repeated itself in the popular songs of 1863: in "Lorena," in "Kitty Wills," in "Juanita," in "Just Before the Battle, Mother," in "When This Cruel War Is Over." "It gave one the shivers," he remembered.[2] The contrast

[1] Thomas E. Watson, *Bethany*, p. 365.
[2] *Ibid.*, p. 364.

1

between these songs and the one the Yankee prisoners sang was too marked to escape his notice.

Sudden, tearful departures and anxious waiting for the return of dead or wounded were woven into the texture of the boy's earliest impressions. Indeed, the decline in the fortunes of the Confederacy seemed to reflect itself in the fortunes of the house of Watson. Tom's father, John Smith Watson, was twice wounded, and there remained in the boy's mind the experience "of going with my mother through all the confusion and dangers of the time, to find my father and bring him home." [3] The preceding year Tom's favorite uncle, William Watson, was sent home with an illness of which he died on December 8, 1862. Later his Uncle Tom Peter came home to his family an incurable invalid. Then, in that winter of 1863, his grandfather, in the midst of the family's woes, suffered a stroke of paralysis that took away his voice and blighted his mind.

It was the stroke which laid his grandfather low that came closest to the boy. For while his father and uncles had departed, returned wounded to die, or set off to fight again, his grandfather had always remained—white-haired, stately, imperturbable, a rock of refuge in the storm.

The house of Thomas Miles Watson was built on his plantation three miles out of the village of Thomson, then in Columbia County. The main portion of the house, the original part, built solidly against the winds of the hilltop, has weathered the winters of a century and still stands, though overshadowed and hidden from the road by the large frame structure later built in front of it. Limited in size by the length of the pine logs of which it was constructed, the house measured only twenty by twenty-seven feet. The logs, hewn square with the broadax, smoothed with the foot-adze, and deeply interlocked at the ends, fitted snugly together without any covering of weather-boards. Through the center of the log house ran a partition, cutting it

[3] T. E. W., *Life and Speeches of Thomas E. Watson*, p. 9.

into two rooms, one of which was heated by a cavernous fireplace on the side. Overhead was a loft, and part of the roof extended to cover a shed room and a back porch. Sometime before the war Squire Watson had added an ell to his house, connecting it to the original structure by a piazza at the front. The addition served as the "company room."

This was the house in which on September 5, 1856, Tom Watson, christened Edward Thomas, was born. "It did not in the least," he once wrote of his birthplace, "resemble a Grecian Temple which had been sent into exile, and which was striving unsuccessfully to look at ease among corn-cribs, cow-pens, horse-stables, pig-sties, chicken-houses, Negro cabins, and worm-fenced cotton fields."

If the house would never have been taken for that of an aristocrat, neither would it have been mistaken as the cabin of a frontiersman, nor the humbler dwelling of the "poor white." It was "just a plain house," according to Tom. Yet of such was the Kingdom of Cotton, for Tom Watson's birthplace was more nearly representative of the Southern Squirarchy than either colonnaded temple or squatter's hut. Since the relinquishment of Southern leadership by the Virginians, the South had drawn the great part of its distinguished statesmen—Calhoun, McDuffie, Yancey, Stephens, Davis—from homes of just this class. Senator George McDuffie, born two miles down the road, was pleased to accept the hospitality of Squire Watson, when, shortly before his death, he had returned to Georgia to visit his birthplace.[4] Robert Toombs and Alexander Stephens, riding the circuit together, could feel equally at home around the Watson table, when they stopped on their way to Augusta from the neighboring towns of Washington and Crawfordville, where they lived. Joel Chandler Harris, growing up about this time in a similar Georgia community, where he had "every opportunity to shiver under the chill of snobbism, if such an atmos-

[4] T. E. W to V M McDuffie, undated copy, Watson MSS.

3

phere had prevailed in his native village," spoke of his neighbors as "the most democratic people the world has ever seen." [5] It was a peculiar democracy, of course—a "Greek Democracy," the statesmen said.

Squire "Long-Tom" Watson was the master of forty-five slaves and of 1,372 acres of land, an estate valued at $55,000 in 1860.[6] His possessions would not rank him with the greatest plantation masters of the state; and yet of the 118,000 white families in Georgia in 1860, only a little more than a third owned any slaves at all, and of these only 6,363 had twenty or more slaves. Squire Watson was, therefore, one of that class whose cause was most closely identified with that of the Confederacy, the class that had most to fear from the loss of the Confederate cause.

Except what he wrote in the form of fiction there are few hints that remain of the first nine years of Tom's boyhood on the plantation, other than some random notes made on the flyleaf of an early diary.[7] Here one learns of such adventures as, "Going to spit in the Alligator's eye," "Breaking pig down in the loins," "Sleeping in the mill house," "Father and Frank Callaher pitting a wounded hawk against Jennie Fuller's rooster." Here, too, one is presented with a list of his fights, fights with Ben Perry, with Billy Farr, with Frank Curtis. Then there comes, "The night of father's departure for the Army," and later, "At a theatre in Augusta during the War, scenes representing horse standing by dead master."

As for the slaves, "They were treated well, upon the same principle that the horses were amply fed." What impressed Tom about his Negro mammy was her unique virtue: "It was said among white men, as well as black, that no temptation could reach her." He recalled also the presence of "a bright mulatto boy on the place, named Sam, whose mother's color was a

[5] Julia Collier Harris, *Life of Joel Chandler Harris*, pp. 8-9.
[6] Columbia County Tax Returns for 1860.
[7] Kept during the years c. 1870–1873, it was more of a journal than a diary, and is referred to hereafter as "Journal 1."

4

smooth universal black, and whose son Sam bore a distinct likeness to my uncle." [8]

"All was steady, all was quiet, all was regular," as Tom remembered the life of the plantation. "Day followed day with respectable monotony; and each found its task done, in order, without haste and without rest." [9] So immutable seemed the multitudinous functionings of his plantation world—each slave with his task, each field with its crop, each season with its duties—that to Tom it was all "like some steady law of nature." Certainly it was a kindly "law of nature" that could produce in such abundance the peace, and security, and plenty of his grandfather's plantation. So, at least, it seemed to Tom.

The end of the War, followed almost immediately by the death of his grandfather, as if by some momentous consequence, was to mark a change so definite and complete in Tom's scheme of things that truly it would seem to him as if nature itself had been perverted. The boy of nine was to find himself rudely jolted out of his warm nest into a world that was at war with itself, where there was no "rock of refuge," where, until he reached manhood, there was little for him but insecurity and poverty.

Those early plantation years, so intimately associated in his mind with his grandfather—who seemed to him a figure of classic serenity and lordly dignity, "tall, venerable, imposing"—became for Tom Watson a symbol of "the days before the War." Perhaps it was out of a compensatory urge, induced by the side-meat and sorghum diet of the lean years after the War, that there grew in his emotional life an irrational core of nostalgia for a lost paradise of childhood. When, as a middle-aged man, he came to write about his grandfather and the plantation, it was with the idolatrous veneration of a boy bereft of an inheritance of grandeur:

My grandfather takes his silver-headed cane and walks around and about the lots, the fields, the orchards, the gardens, the woods—and

[8] T. E. W., *Bethany*, p. 17.
[9] T. E. W., *Prose Miscellanies*, p. 79.

walks slowly, with the calm, dignified air of a master who expects to find everything going as it should; the settled, confident air of one who is used to being obeyed, and who has no anxieties; a stately, self-contained, self-reliant man. . . .

As I look back to it now, it seems to me that my grandfather's farm must have belonged to another world, so complete have been the changes wrought by two generations. It seems to me that there was neither feverish haste upon it nor vagrant leisure, fretful exactitude nor slipshod looseness, miserly gripping nor spendthrift waste. . . .

That old Southern homestead was a little kingdom, a complete social and industrial organism, almost wholly sufficient unto itself, asking less of the outer world than it gave. How sound, sane, healthy it appears, even now, when compared to certain phases of certain other systems![10]

The old order of agrarian rulership that claimed Tom's boyhood loyalties was to retain strong hold upon them all his days, even through the defeat and ultimate decay of the old order. Throughout the triumphant rise of the New South, in which he was to fight his battles, his face remained fixed upon his vision of agrarian bliss. In the Watsonian economics this vision always lay beyond statistics and platforms, and unless it is taken into account there is no understanding the ordeal of Tom Watson in the New South.

* * * * * *

The pioneer generation of Watsons had done its work in Georgia and moved off the scene a century before. In 1768, Thomas Watson and his two sons, John and Jacob, moved to Georgia along with forty families of "the people called Quakers" from Orange County, North Carolina, to which they had "but lately" come from Pennsylvania.[11] This small colony of Friends came to take possession of a reserve of twelve thousand acres in

[10] T. E. W., *Bethany*, pp. 10-19
[11] M. A. Candler, "The Quaker Settlement of Wrightsborough, Georgia," *Magazine of History*, XIV (Aug, 1911)

St. Paul's Parish, thirty miles west of Augusta, granted them by Governor James Wright. The following year, after seventy more families had joined the colony, the grant was extended, a town, called Wrightsborough in honor of the Royal governor, was laid out, and land was allotted to petitioners. Among these petitioners of 1769 was Thomas Watson, whose name comes first on the list, with a grant of five hundred acres.[12] Thereafter, each of the five lineal generations that descended from Thomas, the Quaker pioneer, to Tom, the grandson of Squire Thomas M. Watson, made its home on or near the original Quaker grant.

Colonial Georgia of the later eighteenth century was not the ideal land in which to found the kingdom of peace and brotherly love. Forces that had damned one Utopia could as easily damn another—and still others. The thirteenth colony had put aside the philanthropic purposes of its founders along with their Utopian hopes; slavery was officially admitted in 1749; Indians and Spaniards had to be dealt with frequently in ways neither peaceful nor brotherly; clashes between colonial and Royal interests did not encourage peaceful neutrality. The first colony of Friends to appear in Georgia settled in 1754 upon the site later occupied by the Wrightsborough Quakers. When faced by the threat of an Indian invasion and the proposal of the governor to recall all grants of land and issue new warrants on terms especially hard on non-slave owners, the early Friends gave up their land and moved on.

The later Wrightsborough settlers exhibited more tenacity in their attempt, though not without cost to certain of their most cherished principles. They were frequently warned by their leaders against "superfluity of apparil," "wearing faulds in their coats," and "such vain and vicecious proceedings as frollicking, fiddling and danceing." While peculiarities of speech and dress meant raillery and isolation for Quaker children, other convictions in the matter of slavery and physical violence drew

[12] A. D. Candler, *Colonial Records of the State of Georgia*, X, pp 690-694.

contempt and even hostility upon the heads of Quaker elders.

When war with England threatened, the Quakers were quick to declare their loyalty to the King. Inhabitants of Wrightsborough, among them Thomas Watson and his two sons, signed a resolution repudiating the action of the Savannah patriots who had endorsed the "destroying of a quantity of tea" by the citizens of Boston.[13] The Georgia Quakers, as a sect, remained noncombatants throughout the Revolution, although they disowned a considerable number of their members for fighting. Their position as neutrals and non-combatants seems to have met with little respect from either side, since in 1780 they complain of "being opprest by the violent behavior of the Militia in these parts" and of being "illegally deprived of both liberty and property." No sooner was the War over than their meeting house, being on the property of Sir James Wright, a loyal adherent to the Crown, was confiscated and sold by the state.

Social isolation, military violence, and political oppression were evils to be endured with prayerful humility and long-suffering charity by the faithful among the peace-loving Friends. The constant pinch of economic competition with slave labor, however, was distressing to the firmest in the faith. Owning few if any slaves, the Quakers sank into the lower classes, their frugality and industry degraded by the influence of slavery. As early as 1786 a Quaker petition was presented to the Georgia Assembly "respecting some enlargements to the enslaved Negroes." Much of their feeling in regard to slavery, no doubt, was due to abhorrence in which their religion held the institution. In 1802 a certain Zachariah Dicks, thought among Friends to have the gift of prophecy, visited Wrightsborough and urged the brethren to remove themselves from the midst of slavery, prophesying a terrible rebellion among the slaves and a bloody internecine war within the lifetime of children then living. So powerful were the effects of his prophecy that it produced a panic in the town, and the following year Quakers migrated in

[13] A. D. Candler, *loc. cit.*

8

large numbers to the free Northwest.[14] Thereafter, Wrightsborough was destined to become one of the "dead towns" of Georgia, and the Friends' little kingdom of peace and brotherly love was moribund.

The first two generations of Watsons, whether out of poverty or piety, owned no slaves. They did not migrate to the Northwest with their brethren, but remained on their land, which had been greatly diminished by that time. Later, when the Baptist denomination began to flourish, the Watsons sought consolation in that faith, whose ministers found divine sanction for the institution of slavery. Peter Watson, grandson of the pioneer Thomas, appears to have been the first slave owner. In 1808 his slaves numbered six, and they increased to fifteen by 1821.[15] To what extent the family fortunes grew in the capable hands of Thomas Miles Watson, son of Peter, we have already seen. No longer were the Watsons set apart from their fellow men by the peculiarity of their speech and dress and by their ideas of the ways of God to man: they were right-thinking citizens and God-fearing Baptists. In no way, however, do the four generations of Watsons appear to have distinguished themselves from hundreds of other farmers in Georgia, either in service of the state or the pursuit of the arts.

The three sons of Thomas Miles Watson are said to have had that lanky angularity and sandy-red blondness common in the family. One of them, John Smith Watson, born August 15, 1833, became the father of Tom Watson. He is remembered by one of his sons as "just an average man" and by another son as "not a religious man," but "what would be called a sporting man." [16] He acquired the name of a light-hearted good fellow, always ready to lay a bet on anything from the turn of a card to the age of a horse, to play his fiddle, "call the dance," or to enter into an occasional "scrape" of no very serious nature. When John

[14] M. A. Candler, *loc. cit.*
[15] Tax Records of Columbia County, Georgia, 1808–1821.
[16] William A. Watson to C. V. W., Jan. 17, 1934.

9

was in his twenty-first year he met Ann Eliza Maddox, to whom he was married in January, 1855.

The Maddox family was also of Quaker descent, although the first settlers spelled their name Maddock. Joseph Maddock, in whose name the early business of the Friends with the state was conducted, was the first clerk of the Friendly meeting, and the leader of the migration from North Carolina. Elected a member of the Provincial Congress of 1775, he declined to take his seat, probably because of the hostility of the members to England. When William Bartram, the celebrated English naturalist, visited the colony in 1773, he was entertained by Joseph Maddock, whom he mentioned in complimentary terms as "a public spirited chief magistrate." In the hands of Henry Maddox the fortunes of the family had reached a condition bordering on poverty. Henry and his wife, Letitia Maurice, a native of Wales, lived "in a humble way" on their farm about eight miles out of Augusta on the road to Thomson. Their family was large and it was not convenient for children to remain longer than necessary under the parental roof. So it was that Ann Eliza, when she was about eighteen, left home unmarried to seek work —rather an unusual procedure in her day. She became a seamstress with a wealthy family in Augusta.

After their marriage Ann Eliza and John shared the home of Thomas M. Watson on his plantation three miles out of Thomson for a few years. A little older than her husband, Ann was also of a more sober turn of mind. Like her husband, she had received no more than an elementary school education, but unlike him she read a great deal and was "fond of books"—a peculiarity that her neighbors often remarked. She did not confine her reading to her Bible, but read books with strange names, was "particularly fond of French history," and could entertain her children and visitors by the hour with stories of great and glamorous persons.[17]

There must have been little time for reading and story-tell-

[17] William A. Watson to C. V. W., Jan. 17, 1934.

ing, however, for within the year they were married the first child, Addie Augusta, arrived, and the next year a boy, whom they named Edward Thomas. Some two years later, when his family promised still further expansion, John Watson bought a farm two miles on the opposite side of Thomson and moved there. His six hundred acres were worked by five families of slaves. When John went off to war, Ann Eliza was left not only with the domestic management, but with the direction of a large farm upon her shoulders. By the end of the war three more children, two boys and a girl, had been born, and a fourth was expected. There were seven children in all.

CHAPTER II

Scholar and Poet

A FEW MILES NORTH of Thomson, in the quiet, white-columned town of Washington there gathered on May 5, 1865, a tragic group of men—President Davis and a few of the cabinet officers of the doomed Confederacy. Washington, the home of Robert Toombs, was as fit a place as any in the South for the end of the Confederacy, since it was as near to the heart of the South as a place could well be. These few men, who had directed the destinies of a once powerful government through four years of war, were now helpless fugitives. The last cabinet meeting was held, the last order was written, farewells were said, and the Confederate Government was a thing of the past.

Private John Smith Watson, wounded and penniless, reached home to find his father near the point of death and incapable of recognizing his own son. One June 4 he died, never knowing that the old regime was gone. With one brother also dead and the other an invalid, John, now the head of the house of Watson, traded his farm for his sister's share in the family estate and moved back to his father's house. Calling the slaves together one day and telling them they were free, John found that "not a negro remained on the place the next" and "every house in the 'quarter' was empty." [1] Crops that had been planted in the spring were now in weeds, and the plantation as a whole was in sad

[1] T. E. W., *Prose Miscellanies*, pp. 69-70.

12

need of repair. His slaves vanished, his Confederate money worthless, his state in a condition of turmoil and lawlessness, John faced an uncertain future. In view of these circumstances, John's first action, though characteristic, would seem to indicate that he, like his father, had lived on into the new order unaware that the old one had ended. At a time when many families were glad enough to salvage from the ruins of their houses enough to cover their heads, when thousands were destitute, when building materials were at fabulous prices and money was not to be had, John began the construction of a mansion such as his fathers had only dreamed of. Built directly in front of the old place, the huge new structure reduced his father's rude log house to the proportions of servants' quarters. The façade of John's new house bore all the grandiloquent trappings of a dwelling of the aristocracy—ornate portico, with balustraded balcony and beetling gable supported by great fluted columns. It was as if John had triumphed over defeat and, by simply willing it to be, had not only restored the old order, but realized all it had aspired to. True, the interior of the second story remained unplastered,[2] but the exterior presented a bold and imposing front to the world, and up and down the road for miles there was no house so grand as John Watson's.

In his attempt to maintain a plantation without the foundation of slave labor upon which the system had rested, John was no more successful than others who attempted it. His plan of hiring white labor failed miserably from the first, and the ruinous declines in cotton prices in 1866 and 1867 piled more debt on top of that incurred in building his bepillared mansion. Gazing upon weed-grown fields from his splendid portico, John came slowly to realize that the way of his fathers, much less what they aspired to, was not for him. On May 5, 1868, his place was sold under an execution in favor of his creditors for a mere fraction

[2] Interview with L. C. Smith, Columbia County, Dec., 1933; Mr. Smith's father bought John Watson's house in 1868.

13

of its value.[3] John then moved his family to a modest house on a small farm about a half mile out of Thomson.

By this time John's garment of defiance had worn into bare threads of apathy and despondence. "My father used to be virtually paralyzed for weeks by what he called 'the blues,'" wrote his son Tom.[4] John came to depend more and more upon drink for solace in his attacks of "the blues," and his weakness for gambling grew upon him. Tom once pointed out to a friend a room in Thomson in which he said his father had lost fifteen hundred dollars in one night. By 1868 he was reduced perforce to gaming for more modest stakes. In that year he was in such straits that Tom was forced to drop out of school, until Professor Epenetus Alexis Steed, master of a school in Thomson, agreed to admit him "with the understanding that the tuition could be paid whenever in the future he might become able."

From the time he came to school there at the age of twelve until his death fifty-four years later, with the exception of a few years, Tom Watson made his home in, or quite near, the village of Thomson. In 1856, the year of Tom's birth, a young man named B. L. Neal arrived in Thomson to attend the "Greenway Institute," a school for boys founded in 1853. "Thomson was then in the woods," he writes. "There were two stores, but a yoke of oxen could have pulled all the goods for sale in them at one load."[5] The village had been incorporated only two years earlier, although it was mentioned as early as 1837 as a "place of deposit lately begun on the Georgia railroad." Named for a railroad engineer, the village grew up in the unlovely image of the typical "railroad town"—a serrated line of one-story frame buildings paralleling the rails and separated from them by a wide street.

In Tom's boyhood there still lingered about Thomson something of an aura of frontier days. "In the grocery which stood on

[3] "Book of Deeds, Columbia County," p. 557.
[4] T. E. W. to William W. Brewton, quoted in William W. Brewton, *Life of Thomas E Watson*, p. 376
[5] B L Neal, *Son of the American Revolution*, p. 43.

14

the flat, called the 'slashes,' they could show you the spot where Dick Hattaway had cut the life out of Abe McDonald with a bowie-knife," wrote Watson. "There were places, also, where equally respectable citizens had shot at others equally respectable, but as there were several of these places, and they were lacking in individuality, nobody cared particularly to see them." [6] His uncle "would ride miles to take part in a gander pulling," and his father was an assiduous attender of barbecues, camp-meetings, and all-day-speakings. Tom, who was frequently allowed to accompany his father, was sometimes the witness of eye-gougings, knifings, and drunken brawls that marked the occasions.

The turbulence and violence which characterized the years from 1868 to 1871, however, could not be attributed to a frontier heritage. In those years the state was in the midst of the most thoroughgoing revolution that ever changed the face of its society—military reconstruction. Most of the violence, later investigated by Congress, was confined to two sections, the extreme northwestern counties, and a part of the upper cotton-belt, and was particularly prevalent in Columbia and Warren counties —the two counties out of which McDuffie County was cut in 1870, with Thomson as the seat of government. In these counties "there were several notorious leaders of the blacks, some carpet-baggers, and some native Republicans, who kept their influence over the Negroes by inciting them against the whites. This was the cause of several of the most notorious outrages in the state." [7] Here the Negroes constituted sixty per cent or more of the population, white leaders were disfranchised, and the exploitation of ignorant Negro voters by corrupt politicians backed by Federal guns was so shameless that there grew among white people the conviction that the Negroes must be pushed out of politics by the most effective means that came to hand. Outright payment of cash for Negro votes was the solution for many counties, but

[6] T. E. W., *Bethany*, p. 6.
[7] C. Mildred Thompson, *Reconstruction in Georgia*, p. 366.

in Warren and Columbia the method was intimidation. "Warren County especially was the scene of much lawlessness and great activity from Ku Klux bands," and two mob murders here figured largely in the political controversy over the second reconstruction of Georgia. In Columbia, where the Republican vote was reduced from 1,222 in April, 1868, to one vote in November of the same year, it was judged that "the Ku Klux made their work thorough." In June of the next year General Terry, reporting that there was "no civil law in Warren County, that an insurrectionary organization terrorized the place," sent a detachment of troops to take control.[8] These troops, more than anything else, provoked the native whites to trembling indignation.

The squad of Blue Coats stationed at Thomson was received with bitter protests and demonstrations. A mass meeting of citizens was called a few miles out of the town at Union Church. A Methodist preacher was in the midst of a fiery speech when a squad of horsemen in uniform trotted by. Striking a defiant pose, the orator shouted, "We can't even hold a quiet, peaceable meeting without being spied upon and disturbed by these military masters!" His face flushed with excitement, young Tom stood below the platform with his father. "I remember even now," he said when an old man, "the flame of wrath that leapt into the eyes of that preacher, when he saw the Blue Coat cavalry. . . . I actually believe that if the squad of cavalry had not taken another road on their return to Thomson a great tragedy would have resulted."[9]

Tom attended many such meetings with his father. "It was in this way," he relates, "that I came to know of such Southern leaders as Howell Cobb, Rance Wright, John B. Gordon, Robert Toombs and Benjamin H. Hill." Politics, as Tom Watson first knew the art, was an heroic business of mysterious, white-robed horsemen galloping at midnight, and majestic orators, whose

[8] *Ibid.*, p. 367.
[9] *Columbia Sentinel*, Aug. 16, 1920.

long hair waved in the breezes as the periods rolled. Politics was also a potent magic whereby a distraught and oppressed people might conjure up forgotten, as well as imaginary, grandeurs, unite with intense purpose, and cast off their oppressors. It was the political drama that inspired one of his first unhappy attempts at verse, a poem, "To the South," [10] written when he was about fourteen, which began, "Land of the South, Oh, do not despair," and ended

> Soon will cease the Yankee thy soil to stain,
> Soon will thy ruins cease to be seen,
> Soon will thy fields again be green,
> Yes, soon will come that shining ray
> To lead us forth to glorious day!

Influences more subtle and intimate, and yet, at his age, more important and significant than even social and political revolution, were at work upon Tom's life at this time. A frail, sensitive boy in early adolescence, Tom still had to reckon daily with a mother and father. An insight upon parental influences is gained through a letter which Watson wrote his wife in regard to the rearing of his own son. After recommending the practice of patience, firmness, and sympathetic understanding, he adds:

Had I been trained in this manner, a very different man would be sitting here tonight. . . . On my heart there would not be the scar which many a trial has left there; and my memory would be rid of many a bitter recollection. I have imagined enemies where there were none: been tortured by indignities which were the creatures of my own fancy, and have magnified the gloom of every reverse. . . .

The better part of me is poisoned. A mistaken training leaves a trace from which there is no escape. Between the warp and woof of my life its busy shuttle will carry the black thread till the loom stops.

Had I been firmly governed and not with fitful harshness: had I not been abused, ridiculed, mocked and scorned there would be sun-

[10] MS. Journal I.

shine where now is shadow. I could have joined in the companionship of the world, shared its loves, laughs, friendships and aspirations. As it is I stand where my boyhood put me, fed by my own thoughts, led by my own hopes, scourged by my own troubles.

A sensitive spirit wounded by those who should have nurtured, sees all things in a false color, is proud of its own isolation, magnifies its defects, is unfitted for the intercourse of the world and as far as the necessities will allow retires within itself and imagines that all others are more fortunate, more deserving and more happy. Words fail to describe such a misfortune. A presence that poisons every joy, stains every beauty, checks every impulse. A shadow that follows like a hungry wolf . . .[11]

As an indictment of his parents this letter is indeed a terrible thing, if taken too tragically. But that Tom was correct in fixing the entire blame for his unhappy traits upon his parents there is some room for doubt—if for no other reason than that he "sees all things in a false color." Of some of the specific charges he makes against them—harshness, abuse, ridicule, mockery, and scorn—one or both of his parents were possibly guilty. But the lot of John and Ann was a hard one; Tom was an extremely sensitive boy, and it is not improbable that some of the abuse and scorn he felt were "creatures of his own fancy." The score that he held against his parents, which he confessed to no one but his wife, Tom apparently did not allow to interfere with the discharge of filial duties. One can not be sure which of his parents he held more to account. However, there is perhaps a clue for the psychologist in the fact that, in writing his autobiographical novel, Tom makes himself several years older than he was, and has his father die when he was a baby. It is his uncle who was the hero of the book. Elsewhere he speaks of his mother with a passionate devotion which is unquestionably sincere, and we know that she proved a loyal ally in several crises of his youth.

[11] T. E. W. to Mrs. Thomas E. Watson, Aug. 4, 1883, in the possession of Georgia D. Watson.

Interpreted with discernment and caution, however, this extraordinary self-analysis provides a key to the enigma that was Tom Watson's character, and an insight into the personal tragedy that was alike implicit in his most fantastic crusade and his most statesmanlike action. "I have imagined enemies where there were none: been tortured by indignities which were the creatures of my own fancy . . ." Had these lines, and those that follow, been a deathbed reverie instead of the immature reflections of a young man of twenty-six upon the threshold of a long and varied career (he was then holding his first public office), one might credit their author with a retrospective perspicacity given to few men. He paints his self-portrait exclusively in gloomy colors, "magnifies its defects," as he puts it, and omits all the lighter shades of relief. Still, these dark colors, if disproportionately used, all belong to the subject. They speak of the furtiveness, the vindictiveness, the suspicion of the introvert and recluse, qualities which crowded his life, particularly his later life, with delusions—delusions of persecution, of grandeur, delusions of many kinds. But these are all the darker colors, and there·are many grays and blues and yellows.

There is one record of Tom's appearance as a schoolboy, a "tintype" made when he was about twelve or thirteen. In one hand a dinner-bucket and book; pulled firmly down over protruding ears a wide, white wool hat; his face one gay patch of freckles, his nose small and delicate, his eyebrows and mouth two straight lines, rigidly parallel. Under the wool hat was a shock of thick sandy-red hair. Perhaps it was because his hair was a shade too dark that his schoolmates did not call him "Red," and perhaps it was because of something else. At least four of his schoolmates, now living, agree that he possessed an unusually quick temper and a disposition to attack with waspish fury on small provocation. Tom himself gleefully records numbers of his fights in his diary, fights that as a rule turned out the worse for him. His admirers have it that his combats were usually undertaken in behalf of the underdog—as indeed some of them

19

were. Once when Tom—a boy of fourteen—was working as a clerk in "Dosh" Massengale's grocery store at Norwood, a drunken lout, "of robust size and strength," struck an old cripple in his presence. Snatching up the huge knife that lay on the cheese counter, Tom made for the drunk in good earnest, crying, "Don't you hit him again!" His brother William tells a story of the boy's championship of a Negro whom his father's overseer had beaten. But there are equally reliable stories that bespeak a tyrannical petulance at interference with his plans, a trait sometimes appearing as peevish irascibility, sometimes as sheer red rage. A schoolmate tells of sitting in school one morning, head in his book and feet propped up on the stove, while Tom was adding wood to the fire. Suddenly, without any warning, a heavy stick of wood came down with a sharp crack across his shins. Outraged, the boy looked up to see Tom calmly putting in more wood. This same schoolmate later became a strong political supporter of Watson, following him loyally through many fights. Then one day Tom passed his friend on the street and, without apparent cause, refused to speak. His follower was hurt, but not surprised: "It was like Tom," he said.[12] It is these latter incidents which better prepare one for the day, when in a dispute with his brother Forrest over a jointly owned sawmill, Tom—not figuratively but quite literally—attacked a buzzing circular saw and demolished it with a sledge hammer.

Epenetus Alexis Steed, pastor of the Baptist Church and, with his brother, master of the school Tom attended, so captivated the boy's imagination that he mentioned him again and again in later life. Graduated from Mercer University in 1851, Steed had for several years been professor of ancient languages at a college at Clinton, Mississippi. Steed, wrote Watson, was an "indolent giant" with "a great head, fit to bear a crown"; it also seems that he was a great chewer of tobacco, a great quoter of the classics, and, when in the mood, a great orator. Watson pictures himself watching "through a mist of happy tears" while his master

[12] Interview with B. P. O'Neal, Macon, Ga., Nov., 1933.

"would rise, rise into the very azure of eloquence, and hover above us, like an eagle in the air . . ." Then, after one of these sporadic flights, "he would sink back into jolly indolence," indifferent and unambitious. Yet it was "he, the unambitious" who in his pupil Tom "kindled the spark of ambition that will never die." [13]

Professor Steed seems to have taken a special interest in the boy, arranging for him to defer payment of tuition indefinitely and encouraging him in his reading. Waiting for classes to begin one morning, Tom was astonished to see his teacher break into "a passion of sobs" over his morning newspaper, then arise, and with the words, "General Lee is dead!" dismiss school. When the day came for "examinations" Tom selected the subject, "The Character of Lee," for his speech. In a composition book he kept at the time is a copy of the speech, and at the end, this note: "This was written soon after the death of Lee. Of course it is a very poor 'character.' I only chose the subject because I knew it would engage the sympathies of the audience. This was the first speech I ever composed." He was awarded the second prize.

In this same composition book—which also served as commonplace book and diary—there are quantities of adolescent versifying. Of this verse there is nothing especially remarkable, except, perhaps, its author's confession of his own limitations, as in one stanza from "Glennway Academy," dated January, 1872:

> To the left is Watson who tries to ride
> Pegasus the steed of the muses
> But though he often starts him along
> To fly Pegasus refuses.

The other poems are in a much, very much, more serious vein One refrains from further quotation in deference to the poet' maturer judgment, which appears in the comment above the firs poem, written in the bolder hand he adopted when a college

[13] T. E. W., *Prose Miscellanies*, p. 155.

sophomore: "All these rhyming pieces I wrote when laboring under a severe attack of 'Durn fool.' " However, it is from his poems that we learn of Tom's first romance, and of the charms of "Theo. E. Story, The Moon which forces my tides." Their names and initials are written together again and again, and it is possible, as has been suggested, that Tom was persuaded to reverse the order of his given names to correspond with the initials of his sweetheart, for it was during the affair that he changed his signature from "E. Thomas" to "Thomas E. Watson." Theodosia, who inspired numerous lyrics, was inconstant in her affection it seems: on August 11, 1871, one finds the fourteen-year-old poet imploring the "gentle river" to

> Tell her of this furrowed brow;—
> Tell her of this sunken eye,
> Of youthful vigor too quick fled by.

> *   *   *   *   *   *

> Yes, hated of all, hating all,
> I'll tread life's journey till I fall.

The romance of Theodosia and Tom, in spite of reverses, flourished for several years. But at the foot of his most languishing lyric the irreverent sophomore writes in purple, blasphemous ink: "Puppy Love puke of the most unadulterated kind."

Poetry and romance, however, could never absorb all the interests of a farm-boy who from the age of twelve had owned a single-barrelled shotgun and a dog. In the earlier, rounded handwriting are several accounts of fishing parties, hunts, and camping trips. Leather-bound composition books were apparently not to be had for the asking, for after filling the book with poems and sketches the boy turns back to the front page and with scrupulous neatness crowds every fraction of marginal space with notes from his reading. In and out of the serrate indenta-

22

tions of quatrains run statistics on insanity in Wales and England, wine consumption in France, the speed of meteors, and from page to page in the interstices of limping iambics a history of electrical discoveries—a curiously composite picture of the boy's mind.

To fill out the gaps in the picture of his mental development there are the scrapbooks which Tom kept from early childhood.[14] The earliest of these, made out of what appears to be one of his grandfather's plantation ledgers, is filled with pictures and clippings from *Godey's Lady Book*, newspaper doggerel, comic drawings, an indiscriminate sprinkling of Father Ryan, Edgar Allan Poe, Josh Billings, Joaquin Miller, Lord Byron, Longfellow, and a collection of religious and calendar lithographs of the type entitled, "Au Revoir," "The Kiss," and "Saved." The impression one has is that of a myth-hungry boy groping for nourishment in an environment that had little to offer but unpalatable realities.

Still more revealing, perhaps, is his "List of books read up to 1872." [15] As the oldest son in the family, Tom was undoubtedly needed at the plough and the hoe at this time. For John no longer sat in the shade and directed his labor through overseers; times were terribly hard, debts were pressing, and John had to work his small farm diligently to make a living for his family of seven children. Nevertheless, although his younger brothers were pressed into the farm work, Tom went scot free. This exemption, it seems, was brought about through the intervention of his mother, who was more in sympathy with Tom's love for books than was his father.[16] Had the devout Ann known just how her son was employing a good portion of the precious time she had won for him, she would probably not have pressed his case so zealously. For at the head of his impressive "List of books" he remorsefully entered a "List of 'Yellow Backs' I'm

14 Watson MSS., Chapel Hill.
15 MS. Journal 1, c. 1873.
16 William A. Watson to C. V. W., Jan. 17, 1934.

23

ashamed to say I read long ago." His favorite hero was the amazingly adventurous "Claude": *Claude in the Convent, Claude and the Duchess, Claude to the Rescue, Claude's Last Bullet,* and Claude in other promising situations. There are fifty-six such lurid titles that speak of luxurious afternoons in the hayloft.

But Tom had other literary interests more remarkable in a boy of fifteen. By the time he had reached that age, he recorded, he had read the poetical works (whether complete or not, he does not say) of Homer, Shakespeare, Byron, Scott, Milton, Cowper, Wordsworth, Poe, Tennyson, Gray, Swift, Pope, Moore, Burns, Goldsmith, and several minor poets. His list of novels is more nondescript, but includes a good portion of Scott and Dickens and such books as *Tom Jones, Don Quixote, Robinson Crusoe,* and *Gulliver's Travels.* Augustus Baldwin Longstreet's *Georgia Scenes* appears in this list. Apparently, however, his major concern was with history and biography, for this list bulked larger. He listed Goodrich's histories of Rome, England, Greece, and the United States, Goldsmith's histories of Greece, and England, Prescott's *Conquest of Mexico,* Grote's *History of Greece,* and Gibbon's *Decline and Fall of the Roman Empire.* It is not surprising to learn of Tom's early acquaintance with Alexander H. Stephens' *War Between the States* and Pollard's *Southern History of the War.* Of the biographies the Reverend John S. C. Abbott is the author of at least five. "The Reverend Mr. Abbott may have staggered the wise," wrote Watson later, "but he did not stagger me. I believed it all." [17] His grandfather had given him Abbott's *Napoleon,* and the boy had read both volumes when "the books were almost as heavy as I was." "Had another boy . . . scouted the unalloyed goodness of Napoleon, the unsullied virtue of Josephine, and the unrelieved depravity of Napoleon's foes, there would have ensued immediately a small but interesting case of assault and battery." At the end of his four-page list of books he adds a list of magazines of which,

[17] T. E. W., *Prose Miscellanies,* pp. 67-68.

24

presumably, he was a reader: *Harper's, Scott's, Burke's, Wood's, Littell's, Lippincott's,* and *Arthur's.*

One has the feeling in reading this "List of books read up to 1872" that each title written in that round, guileless hand was set down with a certain flush of pride to mark an accomplishment, another small victory over his world. It is far from clear where he got the books, much less the incentive to read them. His father was certainly no book lover, and his grandfather, he says, "rarely dipped deeper into a book than was necessary to master the pictures." He records the contents of the family library, but it consisted apparently of a mere handful of books. There were doubtless generous neighbors, such as Professor Steed and Miss Belle Hanson, his music teacher, but there was no public library, and Thomson was not a reading community. However cramped the horizons of Thomson, it was at least clear that Tom was bent on not accepting them as his own.

When the school term of 1872 came to a close, Tom made known his desire to go to Macon the following fall to enter Mercer University. He was only fifteen at the time and had not yet finished the local school. Professor Steed was leaving Thomson to take the chair of Latin at Mercer, and it is not improbable that Tom was influenced more by the desire to follow his idol than by anything else. His chances of going to college, however, looked poor indeed at the time. John was on the point of another disaster, the loss of his second farm. After that there would be nothing. Besides, neither he nor any of his family had been to college, and he could not see why this son, who had already been granted more privileges than the others, should be made an exception. Once again it was his mother who came to his support. It was difficult to borrow money because of John's poor credit, but a small loan was obtained, and with the promise of a scholarship at Mercer to take care of the sixty-dollar tuition, Tom enrolled as a freshman in October, 1872.

Mercer University, a small Baptist college, was established at Penfield, Georgia, in 1833. By effecting a "union of agricultural labor with literary study," it proposed "to aid in the education of poor young men preparing for the ministry," which was then "almost without education." The school had its humble beginnings in "two double cabins, with a garret to each, for dwelling, for dining, and for study for both teachers and students." [18] The attempt to unite labor and letters was abandoned, but the school continued until 1862. In that year it was suspended because of the enlistment of practically all its students; it did not open again until December, 1865, and then with only three teachers. Promise of new life came when the city of Macon offered the college a small endowment and a grant of land, and in 1871 the Baptist brethren moved from Penfield to Macon. When the fall term of 1872 opened the faculty was still using the "Mess Hall" for recitations and "prayers" as well as for meals.

One of Freshman Watson's first concerns was with his new masters, the four members of the Mercer faculty. Coolly taking their measure, he set down his conclusions: Dr. Archibald J. Battle, the president, was "a man laboriously cultivated rather than naturally very talented," but still "the best President that could have been chosen from the Faculty." Professor Woodfin, the teacher of Greek, Tom found "charitable, kind, affable," and Professor Shelton P. Sanford commanded respect as the "very well known . . . author of the Analytical Arithmetic." Yet none of these could measure up to Professor Steed, who, "in brilliancy of intellect," he thought, "far surpasses any man in the college," although the youngest member of the faculty. Now that they were at Mercer together, Tom was admitted into such intimacy with his idol that he speaks of their relationship as "chummy." [19]

[18] Dr. R. J. Massey, in *Watson's Magazine*, Vol. IV (April, 1910), pp. 319-323.

[19] A commonplace book, hereafter referred to as "MS. Journal 2." It contains about 600 pages. Watson acquired it when he went to Mercer, and continued to use it until his death. Referring to it, he wrote: "It was not intended that these private records should ever be shown to anyone else. They were just an ambitious boy's effusions, jotted down partly because there was a vague idea that they might one day be very interesting to myself."

"I have just been reading Todd's Student's Manal [*sic*]," wrote Tom on his sixteenth birthday, a few weeks before he left home for college, "and I am resolved 'after mature deliberation' to adopt his plan . . ." Todd's plan was a system of self-discipline that held the student to a rigid daily schedule of study and self-improvement. The office of "Assistant Librarian for the Phi Delta Society" to which he was elected worked the ruin of his good resolutions. If one may credit his prodigious list of books read during the fall term, one may conclude that he abandoned himself to his temptation with a furious sort of zeal. His appetite unsatisfied by reading the new books he found in the library, he read for a second time a large number of those he had listed the year before, including Gibbon's *Decline and Fall* and nearly all the poets.[20] "Forgot all about Todd at college," he added at the end of his resolution.

For all his bookishness Tom did not remain an obscure figure at school. One of his classmates pictures him as he "swaggered across the campus . . . the admiration of less forceful natures," one or two worshipful henchmen in his wake. He was sometimes "bitter" and vengeful, but "a purer piece of grit never inhabited a slight frame. . . . He would have marched up to the Devil and tweaked his nose." His description of himself at this time is something quite different: "I was known to be one of the poor boys, unable to pay the tuition fee of sixty dollars; was very plainly dressed; and was shy and awkward in manner" and of "a retiring disposition." [21] But the incongruity is more apparent than real: the "swagger" and "grit" were ever his means of covering a feeling of inferiority, which he calls "shyness" and a "retiring disposition." The numerous accounts of his college escapades, which he delighted in confiding to his diary, tend rather to corroborate this view of a duality of character than not.[22]

[20] MS. Journal 1, Sept. 5, 1872, and following.
[21] T. E. W., *Watson's Jeffersonian Magazine*, Sept., 1910.
[22] MS. Journal 2.

In Southern colleges of that day it was in the debating societies, rather than on the gridiron, that fame was won. Here such questions as, "Would the removal of the Negroes from the South be beneficial to the people?" and "Does Knowledge exert more influence upon mankind than wealth?" were periodically settled.[23] At the Phi Delta Society Tom Watson was in his native element. Here he could flaunt his learning, brandish in the faces of astonished opponents the purple quotations which he copied in his notebooks and memorized, and—above all—here he could pay devotion to his "Ideal Goddess," Eloquence.

Oratory he evidently regarded as one of the major arts, and it was his most cherished ambition to master it. "Study Eloquence as an abstract beauty," he wrote, and his pursuit of the subject was zealous. He wrote, he read, he practiced. His notes on the lives of famous men were concerned chiefly with their oratorical prowess, and he was forever jotting down observations on the art. For example, there are his twelve "Hints on Oratory—Taught by experience—not books," of which number twelve is, "Pay ardent, unceasing adoration to her as an Ideal Goddess at whose touch the human heart quivers with joy, throbs with enthusiasm, melts with pity, trembles with fear, droops with woe, burns with indignation, or stands still in mute horror." His "Recipe for a public democratical speech" ends with the ingredient, "a grand 'Spread Eagle,' " and under the admonition, "Remember This!" one reads: "when the national heart is heaving with excitement, he who would control its pulsations and direct its energies, must speak in the language of enthusiasm. The power of the orator lies in the sympathy between him and the people. This is the chord which binds heart to heart; and when it is struck, thousands burst into tears or rouse into passion, like a single individual." [24] "Pulsations" and "excitement," these were the materials of his art, and "the lan-

[23] "Minutes of the Phi Delta Society," October, 1873–June, 1874, Mercer University, Macon, Ga.
[24] MS. Journal 2, pp. 1-62.

28

guage of enthusiasm" and "sympathy" were its instruments.

Later in his college career Tom was once called up before a tribunal of the Mercerian Republic, an elaborate system of student government, and charged with creating a "loud, boisterous, uproarious disturbance" in the Mess Hall. When the counsel for the defense had finished, Tom, to the surprise of both himself and the court, leaped to his feet and addressed the jury in his own behalf. "I had thought nothing of what to say but when I opened my mouth there rushed out a torrent of fiery words which swept the jury right along," he wrote, clearly astonished at his own powers. "In a few minutes I found myself ridiculing Cooper. . . . I pointed my finger to Cooper and pronounced the swelling epithets with such a pompous, Ciceronian roll that Tom Burdet and several others burst into a laugh." [25] A fight started. "My case," he wrote, "ruined the Mercerian Republic." He came out of the experience with a new respect for this power he possessed. He wrote out the speech afterward, and in the margin pronounced it "the best speech I probably ever made," "entirely extemporaneous," but "wonderfully effective."

Mercer closed on July 3, and the next day found Tom fifteen miles out from Macon applying for a position as teacher of a country school. After some hesitation on account of his "juvenile appearance" the board accepted him on trial. According to the unequivocal terms (and the spelling) of his contract, adopted by the trustees of the "Centreal Warrior Academy," the teache was required "to keep a good and holsome disciplin at all times, but "The said Teacher shal not be alowed to correct no studan in any way only by a switch the skin not to be cut and not to b abused otherwise." With these limitations upon penal method he was expected to enforce the following rules: [26]

Rule 1st—There shall be no student admitted into this scho that does not come under these obligations.

[25] *Ibid.*, p. 129.
[26] Quoted by T. E. W , *Watson's Magazine*, March, 1910 Cf. also same quoted wi some variation by Walter Wellman, *Review of Reviews*, XXX (Oct., 1904), p. 419.

Rule 2d—All abusive language such as cursing and swearing is attually forbiden.

Rule 3d—There shall no student be alowed to carry consealed weppons.

Rule 4th—There shall be no climbing of fences, resling or throwing rocks at each other alowed.

Rule 5th—No student is alowed to fight in school or on there way too or from school, nor no news to be carraide too or from school.

Opening with five scholars on the first day, the school increased in attendance by August to forty-four, ranging in age from six to twenty-seven. There was Jim Tool, "well grown, with a high narrow forehead and small grey eyes which could look at you an hour without blinking," who thought nothing of licking an ink blot off his copy book, and Ella Gates, who "thanks her stars she has passed her twenty-seventh year." Tom found teaching "not a task but a pleasure," for "while teaching them I am teaching myself." [27] In September he closed his school and returned to Mercer for the fall term.

During the summer he had written to his father of his ambition to become "one of the first men of the State." "It is for this," he said, "that I am studying, it is for this that I am working, and I never mean to stop either the one or the other, until my object is obtained. I have no great wish for money for myself; I only wish for fame; but I intend to make money for you and fame for myself at the same time." [28]

Fame, he fancied, was quite within his grasp when he clipped from the *Macon Telegraph* a favorable notice of his speech (delivered "in a most remarkable manner") at the annual Sunday-school celebration. But his triumph turned to gall and wormwood upon the reflection that it had been won in the borrowed Sunday coat of the Mess Hall matron's husband. [29] No, to enjoy fame one must have money. Money, however, was not immedi-

[27] MS. Journal 2, c. Aug., 1873.
[28] T. E. W. to John S Watson, Aug 1, 1873, Watson MSS
[29] MS. Journal 2, undated.

ately forthcoming. Indeed, it soon appeared that, for all his mother's efforts and his own frugality, this would be his last year in college. The year passed uneventfully.

On June 20 he made a farewell address at the Phi Delta Society, in which he "tried to efface every hard feeling." The Recording Secretary pronounced it in the minutes a very "telling speech." [30] Then he took his leave of college with "barely enough" to pay his way home.

[30] "Minutes of the Phi Delta Society," June 20, 1874, Macon, Georgia.

CHAPTER III

"Ishmael" in the Backwoods

WHILE HIS SON was at college, John, more prone than ever to the "blues" and the indulgence of his weaknesses, had fallen victim to the general economic collapse of the early 'seventies: His last acre of land went in 1873. Haplessly he joined the beginning exodus from land to city, moved to Augusta and there opened a combined boarding house and bar.[1]

The change did not please Tom at all. When a friend, whose father had bought the fine house John had built after the war, called on Tom at the new establishment, he appeared embarrassed and did not ask his friend in.[2] Furthermore, he did not feel at home in the city. "I was a stranger in the city," he wrote, "and my clothes and my manner advertised me as a raw country boy." Vainly he tramped the streets of Augusta that summer seeking work, but work he could not find. It was the first of many rebuffs he was to receive from the city. Unlike his father —he recoiled, as he always did, back to the country. This time it was to the real country.

Having found no work by September, he gathered up his books and sold them at public auction. "As each volume was cried off . . ." he said, "a great gulp rose in my throat." That night he made some memoranda for a "letter to T[heodosia?]." "Youth," he said, "is bidding me goodbye forever. . . . Tomor-

[1] MS. Journal 2, p. 196.
[2] Interview with L C Smith, Columbia County, Georgia, Dec., 1933.

row, though only 18 years have rolled over my head, I shall go out into life as a man . . ." He assured "T," however, that he had "not a doubt of success." [3] But to his diary he admitted more privately that the future "seemed robed in gloom," [4] for it looked as if he were "setting out on a wild goose chase." With six dollars and a half, proceeds from the sale of his books, he boarded the train the next morning. At Lawtonville he got off and walked the remaining eighteen miles through the country to Screven County, the home of his friend Glenn Thompson.

Thompson was soon able to get up a school for the youth in the Little Horse Creek community. Boarding with the Thompsons, Tom promptly fell in love with Laura, his friend's sister, and became engaged to her in less than a month. Fame and fortune, however, were still his chief preoccupations: "Fame," he wrote, was "the Goddess of the Intellectual." Pondering the question of marriage, he decided to remain a bachelor, since "there must be a titanic struggle before Intellect can free itself from the clutches of Poverty." [5] Perhaps it was fame he was seeking when in November he accepted the invitation of the Temperance Society to address its members in the Little Horse Creek Church. The acclaim received for belaboring the demon rum he found gratifying. But temperance lectures and school-teaching held small promise of freedom from the "clutches of Poverty."

January found him back in Augusta in a low state of mind, "attended by shadows," and writing such poems as "Despair," a lugubrious composition, ending:

> Ambition, my cherished ambition,
>   Still comes at my call,—dreary call!
> But a mantle hangs over her features
>   As dark as a funeral pall.

[3] MS. Scrapbook.
[4] MS. Journal 2, Nov. 4, 1874.
[5] *Ibid.*, an entry entitled "Musings."

The poem, he noted at its end, was "written on the banks of the Savannah river while laying [*sic*] out from home and seeking a chance to run away to Texas." [6]

The Texas adventure was happily averted by his mother, who gained permission for him to read law in the office of Judge W. R. McLaws, of Augusta. There he studied until July; then, packing his Blackstone, the gift of Mr. Thompson, he returned to Screven County to take another school for three months at Double Head. He would always remember "those three months with much pleasure." He enjoyed another triumph at the Temperance Convention, and his school closed successfully. "The girls of course cried," he says, and one of his "large pupils, Miss Jennie W.," was even more demonstrative.

In the social life of small and middle-class farmers of backwoods Screven, which centered about the Horse Creek Church, the schoolhouse, and the Temperance Society, Tom was by no means the shy lout he described himself in Augusta. On the contrary, it seems that he was completely at home at such functions as schoolhouse dances and barbecues. He pictured himself "leading into the quadrille a bony, sway-backed damsel," or performing "the double shuffle, the back-step, the pigeon wing, the heel and toe, the limber-leg, the slap-jack, the flip-flop." [7] An accomplished fiddler, he sometimes played for the dances. His repertoire, some fifty separate titles, included waltzes, schottishes, polkas, cotillions, quicksteps, hornpipes, besides "Watson's Medley," made up of "Rosy O'More, Kathleen, Highland Fling, The Girl I Left Behind Me, Blue Danube, Falling Leaves, and Elfin Waltz." [8] Moreover, his talent for composing and reciting such jingles as the following did not detract from his popularity:

> He goes to parties and to balls
> With fiddle music brimmin'

[6] *Ibid.*, "Augusta, 1875."
[7] *Ibid.*, p. 123.
[8] MS. Journal 1, undated.

Who plays in one way for the men—
Another for the women. . . .

By rare good taste and rarer luck
He variegates his fiddling
And whiles away the tedious hours
By heterogeneous diddling.

Whatever there remained of a middle-class agrarian culture
in the post-bellum South, Tom Watson knew at first hand, nor
did he ever forget its language when the right moment came to
use it. "I think that my earnest sympathy for the poor dates
from this period of my life," he wrote. He shared the farmer's
lot completely, and the lot of the farmer at this time and place
was not a perennial barbecue. "Eating at their tables, sitting at
their firesides, sleeping in their beds," he declared, "I gained a
knowledge of these people which no books could give me—these
plain, country people—and I love them." [9]

Having passed the bar examination in Augusta, "with the
compliments of the Judge," Tom received his license to practice
on October 19, 1875.[10] The clerk of the court issued it on credit,
since Tom, so he wrote, "was not able to pay at that time." The
city proving no more hospitable than before, Tom took himself
"immediately" back to Screven to start his law practice. Business
was so dull by March, however, that even teaching seemed more
lucrative, and he gave up the law. "I couldn't stand the crisis,"
he wrote in his Journal. "I sold my horse and took a small
private school till June." [11] When June came, nothing better
offered than to begin another school, this time a public school
in the "Cail neighborhood."

Time hung heavy on his hands, and to dispel the doldrums
he turned to poetry and love-making—both on his customary

[9] T. E. W , *Life and Speeches*, p. 11.
[10] "Richmond County Superior Court Minutes, 1874–1876," pp. 430-431.
[11] MS. Journal 2, "Cameron, Ga., March 4, 1876."

35

scale, that is to say, extensive. There were Molly ("I take you upon my lap and feel your little arms around my neck"), and Fannie ("Oh my! Won't my wife have a heap to scold me about,") and Sally ("But she is married now, and I'll keep her secret,") and Lillie, Laura, Amelia . . . and poems to them all! Particularly there was Jennie, who walked with him under the cypress trees, where "the long moss hung in tresses, waving and sighing sadly in the air," and sang to him "when the night that was around us, no matter how gloomy, was not so dark to me as the world was." [12]

At all this philandering his patrons, chiefly of the Baptist persuasion, were inclined to look askance. Some were scandalized. "It didn't require much wisdom to see that profligacy was ruining me," he reflected. "Those pretty . . . girls of Screven were dragging my good name into the mire. I had well nigh alienated all my well wishers by a reckless career with Jennie W——." In his "Parting Words to Patrons" at the end of school he remorsefully asked "only for a generous silence," and that they "let Forgetfulness with noiseless pinions settle upon every blunder." They were indulgent: he was young and full of life. Then he began publishing some of his poems. A few, like "The Farm" and "John Howard Payne," represented respectably domesticated sentiments. There were others, however, in his judgment, "very Byronical in tone," like "Give Me a Kiss," that "attracted considerable attention in the County." One gathers that the attention was not all laudatory. "People talk of stern manhood! Stern fiddlestick!" he exclaimed, and he wrote another poem: [13]

> Strange tales they tell (*they* tell forsooth)
> About thy wayward froward youth
> And lightly do I reck their truth
> Thy love is all my care
> Let slander hurl her venomed dart

[12] *Ibid.*, c. August or September, 1876; undated MSS.
[13] MS. Journal 2, p. 191 *et seq.*, containing also clippings of the poems.

And strive our lives our hopes to part
I'd shrine thee here within my heart
Though hell should say Beware!

Who was this Pan at large in the Baptist fold? "I was unhappy," he said in his Journal, "and hugged the fancy that I
was an Ishmael of modern times." [14] He played his fiddle, memorized poetry, and "spouted Byron by the hour." He was not
appreciated. He was Byron. He was Don Juan. He was Ishmael.
He was anything but a seedy country school-teacher, and the
world must know about it!

The world and his "Goddess Fame" were still unmoved by
his strivings. When his school (his fifth one) closed in August,
he had hope of getting the State Lecturer's place in the Temperance Society. "I was determined," he said, "to 'go up and
gather lilies.' " But just as the prize seemed in his grasp, the
office was abolished. He was reduced to such circumstances that
he had to trade a silver cup that had belonged to his grandfather for a "cheap cotton garment," though the cup was "worth
about ten times more." [15] "October, 1876, found me utterly
destitute and working as a plow hand for old Jimmie Thompson," he recorded. "At night, my fiddle waked the silence
among the pines. . . . I got morose, moody and sulky as a mad
bull. I used to lay [sic] down under the pines and try to imagine
where the dickens I was drifting to, and what awful change had
come over the spirit of my dream that I was getting so near the
bottom . . ." [16]

In this extremity he appealed to Professor R. H. Pearce, one
of his old teachers in Thomson. Professor Pearce wrote that he
would be glad to advance him board until he got a start as a
lawyer. "Riding back home from the Station where I rec'd his
letter," he wrote, "the glad, fierce feeling of a new life opened
to me rose and swelling till the woods rung [sic] with the

[14] *Ibid.*
[15] T. E. W., *Life and Speeches*, p. 11.
[16] MS. Journal 2, p. 191.

37

whoop that burst from my lips. It was a glorious feeling and right there did my destiny turn the corner." [17] He was a little more than twenty years old.

* * * * * *

In 1870 there had been cut out of Columbia and Warren a county named McDuffie in honor of Senator George McDuffie, who had been born in its boundaries. Although Thomson became the seat of the new County's government and thereby gained much in importance, it was still, in 1876, only a village of seven hundred inhabitants. Nevertheless, in these few years its bar, situated in an old part of the state and drawing talent from more established towns, already enjoyed a tradition that was not to be despised. The presence—even occasional—of Robert Toombs and Alexander Stephens would have lent dignity to the tradition of any bar. Although Toombs still carried on an active practice, both of the old Confederates were in their declining years. More vigorous, if less celebrated, was Judge H. D. D. Twiggs, who was later pronounced "the greatest criminal lawyer of Georgia" by a historian who quoted Watson as saying that "he has never met his equal, and that in some of his flights of eloquence he has fairly rivaled General Toombs." There was also James C. C. Black of Augusta, who belonged "in the front rank of Georgia orators," and W. D. Tutt, a gentleman of remarkably caustic tongue, who "seemed to have caught some of the sparks from the anvil of Demosthenes." [18] Erudition they undoubtedly had, but eloquence was more important.

It was natural that Watson should single out as especial marks for emulation the two most distinguished men. Throughout his youth and early manhood he felt strongly the impact of these two mighty and eccentric personalities. " 'Little Elleck' and 'Bob Toombs' were the Castor and Pollux, the matchless heroes, in

[17] *Loc. cit.*
[18] Lucian L. Knight, *Reminiscences of Famous Georgians*, Vol. I, pp. 412-421.

our neck of the woods," he once wrote. The roads between the homes of his two heroes and his own formed a triangle: Tom at the apex, the house of the aristocrat Toombs, at Washington, and Liberty Hall, plain and ascetic, the very soul of Stephens, son of the "plain people," at Crawfordville. The houses of the two friends still stand, decaying symbols of the two classes whose alliance the Toombs-Stephens friendship represented.

"I came almost from Mr. Stephens' own fireside," Watson said with evident feeling at the sage's death. He knew him, visited in his home, as did almost everybody who came to town, took his advice about law and politics, and fairly worshipped him. Toombs was farther off in his firmament, but a more brilliant star. "I loved Stephens," he said, "but I *gloried* in Bob Toombs!" [19] Once during the year 1864 he asked his mother who caused the war. "Toombs," she answered, and the boy was satisfied.[20] He considered Toombs "truly a big man." "His ideas, views, ambitions, passions, methods, excellencies, and faults were big; his loves and hates, his battles, his triumphs, his defeats were big; his roar of wrath, his shout of onset, his bursts of profanity, his explosions of laughter . . ." Furthermore, he was "an Idol of the South because he carried in his heart the very passions, prejudices, hopes, aspirations, distinctive traits, habits, strength and weakness of the South; and every Southern man felt that here was a man who loved the South with all his mind and soul and heart, hating intensely everything and everybody who hated *her*." [21] Once, shortly after his return from exile, Toombs appeared in Thomson. A crowd had assembled to listen to Stephens, whose address had been somewhat disappointing. When they saw Toombs, it was "As though an electric current had shot through the crowd, the multitude sprang to its feet, and there pealed forth a 'Rebel Yell,' and a roar for, 'Toombs! Toombs! Toombs!' " [22] After the band had

[19] T. E. W., *Bethany*, p. 28.
[20] T. E. W., *Sketches*, p. 15.
[21] T. E. W., *Bethany*, p. 27.
[22] T. E. W., *Sketches*, p. 5.

39

played "Dixie," and the delirium had subsided, he addressed the crowd. Elsewhere Watson describes Toombs in action:

You never saw anything like it! A torrent bursting through a mountain gorge; a wind-storm, with thunder and lightning, tearing through a forest; a volcano in eruption—these were the things Toombs' speech reminded you of; and when you once heard Bob Toombs 'on the stump' you could speak of it in the same tone as that used when one said, I saw Jeb Stuart lead a cavalry charge. It was a thing you could never forget; and nothing else was like it in elemental grandeur.

The example of Stephens, however, more analogous to his own origin and circumstances, was ever uppermost in Tom's mind when he pondered his own future. He observed in his Journal that "This natural born genius talk is all humbug," and that a lawyer must "study 36 hours a day." "With Mr. Stephens the experience was the same. With less of natural talent [than Toombs] he had more of unfaltering perseverance. He commenced poor and worked hard. He lived on eight dollars a month, made his own room, blacked his own boots, and was precious glad when he had any boots to black . . ." [23] His emulation of this example, we may conclude, was indefatigable. Frequently such entries as "Didn't go to bed at all last night" appear in his diary of this period; nor was it because he was an Ishmael fiddling under the pines nor a Don Juan among the cypresses. He was "burnishing up" his "legal armor for the Superior C[our]t," or "up till 2 o'clock studying Kent and the Code and reading Jean Ingelow." [24] He had certain debts that must be paid: "So I dressed plainly, ate my cold dinner in my office, diligently attended to what cases came my way, studied hard, lived cleanly in every respect, and gradually gained ground."

Indeed the move from Screven to Thomson had worked a regeneration in him, and his every effort was to become a model

[23] MS. Journal 2, undated.
[24] Ms. Diary, 1878, Feb 19 In possession of Georgia Watson, Thomson, Georgia.

of decorum and industriousness. When Mrs. Pearce, in good-natured raillery, told him that "fiddlers never amount to anything," he put aside his instrument firmly, and nothing could induce him to play it for some time.[25] Shortly after he arrived in Thomson, there had appeared in the *Sunny South*, a literary weekly published in Atlanta, a story called "Jerome Montemar or In the Days of Napoleon," by Thomas E. Watson.[26] The story was not given a prominent place, but its appearance here represented a considerable rise in eminence for its author, whose only publishers had previously been obscure rural papers. He does not appear to have followed up his advantage. He was no longer an author. He was a rising barrister.

When a "revival" came along, he even tried religion, embracing it with the impulsiveness and emotionalism that characterized his conversion to anything from an economic doctrine to a political platform. The evangelist, he wrote, "got hold of me in such a way that, I not only cried and 'took on' myself, but I picked out the hardest old case in the congregation, pried him loose from his seat, dragged him down the aisle, and landed him on the mourner's bench." So fervent a convert was he that he agreed to "make-up" with one of the brethren whom he had thrashed on the street a few months before. Meeting him in public he impulsively offered him his hand. The hand was refused. "I had to meekly swallow the affront," [27] he said. He was never one to swallow affronts in good grace and piety. "I am not what the French call a religionist," he remarked in later life. "But I think that a man who underrates the powerful hold of religion is without reasoning power. . . . As Napoleon said: 'If we didn't have a religion we would have to make one.' " [28] Toward the clergy generally, of whatever persuasion, Watson nursed an impatience he could not always conceal. The deism of Voltaire and Jefferson was at the root of the feeling.

[25] Interview with Mrs. Lula Farmer, daughter of R. H. Pearce.
[26] *Sunny South*, Nov. 18, 1876.
[27] T. E. W., in the *Jeffersonian*, Sept. 30, 1909.
[28] Interview with Watson in Atlanta *Journal*, Sept. 26, 1922.

41

Before his first year of practice was over he recorded: "My practice has been good, yielding me $101.70 in cash. I have met single handed every member of the Bar and have no reason to complain of the result." Then later: "Tutt's rough, brilliant blows have often been galling but I see now I could have had no better schooling." [29] He was "not such a fool," he says, as to sign an agreement with established lawyers binding himself to charge the same fees they charged. He was willing to "work all day for two dollars" and accept any job, however menial. On January 19, 1878, he noted in his diary: "Go to Appling to Justice's Court. I represented Plaintiff B. P. O'Neal. . . . get judgment for $7.00 and costs . . . altogether, I've ridden Little Nell 50 miles today." His victories were not always won in perfect amity and dignity before the bar. For example, this entry was made a week later: "Go down to Pope Hill in Jefferson County. Gain my cases but get into a fight. Jim Cardue calls me a liar in the court room and I slap him. Outside he renews it. I hit him again and he whips me. Result—on my part,—a scratched up face, on his a blue brow and split nose. A 55 mile ride." [30] This altercation is by no means an isolated example. His gross earnings for the first year's practice were $212.

Heavily upon his pride lay the humiliation of his family's poverty. The memory of what they had been and the oppressive consciousness of their present plight was forever haunting him. Before the year was over he set out to rescue them. First there was his younger brother, William, eking out a wretched existence as a share-cropper on the land of "Shep" Wright, a wealthy planter. William, known as "Top" in the community, had been to his brother with tales of Wright's mistreatment and sharp dealing beforehand. When Top later reported that the planter had beaten him like a slave because he had whipped his son in a fist-and-skull fight, Tom saw red. He borrowed a pistol and waited for Wright to come to town. Wright, said to have been

[29] MS. Journal 2, pp. 192 and 267.
[30] MS. Diary 1878.

42

"a noted fighting cock," appeared on horseback one Sunday morning. Armed with his pistol, Tom wrenched the planter's riding switch from his hand and in the presence of a dozen citizens administered him a whipping. "The distance which the noise of the 'cussing' is said to have travelled, that Sabbath morning, staggers belief," reported the assailant. Tom was arrested, but the prosecutor offered to drop the case if Top would agree to surrender his half of the crop he had been working. "We were poor boys," wrote Watson, "and we agreed." [31]

The incident sank deep into his conscience. The rôle of agrarian avenger, when he assumed it again, seemed almost as much a heritage as it was a conviction. Once in boyhood he recorded with pride in his Journal how he had browbeaten "one of the white croppers" on his father's plantation by arrogantly marching up, gun in hand, helping himself at the water bucket on the front porch, and sauntering off without so much as glancing at the astonished cropper.[32] Some little turning of the economic tables had worked a revolution in the attitude of the arrogant young planter's boy. He now saw croppers in a different light.

During the year he paid his family a visit. The pitiable condition in which he found them gave him a profound shock. His father had sunk into a "hopeless stupor"; his "energy was gone and he continued to drift downward . . ." So far had John declined that there was really not much further for him to drift. He had moved to a wretched shack on a little piece of sandy soil in Richmond County. The family including his three sisters, Tom wrote with horror in his Journal, "had lived in a miserable shanty skirted by a long marsh until the chills and fever entered and took possession of every one of them." [33] One detail, possessing a peculiar significance for him, stuck in his mind a long time, and thirty years later he wrote: "The smoke-house, larder,

[31] MS. Journal 2, p. 195.
[32] *Ibid.*, p. 128.
[33] *Ibid.*, p. 196.

43

pantry, buttery, etc., consisted of a home-made book-case that had belonged to my stately old grandfather." [34] These things could not be. He found it all "deeply mortifying and determined to lose no time in coming to their relief."

By an arrangement of credit whereby he was to make six payments of $500 each over a period of five years, he was able to purchase the "Sweetwater Place," a farm of seven hundred acres that John had left at the death of Thomas M. Watson. In more than one sense, then, the return of his family was a homecoming. His responsibilities were now greatly multiplied, but upon Tom there settled for once (and briefly) a consciousness of peace and contentment. "It was a curious feeling of gratification when I rode over the redeemed 'Homestead,' " he wrote shortly after buying the place.[35] He often sat on the "piazza" after an early supper and listened to the hands come in from the fields, and to "my waggon" rattling along the road from town. "At such a time," he said, "one drinks in a world of quiet pleasures—pleasures which leave no bitter taste behind." [36] He took a particular pleasure in hunting out "old Abe Watson," an old Negro that had belonged to his grandfather, and served as plantation foreman. Tom installed him on the place as a tenant. This was "much to [his] satisfaction," he wrote. Unconsciously, perhaps, Tom was seeking the restoration of an imaginary paradise. It was a more plausible restoration than John's lost mansion, from which he had declined so precipitantly to a shanty— but it was sought from the same motives. "Old Abe" he seized upon immediately as an authentic architectural detail, one that his "stately old grandfather" had given his stamp of approval. "It was a curious feeling of gratification . . ." he wrote. "I gave him a little money to buy 'Christmas' with. He goes to work as earnestly this new year as if he had been making money." [37] Of course, there were other motives than nostalgia, and it was not

[34] T. E. W., in the *Jeffersonian*, Sept. 30, 1909.
[35] MS. Journal 2, p. 196.
[36] MS. Diary 1878.
[37] MS. Journal 2, p. 196.

to be regretted that Abe was an "earnest" tenant, as well as an architectural ornament.

But contentment, even of paradisaic fulfillment, was not congenial to the Watson temperament, not for any appreciable length of time at least. Under the date, February 24, 1878, one finds the following entry in his diary: "I can think of nothing all day but Georgia Durham. I go to sleep in a pine thicket and still in my sleep I think of her." [38] His passion for her would give him no peace: "I suffered I think, as much as human nature can suffer. For months I lay in my office on a big sofa perfectly benumbed. My mind was chained down to one subject and it was utterly impossible to think of anything else. I became morose and moody and well nigh desperate." [39] Here once again is the familiar Watson—thwarted, disconsolate, rebellious.

Tom's courtship was ardent and not without romantic incident. During the sixteen months it lasted there were obstacles innumerable: Georgia's long engagement to a rival suitor, her threatening illness, her reluctance to leave her foster-father, whose heavy drinking made him dependent on her care, Dr. Durham's own objection to her early marriage. After several postponements, each of which plunged Tom further into distraction, they were married on October 9, 1878.[40] His diary is silent for a period and then he writes, "I am as happy as a man ever can be."

Georgia Durham was the adopted daughter of Dr. George W. Durham, a physician of Thomson. Around her origin, upon which there is considerable speculation (some conflicting) but no reliable evidence, there remains much obscurity.[41] In a fragmentary manuscript that is apparently the beginning of a novel, Watson gave the story current in the family a highly romantic color. He pictures Georgia as the orphaned victim of sectional hatred that separated the families of her parents at the begin-

[38] MS. Diary 1878.
[39] MS. Journal 2, undated.
[40] MS. Diary 1878.
[41] *Vide* William W. Brewton, *Life of Watson*, pp. 106-113.

ning of the War and made her the secret charge of an old slave couple.[42] All that seems to be unquestionable, however, is the fact that Dr. Durham, then a young surgeon of the Confederate Army stationed near Savannah, became attached to the child in some way, adopted her, and brought her home to his wife during the War.

"If I have a Sister Spirit on earth," Tom wrote during his courtship, "it is she." All that we know of her character, however, seems to indicate that it was in many ways the very antithesis of her husband's, for that she was serene, patient, and reserved seems to be the opinion of those who knew her best. Never taking an active interest in politics, she rarely accompanied her husband on his campaign tours, but when she did she usually received her share of attention from newspapers. "She is small and her figure is almost girlish," said one. "Hands, voice, expression all bespoke the sheltered gentlewoman. Nothing more anomalous than this high-bred daughter of the South affiliated with the party that held Jerry Simpson, 'Sockless Jerry,' could be imagined." Another trait of the "sheltered gentlewoman" of the Old South that she possessed to a marked degree was her shrewd business ability. Like many mistresses of the old plantations, Mrs. Watson, for all her fragile gentility, became the business executive of several large farms, employing and discharging scores of tenants, keeping accounts, buying supplies, directing work, relieving her husband of a vast amount of routine, yet managing to appear quite "sheltered." Watson's letters to his wife put beyond question the ardor of his devotion to her, an ardor which—until a much later period—seemed to proceed out of a deeply romantic passion.[43] It is not often one finds a husband writing love lyrics to his wife after twenty-seven years of married life.[44]

[42] MS. in the possession of Georgia Watson, Thomson, Georgia.

[43] Letters of T. E. W. to his wife between 1883 and 1908 in the possession of Miss Georgia Watson.

[44] "Lines written on the back of a photograph of Miss C. D. in May 1878—Copied April 19, 1905," MS. Journal 2, p. 572.

After living for a short time in the home of the Durhams, the Watsons moved to a house of their own. Here within the next seven years their three children, a boy and two girls, were born. These years, strenuous ones for Tom, were crowded with a thriving practice, a practice that grew with his reputation, and grew rapidly. In April, 1881, he wrote: "I have won a steady and lucrative practice in four counties. I meet the best men from the Bar of the Northern as well as the Augusta Circuit, and I am strong in the faith that nature intended me to be the peer of the best." [45] Not long after he had returned to Thomson he had written, "I love my profession strongly." Well he might, for in the first three years of his practice he had doubled his income each year, and thereafter it shot up proportionately. At the end of the year 1887, eleven years after he had arrived penniless at Thomson, he estimated his "assets" at $30,585, most of which was in land. [46] Those were lean years in rural Georgia. In four more years, it is said upon fair authority, his practice "carried him all over the State, and his income was probably larger than any other country lawyer in the State, with the exception of General Toombs and Benjamin H. Hill." [47]

It is not the purpose here to trace the progress of Watson's rise to eminence as a lawyer, nor even to examine the legal problems involved in his more sensational cases, of which there are many. What is more important is the fact that his practice was almost entirely rural, that it was concentrated in his congressional district, that his juries and audiences were usually made up of farmers who were also voters, and that his practice, as soon as he could command a choice, consisted very largely of criminal cases in which he acted as counsel for the defendant. With these facts in mind, a brief examination of his jury methods might not be entirely without interest.

One of Tom's happiest gifts was a certain talent for robust

[45] MS. Journal 2, p. 287.
[46] "T. E. W. Account Book, 1888–1893," Watson MSS.
[47] William J. Northern, *Men of Mark in Georgia*, IV, p. 223

metaphor and Gargantuan simile struck óff with spontaneity in the genuine rural idiom. Judge Twiggs, a distinguished opponent, several years his elder, was frequently the butt of these aphorisms. In one case involving the identification of a stolen hog, Tom said, "Why gentlemen, he wants you to believe that if a piece of his middling were boiled with collard greens he could tell that it was his by testing the potlicker." And later, "I presume from what he says, that he could with all ease tell you the sex of a hog, male or female, merely by smelling of the gravy." [48] One of these figures, we may imagine, was sufficient to set the jury rolling in the aisles, but in the same speech we find, "The distinguished Judge [Twiggs] has a mind so imaginative and a fancy so poetic that he could weave metaphors round a wheel barrow and draw music from a fence rail." Then, while cross-examining a witness, "If the truth, the whole truth were to strike this witness fair and square it would split him worse than lightning would split a rotten potato." Once after recording one of his gems in his Journal, Tom added, "This little sentence burst out impromptu during a reply of mine to H. C. Roney. It surprised myself and its effect on the hearers was electrical." And after another speech, "I almost forgot where I was and seemed to tread on air." [49]

Much less spontaneous and original—and consequently possessing less real humor—was his collection of anecdotes, also robust. These were assembled over a number of years, filling at least two notebooks, and were used in political speeches as well as before the bar. They are recorded in elliptical phrases which, nevertheless, make their nature fairly apparent—as in the following samples: "Keeps a stud horse and plays the fiddle," "Kissing the wrong place in the dark," "The cricket and the tumble bug," "Zeb Vance's poor man—p——s on the fire and calls

[48] MS. Journal 2, p. 286. In these pages Watson kept many brief accounts of his cases, complete speeches of some of his early ones.

[49] *Ibid.*, c. 1879.

48

his dog," "Hold up your right *leg* then—hold something." [50]
These anecdotes represent a type of folk humor, as anyone
familiar with the section will recognize, and they did not go
unappreciated.

As an example of his juristic technique and forensic methods,
there is the case of Jack Peavy. [51] This case came fairly early in
his career; in itself it is relatively unimportant and little known;
it is not selected to illustrate Watson's legal skill, but for what
it may reveal about the lawyer himself, his methods, his clients,
his juries.

Peavy, it seems, had boarded a train in an intoxicated condition and made himself such a nuisance that the conductor had
ejected him from the train. Whereupon, it was charged, Peavy
attempted to shoot the conductor, but instead was shot by the
conductor. Peavy then escaped. Discovered later by a constable's
posse he was again wounded, this time by an incredible number
of buckshot, placed under arrest, and later tried for assault with
intent to murder. Watson was appointed to defend him. It appears that Peavy did not enjoy an enviable reputation in Warrenton, where he was tried, and that public sentiment was
strongly against him. It was, naturally, Watson's first concern
to propitiate and if possible to convert this prejudicial atmosphere into one favorable to the defendant. He began with what
appears to be an unconscious travesty upon Anthony's oration on
the fallen Caesar—baring the wounds of the victim. *Pianissimo.*

Why, gentlemen, Jack Peavy has been shot till his hide wouldn't
hold shucks. If he was a cow his skin wouldn't be worth tanning.
His coffin will be a lead mine. It's a wonder to me all the little boys
who are learning to shoot don't practice on his carcass. The law certainly would not interfere . . . No! Let the brave work go on! Bar-
nett shot *him* and the law accuses Peavy. A constable's crowd shot

[50] Notebooks in the possession of Georgia Watson, and also among the Watson
MSS. at Chapel Hill.
[51] MS. Journal 2, p. 305. The case was apparently tried in 1882.

49

him without warning till the wife of his bosom might have tracked him seventeen miles by the life blood as it drained his veins. And the law makes no complaint.

This having taken effect, he proceeds with another trend. *Crescendo.*

The further we go the more clearly will we see one of these cruel class differences that disgrace the justice of men.

Suppose Gen. Toombs passing on this Washington train had cursed. Is there a man on the jury who believes that this young conductor would have collared him and have spoken to him as he did Peavy? How absurd. Toombs, sacred by reason of his class, his cloth; powerful in the golden strength of his hundreds of thousands. . . .

But Peavy! That's another matter. Slouch hat and homespun dress inspire the youth with no such awe. Hear how his conduct speaks: "I will collar him like I would a slave, speak to him as I would to a slave and if he dares resent either I'll shoot him like a dog. Such men have no rights that I am bound to respect."

And finally for the "grand spread eagle." *Fortissimo.*

Peavy answers the shaking of the pistol in his face by saying, "You —. You damned son of a bitch," and is shot. At least he had endured all he could and his whole nature rose up in arms. "You have collared me as if I were a cur. You have talked to me like you would a servant. You have insulted me before all the passengers— put me off the train after I had bought my ticket and now you threaten me while I am down. I'll stand no more. Your rank and your riches give you no right to wipe your feet on me. God Almighty breathed into my nostrils as well as yours. My blood came from the dust and so did yours. I throw my defiance in your teeth and meet you face to face—

> "What tho on homely fare we dine,
>   Wear hodden gray and all that;
>   Give fools their silks and knaves their wine—
>   A man's a man for all that."

50

Jack Peavy was cleared. "By the time I had spoken half an hour," wrote Watson, at the end of the above account, "the popular tide was with us and many a manly eye was dim."

Out of such victories as this—and it was multiplied a hundred-fold—was built the legend of his invincibility. It became a widely prevalent belief that there was a sort of rule, or at least an agreement of honor, that Tom Watson should not assist in the prosecution of one charged with murder, for if he did, it meant certain death for the defendant. His talent was reserved for the defense. He was a tribune of the people, and hundreds had found shelter within his voice.

And might not a whole people find shelter there likewise? Were not they all so many Jack Peavys in "slouch hat and homespun?" Were they not forever being collared and booted about by arrogant young conductors of the railroads who charged them such outrageous rates to carry their cotton? Or by some upstart millionaire of Wall Street, "sacred by reason of his class?" By city folk in general? And might they not, with the words Tom had put in Jack Peavy's mouth, some day rise in their wrath and say, "I'll stand no more?" And with such a voice and such a tribune for their leader, might they not become so many Jack Cades?

CHAPTER IV

The "New Departure"

MEN, MANNERS, AND EVENTS in the South during those two decades that lie between the restoration of home rule in the early 'seventies and the agrarian revolt of the 'nineties have been strangely neglected by historians and men of letters generally. Perhaps it is because Reconstruction, which immediately preceded this period, and the Populist movement, which marked its close, have offered materials so rich in tragic and melodramatic appeal that the interlude has been poorly attended. Perhaps it is because the great circus of the Gilded Age at Washington completely out-shone it in competitive attraction. Be that as it may, the South also had its "Great Barbecue." True, it was somewhat delayed by an ungentlemanly squabble over who should play the host, and its conviviality was unhappily marred by a most un-Southern inhospitality in the matter of invitations, and by a few, a very few, haughty old patricians who contemptuously spurned the invitations and stayed at home to munch cold victuals. But the Barbecue went on.

Out of the almost unanimous silence on this epoch has grown much erroneous thinking about the South and Southern history, particularly about that era in which Watson and the Populists played an important part. To understand the significance of their rôle, one must at least be warned of the more prominent misapprehensions concerning the epoch out of which they arose, which, in fact, produced them.

52

After the surrender, as after any war and especially an unsuccessful one, there followed a great deflation of political fervor and moral enthusiasm. Southern leaders had been disfranchised. Some were in prison, some in exile. Nothing but widespread poverty prevented a larger emigration than actually occurred to Latin American colonies. The South was a "conquered province." How, then, could its citizens be expected to exhibit a great deal of interest in the question, "When is a state not a state?" which was troubling Thaddeus Stevens of Pennsylvania and Charles Sumner of Massachusetts? A few old heads recognized "Reconstruction" for what it was—a Yankee euphemism for capitalist expansion. But their number was small, and their counsel generally regarded as occult. The last demonstration of political genius made by the old ruling class was in assisting the overthrow of the Carpetbagger regime. But that was accomplished in the guise of Brer Rabbit rather than in that of Brer Lion: "Sir," General Toombs is reported to have said to a Federal detective while the general was engaged in paying off Negro voters, "Sir, are you not touched by this spectacle of the unbought suffrages of a free people?" [1] In 1870 he had joined hands with Governor Joseph E. Brown to overthrow the corrupt Bullock administration; with unwonted cynicism he had written Stephens, "Rather a strange conjunction is it not? But you know my rule is to use the devil if I can do better to save the country." [2]

Adversity had minimized old differences and old hatreds momentarily, and all Southern people felt powerfully drawn together against a common enemy. Their mood is clearly reflected in a letter that Augustus Baldwin Longstreet wrote to Stephens: "When I think of you and Toombs as you are now, and as you were twelve or fourteen years ago, I feel like *killing the fatted calf, and waking up music and dancing.* . . . Well,

[1] C. Mildred Thompson, *Reconstruction in Georgia*, pp. 273-274.
[2] Ulrich B. Phillips, *Life of Robert Toombs*, p. 264.

as Ransey Sniffle says, 'We are all friends now.' " [3] Whigs, Know Nothings, Unionists, Secessionists, even some Republicans were all one in a conservative embrace. It so happened that the common repository for these generous and powerful emotions of a people was the Democratic party. But no sooner had the spontaneity of this impulse begun to pall than the more sensitive souls began to feel the embrace distinctly embarrassing.

In 1872 Stephens and Toombs, in an ineffectual effort to prevent Southern Democrats from joining with the Northern wing of the party in a "New Departure" to nominate Horace Greeley, the Liberal Republican of New York, for president, had lost their fight for the control of the Georgia Democratic party. Renewing the struggle upon the same issues the following year, Stephens was defeated as a candidate for senator by General John B. Gordon. He then accepted as a sop a seat in Congress, but his relations with the "New Departure" Democrats remained estranged. The old invalid was expected to die any day now, but instead he cheerfully corrected the proofs of his obituary (just as Toombs predicted), and went on living, an irrepressible mummy in a roller chair, "An immense cloak, a high hat, and peering somewhere out of the middle a thin, pale, sad little face." [4]

Toombs, example *par excellence* of the unreconstructed Rebel, had returned from his two years' exile abroad in a much more belligerent mood than Stephens had exhibited upon his release from prison. In fact he returned as a citizen of Georgia only, for he never applied for United States citizenship. In 1876 the old Rebel was no more pleased with the doings of his new party than he had been four years previously. On October 30 he wrote Stephens, "The mongrel crew who call themselves Democrats . . . want Tilden elected for the same reason that Falstaff rejoiced at Prince Hal's reconciliation with the old King—'Hal,

[3] John Donald Wade, *Augustus Baldwin Longstreet*, p. 354.
[4] Louis Pendleton, *Alexander H. Stephens*, pp. 386-387.

rob me the exchequer.' " [5] But Toombs' recalcitrance was not yet reduced to impotent mouthings. One of his chief abominations was the Constitution of 1868, the product of "aliens and usurpers." The sanction this document gave to the policy of state aid to railroads and public corporations was perhaps the main cause of his displeasure. It was known that he never invested a dollar in railroad stock, and his vehement denunciation of railroads was regarded by many at the time as a paranoia. His personal power in the state was such that he was able to dominate the Constitutional Convention of 1877 and to force the adoption of his ideas in the new constitution. "Toombs is attempting a new revolution" was the cry of hoards of railroad lobbyists, promoters, developers, expanders, and captains of industry who descended upon Atlanta to stop this "war upon the rights of property." "It is a sacred thing to shake the pillars upon which the property of the country rests," one of their number solemnly charged. "Better shake the pillars of property than the pillars of liberty," thundered the old man. "The great question is, Shall Georgia govern the corporations or the corporations govern Georgia? Choose ye this day whom ye shall serve!" In spite of the powerful opposition of Joseph E. Brown and others, the convention made its choice at the dictation of Robert Toombs. His motion to strike out the section against dueling was defeated, but not his proposals to prohibit state aid to railroads, irrevocable franchises and immunities, the purchase of railroad securities by the state, and monopolistic combinations of railroads.[6] Toombs had won the day, but it was to be his last one. Barred from holding federal office, he constituted himself ex-cathedra censor of public morals, resorting to strong drink, strong language, and blacker prophecies as the years passed. By a stranger conjunction than Toombs' brief alliance with Joe Brown, young Henry Grady became almost the amanuensis of

[5] Ulrich B. Phillips, *op. cit.;* p. 268.
[6] *Ibid*, p 269-272; Samuel W Small, *Proceedings of the Georgia Constitutional Convention . . . 1877, passim*

the General, patronizingly jotting down his jeremiads and reporting them amiably to the public.

Upon the restoration of home rule in 1872 the Carpetbaggers, it is frequently said, were succeeded by the "Bourbons," the impression being, it seems, that the "Bourbon Democrats," having overthrown the Reconstruction administration, were able in some way partially to rehabilitate the old order while paying dubious respect to the new. Having caught the fancy of a suspicious North and having been adopted by the South itself (though in a somewhat different sense),[7] the term *Bourbon* has enjoyed a remarkable success as a political epithet. Indeed, in this sense it has become a part of our language, *Webster's New International Dictionary* defining the word as, "A ruler or politician who clings obstinately to ideas adapted to an order of things gone by;—sometimes applied to Democrats of the southern United States." Yet, since the American aborigines were called *Indians* there has probably been no more fallacious misnomer in our history than this term *Bourbon*—at least when applied to the men who governed Georgia.

The nature of the new rulers of the South might be made fairly plain by a recitation of statistics demonstrating the rapid advance of industrial development. Some insight should be gained by a study of the rulers themselves. During the interval between 1872 and 1890 either Joseph E. Brown or General John B. Gordon held one of Georgia's seats in the United States Senate, and after the expiration of his second term as Governor in 1882, General Alfred H. Colquitt held the other; during the major part of that same period either General Colquitt or General Gordon occupied the governor's chair. So regularly were these high offices bandied about among the three men, that they came to be spoken of as the triumvirate—"the Bourbon Triumvirate."[8]

The career of Joseph Emerson Brown is one of those anom-

[7] Thus, Joseph E. Brown in 1880 refers to "the sentimentality of the South and the Bourbonism of the past." Herbert Fielder, *Life and Times of Joseph E. Brown*, p. 550.
[8] Isaac W. Avery, *History of Georgia*, pp. 370-372.

alies that render unsafe broad generalizations about the Old South as well as the New, for his is the story of a self-made man, one of the first "success-stories" of the ploughboy who became a multimillionaire and a senator. His rise began in the Old South. At the age of nineteen he emerged from the primitive, poverty-ridden backwoods of north Georgia wearing homespun and driving a yoke of steers. Six years later he was graduated from the law school of Yale College and returned to Georgia to take up the career of lawyer, farmer, and politician. At twenty-eight he was a state senator and shortly afterward a circuit judge. In 1857, at the age of thirty-six, he was advanced to the governor's chair largely by the votes of the small farmer (whose influence in antebellum Georgia was by no means negligible). The news of his nomination reached him in his wheat field, where he was lending a hand with the harvest.[9]

The contrast between the personality of the young governor and those of such men as his predecessor, Governor Johnson, or Senator Toombs was striking. His composure, one of his admirers tells us, was "perfect, though his manners, while not easy, were not awkward." His face was "pale, bloodless," his mouth "wide and thin-lipped, something like Henry Clay's, though not so extensive," his clothes "plain black without attempt at fashionable fit," his voice "very clear and not at all musical." In speaking he showed "no rhetorical finish," was "disregardful of ceremony," and kept himself "free from any sentiment of reverence for custom or authority unless his judgment approved." His pronunciation, marked strongly by the provincial drawl and the rural peculiarity of accenting the last syllable, won him the name of "Old judgment." Governor Brown's first regime of four years was said in 1881 to have given Georgia "the largest measure of material growth she has ever had." Whether fighting banks, legislature, press, or "custom and authority," Brown was the same "native-born belliger-

9 Herbert Fielder, *op. cit.*, pp. 91-92; I. W. Avery, *op. cit.*, pp. 7-46; U. B. Phillips, *op. cit.*, p. 171.

ent," relentless, stubborn, self-confident. As war governor he was also a capable administrator, although his conflict with the Confederate government over conscription and state rights (in which he took the side of Stephens and Toombs against President Davis) was a serious matter.[10] Brown's political career did not end with the War. For a quarter of a century after the surrender his influence was powerfully felt in Georgia and in the South. Then, might not this man, farmer, eight-years' governor of Georgia, ardent defender of state rights, ally of Stephens and Toombs, with justice be called a "Bourbon"?

After the War, Governor Brown grew a long gray beard of the sort that masked the faces of a great many statesmen of the Gilded Age. "The statesman like the business man," wrote Governor Brown in his letter of resignation, June 29, 1865, "should take a practical view of questions as they arise . . ." The advisor in this case profited more than the advised. "We have never in the South had a more practical man than Governor Brown," said one of his admirers.[11] For his advice to the South of entire acquiescence in the abolition of slavery and a cordial support of the full Radical reconstruction policy, Brown became perhaps the best-hated man in Georgia, bringing down a tirade of abuse from such men as Ben Hill, who pronounce him "parricide" and "traitor," though in taking this position, Brown merely anticipated Hill about three years and Southern Democracy about five.[12] Governor Brown simply showed more alacrity in combining profitably the "practical view" of the business man with the duties of the "statesman." He became a Republican temporarily, and was duly rewarded for his practical views by the Bullock administration with the office of chief justice of the state supreme court. In the name of "development" and "progress" the reconstructors (like their brethren in Wash-

[10] I. W. Avery, *op. cit.*, pp. 48-49, 167-170, and also Chapters XX-XXXI; H. Fielder, Chapters III-X, especially pp. 355-398.

[11] I. W. Avery, *op. cit.*, pp. 339-340.

[12] Haywood Pearce, *Benjamin H. Hill*, pp. 214-215; I. W. Avery, *op. cit.*, pp. 370-371.

ington) drew out of the public treasury munificent doles with both hands for the industrialists. Some $4,450,000 worth of such bonds were later declared fraudulent and repudiated, but not all.[13] Chief Justice Brown was closely associated with many of the beneficiaries of these policies.

In December, 1870, Brown resigned his office as chief justice to take charge of the Western and Atlantic Railroad. The lease of this state road had been awarded the company of which he was president as one of the last acts of the Bullock legislature, just before the "Carpetbag" Governor fled the state. Later investigation declared the obtaining of the lease and the formation of the company to be fraudulent, but the lease was not broken.[14] During the next decade Brown was occupied largely with a multiplicity of industrial developments. At one time he was president of the Western and Atlantic Railroad Company, the Southern Railway and Steamship Company, the Walker Coal and Iron Company, and the Dade Coal Company, and part owner of the Rising Fawn Iron Works.[15] His mineral interests alone covered a large part of several counties.

The labor supply that Governor Brown used in the Dade coal mines, one of his larger interests, is worth passing attention as a commentary upon the rise of the progressive spirit in the South and the patent advantages of the new freedom over the old feudal system. The practice of leasing state convicts to private individuals and corporations had arisen during Reconstruction, when for the first time large numbers of Negro convicts began to appear. The state, it was claimed, was too impoverished to maintain them in idleness. Governor Brown was willing to relieve the public of a large part of this burden, and pay the state something

[13] C M. Thompson, *Reconstruction in Georgia*, Chapter IX; H. Fielder, *op. cit.*, pp. 465-480; Alex M. Arnett, *Populist Movement in Georgia*, p 26

[14] The question of fairness in this lease is still controversial. Cf. C. M. Thompson, *op. cit.*, pp. 251-254, which puts a damaging construction upon the testimony, and H. Pearce, *op. cit.*, pp. 218-230; which takes a different view; also Fielder, *op. cit.*, pp. 480-483; A. M. Arnett, *op. cit.*, pp. 26-27; Rebecca L. Felton, *Memories of Georgia Politics*, pp. 62-63; pp. 68-78.

[15] I. W. Avery, *op. cit*, p. 606; H. Fielder, *op. cit.*, pp. 488-490.

over six cents per working day for the convicts, whom he worked in his mines for ten to twelve hours a day, until those limits were removed in 1876 by a grateful legislature. True, there were a few ungrateful critics among the Independents, one of whom denounced the system as "barbarous": "Juveniles and old, hardened criminals, men and women, black and white, the obdurate and unconquerable, are all huddled and chained together. You have a system that is degrading—that is barbarous—that is devilish." [16] The public, however, was inclined to understand the viewpoint of Mr. Brown, who admitted that "We make some profit at the Dade Coal Mines, and there we use convict labor," but, he asked, "Is it a crime for a citizen to put his money into the development of mineral interests, especially if he should succeed in making money by his energy and enterprise?" The moral advantage was obviously all on the side of Mr. Brown's argument, for he had undoubtedly succeeded in making money by his energy and enterprise, and he had been among the first to give cordial welcome to the abolition of slavery. The number of convicts increased from 432 in 1872 to 1,441 in 1877. This was due, according to the governor, to "increased vigilance and rigid convictions by the judiciary." [17]

As a citizen, Governor Brown had many other exemplary moral qualities. He was a devout churchman, strictly temperate, using neither tobacco nor alcohol. He was a prominent philanthropist, donating thousands to charity and education for the poor. Withal he presented, like his Northern prototype, Jay Cooke, a grave and deacon-like appearance. His biographer gives this engaging picture of his hero: "He works with the regularity of a perfectly adjusted machine; is temperate in the application of supporting diet, as is a skilled machinist in the application of steam; and sleeps by the force of controlling will power as promptly and soundly as the wheels and levers of the machine

[16] R. L. Felton, *op. cit*, pp. 437, 458, 583-596.
[17] "Report of the Investigating Committee on Convict Lease," Georgia Legislature, in *Georgia Laws*, 1908, pp. 1059-1091; H. Fielder, *op. cit.*, pp. 488-489; A. M. Arnett, *op. cit.*, p. 28.

stop and rest when the steam is shut off." Among Southerners this was verily a new type of man, and they watched him, fascinated—as they were fascinated by the new factories and railroads.

A more paradoxical figure than even Governor Brown was General John Brown Gordon, the second member of the "Bourbon" triumvirate, who, although unheard of before the War, was for forty years thereafter the very incarnation of the Lost Cause and the Old South in the public mind. To his contemporaries he was the authentic folk hero, and a much more superbly cast one than the North had in Grant, for General Gordon possessed a magnificent figure, a faultless bearing, "especially when mounted on horseback," a manner that was chivalrous, genial, and courtly. Upon his face he bore the scar of a wound, but, happily, "instead of marring his countenance, this sabre-wound [less poetically, a Minié-ball mark] only intensified its nobility of expression." Just as his contemporaries were captivated by the man's personality, so the affections of later generations have been engaged by his *Reminiscences*. In all its pages, full of fratricidal carnage as they are, there is not so much as a fleck of gore: invariably, "the fatal grapeshot plunged through his manly heart," and the "chivalric chieftan" died "riding at the head of his regiment, with his sword above him, the fire of battle in his eye and words of cheer for his men on his lips . . ." [18]

At the time of Georgia's secession, Gordon was in the mountains of the extreme northwestern part of the state engaged in the development of coal mines. Rumors of war brought this young Hotspur down from the north hills to Atlanta at the head of a picturesque company of mountaineers, whose "only pretense at uniformity was the rough fur caps made of racoon skins, with long, bushy, streaked racoon tails hanging behind them." They announced that they were the "Racoon Roughs" and that they had come to fight. After their services had been

[18] L. L. Knight, *op cit*, II, pp. 872-873; John B. Gordon, *Reminiscences of the Civil War*, pp. 40, 61, 65.

three times refused and they had been loaded into a train to be shipped back to the mountains, they uncoupled the cars from the engine, and grimly repeated that they were looking for a fight. At the head of these men Gordon, only twenty-nine at the time and entirely without military training, galloped to fame. At Manassas he was when it was won, and at Malvern Hill and five times he was wounded at Antietam, but he was known to have a "charmed life," and on he fought through Gettysburg, the Wilderness, Spottsylvania, Monocacy, and he had been at Lee's last council of war, and led the last charge at Appomattox, "and evermore he hadde a sovereyn prys."

When he returned to Georgia, it was with the rank of Lieutenant General and the distinction of being the most important military figure in the history of the state. Was it not "Georgia's Gordon that divided with his great chieftan, Lee, the sad celebrity of that heroic but irreparable conclusion of the grand drama," and was he not "the second figure to Lee in the dismal glory"? Anything it was the state's to give was the hero's for the asking. First it was the governorship in 1868, but that honor was snatched from him by General Meade, military governor. Next he busied himself with the exploits of the Ku Klux Klan, taking a leading part, it is said. In 1872, as a "New Departure" Democrat, he was elected to the Senate, defeating Hill and Stephens, who "could not withstand the plumed knight of Appomattox"—as indeed, who could! [19]

General Gordon, as one historian has slyly put it, was one of those statesmen, "so prominent in his day, who combined a laudable desire to advance the common weal with large personal ambitions." [20] But his ambitions, other than political, were not those of the planter aristocrat his manner proclaimed, but rather the acquisitive zeal of the rising capitalists and industrialists whom he served. The General's ambitions were munificently gratified, for he became one of the leading railroad promoters of the

[19] I. W. Avery, *op. cit*, pp. 264, 323; Knight, *op. cit.*, II, p. 873.
[20] A. M. Arnett, *op. cit.*, p. 29.

South. The publication of the Collis P. Huntington letters in 1884, which was then second only to the Credit Mobilier scandal as a soiler of Congressional names, revealed Gordon pretty clearly as "one of our men." [21] The New York *World* commented that "A careful examination of the [Huntington] letters shows that . . . Senator Gordon, of Georgia, who posed as the representative of everything respectable in the South, was a servant of the corporation." And yet, in hastily attributing conscious duplicity to General Gordon's actions, one is likely to credit him with a complexity of mind of which he was innocent, for it must be remembered that the General was an authentic hero, and heroes have never been notorious for complex mentalities. Very probably his conscience was no more disturbed by the Huntington affair than President Grant's was by the "gift" of a fifty-thousand-dollar house in Philadelphia, and certainly the former scandal created no greater ripple on the public conscience of Georgia than the latter did on that of the nation. As a further comment upon the times it should be observed that Gordon was subsequently elected governor of the state, and later returned again to the Senate—without so much as a mention of the scandal on his part. The taste for irony was not cultivated in the Gilded Age, and the South apparently saw nothing incongruous in the "Hero of Appomattox" helping a buccaneer capitalist maraud the nation. As a crowning irony, they elected Gordon commander-in-chief of the United Confederate Veterans, an honor he held from the origin of the Veterans' Association in 1890 until his death in 1904; and his mere appearance at the annual reunions always evoked the effect of a tattered battle flag. North and South the General went reciting his oration, "The Last Days of the Confederacy," the burden of which was that both sides had been "right." As an unveiler of monuments, the General knew no peer in his latter days.

[21] The letters are quoted by R. L. Felton, *op. cit*, pp. 82-83, 89, 100, 115; also see *Congressional Record*, 44th Cong, 2 Sess, p. 589; Report and Testimony taken by U. S. Pacific Railroad Commission, *Senate Executive Document* No. 51, 50 Congress, 1 Sess., Vols. II, IV, V; New York *Sun*, Dec. 29 and 30, 1883.

The personal characteristics of General Alfred H. Colquitt, the third member of the triumvirate, present by far the most plausible claim to a legitimate application of the term "Bourbon." In the first place Colquitt was a gentleman of "family." Walter T. Colquitt, his father, was a man of distinction and many accomplishments, legislator, judge, Methodist minister, and "magic-working orator." As a "fire-eating" secessionist he possessed a name that was said to have been a "household word," and as a planter he was the owner of many acres. His son Alfred was said to have been "a worthy son of an honored sire," and to have continued the planter tradition as the master of one of the largest plantations in the state after the War. He was a graduate of Princeton. In 1849, the year Brown entered the State Senate, Colquitt was Assistant Secretary to that body; four years later he was sent to Congress as a state rights man. After the War, in which he served as a brigadier general, he was regularly referred to by orators as the "gallant Hero of Olustee."

Governor Colquitt's connections with Brown and Gordon were financial as well as political, for besides his planting interests, Colquitt was an industrial promoter. In one ambitious venture, the Georgia Pacific Syndicate, with a capital of twelve and one-half million dollars, he was associated with General Gordon, who was president of the Syndicate. He was wont to welcome expanders and financiers from the North and East with open arms.[22] It is true that his chief interests remained those of the large planter, but there were certain forces at work —as will appear later—that were placing a barrier between the interests of the average farmer and those of the few large-scale planters who remained after the War. At any rate Governor Colquitt was not one of those Bourbons, who "clung obstinately to ideas adapted to an order of things gone by": his eye was fixed upon a shining land of the future, the vision that glittered

[22] L. L. Knight, *op. cit.*, II, p. 880; I. W. Avery, *op. cit.*, p. 635; A. M. Arnett, *op. cit.*, pp. 30-31.

and shimmered before the dazzled eyes of Mark Twain's Beriah Sellers when he left home for Washington.

Of the compeers of the "Bourbon Triumvirate," the lesser rulers of the 'seventies and 'eighties, much could be learned that is instructive, but for the most part the telling would suffer from tedious repetition of the three foregoing stories of Brown, Gordon, and Colquitt. For however their stories may differ in certain particulars, the subjects were of a kind, and their preoccupations were not primarily with "things gone by." Of the three governors during these two decades, other than Gordon and Colquitt, one was a lawyer, the second a merchant, lawyer, railroad director and banker, and only the third, Stephens, was personally representative of the great body of small and middle-class farmers who made up the state. And Stephens served only six months. Likewise, the other two senators were representative of the commercial interests. Of the congressmen of the period, thirty were lawyers, business men, or both; three were planters; and one of the number was a combination of small farmer, physician, and preacher. Even the state legislature, the members of which were supposedly in closest touch with the overwhelmingly agrarian constituency of their counties, showed a declining minority of farmer representatives.[23]

It would seem, then, in view of these facts and certain others that will appear later, that new masters were riding the saddle in the South. Whether or not the Civil War had been fought to work the ruin of the agrarian power of the South, and whether or not the Reconstructors had been the advanced missionaries of capitalism, the results—victory for the industrialists and unimpeded expansion—were the same. Nor, as has been seen, did the restoration of home rule mean the restoration of the old order: there were speedily found in the South willing and ready hands to carry forward the torch of "progress." These willing hands were not all recruited in Georgia. A reëxamination of the post-

[23] A M. Arnett, *op. cit.*, pp. 31-32.

war careers of other Southern leaders of the time, might throw a new light upon this period.

One is reminded that the new rulers were, and are still, called "Bourbons." Are we laboring a mere matter of terminology? "Gov. Colquitt and Gen. Gordon," writes one historian in perfect good faith, "stood as *striking types of the most cherished sentiments and practices of our ante-war civilization.*" [24] Instead of a mere mistaken terminology, then, might not the confusion be more fundamental? Might it not be that a golden voice, a flowing beard, a courtly manner have been accepted at face value for "the most cherished sentiments and practices"? At any rate, it would seem wise to avoid the term "Bourbon." In its place, and with the realization that all political epithets share the fault of slovenly thinking, the slogan adopted in 1872, the "New Departure" Democrats will be employed. For several reasons it seems more appropriate: the New Departure marked the Democratic party's first acquiescence in a national platform in the policy of reconstruction; in Georgia it marked the delayed acceptance of Governor Brown's advice to combine the "practical view of the business man" with the duties of the "statesman"; and it marked also loss of control of the party by such men as Toombs and Stephens, and incidentally the defeat of Stephens by General Gordon in the race for the Senate. It was, indeed, a "New Departure."

Having been kept away from the table like naughty children, the South, that is, a small but growing class of Southern men, now rushed in as if by signal to help themselves at the Great Barbecue. Some of them forgot their manners and snatched food with both hands, and all of them forgot that they were crowding out about ninety per cent of the home folks, the farmers, who were not invited, and got none of the 'cue. But the New Departure was tacitly accepted as a blessing to all, and for a while the South followed behind its leaders, who bravely pushed forward into the era of progress.

[24] I. W. Avery, *op. cit.*, p. 604. Italics mine.

It is important to observe that the feud between the old leaders and the new rulers went on over the heads of the submerged masses of the state. Neither the old agrarian leader of the type of Toombs nor the new industrialist Brown was the spokesman of that forgotten majority. The agrarian masses, still leaderless, had not yet stirred from their sleep.

The submissive loyalty that the leaders of the New Departure commanded in Georgia conformed to a pattern found in all Southern states after home rule was restored. "The 'Solid South,' " wrote Henry Watterson in 1879, "is a reaction against proscription, attended by misgovernment, and a protest against the ever-recurring menace of Federal interference." [25] Thus the new discipline was feudal rather than democratic. It was based upon fear—fear of the Negro menace, the scalawag menace, the Federal menace, menaces real and imaginary. As the price of protection, it demanded unquestioning allegiance. White men could not divide on lines of class interest, nor could differences over measures and candidates be expressed at the ballot box. Such matters were settled by the small clique that ran the machine. Democratic forms were observed, but their observance was entirely perfunctory. Party platforms contained nothing but such platitudes as all white men could agree upon. Incompetency and weakness in candidates had to be overlooked for the sake of white solidarity. Suspected graft in public office could not be exposed for fear of Negro domination. Ballot-box stuffing had to be tolerated when white supremacy was threatened. Such was the moral intimidation of this feudal discipline that it was widely felt that to scratch a ticket was "treason to the white race," and to make open declaration of independence was "an effort to africanize the state." [26] In this atmosphere national issues, to say nothing of local ones, were almost lost sight of; politics became

[25] Henry Watterson, "The Solid South," *North American Review*, CXXXVIII (1879), p. 46.
[26] Holland Thompson, *The New South*, pp. 10-12; W. H. Skaggs, *The Southern Oligarchy*, *passim*, esp. pp. 107-108.

a matter of personalities, and public affairs the business of a few politicians.

When one recalls the long tradition of independence and political conflict behind these people, one is surprised that they submitted as long as they did. For not only had they seceded from the Union, but threatened secession from the Confederacy, and even the presence of an invading army could not stop these incorrigible individualists from casting ballots and debating the very existence of their state. Now that peace was restored, they were asked to render a blind obedience that heretofore they had refused even in war.

The Southern Piedmont, that long peninsula that had always resisted the tides of Southern opinion, was the place where revolt first lifted its head after the War. An isolated region of small farmers and few Negroes, it was less swayed by the banner of "respectability" and the bogy of "Negro domination" than the lowlanders. When the farmers of the Seventh Congressional District, the western half of the mountain area, were told by the party convention in 1874 that they must elect L. N. Trammell as their congressman, a cry of "ring-rule" arose. It was widely believed that the candidate was a "Bullock Democrat" and that his nomination had been engineered by Joseph E. Brown.[27] Dr. William H. Felton, a picturesque figure of fiery eloquence, who combined the professions of physician, Methodist preacher, and farmer, entered the race as an independent Democrat. When Felton, with the help of his wife, exposed his opponent's part in the fraudulent bond-issue of the Bullock regime, the machine hastily put forward a second candidate, but neither candidate nor the influence of Brown's railroad could prevail against Dr. Felton's fierce attacks upon "the court-house rings" and "supreme caucuses." Felton was elected again in 1876 and 1878. In the latter year the eastern half of the mountain country, which made up the Ninth District, joined the Independents by sending

[27] R. L. Felton, *op. cit*, pp. 144-147; I. W. Avery, *op. cit.*, pp. 511-512.

to Congress Emory Speer, a more conservative man than Felton, but still an Independent.[28]

To a certain extent these early Independents seem to have been influenced by the Granger movement. The Grange appeared in Georgia in 1872, and in three years built up a membership of 18,000, the largest in the South Atlantic division. Its political influence in the South was much weaker than in the West, but the Independent leaders used its vocabulary: "Men talk of the improvement of business, the revival of business, and all that," exclaimed Dr. Felton. "Do you find it in the homes of the farmer . . . among the mechanics and wealth-creators of the country? No, sir! Absolutely, the rich are growing richer and the poor are growing poorer from day to day." None the less, in dealing with both early and late agrarian movements in the South, as distinct from the West, it is important to remember that they had behind them a longer tradition, and that in many ways the later movements may be thought of as continuous with, or growing out of, the old. In Georgia, Toombs and Stephens served as the nexus between ante- and post-bellum agrarianism. Both were actively sympathetic with the Independents of the 'seventies, and Toombs in his attack upon special privilege, corporations, and trusts in the constitutional convention of 1877, already referred to, sounded remarkably like the Populists two decades later.[29]

Despite the opposition of agrarians, however, the party of the New Departure won a great victory in 1876. Governor Colquitt was elected by the largest majority ever given in the state, and Georgia was presented with a silken banner that signified that she "led the Democratic hosts of the Union." Nevertheless, it was only shortly after this victory that insurgency began to take on the aspect of a state-wide movement.

[28] R. L. Felton, op. cit , passim. I W. Avery, op. cit., p. 513; L. L. Knight, op. cit., II, p 901

[29] R L. Felton, op. cit., pp. 193, 253-254; and Watson Scrapbooks.

First of all Governor Colquitt touched the public conscience upon a point at which it was most sensitive at this time. Despite the legislation of 1874 seeking to put an end to such practices, he endorsed the bonds of the Northeastern Railroad. The wave of protest against his action brought on an investigation that, although vindicating the Governor, merely whetted the public's appetite for further disclosures. There followed a series of investigations, embracing the whole executive department, and as disclosure followed disclosure indignation mounted. As one apologist of the administration artlessly put it, there seemed to be a "morbid plethora of public virtue." The comptroller-general was impeached and convicted on eight counts; the state treasurer was also impeached, but, upon restoring misappropriated funds, was not punished; the commissioner of agriculture resigned following less important disclosures concerning his department; and, on top of these investigations, came the sensational report on the convict lease system.[30] The temper of public feeling may be judged from the tone of Ben Hill's "Address to the People of Georgia," in which he said that the recent scandals threatened "to disgrace our politics, to impoverish honest people, to enrich official rogues, and to threaten our popular institutions with ignominious shame, rottenness and ruin."[31] Up to the year 1880, however, efforts to implicate Colquitt personally in the scandals of his administration had been successful only in spreading the opinion that he had yielded to corrupt associates, and that a general house-cleaning was needed. It was after the pre-convention campaign had started that the event occurred that brought smoldering revolt to sudden flame.

In May, only three weeks before the end of the session, General Gordon suddenly resigned his seat in the Senate, to which he had only recently been reëlected, and Governor Colquitt immediately appointed ex-Governor Brown, who was on his way to Washington before the public learned to its amazement what

[30] I. W. Avery, *op cit*, pp. 540-552; R. L. Felton, *op. cit.*, p. 295.
[31] *Ibid*, pp. 290-292; L. L. Knight, *op cit.*, p 898.

had happened. The charge of "bargain" and "trade" was the spontaneous cry of the insurgents; public meetings were held at which the transaction was denounced as "base and treacherous conduct," "eternal infamy," and a "stench in the nostrils of honest men." It was widely believed that a deliberate bargain had been struck whereby General Gordon, for creating a vacant seat in the Senate, was to be rewarded with the presidency of Brown's railroad, and Colquitt, for appointing Brown to fill the vacancy, was to have the support of Brown in his campaign for reëlection. Although these charges were ridiculed, popular belief in them was later strengthened by the fact that Gordon, instead of taking the railroad position in Oregon, which he said had persuaded him to resign his seat, returned to Georgia to engage in large-scale railroad promotion.[32]

But to understand the intensity of public indignation over these machinations one must appreciate the odium which attached to the name "Joe Brown" in that day. With the same facility the Northern capitalist showed in matters political, Brown had shifted his allegiance from one party to the other; although he had returned to the Democratic party and rendered valuable services to the party machine, his old connection with the Carpetbag Republicans had never been forgotten. A Georgia novel of the time, while defending Brown, lamented that "It was currently believed, by some, that he was always engaged with governors, legislatures, city councils, railroad officials, and great speculators, in certain mysteries" and that "if the mask could only be torn off, this saint of the church . . . would be found to be the wiliest hypocrite, the most hardened, skilful, practiced, unconscionable knave on the face of the earth." [33] Yet it was upon an alliance with Brown that the New Departure had to stand or fall in the election of 1880.

General Gordon, apparently forgetting the urgency of the

[32] R. L. Felton, *op. cit.*, pp. 295-311; I. W. Avery, *op. cit.*, pp. 561, 635; H. Fielder, *op. cit.*, pp. 522-524.
[33] William Dugas Trammell, *Ça Ira* (New York, 1874), pp. 30-35, 303. The character called "Malcomb" is easily identified as Joseph E. Brown.

Oregon railroad position that had not permitted him to remain in the Senate three weeks longer, hurried home to join Governor Colquitt in a state-wide campaign of "vindication." "The coming campaign," observed an editorial in one of the opposition papers, "will be Colquitt, Brown, and Gordon against any man who will step to the front. Brown with his money, Gordon with his buttons, and Colquitt with his religion will make a combination that can not be beaten." [34] As the date of the nominating convention approached the invincibility of this combination appeared more and more probable.

[34] Columbus *Daily Times*, May 25, 1880; R. L Felton, *op. cit.*, pp. 276-282.

CHAPTER V

Preface to Rebellion

WHEN THE NOMINATING CONVENTION met in Atlanta on August 4, it quickly became apparent that, although the votes were divided among five candidates, every one of the 549 delegates had come resolved on one of two purposes—to nominate Governor Colquitt or to defeat that nomination. From the first ballot Colquitt was shown to have a large majority, but not the two-thirds which, according to the rule adopted, was necessary to make him the nominee. Nor would the determined anti-Colquitt minority be persuaded to yield the handful of votes that would increase his vote to two-thirds. Throughout barrages of oratory, appeals to patriotism, and prophecies of the certain doom of "white supremacy" the opposition held its ranks firm. Ballot after ballot only served to emphasize its solidarity and to fix the majority firmer in its determination to nominate Colquitt.

On the third day one of the minority chiefs came forward with the proposal that a committee of representatives from both sides be appointed to select a compromise candidate. In answer to this proposal Patrick Walsh of Augusta, the leader of the Colquitt forces, rose to speak. An Irishman, though "with nothing in him of the mercurial and flashing," Walsh was representative of the new type of Southern leader, the aggressive, self-made business man. Stocky of body, with a massive head set solidly upon a stout neck, he was of manner blunt and "as direct as the course of a cannon ball." In Augusta he managed the strategic Catholic vote so expertly that he was able to boss the politics of his district.[1] His speech in answer to the proposed compromise was a quick succession of hammer-blow sentences that were intended to crush out any hope the minority might have left. He concluded: ". . . and we do not intend to depart from the city of Atlanta until we have nominated Alfred H. Colquitt! (Great applause.) We have come here to do that if it takes us until Christmas to do it. (Renewed cheering.)"

After a ballot had been taken and the excitement over Walsh's ultimatum had partially subsided, it was discovered that an extremely young man was addressing the house, his voice, "shrill and ringing," almost drowned in the ebbing excitement. He made a second start. It was not his renewed proposal of a committee to select a compromise candidate that gained him attention. It was perhaps the striking contrast he presented to the preceding speaker and to the surrounding graybeards: his boyish figure, "so slight it seemed you could circle his chest with two hands," his freckled, immature face, and something audacious in the way he tossed his shock of red hair. When he paused after reading a list of possible candidates and mounted his chair to conclude, he had the attention of the whole house. He was answering Walsh's ultimatum:

Sir, I am tired of hearing the cry of generosity, when I see no generosity (applause); I am tired of the cry of harmony when I see no harmony. (Applause.) I have not come here to be fattened on chaff, nor filled with taffy. You might as well attempt to gain flesh on corn cob soup in January. (Laughter.)

Mr. Chairman, I have said, and I say now, that I am here with no bitterness of partisan rancor. I have fought this much-named gentleman, A. H. Colquitt. I have fought him honestly. I have advocated Rufus Lester. I have advocated him honestly. But high and serene above them both, above my opposition to Colquitt, above my support of Lester rises my love, my devotion to my state, like the tranquil star

---

[1] Augusta *Daily Chronicle and Constitutionalist*, July 2, 1882; Augusta *Chronicle*, Sept. 20, 1890; Athens *Watchman*, Watson Scrapbooks.

that burns and gleams beyond the reach of the drifting clouds. (Cheers.) But Sir, under the course of the gentleman from Richmond [Walsh], I am debarred from this privilege. He tells us that we must yield to him, and that unless we nominate Colquitt that this party will permit no nomination. Mr. Chairman, this is not the language which a friend addresses to a friend. It is not the language a brother addresses to a brother. It is the language of a master to his slave. (Cheers.)

We are the slaves of no man. We haven't come here to bulldoze anybody and we haven't come here to be bulldozed. (Cheers.)

Sir, a silken cord might draw me, but all the cables of all the ships that walk the waters of all the seas cannot drag me. (Cheers.)

Sir, the gentleman's position means that we must take Colquitt or the party will be disrupted. Sir, if it must come, let it come. (Cheers.) We love the party, honor it, are devoted to it, but we will not yield when the gentleman's speech has made it a loss of self-respect to surrender.

If they will split the convention, we will be here to the end (applause); if they will sink the ship, we will remain in her shadow to the last. (Applause.) We would deprecate it. We would deplore it. But if she can only be saved on terms as unmanly as these then—

> "Nail to the mast her holy flag,
> Set every threadbare sail,
> And give her to the god of storms,
> The lightning and the gale." [2]

As he took his seat, the name of Tom Watson flew from lip to lip, and those who had never heard of the red-headed young man from McDuffie County were not long in learning who he was. The noisy demonstration of the minority stopped proceedings while delegates from all over the house pressed around Watson to congratulate him. Colquitt newspapers, unable to ignore the news value of "the youngest member of the convention"—he was not yet twenty-four—creating the greatest sensation of the day, printed his speech in full, and papers all over the state took up the story of the young man who "made the

[2] Atlanta *Daily Constitution*, Aug. 7, 1880.

most brilliant speech in the convention" and "gave so many black eyes to the bulldozing majority and its arrogant leader." [3]

Thus Tom Watson made his political debut as a rebel, flying all the colors of revolt. It was not his last appearance in that rôle.

Upon the motion of Walsh, Watson's resolution was promptly tabled, and a Colquitt man provoked a burst of victorious laughter by shouting, "I move the molehill now come to the mountain." [4] If the majority was unterrified by prospects of "sinking the ship," the "molehill" showed no signs of moving. The response of the minority to Watson's speech had removed all but the faintest hope of reconciliation. Four days later the convention was facing the same stalemate. One delegate, fixing upon Walsh and Watson as the opposite poles among the irreconcilables, admonished: "I would respectfully ask these gentlemen what, in this state of things, is to become of the democratic party whose interests require a nomination?" Watson, for his part, protested that he did not occupy the extreme anti-Colquitt position; he had come with no personal bitterness against Colquitt, nor would he have refused to accept him rather than split the party. He continued with emphasis:

. . . we were shown from the first that we must take Colquitt. They would try no other course. We were tied to the names before us. Hemmed up, penned out, starved out. It was then I said that these gyves being upon me I could never go to Colquitt, and I never will. (Applause.) Upon this record I am willing to go back to my people, and if for this record I am sacrificed I shall always think that I am entitled to a decent burial and an honorable epitaph. (Applause.)

So formidable was the impasse that the convention adjourned without making a nomination. Colquitt was "recommended" by the vote of the majority, but no official Democratic nominee was

[3] Clippings from Augusta *News*, Louisville *News and Farmer*, Macon *Telegraph*, and Savannah *News*, MS. Journal 2, pp. 282-283.
[4] I. W. Avery, *History of Georgia*, p. 580.

76

put before the state—a circumstance unique in the history of the party. The minority, resolving itself into a rump meeting, then "recommended" as its candidate Thomas M. Norwood, a former United States senator.[5] With the "White Man's Party" now split, the people, for the first time since the War, were permitted to select their governor at the ballot box.

* * * * * *

In the days when Watson began the practice of his profession, the hustings were as naturally the haunt of lawyers as the bar, and almost from the time the young lawyer began to ride the circuit he found himself "in politics." Where the Superior Court convened, the political lions congregated, and one had to take sides. Thus, at the session of 1879, in Crawfordville, Watson noted: "Am introduced to Seab Reese, the Solicitor, and admire him. He is lordly in bearing, smokes like an engine, and drinks like a horse. Am in a game of whist with him till a late hour." The same year he and his partner Johnson attended a banquet in Augusta to celebrate the victory of Judge Claiborne Snead over the Augusta "ring." "Here were poets, editors, reporters, cotton-men, and preachers. . . . I was called on, responded, and was cheered loudly and long." But a more glorious triumph came at the home of his idol, Alexander Stephens. "Spent the evening at Liberty Hall," he recorded, "sitting with a party of gentlemen and Mr. Stephens on the back piazza eating peaches and talking politics." There had been a great barbecue and much speech-making. "It was a glorious day to me. My speech took well. Mr. Stephens complimented me especially." That night he lay vainly awaiting sleep. "It seemed to me that a thousand associations of greatness were buzzing around me. I could hear Mr. Stephens' voice, shrill and clear talking all the while downstairs." [6]

[5] Atlanta *Daily Constitution*, Aug. 10-14, 1880.
[6] MS. Journal 2, pp. 209-214.

To the old Confederate Watson looked eagerly for leadership. During a visit in July, 1878, he had watched the aged invalid open a copy of the Augusta *Chronicle*, Patrick Walsh's paper, glance at the leading editorial, and, flinging the paper away from his wheel-chair, remark, "Well, I see this fellow means a fight." [7] Watson supported Stephens against Walsh that year. In 1880, though taking no active part in the campaign, Stephens opposed Colquitt's nomination, saying he was "not fit for Governor." [8] General Toombs, another of Watson's idols, confessed to Stephens that he felt "deeply humiliated for the State to have two such Senators as Gordon and Hill, both venal and corrupt." [9] He joined actively in the campaign against Colquitt in 1880. In view of the position of Stephens and Toombs on the issues of that year, there was little doubt what Watson's attitude would be.

"For myself," he wrote, "I had never admired Gov. Colquitt and the appointment of Brown turned me strongly against him." Watson became a candidate for delegate to the convention: "I worked with great ardor. The issue was squarely Colquitt and anti-Colquitt. I was elected—running ahead of my ticket who were all chosen excepting Hardaway . . ." [10]

Because of the hearty endorsement given him by his constituents and the militant and uncompromising position he assumed in his speech before the convention, Watson's secret confession comes as something of a surprise: "After the split," he wrote, "I hesitated long what to do." After all, there was an important difference between insurgency against the machine candidate within the party, and party revolution. More than one timorous delegate withdrew from the minority convention when it was decided to nominate a separate candidate. The business man's party of the New Departure enjoyed enormous pres-

[7] *Loc. cit.*
[8] R. L Felton, *Memoirs of Georgia Politics*, p 286.
[9] Toombs to Stephens, Mar. 25, 1880, U B. Phillips., ed , *Correspondence of Robert Toombs, Alexander Stephens, Howell Cobb*, pp 739-740
[10] MS. Journal 2, p 281.

tige for having overthrown the Carpetbag regime, restored "home rule," and saved "Anglo-Saxon civilization." Though fighting under the standard of the same party, the insurgent wing was seeking the overthrow of the machine that commanded and exploited this loyalty. It had also to bear the odium of "bringing the Negro back into politics," from which he had been largely eliminated in the early 'seventies at the cost of unquestioning white solidarity. Now he would be called in to decide between the two white factions.[11] The experience of Reconstruction was fresh in the minds of the people, and to many the insurgents represented nothing more than a relapse to moral anarchy. Still another handicap of the insurgents was the weakness of their candidate, Norwood, who seems to have been ineffectual as a speaker, deficient in popular appeal, and lacking in sympathy for the Negroes, whom he had antagonized by previous utterances.[12] Aside from these there were doubtless more personal reasons to account for Watson's hesitancy in making the plunge. He had to consider his future. At the very outset of his political career he was about to enter into open strife with the most powerful machine politician in his district, Patrick Walsh. He made his decision: "Finally concluding to go the whole hog, I took the stump . . ."[13]

With young George F. Pierce as his colleague, Watson campaigned county after county. Favorable reports came from his home. "McDuffie will soon be a grand Norwood Club," it was said. "The county will strongly endorse the course of Mr. Watson. In fact, we are all Watson men." In Augusta "the brilliant young orator" was received with great enthusiasm; crowds followed him to his hotel for a second speech. He regretted the split in the party, but the Colquitt faction, because of its failure to abide by its own two-thirds rule, was alone responsible for the disruption. The arrogant and dictatorial attitude of the machine

[11] I. W. Avery, *op cit*, pp. 585-586.
[12] Atlanta *Daily Constitution*, Aug 24, 29, 1880; R L. Felton, *op cit*, pp. 273-274; I. W. Avery, *op. cit*, p 591.
[13] MS. Journal 2, p. 281.

politicians more than justified revolt. As for Colquitt, Watson attacked the numerous scandals associated with his administration, the high taxes he had levied, and questionable appointments he had made. He also elucidated the evils of the disgraceful convict lease system, showing the governor's responsibility for it, and how Senator Brown and others were exploiting hundreds of these state slaves, for whose labor they paid only seven cents a day. This part of his speech was "well received by the colored people." One statement of Watson's at this time gains added significance in the light of later years. "He was a Democrat," he told them, "but when Democratic principles are forsaken he would seek some other home and there rest his cause." [14]

In addition to its precedence in the field, its well organized machine, and its possession of office, the party of the New Departure had other considerable advantages. On Colquitt's campaign committee was an aggressive group of young capitalists, "leaders among the business princes of middle Georgia and especially Atlanta." Chairman of that committee was young Henry W. Grady, the magic of whose personality already gave him a widespread influence. Grady "threw himself into the struggle with his whole heart"; his "enthusiasm was irresistible, and he finally took the undisputed command." [15] With his paper, the *Constitution*, most of the press lined up for Colquitt. Despite his evil name in the state, Joseph E. Brown, now senator, with his multiple railroad interests, religious philanthropies, educational endowments, and hundreds of employees, was perhaps more of a help than a hindrance. In winning the coveted Negro votes, Colquitt, as a Republican paper put it, "was assisted by that excellent man, Joseph Brown, who, having been a Radical at one time, understood the business." [16]

Unlike his opponent, Governor Colquitt carried on a vigorous

[14] Clippings, *Ibid.*, pp. 282-285.
[15] I. W. Avery, *op. cit*, pp. 254, 269.
[16] R. L. Felton, *op. cit*, p 273.

speaking campaign in all parts of the state in his own behalf. He was seeking "vindication," he said. One of his chief complaints was that his opponents abused him "about going to Sunday schools." [17] He was "being persecuted for Christ's sake, and he called upon all religious people in the state to rally to the maintenance of pure religion against infidelity." Always at his side was the redoubtable "Hero of Appomattox," General John B. Gordon, whose golden voice was Colquitt's greatest asset. "Why should Colquitt be questioned?" asked the General. "Is he not the hero of Olustee! Colquitt is persecuted because he floated the banner of the King of kings." [18]

The state had seen heated campaigns before, but the contest of 1880, wrote a historian of that period, "was such a tornado of violence as to make all previous disturbances mere child's play." Both the corrupt practices of the Carpetbaggers and the methods of the Ku Klux Klan were again brought into play. Charges and counter charges of corruption, intimidation, and violence were made, many of which were unquestionably true. The Colquitt machine, however, was more successful, for Colquitt won by various means the great majority of the Negro vote. Combined with a minority of the white vote it outnumbered the poll of the insurgents.[19] The revolt was crushed, but the leaders of the New Departure had been seriously challenged and they were stirred by apprehensions for the future. In spite of numerous handicaps the insurgents won about thirty-five per cent of the popular vote.

"Goodmorrow, Tutt,[20] of McDuffie! Regards to Colonel Watson," taunted Henry Grady's paper, announcing the returns from that county. Watson's ticket had not won a third of

[17] Atlanta *Daily Constitution*, Sept. 29, 1880.
[18] R. L. Felton, *op. cit*, p. 268; I. W. Avery, *op cit.*, p. 593.
[19] Atlanta *Daily Constitution*, Sept. 29, Oct. 9, 1880; I. W. Avery, *op. cit.*, p. 591; R. L. Felton, *op. cit.*, pp. 273-274; W. H. Skaggs, *The Southern Oligarchy*, p. 141, quoting Watson, and pp. 107-108.
[20] W. D. Tutt, a rival lawyer, had supported Colquitt; both Watson and Tutt had directed personalities against one another during the campaign.

the votes cast in his own county. Watson was remarkably unperturbed, even nonchalant. "Jordan White swears that I made more out of the campaign first and last than any man in the State," he noted in his Journal. Then he added sententiously, with the cynicism that is the privilege of the very young, "Young men are not affected so much by results. They are not held responsible. They make a certain show-parade. They are judged by its worth." [21]

The episode of 1880 was a proper prologue for the drama of the next four decades in which Tom Watson figured as protagonist. The theme was clearly announced: the Solid South against the insurgent rebels, the new capitalists against the old and new agrarians. The Negro was introduced in his inevitable role, a black Nemesis. The chorus of shibboleths would remain the same: race chauvinism, religious superstition, military fetishism. The action was derived from that of Reconstruction. The capitalists would become more class conscious, and, as their alliance with the Northeast was strengthened, more self confident and ruthless. The agrarians would become much better organized, and, as their alliance with the West was strengthened, more militant, and, with increasing repression, more desperate. The conflict would multiply a hundredfold in bitterness and intensity.

Looking back wearily from the distance of twice his age at this time Watson spoke of himself as a "namby-pamby Democrat in 1880." "I was a Reformer, all right," he declared, "and was going to get the reforms inside the dear old Democratic party. . . . The burden of my little song was: Bad men have come into the party and have had things pretty much their own way; but we must drive these bad men out; put the good men in control, and thus get reforms inside the Democratic party." [22] Here was speaking the disillusioned man of fifty whose primary

[21] MS. Journal 2, p. 281.
[22] Quoted by Sara Lois Gray, "Thomas E. Watson" (Master's thesis, Emory University), p. 32.

concern was "results." At half that age his preoccupation was still "a certain show-parade." When the campaign was over he wrote: "Stump speaking is glorious! The inspiration of the band, the cheers of the crowd, the ready echo to every blazing sentiment and sparkling anecdote leads the orator to a brilliant feast on the Field of the Cloth of Gold." [23]

[23] MS. Journal 2, p. 252.

The Temper of the 'Eighties

THE COLLAPSE OF THE INSURGENT MOVEMENT in 1880 removed the last formidable barrier from the path of the New Departure for a decade more and marked the beginning of a new era. The political peace and acquiescence of the 'eighties contrasted gratefully with the war of the 'sixties and the revolution of the 'seventies. Energy and imagination, wearied by stale feuds and recriminations, turned hopefully toward the glittering prizes promised by capitalists and industrialists. The new decade afforded no rôle for the agrarian rebel, whether a Bob Toombs of the older generation or a Tom Watson of the new. The career opened so brilliantly by Watson in 1880 was virtually closed to him for the next ten years, for Watson in any other rôle than rebel was miscast. It was during this period of marking time, however, that ideas that were perhaps the product of opportunism and temperament took firm root in him and his class, found nutriment in the soil of rebel tradition, and burgeoned into a hardy native growth. It was in this period, too, that the economic setting was prepared for what Watson in a moment of optimism pronounced "Not a Revolt; It Is a Revolution."

In an address before the General Assembly on November 13, 1880, the night before the senatorial election, Joseph E. Brown frankly interpreted the issues at stake, and unconsciously enunciated the dominant mood of the 'eighties. Reminding his audience that "The voters of General Toombs's own county decided in favor of Governor Colquitt and myself by over 700 majority," he candidly announced, "I accept the issue, then . . . If the people of Georgia think that a man should be sent to the Senate to represent that sentiment of the old ruling class . . . then I admit that my honorable opponent [Lawton] is a fit represen ative." On the other hand if they agreed with him that "we live in a new era, and the new South must adopt new ideas, must wake up to new energy," he was their choice. As for General Toombs, since "the country must move forward, we are obliged to leave him there and let him cuss. (Prolonged laughter and applause.)" As to the class he represented, he left no question: I seek "to build up the manufacturing interest of the country. . . . We have in the future no negroes to buy; we are making money; we shall want investments." With this in view he had, he explained, during his temporary office in the Senate, talked to many Northern capitalists: "Again, I stated that we had the advantage in cheap labor, and that the raw material is produced in the fields around the factories themselves. . . . When I told them of the profits made by our Augusta mills, and the high price the stock bore, some gentlemen of capital said they desired to look further into the matter . . ." [1]

The greatest triumph of Brown's address, which was intended as a sort of vindication, was his reading of a letter written by General Robert E. Lee said to have "had the startling authority of a miracle." According to Mr. Brown, General Lee "entertained the same views and gave the same advice," a coincidence that proved "the old hero was of good judg-*ment.*" "Which will you follow," asked the candidate, "Toombs . . . or Lee?" One of these gentlemen was disfranchised, and the other was dead and past denying this strange disciple. Georgia followed Joseph E. Brown.

It was an unerring instinct that led the new masters to discern the need for some pageantry of dedication, some ceremony

[1] Herbert Fielder, *Life and Times of Joseph E Brown*, pp. 536-559.

of fealty here on the threshold of the new order. It was the Southern way. So it was that "a grand parliament of industry" was decreed, the International Cotton Exposition, "the first World's Fair in the South." Senator Joseph E. Brown was the first president of the Exposition, Governor Colquitt the second. "Businessmen took hold of it eagerly," and the work moved forward.[2]

Atlanta, variously styled by enthusiasts of the time "the offspring of railroads," "the Chicago of the South," the "City of Conventions," or "the Giant Young Metropolis," was thought of as the capital of the New South. "A nervous energy permeates all classes of people and all departments of trade," it was observed in 1881, "and the spirit of enterprise never sleeps."[3] Appropriately, it was selected as host for the Exposition.

The Exposition opened on October 5, 1881, "with imposing ceremonies." Senator Zebulon B. Vance of North Carolina extended a "soulful Southern welcome" inviting visitors "to see that we have renewed our youth at the fountains of industry and found the hills of gold in the energies of an imperishable race." Senator D. W. Vorhees, of Indiana, replied by welcoming the South to "the arena to contend for the first time for the supremacy in all the industrial pursuits," a strife "over which the angels of heaven have joy."[4] Through the Exposition building, with its twenty acres of floor space, its eighteen hundred exhibits, and its hymns of enterprise, salesmanship, and profit, Southerners thronged for three months. Young men, recalling Ben Hill's advice not "to pine away or fret to exhaustion for imaginary treasures hopelessly lost," but to "reach out their hands and gather richer treasures piled up all around them," saw new careers open to them. Northern capitalists verified rumors of cheap labor and fat profits. Out of the enthusiasm engendered the *Industrial Review* was founded; the very Ex-

[2] I. W. Avery, *History of Georgia*, p. 650.
[3] E. Y. Clarke, *Atlanta Illustrated, passim*
[4] I. W. Avery, *op. cit*, pp 648-649

position buildings were converted into a cotton factory; between 1880 and 1885 the number of cotton spindles in the Southern states doubled.[5]

Poets, novelists, preachers, educators, journalists, historians—professionals once in the service of an agrarian state—swung rapidly into procession behind the new leaders. "Set by the steam-god's fiery passion free," wrote Paul Hamilton Hayne, in "The Exposition Ode":[6]

> I hear the rise and fall
> Of pondrous, iron-clamped machinery
> Shake, as with earthquake thrill, the factory halls. . . .
> Quick merchants pass, some debonair and gay,
> With undimmed youthful locks—
> Some wrinkled, sombre, gray;
> But all with one accord
> Dreaming of him—their lord,
> The mighty monarch of the realm of stocks.

A novelist, through thinly disguised fiction, celebrated the exploits of Joseph E. Brown, and proclaimed him "the most representative man of our new civilization" and "perhaps the richest man in the state."[7] Historians echoed with chapters upon the "splendid demonstrations of individual management, and formidable coalitions of capital and genius," "dramatic audacities of railway enterprise," "enterprise full of romantic eventfulness."

Fifteen religious institutions of five denominations in the South were recipients of gifts from Joseph E. Brown ranging from $500 to $53,000. His smaller charities were "simply innumerable." In 1883 the trustees of the University of Georgia, after some caviling by legislators over "tainted money" and

[5] P. M. Wilson, *Southern Exposure*, pp. 141-143; *Appleton's Annual Cyclopaedia, 1881*, pp. 260-271; H. Thompson, *The New South*, pp. 89-90
[6] Atlanta *Constitution*, Oct. 6, 1881.
[7] W. D Trammell, *Ça Ira, passim*, especially pp 303-304

constitutional questions, accepted a donation of $50,000 from Brown, with one dissenting vote—that of General Toombs.[8] That same year the General Assembly heard a report on the proposed establishment of a state school of technology: "In the development of manufactures, therefore, lies the hope of our people." Since "Georgia needs some such agency to arouse the spirit of her people on the subject of manufacturing enterprise," a state school should be established in which "everything is simply subordinate to the leading idea of technical education."[9]

By the turn of the decade "the large majority" of the newspapers of the state was one chorus of approval for the New Departure. No other paper, however, approached in this respect the importance and significance of the Atlanta *Constitution*. This was not because it had a phenomenal circulation, four times greater than the population of Atlanta, but because it was the organ of Henry Woodfin Grady, whose personality loomed larger than any paper and pervaded the whole South.

A sword may be surrendered with more grace and dignity than a point of view. Following the example set by General Lee (later institutionalized by General Gordon) Southerners had bowed to military defeat without serious loss of face, but it was not until later that they learned from Henry Grady how words could be swallowed without leaving a brown taste. "The South," Grady said and declared he could prove, "found her jewel in the toad's head of defeat."

The new railroad barons, mine owners, and captains of industry were, generally speaking, a grim and bearded lot, with unenviable reputations for sharp dealing, and, as the eulogist of one of them remarked, "with a narrowed range of thought in some matters due to lack of early culture." As peerless champion of that group (yet always with a word for the "Heroes in Gray"), now stepped forward an almost uniquely clean-shaven

[8] H. Fielder, *Life of Joseph E. Brown*, pp. 568-587; I. W. Avery, *op cit.*, pp. 605-606.

[9] *Georgia House Journal*, pp. 230-255, July 24, 1883.

young man of infectious enthusiasm, radiant, eloquent, and perennially boyish. Grady played the part of an irrepressible good caliph-at-large in Georgia, dispensing a gospel of optimism, charity, and fun. His zest for fun-making led to such extravagances as his "leg artist" contests, endurance walking competitions in which his reporters participated. There followed a craze for such matches in the early 'eighties. It was said that "He was related by some act of kindness to every individual in his native state." [10] To question the motives of such a man would be churlish.

At the young editor's side, though keeping always shyly in the background, was the most lovable literary figure in the South—Joel Chandler Harris, chief editorial writer of the *Constitution*.[11] There was no resisting this partnership of major prophet of the New South and tenderest chronicler of the Old South. Southerners generally quite lost their hearts to them.

Grady's services to the new order were manifold. There was much to be done. It was necessary that the acquisitive instincts not only become respectable, but that they be regarded as ambition. Speculation should be awarded the prizes of courage and valor, and the profit motive mile-posted as the road to the good life. The lives of those men who traveled that road had to be invested with a glamour that would evoke emulation, their destination recognized as "success," and the changes they wrought be regarded as "progress." Indeed it was important that the meaning of life be discovered in the vicissitudes and triumphs attending the competitive struggle for business profits.

"It is a revelation to any provincial to enter the gallery of the stock exchange and gaze upon the floor below," wrote Grady from New York. The sight "kindles the blood of an onlooker as a battle would." Grady delighted in relating such stories as that of a man who "had gone to Colorado a few years before as

[10] J. W. Lee, *Henry W. Grady, The Editor, the Orator, the Man, passim*; also Joel C. Harris, *Henry W. Grady*, p. 90.
[11] Mrs. Julia Collier Harris, *Joel Chandler Harris, Editor and Essayist*, pp. 36-37.

a newsdealer and was now worth not less than $10,000,000, and owned a bank, a railroad, and the Little Pittsburgh mine," or that of "the man whose brother's son had bought a mine for $25 and sold it in a month for $400,000," or one of "a fellow who had [been] furnished with money to buy his meals with a few months ago, and was now worth over a million." [12]

Nor was Grady daunted by more prosaic subjects. "I have the greatest interest in the history of these self-made men," he wrote. "Atlanta is the home of this sturdy genus, and I have thought that this was one secret of her wonderful advancement. . . . They enrich the blood, quicken her pulses and give her vitality, force and power." He was wont to dwell on the stories of their rise from obscurity to wealth—one of "the great dry goods merchant, who sells nearly a million a year," another of a business man "now prosperous and rich and growing richer"— polishing them till they took on the lustre of his imagination. "They have sunk the corner stone," he declared, "of the only aristocracy that Americans should know." [13]

A more tangible service, perhaps, was the perfect flood of publicity that Grady gave to Southern resources for industrial development. His oratorical poems picturing "mountains stored with exhaustless treasures, forests, vast and primeval, and rivers that, tumbling or loitering, run wanton to the sea" were one long hymn of invocation to preëmption and exploitation.[14] "He did not tamely promote enterprise and encourage industry," wrote an admirer; "he vehemently fomented enterprise and provoked industry until they stalked through the land like armed conquerors." [15]

"I am no pessimist as to this Republic," announced Grady. "I always bet on sunshine in America. . . . The trend of the times is with us. The world moves steadily from gloom to

[12] Atlanta *Constitution*, March 24, 1880.
[13] *Ibid.*, Aug. 15, 1880.
[14] J. C. Harris, *Henry W. Grady*, p. 182.
[15] Quoted by Oliver Deyr in his "Introduction" to Henry W. Grady's *The New South*

brightness." [16] The spell of this radiant optimism spread over the South like a warm April sun after the season of rain.

* * * * * *

Despite the wholesale regimentation of public opinion behind the New Departure persistent rumors of revolt arose in the winter of 1881. These rumors centered around Dr. William H. Felton, the old Independent warhorse. Senator Benjamin H. Hill, after an attack by Felton for his defection to the New Departure, answered with a diatribe against the Independent movement. His argument, published by Grady, is worth attention as a model of the dialectic employed by the new masters against dissent throughout the next two decades:

Factories are springing up in all directions. Our industries are being multiplied as never before. Thousands of the best men of the North have gone home from the exposition enthused with the brightening prospects of all business in the State. Our taxes were scarcely ever so low. Our credit was never so high. Capital and people and machinery are flowing in, and everybody is brushing away the tears of war, and laughing with a new hope in a new era! All this, all this has been accomplished under the rule of the men who are denounced by trading politicians as narrow-minded, intolerant Bourbons. . . . Must our peace be destroyed, race collisions again provoked, and our budding prosperity arrested merely to gratify a few men who are willing to run with all parties and be true to none?[17]

Yet this was the woe the Independents would wreak by their "blatant pretenses of reform, and still more blatant outcries against that mythical monster—the Bourbon Democracy of the South."

Hill's diatribe, widely quoted, was considered a severe blow to the Independents, but it did not deter them from organizing

[16] J. C. Harris, *op. cit*, p. 156.
[17] B. H. Hill, Jr., *Life of Benjamin H. Hill*, p. 822.

91

and issuing a call to all who agreed "that neither the Republican party nor the Democratic party as at present organized can subserve the vital interests of the people" to meet them in convention.[18]

As time for nominations for the election of 1882 drew near, the eyes of Independent and New Departure leaders alike turned toward the dwarfed invalid of the brilliant eyes in the rolling chair at Liberty Hall. Alexander Stephens occupied a strategic place between the rival parties. His pathetic, gnarled figure, his long public record before, during, and after the War, and his present position, which was committed to neither party, commanded a following that might turn the balance one way or the other.

No one waited more eagerly for the Sage's decision than Tom Watson. When it was announced that "It is now definitely known . . . that Mr. Alexander H. Stephens will retire from politics at the end of the present term of Congress," [19] his young disciple's emotions overflowed into verse: [20]

> Hushed is his voice of silver
> Its echoes die away
> And the clouds of night arise
> Around his closing day.

Older politicians were not so quick to despair. Just as Talleyrand would meet a political quandary by taking to his bed, Stephens would decline to run and announce his retirement from politics, ". . . yet [he] never failed to run as soon as the coast was clear." [21] Even at that time he was corresponding with leaders of both parties. Following closely the development of the plans of the Independents, he had given them particular encouragement; yet when he was nominated for governor by their

[18] R. L. Felton, *Memoirs of Georgia Politics*, pp. 335-341.
[19] Atlanta *Constitution*, March 9, 1882.
[20] MS. Journal 2, p. 73.
[21] R. L. Felton, *op. cit.*, p. 351.

convention of May, 1882, he forgot his letters to their leaders and declined to run.[22] When it became apparent that he was giving ear to Brown and Colquitt, it was said that "Mr. Stephens in his mental and physical weakness is a mere tool in the hands of designing men." [23] The New Departure papers, indeed, made no secret of their hopes: "The *Chronicle* believes that Mr. Stephens' nomination [for Governor] will heal all breaches in the party and that the very mention of his name will destroy all elements of Independent opposition." [24] The Democratic Convention in July would reveal Stephens' position.

Watson, himself a candidate for the Legislature, arrived in Atlanta before the Convention opened. He was recalled by the papers as "the young man eloquent of 1880." The fact that he came from Stephens' district, it was thought, "answers the question as to his gubernatorial preferences." Stephens established himself at the Kimball House, chief headquarters for delegates and candidates. Young Watson found excuse for loitering in his room by the hour every day. He thought the old statesman's "pallid, shrivelled face was beautifully benevolent, and his eyes were radiant with the tenderness of a noble heart." He listened as Stephens dictated a letter of reconciliation to his old enemy, Ben Hill, then on his death bed, and the incident fired his imagination.[25] The papers reported that "among . . . [Stephens'] many visitors in the early morning was Senator Brown. They held sweet converse for a lengthy time . . ." [26]

Another guest of the Kimball House trod its corridors in no such benevolent and conciliatory frame of mind. Unregenerate and unreconstructed, General Robert Toombs made no secret of

[22] *Ibid.*, pp. 343-344, 362. Mrs. Felton writes: "The aged Statesman, under the influence of continual hypodermics, aided by stimulants which were constantly kept up, was led along until he actually forgot what he had written to Judge Hook, to Dr. Felton, to his most intimate friends in Georgia, and to myself—his constant correspondent."

[23] Macon *Telegraph* quoted by Augusta *Chronicle and Constitutionalist*, July 4, 1882.

[24] *Ibid.*, July 4, 1882.

[25] T. E. W., *Sketches*, pp. 282-283.

[26] Augusta *Herald*, July 18, 1882.

his opinion of his old friend Stephens' dalliance with the New Departure. Puzzled by this difference between his heroes, Watson nevertheless divided his adoration impartially between them. But never was the hero-worshiper in Tom so evident as when Toombs was its object. Around and about the lobby and bar of the hotel he followed the General, an assiduous Boswell. Never, he noted, did "the inborn, imperial superiority of Toombs make itself so conspicuously self-evident as it did in his lordly bearing *at the* breakfast table." Here, surely, the image he guarded so jealously in his heart found a living reflection—set with a seal "To give the world assurance of a man." It was the way he liked to think of his grandfather, "tall, venerable, imposing." Here, too, was a satisfying image of the rebel: "His hair was iron-gray, abundant, disordered, like the mane of a lion, but becoming to him as in his prime. Decidedly he was the most leonine old man I ever beheld. He was a ruin, but majestic and impressive."

In the evening the General, deep in his cups, entered the bar at the head of a procession of admirers, obviously enjoying his position. "Wherever he stopped," observed Watson, "a group would gather to hear him talk. . . . It was like going to see Vesuvius in eruption." Spotting a Northerner in his audience, Toombs seized upon the mention of his late opponents as occasion for an explosion against the North:

"Hate it? Of course I hate it. Why shouldn't I? Am I more or less than human? Haven't they given me cause enough? Didn't they drench my country with blood and sweep it with fire? Haven't they deprived me of the rights of a free man? . . . But I am an old man. My day is passed. The people seem to have lost heart. The South is ruled by as cowardly and venal a lot of place-hunting politicians as ever lived. Like putrid bodies in the stream, they rise as they rot. . . . They lick the feet of Tammany corruptionists, and grovel in the dust before Northern money. But Southern pride and principle will one day assert themselves. . . ."

Someone rashly interrupted to remind the General that his friend Stephens counseled peace and reconciliation.

"I don't give a damn if he does!" blurted Toombs. "Henry Grady cries peace too, and so does Jack Gordon and Ben Hill and Lushe Lamar. What do I care for the talk of politicians and opportunists. They may cry 'Peace' till the heavens fall . . ." [27]

Such quixotic incorrigibility could not fail in its appeal to a youth of Watson's temperament and predilections: "No matter how much you might revolt in judgment at what he said, he carried you with him for the moment." He was attracted and repelled at the same time: it was magnificent to be incorrigible, but it was practical to be conciliatory. "Nobody pinned faith to what he said," he reflected; "nobody altered his course a jot because of any opinion he expressed . . ." [28]

Alexander Stephens was nominated Governor by the New Departure Democrats, and the Convention adjourned. Toombs expressed his conviction that his friend was "either the veriest demagogue in the country or in his old age he has lost his grip." He believed his Independent opponent would beat him, "and ought to beat him." [29] Watson, out of personal loyalty, pledged himself as a "Stephens man," and returned to McDuffie County to take up where he had left it a particularly warm campaign on his own account.

[27] Conversation quoted by T. E W., *Sketches*, pp. 282-287.
[28] *Loc. cit*
[29] R. L. Felton, *op. cit*, pp 371-372

CHAPTER VII

Agrarian Law-making

"SINCE THE CONVENTION of 1880 I had had a fixed determination to run for the Legislature this year," wrote Watson in 1882. This was by no means an unreasonable ambition in a young lawyer of his attainments. It was rather the conventional, the expected thing—a step toward the judge's bench. The actual Representative was retiring at the expiration of his term, with the hope of being elected the next Superior Court judge. Watson expected an easy victory. An aspirant for office was frequently elected without mention of a single issue of race, class, creed, or party—simply by agreement in the primary of the "White Man's Party." At first it seemed that this procedure might be followed with Watson's candidacy, for no opponent appeared at the beginning. He did not believe there would have been any opposition had not his shooting scrape with W. D. Tutt brought on "various obstacles." Indeed this affair but introduced the first of the issues customarily circumvented—all of which Watson succeeded in stirring up to a dramatic pitch in this his first contest for office.[1]

Feeling between Watson and Tutt had been brewing for over five years. The day Watson arrived in Thomson to begin his law practice in 1876 he was greeted at the railway station by loud guffaws provoked by a remark at his expense from Tutt. "If I had had my gun," Watson told a friend, "I would have

[1] MS. Journal 2, p. 292.

shot him right there." [2] Although Tutt was several years his senior, and was already established as a highly successful lawyer, Watson's aggressive rise in the profession was not long in challenging Tutt's place of preëminence at the local bar. Watson's success appears to have been won largely at the expense of his rival. In the three and a half years preceding March, 1882, his "Lawyer's Record Book" [3] accounts for twenty-nine cases in which he and Tutt represented opposing interests, only twenty-two in which Tutt was not his opponent, and just one in which they collaborated. Many of these were criminal suits, in which popular excitement ran high, feelings were strained and taut, and rivalry bitter and personal. Watson was by far the more successful of the two in their clashes, and it was but natural for the older man to resent the impertinence of an upstart's rivalry.

Feelings were not improved during the campaign of 1880, when both men indulged in personalities in their speeches. In answer to Tutt's charge that the Independents were only disappointed office seekers, Watson replied that Tutt had himself deserted the Independents and was

Stiff in opinion, stubborn, always wrong,
Everything by turns and nothing long.

It also appears from his private Journal that Watson had secretly aspired to a seat in the Senate, but had been forced to content himself with a candidacy for the Lower House when the Democrats nominated Tutt for the Senate. [4]

In March, 1881, Tom, his brother Julius, and Tutt were jointly indicted for "carrying concealed weapons." At the trial the following January the Watson brothers pleaded guilty, Tutt not guilty. The court fined each of the three twenty-five dollars. [5]

[2] Interview with Mr. J. L. Cartledge, Augusta, Ga., Aug. 24, 1934.
[3] Watson MSS., Chapel Hill. Apparently all cases were not recorded.
[4] MS. Journal 2, p. 287; dated April, 1881.
[5] "Minutes, Supreme Court, McDuffie County, Sept., 1876 to March, 1884," Thomson, Georgia.

Serious trouble was expected almost any day now. The rivals had already clashed in two cases in March when Watson conceived the idea that Tutt had done him an injury by accepting a case in his absence that he thought should have been his. At a chance meeting in a law office in Thomson words were exchanged. Watson was insulting. Tutt struck him. Watson drew a gun and fired, striking Tutt, who had raised a chair before him, on the hand. Watson was disarmed, and the two were separated.[6]

On March 22 Watson was indicted for "assault with intent to murder," and only two days later appeared for trial before Judge Claiborne Snead. He had engaged, from the many who offered to defend him, three competent lawyers, among them, James C. C. Black, of Augusta. A jury was impanelled and sworn, and the case proceeded until the State closed. Then friends of both parties suggested a "settlement." Watson, apparently seeking a vindication, "opposed it bitterly and only gave in at the last moment upon condition that I should state my side of the case." [7] This done, Judge Snead withdrew the issue from the jury and ordered that "good cause having been shown, the said case be and is hereby settled." [8]

While this unusual, and probably illegal, procedure was applauded by many, it gave the faction that was organizing against Judge Snead a live issue to display before farmer voters. Class consciousness among farmers, promoted by hard times in the 'seventies and fostered by the insurgency of 1880, had not attained the militancy and discipline it was to acquire in the following decade, but the feeling was present. It was an anomaly that Tom Watson, future leader of the movement, should by a trick of circumstances, become one of its first victims. "People said," he observed in his Journal, "had it been anybody but a lawyer [e.g., a farmer] the case would not have been stopped." Also I found

[6] W. W. Brewton, *Life of Thomas E. Watson*, pp. 152-153.
[7] MS. Journal 2, p. 292.
[8] "Minutes, Supreme Court, McDuffie County, Sept., 1876, to March, 1884," Thomson, Georgia.

"a pretty general feeling that on account of the difference in our ages, I had acted hastily in giving him the lie." Judge Snead inflamed antagonism further by imprisoning one W. O. Harrison for misconduct as bailiff, when that gentleman gave too free expression to his opinion of the court's conduct in the case.[9]

In the midst of the excitement thus provoked there appeared a second candidate for the Legislature, E. A. Shields. Obviously he intended to capitalize on the feeling produced by the Watson case, for he was openly an anti-Snead candidate, out for the farmer's vote. Watson was now thrust into an extremely embarrassing alignment with Judge Claiborne Snead, whom he had no wish to defend, whom to defend would probably mean defeat, yet who, in the eyes of the public, had done Watson a considerable kindness, and had done it probably at the cost of his own political ruin. Caught in this dilemma, Watson refused to pledge himself outright against Snead, but instead resorted to the expedient of assuring voters that he "was willing to vote against Judge Snead in the next election if the people so instructed but would not run anti-Snead." [10]

After canvassing the county "laboriously and thoroughly," he concluded that the white vote was about equally divided between him and his opponent, and that therefore the Negro vote would decide the contest. The black population, indeed, represented a majority, there being 5,522 Negroes to 3,367 whites in the county.[11] Though their vote had been intimidated and manipulated, the Negroes were not yet disfranchised. They had been thoroughly organized by the Republicans, and it was through the Executive Committee of that party that Watson had to approach the Negroes. He found that his opponent had been endorsed by one of their meetings, but that, owing to small attendance, final action had been postponed until a later meeting called for the purpose of deciding between the candidates. At

[9] MS Journal 2, p. 292.
[10] *Ibid.*
[11] U. S Census, 1890.

99

this meeting Watson spoke, making a favorable impression chiefly by favoring free schools for Negroes, and by condemning the iniquitous convict lease system, of which the Negroes were the main victims. A resolution was adopted endorsing his candidacy, but it apparently gave the impression that Watson had endorsed the Republican platform, for after the meeting was adjourned, but while the crowd was still present, he added that "he did not endorse their platform, and had not been asked to do it." Their resolution endorsing him was not changed, however.[12]

The Negro meeting on Saturday was followed by an uproar created by the charge of the Shields supporters that Watson had stolen the Negro vote by endorsing the Republican platform. Thus he faced a second dilemma: he would have to repudiate the charge completely, but in doing so he would run the risk of losing the Negro vote. On the following Monday a white convention assembled at Thomson to nominate W. D. Tutt for the Senate. Affidavits signed by a witness of the Negro meeting were distributed by Watson, and he appeared at the Convention to demand a hearing. His exertions were telling on him. "I was so sick I could hardly stand up," he wrote, "but I went to the convention . . . and achieved the greatest oratorical victory of my life. I went out of the Court House with a triumphant and enthusiastic majority." Shields then withdrew from the race, but Watson was given no respite. Dr. James S. Jones, who had twice represented the county in the Legislature, was forthwith put up as a second opponent, a formidable one, according to Watson, for "It was confidently asserted that he would sweep the field." [13]

Other issues and more important offices were now forgotten. "The principal interest of the campaign," it was reported, "seemed to be who should be our next Representative in the Lower House." Watson's supreme talent for self-dramatization was one explanation of the excitement produced by a relatively

[12] Affidavits signed by "S. Norris," MS. Journal 2, p. 295.
[13] MS. Journal 2, p. 292.

insignificant contest. No better example of his use of that talent can be found than that displayed at a mass meeting held to decide whether the race between Watson and Jones should be decided by a nominating convention of white Democrats, or by an open race with no nomination. Watson favored an open race before the public, Jones the nomination. "The Watson men," it was reported, "beyond all question held the day." The meeting was then adjourned, but the people remained to listen to an address by Watson.

What of the charge that he was out to get the Negro vote? "Colquitt could get it, Stephens could get it, Roney could get it . . . and it was all right. But when he got it, it was all wrong." Clearly all the hue and cry against him was persecution, pure and simple. "I know now," said he, "that 'tis written, Before the ascension lies Gethsemane's Garden. I know now that the pathway is lined with brambles, and at each foot step I have pressed the thorns." By the time he had reached his conclusion, his cause had acquired for him, and it would appear for his listeners also, the proportions of a mighty crusade of good against evil, of right against black injustice. "No, gentlemen, they are in for anything to put me down. (Cries of That's so.) But with the fine support I find in your midst they'll never do it. I hear the tread of the people, as aroused up by this crusade, they come to see that justice shall be done. The whole people shall decide the contest." [14]

As if the campaign thus far had been only a preliminary skirmish, Watson notes that "From this time the race became very bitter." However, he was "more completely determined than . . . [he] had ever been on anything." During the next two months of campaign there are occasional glimpses of his activities: at a barn dance in Wrightsboro, "Standing up fiddling away for dear life, Willie Hadley bending down in front to beat the strings with straws, one negro playing second fiddle and another knocking the agony out of a tambourine." The

[14] Clipping, dated "Thomson, August 16, 1882," in MS. Journal 2, p. 293.

girls would "dance with no boy till he promised to vote for me." Or in Dearing District at the swimming hole: "Like the balance I climbed the stumps and leapt off for a dive." Or underground in the gold mines on the Ridge: "When Election day arrived, the mines stopped and Ed Carline voted every man for me." Campaign adventures fairly intoxicated him: "I stopped at all kinds of places, got all kinds of treatment, went through every grade of hope and doubt, elation and despondency; received enthusiastic praise, bore malignant abuse; was devotedly followed by friends; was desperately opposed by foes"—and, insatiable romantic that he was, nothing could have pleased him more.[15]

He was elected by a majority of 392 votes.

* * * * * *

The new assembly convened November 1, only a few weeks after the campaign ended and before Watson had recovered from a summer illness. He complained of being "sick most of the time," and was incapable of his usual exertions and not a little unhappy during the winter session. The *Constitution,* however, found him "looking as game and handsome as he did when he 'nailed to the mast her sacred flag,' " in the Convention of 1880 and added that "Tom is a whole team and dog under the wagon besides." Despite his health, he attended regularly and spoke frequently. Reports of debates in which he participated almost invariably singled him out for special comment and quotation. At twenty-six he retained much of the appeal of the rustic poet that his earlier pictures carry, and he was described as "slender," "debonair," "impetuous," and "boyish." He was given place on four House committees, one of them the General Committee on Judiciary.[16]

Walking to and from the Capitol, Watson daily passed the entrance to a narrow stairway, on what is now Henry Grady

[15] MS Journal 2, pp. 294-295.
[16] *Georgia House Journal,* 1882, pp. 68-72

Square, marked 48 Marietta Street. The address graced the letterhead of Woodrow Wilson, attorney at law, licensed all of ten days before Watson arrived in the city. Of Watson's own age, Wilson like him had passed part of his boyhood in Augusta and had turned to law. Yet they now faced different problems. "Buried in humdrum life down here in slow, ignorant, uninteresting Georgia," Wilson complained yearningly of his plight to a friend "away off there in Europe, surrounded by everything that is attractive in the old world, deep in the work of a great university." His every contact with this sterile society, "where the chief end of man is certainly to make money" was "utterly disillusioning." He reflected that the practice of law "for purposes of gain is antagonistic to the best interests of the intellectual life"—and anyway not a client appeared. He could watch from his office windows, "which look out upon the principal entrance of the big, ugly building which serves new Atlanta as a temporary capitol, the mixed crowds going to secure seats in the galleries of the House of Representatives . . ." Having plenty of time, he occasionally joined the crowd in the galleries himself and watched the lawmakers below—"country lawyers, merchants, farmers, politicians, all of them poor, many densely ignorant. . . . As different as the poles from the British Parliament, wherein a class of men from leisured families, disciplined for leadership, ruled the state." [17]

Inaugurated on November 4, Governor Alexander Stephens entered his new office without the satisfaction of having "destroyed all elements of Independent opposition" as the leaders of the New Departure had hoped. The vote, in fact, came much nearer justifying General Toombs' prediction of an Independent victory than had been expected, for in spite of Stephens' personal popularity his Independent opponent received thirty-two per cent of the votes cast. Opposition to the New Departure was reduced but not destroyed.[18]

[17] Ray S Baker, *Woodrow Wilson*, Vol. I, pp 150-157. Copyright, 1927, by Doubleday, Doran & Co , Inc
[18] *Georgia House Journal 1882*, pp. 38-39.

The death of Senator Benjamin H. Hill on August 15 had left a few months of his term to be filled, and the more important question of who was to succeed him in the long term had to be decided. This question above all others agitated the new assembly during the first two weeks. The statement that the contest was "simply unprecedented in its bitterness and passion" is probably an exaggeration, but it seems true that the issue was "the same one that has been presented for the last several years" —namely, the New Departure oligarchy against its more or less unorganized opposition. If ex-Governor Colquitt's candidacy proved successful, each member of the New Departure Triumvirate, Gordon, Brown, and Colquitt, would have his turn in the Senate in as many years.

Senator Brown, who owed his first entrance to the Senate to Colquitt, was bringing to bear the multitudinous resources at his command in behalf of Colquitt's candidacy. Demurring to the charge that he was "chief boss" of Georgia politics, he added that if it was true, "then I have a right to be proud of the results of my labor, and I have a right to expect the plaudit of 'well done' from the democracy of Georgia." He also expected the prompt election of Colquitt as his junior Senator.[19]

Henry Grady, as might be expected, also marshaled his influence behind Colquitt. The power he wielded was already formidable.[20] Grady opposed particularly the election of J. C. C. Black, the lawyer who had defended Watson in his trial and who was now the opponent of Colquitt.

At the election in the assembly Watson seconded with his most florid oratory the nomination of Black, "a leader whose plume is as white as the plume of Navarre." As for himself, he said, he had "rather be a mourner at the defeat of right, than

[19] J. E. Brown to editor of the *Constitution*, Nov. 12, 1882.

[20] Later it was said: "He was almost an absolute dictator in Georgia politics. No man cared to stand for election to any place, high or low, unless he felt Grady was with him. He certainly was the most powerful factor in the election of two governors and practically gave more than one United States Senator his seat" Quoted in J. C. Harris, *Henry W. Grady*, p. 79.

to be king at the carnival of victorious might." He found himself among the mourners. Colquitt easily won over his three opponents.[21]

With Brown and Colquitt in the Senate and Governor Stephens keeping step to the new music, there was little left for the New Departure to ask that it did not have. "Let us bury all personal differences," urged the conciliatory Grady, "and have a general peace. The elections are all over; good men are elected . . . and there is little cause for complaint, but much for congratulations."[22] As a personal gesture in this direction, Grady invited leaders of all factions in the recent contest, Tom Watson included, to a "unique entertainment" at his home on Peachtree Street, said to have been "the center of the social life of the city." Invitations read "Dinner at 6, fiddling at 9." After dinner Watson and three other members of the House were announced as contestants for a fiddling prize. In a hilarious contest Watson was judged winner and awarded "a floral fiddle, with tube rose body and smilax springs," afterwards sent to Mrs. Watson. The famous Grady hospitality flowed, and under the tutelage of this master reconciler, reconciliation went on apace. It would require all the arts of a master to keep this champion fiddler in tune with the new music, but until the baton finally slipped from Grady's hand discord was prevented.

In both his campaign against Colquitt and the New Departure in 1880, and in his pledges to the Negro voters two years later, Watson had attacked the convict lease system. Agitation against the Georgia system of leasing state convicts for exploitation by private individuals and corporations had been carried on by Independents for several years with no ameliorative result, because, it was said, "men of high standing and great influence, governors and United States Senators, were making fortunes out of it."[23] In 1880, the state had granted a twenty-year lease.

[21] *Constitution*, Nov. 15, 1882; *Georgia House Journal* 1882, pp. 220-223.
[22] *Constitution*, Nov. 15, 1882.
[23] New York *Daily Tribune*, Aug. 28, 1887, quoted in R. L. Felton, *Memoirs*, P 599

105

George W. Cable, the novelist, after extensive investigation of this penal system in the Southern states, concluded that in Georgia the system was found "peculiarly vicious." He went even further to say that, "Here may be seen a group of penal institutions, the worst in the country by every evidence of their own setting forth: cruel, brutalizing, deadly; chaining, flogging, shooting, drowning, killing by exhaustion and exposure . . ." The crushing burden of this injustice was borne by the Negroes: although they were a minority of the state population, there were in October, 1880, 1,071 Negroes serving terms, and only 115 whites.[24]

Upon this mudsill of human misery and degradation was built a considerable part of the great fortune of Senator Joseph E. Brown. As already mentioned, three hundred of the convicts, leased for twenty years, went to labor in his Dade County coal mines. For the labor of its prisoners the state received about seven cents per working day.[25]

It would seem that Governor Colquitt could see no crime in such profitable enterprise. In his final message to the General Assembly, November 2, 1882, the Governor, referring to the penal system, said that "in the three great essentials of good discipline, economy, humanity and reform, Georgia stands pre-eminent."[26]

Just two weeks later Watson arose in the House to speak on penal institutions. He advocated the abolition of the convict lease system, which, he said, "commercialized the State's sovereign right to punish her criminals to money-making companies whose only interest was to maintain the convict at the lowest possible cost and to work him at the utmost human capacity."

[24] George W. Cable, "The Convict Lease System in the South," *Century*, Feb., 1884; Vol. V, pp 582-599; *vide* also J. N. Hammond, in an answer to Cable, *Constitution*, Jan. 13, 1885.

[25] H. Fielder, *op cit.*, pp 488-489; A. M. Arnett, *Populist Movement in Georgia*, pp. 27-28; I. W. Avery, *op. cit.*, p. 606. It was admitted by the critics of the system that the convicts employed by Brown were not as badly treated as were the convicts of other lessees

[26] *Journal of the House 1882*, p. 35.

He also condemned the "very atrocious crimes committed against the convicts by the whipping bosses of these lessee companies." Instead of proposing the abolition of the system, which would probably have received no serious attention, he offered a resolution calling for a special investigation and report by the Committee on the penitentiary on "whether in the lodging, chaining and working of the convicts any distinction and classification is made between males and females, white and colored, those convicted of crimes involving moral turpitude and those convicted of offenses not so involving moral turpitude." [27] The resolution was agreed to on November 17.

In December the Committee reported that "The camps at Dade Coal Mines, under the control of Company No. 1, were found to be in a healthy condition. . . . Your Committee take pleasure in commending the management of this branch of the penitentiary." [28] In less than a month after his inauguration, Governor Stephens pardoned Edward Cox, General Gordon's sub-lessee of convicts, convicted of the murder of Robert Alston, an outspoken enemy of the convict lease system.[29]

After the exploited convict, the tenant farmer became Watson's chief concern. The first bill he introduced in the House was one to amend the Code "so as to allow tenants distrained, if unable from poverty to give bond and security, to file a bond *in forma pauperis* . . ." [30] As the law stood, once the landlord obtained a distress warrant against the tenant's crop and equipment in order to collect debt or rent, the tenant was compelled to give bond of twice the amount sued for in order to contest before the court the justice of the landlord's claim, or to retain his possessions pending litigations.[31] The poverty of the average tenant, who was habitually in debt and often possessed nothing but his

[27] MS. House Bill 59, 1882, on file in Georgia Department of Archives and History, Atlanta, Georgia.
[28] *Journal of the House 1882*, pp. 511-512.
[29] R. L. Felton, *Memoirs*, pp. 372-373, 491-496.
[30] *Journal of the House 1882*, p. 87; MS. bill missing from State Archives.
[31] *The Code of the State of Georgia* (Macon, 1873), Section 4083.

107

labor, did not permit him to give bond and frequently left him at the mercy of his landlord, against whom he could not even appear in court. Watson's bill proposed to enable the tenant to contest the landlord's claim and to retain the property levied upon until a judicial decision was rendered. While the bill was recommended by the General Committee on Judiciary, it was recommitted to the Committee in the next session and failed to pass.[32]

With these and other failures irritating his pride, Watson returned to Thomson at the end of his first session in a mood of dissatisfaction, if not frustration. In his Journal he wrote that he "found no pleasure in the Legislature and was not all satisfied with my share in the programme." His imagination had been somehow offended, cheated, like that of young Wilson looking down from the galleries. It was no forum of Periclean Greeks upon whom he had lavished his periods.

It was between sessions, on March 4, only shortly after Watson had paid the old invalid a visit in Atlanta, that Governor Alexander Stephens died. Watson's tribute to his boyhood hero at the memorial day in the Legislature seems a sincere expression of affection, and he returned to the summer session saddened by the loss.[33] From his office window across the street Attorney Wilson gloomily watched the crowd file into the galleries for the inauguration of Henry D. McDaniel, elected to fill the unexpired term of Governor Stephens: "They were probably not much entertained," he wrote his friend in Berlin, "though they may have been considerably diverted, for our new Governor cannot talk." The state was about to "replace a governor who could not walk with a governor who could not talk."[34]

Any special favor that Watson may have won in the eyes of Negroes and white tenant voters by his championship of convicts

[32] *Constitution*, Nov. 15, 1882; *Journal of the House 1882*, p. 282; *Journal 1883*, pp. 132-133.
[33] T. E. W., *Life and Speeches*, pp. 30-31.
[34] R. S. Baker, *op. cit.*, Vol. I, pp. 154-157.

and impoverished tenants during the first session was placed in jeopardy by two of his actions during the summer session. According to the chairman of the Committee of Privileges and Election, "the strongest case" with which he had to deal in the session of 1882, was a contest for the seat of Camden County made by Anthony Wilson, Negro, against Daniel R. Proctor, white, who had been at first awarded the seat.[35] Wilson contended that, having received a majority of the votes over his white opponents, he was entitled to the seat. The Committee supported his contention. Heated opposition to the committee report was led by Tom Watson. While admitting that Wilson had a majority of the votes, Watson held that "he did not show it by strictly legal testimony." [36] So strong was the opposition that the question was postponed till the next session. Wilson was then awarded the seat. The charge was later made that Watson's position was dictated by race feeling, but this is not supported by evidence.

The first bill Watson offered in the summer session proposed a tax of one dollar per head annually on dogs, the proceeds to go to the support of education.[37] In his defense of the measure he appealed to "our brother in black" for his support. Wilson replied that "The colored people don't want this law . . ." A commentator explained that "The tax payers of the state were with him [Watson], but the colored voters at home doubtlessly overawed the average country member, and the dog and the Negro is [sic] still on top. The Negro voter is a power in Georgia politics and the lamb must go." [38]

Farmers were only beginning to awaken to the injustice which the general property tax system worked upon them. They undoubtedly paid out of all proportion to the value of their

[35] Printed circular, Northern Scrapbook, Vol. III, p. 147.
[36] Journal of the House 1882, pp. 372-377; Constitution, Aug 24, 1882.
[37] MS. Bill No 425, on file in Georgia Dept. of Archives and History, Atlanta; Journal of the House 1883, p. 36.
[38] Clippings, undated, MS. Journal 2, p. 344.

property or their ability to pay, while personal and intangible property of the city dweller escaped with a mere pretense of taxation.[39] Resentment was also beginning to arise against the gross thievery of the railroad financiers, and against their rate discrimination against the farmer in favor of the city. While the railroads had been made subject to state taxes in 1877, they still paid no taxes to the county through which they passed. In view of these circumstances considerable interest arose over a bill to require railroads to pay taxes to counties in which their property was located, "just as individuals are now required by law to do."

Watson supported the bill with "fervent argument." Appealing to the doctrine of Robert Toombs, he contended that "the convention of 1877 saw the fallacy of the old system of dealing with railroads and placed them on a footing with other property in the state. This bill merely carries out the theory of the constitution, and proposes no more than just taxation of the roads." One member, who denounced the bill as "one of these extemporaneous routes of demagoguery," employed an argument then frequently heard: reform and taxation would discourage capital and enterprise. "The North has the surplus money," ran the formula. "Let us encourage its investment in railroads in Georgia and the South." Watson ridiculed the inconsistency of the champions of the railroads; "in one breath making them giants of power and in the next breath weak subjects for protection." [40]

It was only a few days before the railroad bill was taken up for final vote that "quite a ripple of interest" was created by the announcement of the clerk of the House that he had free passes for all members over the Air Line Railroad, good throughout the session and ten days after adjournment, and it was at that same session that the House accepted the invitation to the Louisville Exposition, transportation paid, from Joseph E. Brown, "president of the most powerful railroad corporation South and

[39] L. F. Schmeckabier, "Taxation in Georgia," *Johns Hopkins Studies*, Vol. XVIII, p. 232.
[40] Atlanta *Journal*, July 19, 1883; undated clippings, MS Journal 2, p 341

110

Senator from Georgia." [41] The railroad tax was defeated in the Senate.

Watson fired two parting shots at the railroads in the form of two bills, one changing the Code to provide that mere presence upon railroad right of way did not constitute contributory negligence in case of injury inflicted by the railroad; another redefining "trespass" to except cases of presence upon the right of way, unless damage of property or infringement of franchise were committed.[42] Both bills were introduced toward the end of the session, and both died in committee. When a bill for incorporating a navigation company appeared, Watson obtained the passage of amendments putting freight and transportation charges under control of the state, and striking out a clause giving the company monopoly of navigation on the river.[43]

His attacks on the sanctity of corporations, however, were by no means to be extended to the sanctity of the institution of private property. When it was proposed to condemn certain property "in order to complete the symmetry of the new state capitol," Watson was prompt to object: "It is dangerous to condemn private property for the sake of mere symmetry, just to make the ground look pretty. I am against the amendment." When the conflict was between the farmer and property, it was the worse for property: when between beauty and property, the worse for beauty.

Doubtless Watson derived a certain amount of satisfaction from clipping newspaper comment and sending it to his wife, such flattery as the article describing him as "the most brilliant young man in Georgia," or the one that said, "There was no more brilliant and brainy young man in the Legislature last session . . ." But his prevailing mood continued to be restlessness and disillusionment. He could review only a brief record of failure and temporizing and his impatience with time-servers

41 Augusta *Chronicle*, July 6, 1883; *Journal of the House 1883*, pp. 814-816.
42 MS. House Bills Nos. 1048 and 1049, Georgia Dept. of Archives and History; *Journal of the House 1883*, p. 818
43 *Constitution*, Dec 6, 1882.

111

grew. The same mood was expressed by one of his colleagues, a young man "of fine intelligence" who complained that he was "utterly dissatisfied and desirous of quitting the Legislature and going home to private life," because "there was nothing occurring in which he took an interest . . ." [44] Whether for the same reason or not Watson resigned his seat in the Legislature before his term expired the next year.[45]

"The galleries are deserted and there is a languid dullness around the capital generally," it was reported a month before the turgid summer session dragged itself to a close. Watson did not conceal his impatience. Instead of dashing off to the Louisville Exposition as Senator Brown's guests, the legislators, he thought, should remain on the job and complete their business. In a rebuke to the House he announced that he intended to take his leave if the session were not adjourned on a certain day. On September 17 he did leave, but the session dragged on—drawing its *per diem* pay.

On his deathbed General Toombs was told that the assembly was still in session.

"Send for Cromwell!" growled the General.[46]

[44] The young man was Charles R. Pendleton. N. E Harris, *Autobiography*, pp. 234-235.

[45] *Constitution*, Aug. 14, 1884. His resignation was probably an attempt to qualify as a presidential elector.

[46] Ulrich B. Phillips, *Life of Robert Toombs*, p. 273.

CHAPTER VIII

Henry Grady's Vision

As THE CURTAIN was rung down on an old era, it had hitched on a quartet of aged figures taking belated curtain calls. Awkwardly they bowed off the stage, one by one: Herschel V. Johnson in 1880, Ben Hill in 1882, Stephens in 1883. General Toombs, confined to his bed and soon to follow them, continued to be heard from only as a discordant rumble off stage. As if to clear the stage drastically of old scenery, the old Kimball House burned to the ground on August 13, 1883, and that same year a new capitol was decreed. A new spirit quickly peopled the scene with new men.

One September morning in 1882 young Wilson was transported out of his lethargy by the sudden appearance at his office of a young man with the face of a poet and the breezy manner of a salesman—Walter Hines Page. They enthusiastically discovered themselves "interested in the same things, with much the same point of view." Both were "men of the New South, impatient with old slogans." Page assumed the rôle of prophet and mentor. He was touring the South for the New York *World*, which belonged to Jay Gould, and scattering glad tidings—the same tidings Grady broadcasted. A recent interview with Jefferson Davis had moved him to reflect that "Cotton mills and railroads are of more consequence . . . than constitutional questions irrevocably settled." He fascinated Wilson with his talk of Johns Hopkins, where the young lawyer was soon

113

to go. Off to North Carolina went Page to carry his message home. "Wake up, old commonwealth," he shouted. "What North Carolina most needs are a few first class funerals." He called to witness "any man who has made his own way by his own independence and industry in trade or manufacturing, if these be not true." [1]

Walter Page, Woodrow Wilson, Henry Grady—these alert young men, like hundreds of Tom Watson's contemporaries, were riding the crest of time's wave, as bright young men are wont to. They were ingratiating themselves with the great captains of industry or the new captains of education, making themselves instruments of their own *Zeitgeist*. But the great tidal wave of Industrial Revolution, while bearing his alert contemporaries on its crest, swept over Watson and his class, inundating them silently for a decade. With as bright a mind as the keenest of them and as much ambition as any, Watson was born of a certain tradition, and his loyalty to that tradition and to his class was the most important thing in Tom Watson's life. At the name of Jay Gould he would shrink, instinctively, perhaps recalling something that Bob Toombs had said or done. As for the captains of education, they were quite out of his reach.

Until near the close of the booming 'eighties Watson remained a hesitant spectator. Sometimes he made timorous advances, mouthing a phrase of Grady's in a speech or lending a hand with an election; yet he never did embrace the new creed for his own. He always recoiled before a gesture became an alliance. There was the case of the state convention of 1884. When his name was presented for presidential elector from the tenth district, the objection was raised that his office as a member of the House would disqualify him. Although he had resigned his seat beforehand, Watson promptly withdrew his name.[2] The electoral bandwagon moved on without him.

[1] B. J. Hendrick, *The Training of an American*, pp. 146, 158-168; Ray S. Baker, *Woodrow Wilson*, Vol. I, pp. 144-145.
[2] *Constitution*, Aug. 14, 1884.

114

The victory of Grover Cleveland furnished fresh impetus for the New Departure. The news of the election brought the people pouring into the streets of Atlanta "wild with joy." Bloody shirts saturated with oil were set ablaze in front of the capitol with "the wildest demonstrations." Henry Grady, as master of ceremonies, was in his element. At the head of a procession of drums, he burst into the House of Representatives, seized Speaker Lamar in his arms, snatched the gavel from his hands, and declared the House adjourned in the name of Grover Cleveland.

At the head of the procession Grady remained, and behind him it swelled in numbers as the 'eighties advanced. Thousands were enchanted by his vision of the New South: "I see a South the home of fifty millions of people; her cities vast hives of industry; her country-sides the treasures from which their resources are drawn; her streams vocal with whirring spindles . . ." His journey to Dallas to deliver an address was one prolonged ovation, "and his appearance created an enthusiasm that is indescribable." "No such tribute as this has ever before been paid, under any circumstances, to any private American citizen . . ." [3] Grady symbolized to the South a hope that was almost pathetic in its desperation.

In the North his message was thrice welcome. "We have sowed towns and cities in the place of theories, and put business in place of politics," he told the New England Club in New York. "We have challenged your spinners in Massachusetts and your ironmakers in Pennsylvania . . . wiped out the place where Mason and Dixon's line used to be, and hung out a latchstring to you and yours. . . . We have fallen in love with work. . . . We are ready to lay odds on the Georgia Yankee as he manufactures relics of the battle field in a one-story shanty and squeezes pure olive oil out of his cotton-seed, against any down easterner that ever swapped wooden nutmegs for flannel sausages in the valleys of Vermont." He rejoiced that the two civilizations, which

[3] J. C. Harris, *Henry W. Grady*, pp. 16-17 and 91.

115

"Did lately meet in the intestine shock
Shall now, in mutual well beseeming ranks,
March all one way."

"Every train brings manufacturers from the East and West
seeking to establish themselves or their sons near the raw material in this growing market," he told eager Southerners, and
with open arms he added, "Let the fullness of the tide roll in." [4]
Such hospitality did not go begging. In the middle 'eighties,
along with the profit seekers, came an invasion of journalists,
whose books and articles poured from the press. A. K. McClure
was delighted with Atlanta, which was "the legitimate offspring
of Chicago," with "not a vestige of the old Southern ways about
it." The "old regulations Southerners in this region . . . have
either died untimely in despair, or have drifted into the current
and moved on with the world." "Here the most advanced leaders of the whole South have their homes," he discovered, young
men who "have learned that 'hardness ever of hardiness is
mother,' " who were contemptuous of "effete pride," who had
"revolutionized Georgia" and were overrunning the South.
"There are more potent civilizers in Georgia than I have met
with in any portion of the South," he declared. "The more intelligent young men of from twenty to thirty years" were "the
foremost missionaries of the new civilization in the South." [5]
William D. ("Pig-Iron") Kelley of Pennsylvania was quite as
enthusiastic. "That they are a prosperous people is attested by
everything you behold in Atlanta," he observed; particularly
by "the elegant residences of Atlanta's millionaires." He was
widely quoted for his saying that the New South was "the coming El Dorado of American adventure"—whatever that may
have meant.[6]
But it was the Southerner himself, first and last, who was

[4] *Ibid.*, pp. 88, 114.
[5] A. K. McClure, *The South; Industrial, Financial, Political* (Philadelphia, 1886),
pp. 58-76.
[6] W. D. Kelley, *The Old South and the New* (New York, 1888), pp. 13-14, 162.

116

most impressed by his own exploits—and for the most part they were his own.[7] At Vanderbilt University, recently endowed by the Commodore, a professor observing that "The wealth of the Southern States has increased forty-one per cent. in the last five years," blandly prophecied that "Southern millionaires there will yet be, and not a few, who will use their wealth, righteou:.y gotten by their own honest labor, to develop their land and bless the race."[8]

Patrick Calhoun, at some risk of raising the ghost of his grandfather, enthusiastically proclaimed that "The future of the South is commercial and manufactural. She will exchange the modest civilization of the country gentleman for the bustling civilization of the towns."[9] Henry Watterson, most accurately catching the spirit of his times, wrote, "The South, having had its bellyful of blood, has gotten a taste of money, and is too busy trying to make more of it to quarrel with anybody."[10]

No one who has pored for months over the mass of pamphlets and books that issued from the South in the 'eighties can find it in his heart to condemn utterly the motives and hopes they represent.[11] For all the greed of gain and sordid acquisitiveness that animated the average capitalist, his cause was almost ennobled when it became the delusion of the mass of impoverished, defeated, and dispirited Southerners that it was likewise their

[7] Broadus Mitchell, *The Rise of the Cotton Mills*, p. 102. "The impulse was furnished almost exclusively from within the South, against much discouragement from selfish interests at the North . . ."

[8] W. F. Tillett, "The White Man of the New South," *Century Magazine*, Vol. XXXIII (March, 1887), pp. 769-776

[9] *Constitution*, May 23, 1883.

[10] New York *Herald*, July 19, 1887, quoted in Allan Nevins, *Grover Cleveland*, p. 323.

[11] Of a countless number the following are a few samples: Richard H. Edmonds (ed. of *Manufacturer's Record*), *The South's Redemption* (Baltimore, 1890); George B. Cowlan, *The Undeveloped South* . . . (Louisville, Ky., 1887); Edward Atkinson, *The Future Situs of the Principle Iron Productions of the World* (Baltimore, 1890); *South Carolina in 1884* . . . *A Brilliant Showing* (Charleston, 1884); *A Story of Spartan Push The Greatest Manufacturing Centre in the South* (Pamphlet from an article in *News and Courier*, July 28, (?), by E P. McKissick); J. C. C. Newton, *The New South and the Methodist Episcopal Church South* (Baltimore, 1887).

117

cause, their hope, the light that would lead them out of darkness. With pathetic fervor and remarkable unanimity Southern people of all classes rallied to the new slogans. Most moving, because most deluded in its unconscious pathos, was the response of the agricultural masses.

At a meeting of the State Agricultural Society in Atlanta an unknown farmer rose to speak. He was "chosen from the rank and file of this society," he said, and he described himself as "no kid-glove farmer," but the owner of a hundred-acre farm in Bartow County. "I emphatically earn my daily bread, and having no other resource, I support my family on this vast estate." He confessed to one extravagance, "taking the *Daily Atlanta Constitution*, as I am determined to keep up with the times." That he did so is evident from his address, yet in place of Grady's cheerful optimism, his farmer disciple embraced the new creed with something like despair: [12]

We must get rich! Let the young south arise in their might and compete with them [Yankees] in everything but their religion and morals. Don't mind old fogies like myself and others of the same age who are sulking in their tents.

Life is real, life is earnest;
In this modern fight of life,
Be not like your old ancestors,
But let money be your strife.

We have the cotton and can make cheaper goods than they can. We have the wool, and will have sense enough to use it. We can make iron at less cost than they can and must manufacture it into implements we are obliged to have . . .

Get rich! Sell everything marketable and live on the culls. Let every yellow legged chicken, dozen of eggs and pound of butter look in your eyes as fractions of a dollar, and act accordingly. Get rich! if you have to be mean! The world respects a rich scoundrel more than it does an honest poor man.

[12] *Constitution*, Aug. 16, 1883

118

Poverty may do to go to heaven with. But in this modern times . . .
Get rich! and the south will no more beg for settlers; the sails of
your vessels will whiten every sea; emigrants will pour in; capitalists
will invest. . . .

Get rich! and Georgia . . . will not only be the empire state of
the south, but in less than half a century will be the empire state of
the whole union.

Henry Grady featured this speech prominently in the *Constitution*, and Tom Watson clipped it for his scrapbook. Watson
was no weathercock in these new winds of doctrine, but he could
not remain wholly insensitive to them. One can follow the current of his mind in his Journal. In 1882 he was writing, "The
Past! No wonder it is seemingly better. There lie our brightest
and purest hopes, our best endeavors, our loved and lost." [13]
And in invocation he cried, "Come back to us once more oh
dream of the old time South!" A year later the theme was
different: "In the name of the future let the dead past bury its
dead. The world moves, let us move with it. Let us get out of
our Egypt." Prophets were not wanting, and "Should our path
be blocked by the sea, the master will divide it. Should our lips
grow parched with famine the rock will give forth water, the
desert manna." The South must prepare for prosperity. "It will
come by the stream where the factory moves. It will come
through the streets busy with hurrying feet." That was about as
near as Tom Watson ever came to being seduced by the heady
romanticism of the Southern middle class—and that was pretty
near, indeed, for the future leader of the revolt against it. At the
same time he could not stomach the popular nationalism of
"some Southern newspapers and politicians who say they are
patriotic enough to support this Tariff because it builds up the
interests of the *Whole* nation; because it fosters American manu-
factories. If this be patriotism, I am no Patriot." [14]

[13] MS. Journal 2, p. 296.
[14] MS. Journal 2, pp. 317-331. Speech delivered July 4, 1883. Broadus Mitchell
writes that "The wish for nationalism and for industrialism on the part of the
South were necessarily one." *The Rise of the Cotton Mills in the South*, p. 237.

119

Patriots of the required stripe were not wanting, however. In 1886 a gubernatorial candidate was required. Henry Grady, with a magician's finesse, resurrected General John B. Gordon in New York (and somewhat out at the elbows), put him in a new suit, and presented him as the people's savior.[15] The stage was faultlessly set. Poor old Jefferson Davis, having dedicated a Confederate monument in Montgomery two days before, was brought to Atlanta with Winnie, his daughter, to unveil a statue of Ben Hill. Longstreet appeared in Confederate uniform. The rebel yell was lifted, and General Gordon was ushered in—"the Hero of Appomattox!" It was as simple as that . . . in the 'eighties.

Since his questionable resignation from the Senate in 1880 General Gordon had led an adventurous life. There had been adventures before; the Southern Publishing Company, with its "Southern books that will not slander our people," and the Southern Insurance Company, whose "dupes were scattered from Baltimore to Texas."[16] Only after 1880, however, did the General really strike his stride. After a vertiginous whirl among several schemes, in 1883 he resigned the presidency of the Georgia Pacific Railroad to give his attention to the International Railroad and Steamship Company. It was certain to make Florida "the great commercial center of the Western World." Thousands of pamphlets, bearing a full-page picture of the General, were struck off as advertisements. After a noisy splurge the enterprise suddenly collapsed; the property was attached, and the General was off to greener pastures.[17] Meanwhile he managed to keep a hand in the convict lease game. A contemporary thought the General was "the living realistic 'Mulberry Sellers' of America," with sufficient "skin games and south sea bubbles" on his record "to furnish material enough for a dozen

[15] Information obtained from Raymond B. Nixon, now preparing a biography of Grady.
[16] R. L. Felton, *Memoirs*, pp. 484-485; 494-495, 502.
[17] John R. Jones (one of Gordon's engineers) to the editor of the Macon *Telegraph*, in R. L. Felton, *op. cit*, pp. 538-540.

first-class farces." [18] It was not until 1884, only two years before his race for governor, that Gordon's complicity in the Gould-Huntington scandal was revealed. Even then, following Grady's lead, the state papers ignored the revealing letters, and those who heard seemed unimpressed.

Nothing in such a record recommended the General's candidacy to Tom Watson, and it was he who led a victorious fight against Gordon in McDuffie County, "one of the most valiant and significant in the campaign." It was Watson who made the speech in reply to General Gordon when he visited Thomson. Gordon's opponent in the race was personally unknown in the county, yet "all the enthusiasm, all the winning strength were found for him from the ranks of the people of the country." [19] At the nominating convention Watson cast the vote of his county against Gordon; but the majority of votes were cast in the opposite way. The Triumvirate was again in the saddle—both seats in the Senate and the governor's chair—and Grady enjoyed another triumph.

The following year President Cleveland visited the Piedmont Exposition in Atlanta. While Mrs. Cleveland received at Mrs. Grady's home, and the President dined at Governor Gordon's and at Senator Colquitt's, throngs of Southerners crowded the city to cheer Cleveland. Everywhere talk of the New South was poured into the porches of his ears, "and Grady was at his elbow to explain the significance of the phrase." It was on the advice of Lamar and Garland that "Cleveland distributed patronage in the South in such a way as to discourage the Bourbon or unreconstructed element, and bring forward the younger men." [20] Lamar had first learned of Cleveland's election from Gordon, who wired, "Turn the rascals out." [21]

Despite his half-studied detachment in the 'eighties, Watson managed to command the continued respect of the politicians

[18] T. M. Norwood, letter in Augusta *Chronicle*, Sept. 29, 1890.
[19] Augusta *Chronicle*, June 10, 1886.
[20] A. Nevins, *Grover Cleveland*, pp. 319-323.
[21] Wirt A. Cate, *Lucius Q. C. Lamar*, p. 403.

121

and his share of the public's attention. In 1888 he was put at the head of the electoral ticket of the state. He and his fellow elector from the state at large, John Temple Graves, were mentioned as "the two most prominent young men in the state." Their combined weight was 227 pounds, 127 of which belonged to Watson. Graves, however, was said to have the edge on personal beauty, for though admittedly homely he was said to be a "perfect Adonis" when compared to his colleague. Together they toured the state, whipping up a torpid enthusiasm for Cleveland. Watson emphasized the tariff question. "The success I met with was extremely gratifying," he wrote in his Journal. "The Savannah trip was an ovation—one of the proudest occasions of my life." [22] Indeed, the newspapers outdid themselves to describe his speech, "its beauty and brilliancy and the marvelous impression it produced. . . . On every hand was heard, 'A second Aleck Stephens.' 'I thought Stephens was dead.' "

For an incipient rebel, Watson was singularly orthodox in his utterances at this time. His prayer, he said, was "Good Lord, protect the people, and keep the south solid." At Warrenton, however, he gave solemn pronouncement to a warning that must have given pause to machine politicians of the New Departure. "There are certain men in Congress and certain influential newspapers in the state," he said, "which are advocating principles diametrically opposed to the sentiment which prevails almost unanimously throughout the south. And if the seeds of dissension sown by these parties are not uprooted . . . the result will be that the solid south . . . will be disrupted and ruin will follow to the party." [23]

One who sought confirmation for such dire prophecy on the surface of the contemporary scene would be largely disappointed. On the other hand, one would find abundant evidence—on the surface—that the new creed held full sway. Especially was this true in the cities, and the would-be cities. The urban South was

[22] MS. Journal 2, p. 407.
[23] Macon *Daily Telegraph*, Oct. 6, 1888.

doing its level best to play the sedulous ape to the industrial North—succeeding but poorly perhaps, but doing its best. Jigsaw gingerbread flourished where charred colonnades had fallen. Cast iron fences triumphed over white wooden pickets; in place of the boxwood an iron stag was planted. Frock coats and tails were discarded for smart business suits. In Augusta it was said that the New South idea "is as much of a craze as high collars and lawn tennis." Augusta boasted of being "the Lowell of the South." Columbus aspired to be "the Pittsburgh of the South." Atlanta was already "the legitimate offspring of Chicago." A recent writer has caught the attitude in an inimitable phrase: " 'Yes sir-ree, it's a regular little old metropolis—New York of the South we call it, 89,000 people in the last census—and *Progress?* Gen-tle-men, *Progress? I'll* say *Progress!*" [24] So on down the line: "Sandersville is fast assuming 'big city' proportions. . . . Capitalists are invited to investigate." "That booming town of Wadley . . ." "Even Odum Booms . . ." [25]

To the far corners of the land the ruling genius of the New South sped on winged feet. At Dallas Grady told hopeful farmers that "plenty rides on the springing harvests," and in Boston, in the last speech of his life, he told the Bay State Club that as soon as the carping critics, "those noisy insects of the hour, have perished in the heat that gave them life, and their pestilential tongues have ceased, the great clock of this Republic will strike the slow-moving, tranquil hours, and the watchman from the street will cry, 'all is well with the Republic; all is well!' " [26]

This is what our observer would have found on the surface of the contemporary scene. None the less, had he looked below the surface, had he left the railroads and the cities, had he talked to anyone but Atlanta "boomers" and "sooners," had he listened to anything but the din of the New South talk in his ears, he would have discovered beneath these tranquilly oiled waters the seeth-

[24] John D. Wade, "Old Wine in New Bottles," *Virginia Quarterly Review*, Vol. XI, pp. 239-252
[25] Macon *Telegraph*, April 3, 5, 6, 8, and 9, 1890; Augusta *Chronicle*, 1888–1891.
[26] J. C. Harris, *op cit* , pp 96, 206.

ing stuff of nascent revolution. Had he met the right men, he would have discovered that Grady's carping critics had by no means "perished in the heat," and that they were only beginning to find their "pestilential tongues."

The earliest critics of the new order in the South raised their heads amid the first fine flush of their enemy's victory. As a consequence, they were ignored then—as they have been ever since. Indeed, they were really very few in number. It is not without significance that the first of them, in Georgia, was a Confederate colonel. Charles Colcock Jones, the distinguished historian, whom Bancroft called "the Macaulay of the South," was of the stripe of Bob Toombs. The Colonel never really laid down his arms. It was not until 1887, however, that he published his addresses on *The Old South*.[27] His elaborate rhetoric and ecclesiastical tone belong to the man and his day, and were doubtless smiled at in the bustling 'eighties:

In this epoch of commercial methods—of general and increasing poverty in the agricultural regions of the South—of absorption by foreign capital of favored localities, and of the creation in our midst of gigantic corporations intent upon self-aggrandizement, in this era of manifest modification, if not actual obliteration of those sentiments and modes of thought and action which rendered us a peculiar people —I call you to witness that there is a growing tendency to belittle the influences, the ways, the services, the lessons, and the characteristics of former years. . . . I call you to witness that by adulation and fulsome entertainment of itinerant promoters and blatant schemers, seeking to inaugurate enterprises which are designed to benefit those only who are personally interested in them, the public has been sadly duped to its shame and loss. . . . I call you to witness that a reign of plutocrats—a subjection of men, measures and places to the will of millionaires and plethoric syndicates—is antagonistic to the liberty of the Republic and subversive of personal freedom. . . . I call you to witness that the alleged prosperity of this commonwealth, except in

[27] *The Old South: Addresses Delivered before the Confederate Survivors Association . . . by His Excellency, Governor John B. Gordon and by Col. Charles C. Jones, Jr, LL D.*, Augusta, Georgia, 1887.

limited localities is largely a matter of imagination. . . . I call you to witness that behind this fan-fare of trumpets proclaiming the attractions and growth of the New South may too often be detected the deglutition of the harpy and the chuckle of the hireling.[28]

The second critic of the early period came of a different school. He was an Independent of the Reconstruction era and the early 'eighties, Thomas M. Norwood, former Senator from Georgia. In 1888 appeared his *Plutocracy, or American White Slavery, a Politico-Social Novel,* a diatribe against the *nouveaux riches* with generous excerpts from Independent hustings. The following is a sample:

Oh, ye generation of hypocrites and robbers! Spin your false theories; run your printing presses; buy your scribblers; weave your sophistries; juggle with figures; falsify balance sheets; delude your victims; rob labor; roll your millions up to billions; but remember, "for all these things," sooner or later, the *People* "will bring you to judgment!" And may they show that mercy they have not received![29]

Here are clearly represented two traditions of rebellion: the tradition of the Lost Cause—stately, measured, dignified, conscious of righteousness, but fundamentally conscious of defeat, of irreparable defeat. Second, the tradition of the game Independent—shrill, vituperative, a bit febrile, conscious of impotence and frustration. Growing out of the two, organically a part of both—relying upon its heritage for dignity, yet also a little shrill with vituperation—now appeared a new and third tradition, that of the Populist rebellion. But the new rebellion had something the two older traditions lacked. It had a tough-minded realism, a fact-encrusted hardness that was modern. It

---

[28] "The Old South and the New South" (an address delivered April 26, 1889), *Library of Southern Literature,* Vol VII, p. 2851.

[29] P. 315. The novel was published in New York. It was later said to have been regarded by the Populists of Georgia "something as *Looking Backward* is by the Nationalists." Macon *Telegraph,* Aug. 26, 1890. Norwood regarded the Alliance movement as "the grandest since the declaration of independence or the destruction of the Bastille and the overthrow of the Bourbon dynasty." *Constitution,* Aug. 30, 1890.

was not afraid of soiling its sleeves in a catch-as-catch-can tussle, and it had a gay, half-joking fighting spirit born of an undaunted consciousness of rags and tatters, a consciousness of nothing-to-lose and something-to-gain.

In the late 'eighties Tom Watson was already becoming the embodiment of the new Rebellion. Somehow, with Grady still at the helm of the *Constitution* and the other papers following pretty much in his wake, his speeches, or the parts of his speeches that were in this vein, very seldom got into print, or were toned down when they did. So it is that one must turn to his private journals where he made fragmentary notes for speeches in order to find the earliest manifestations of the new spirit of revolt. The following notes were made for a speech delivered in 1888.[30] The speaker, be it noted, was no bearded superannuate addressing moist-eyed Confederates, nor an embittered Independent indulging in vindictive retrospection. He was a red-headed Populist—in all but name—with fire in his eye and mutiny in his voice, and he was speaking from the stump to a crowd of ragged, impoverished farmers with the raw corn liquor of revolt racing in their veins:

"New South" idea. If it means apology, abject submission—sycophancy to success—perish the thought, etc. . . .

Shame to Southern men who go to Northern Banquets & glory in our defeat. Instances.

Unpaternal. Parricidal. . . .

Mr. Grady in his great Dallas Speech thinks that "Plenty rides on the springing harvests!" It rides on Grady's springing imagination. Where is this prosperity? Comment on actual conditions of Farming class.

It seems that Grady was fond of talking about his "dream farm." He would sometimes retire to his office with instructions to tell all callers that he had "gone to his farm." "The farm was a dream," his biographer Joel Chandler Harris explains, "but

[30] MS. Journal 2.

126

he no doubt got more enjoyment and profit out of it than a great many prosy people get out of the farms that are real." [31] That was just about what the wool-hat boys calculated. Anyway, it was little enjoyment and no profit at all they got out of *real* farms. Watson could not resist pointing a moral.

It takes these city fellows to draw ideal pictures of Farm life—pictures which are no more true to real life than a Fashion Plate is to an actual man or woman. . . .

In Grady's farm life there are no poor cows. They are all fat! Their bells tinkle musically in clover scented meadows & all you've got to do is hold a pan under the udder & you catch it full of golden butter.

In real life we find the poor old Brindle cow with wolves in her back & "hollow horn" on her head & she always wants to back up where the wind won't play a tune on her ribs & when you milk her you get the genuine "blue milk" . . . .

In Grady's farm life—lands all "Rich—richer—richest." Crops "Good, better, best." Snowy cotton, rustling corn etc.

In reality—barren wastes—Gullied slopes—ruined lowlands, Barn leaning up against crib, Gin house on crutches. Diving down in grass for cotton. . . . Billy goat would have to labor 12 hrs a day for his living.

Grady's speech an indictment against us.

He only comments on *our* Sins! Nothing said of those who sin against us.

Plead guilty—Admit errors of one crop system—of carelessness—Indolence. . . .

But what of the Trespasses against us?

Banking Laws. Brazil helping her farmers with $6,000,000. Contrast.

We denied access to currency which is life blood of enterprise—cite as example Bank of Augusta—Lavish loan to Georgetown & Lane R. R. Bankruptcy.

Yet finest farm in Georgia couldn't have got any of that money which was poured into a little hippitehop R R commencing in a cabbage patch & ending in a cow pen—Results.

[31] J. C. Harris, *op. cit*, pp 19-20.

127

Tariff laws—81½% on us.

Diversified crops will help—not cure.

These very evils—Bankruptcy laws & Tariff rates are mainly the cause of these lesser evils of which Mr. Grady speaks. . . .

Carelessness & Indolence largely the consequence of repeated failure, constant discouragement—Apathy stealing over energies of the people!

Organization needed—

Party for Pompey—Party for Caesar—No Party for Rome.

Henry Grady did not print that speech on the front page—as he had the speech of his farmer disciple in 1883. He did not print it at all, in fact. Nor did he print the following speech that Watson made a year later: [32]

And yet the city orators say that the great clock of the Republic will keep time as usual & that the Watchman upon the Tower will sing out "All's Well with the Republic, All's Well."

There's no foretelling what the Watchman may say—I would first wish to know who the Watchman is—if he is floating with the tide which carries prosperity to certain classes at the expense of others —If he is the known champion of Rail Road kings, & R. R. combinations. If he is cheek by jowl with the heretofore dominant influences which have sought to fasten upon us forever the curse of High Tariff, & has prostituted his paper & his talents. . . .

Then indeed such a watchman may cry out "All's well."

Rather, O my countrymen, listen to those who tell you of the danger which threatens—who warn you to put on your armor, & man the walls . . .

[32] MS. Journal 2, p. 409.

CHAPTER IX

The Rebellion of the Farmers

THE SOUTHERN FARMER HAD LISTENED apathetically to preachments on diversified crops, scientific method, and improvements from Grady and others of his sincere well-wishers ever since the War. He grudgingly acknowledged the pertinence of their advice, but he observed that Southern agriculture continued to sink lower and lower in a morass of despair. Vaguely, but with mounting conviction, the farmer realized that these preachments did not touch the heart of his trouble. Indeed, an eighteenth-century observer, writing of the plight of the *métayer* under the old regime in France, came nearer the truth when he said, "It is as impossible for one of these wretches to be a good farmer as it is for a galley convict to be a good admiral." [1]

The Southern farmer had lost his independence, his industrial autonomy. In the grip of the lien system—which more universally characterized the post-bellum economy than ever slavery described the ante-bellum system—the farmer, former masters, the majority of them, along with former slaves and yeomen, had been reduced to a state of peonage to the town merchant. The lien system converted the Southern economy into a vast pawn shop. Its evil effects did not end when the farmer signed away his future crop, for that act merely started a vicious circle of compounded evils. It meant that until he paid the last dollar of his debt, and his crop was often found inadequate for that, he

[1] Leo Gershoy, *The French Revolution and Napoleon*, p. 42.

was dependent for his every purchase, clothing, food, implements, fertilizer, everything, upon his creditor merchant, who charged him from twenty to fifty per cent more than the cash price and dictated the amount and quality of the purchase. Moreover, the merchant bound his lien thrall to the one-crop cotton system "by a law as inexorable as any ever promulgated by the most despotic earthly government" in order to insure his investment by a cash crop, and at the same time to increase the farmer's dependence upon him for his exorbitantly priced foodstuffs. By submitting to the one-crop system (and there was no choice) the farmer further depleted his lands and became more dependent upon the merchant's high-priced fertilizer and food, and further increased the surplus and decreased the price of the very product upon which he staked all. At the same time he signed away his right to buy in the cheapest market, the farmer pledged himself to sell in the lowest market. By the very nature of the system he was made an easy victim of every brand of chicanery and false dealing known to business, for the power was all on one side, and mercy and probity are virtues rarely compounded with absolute power. Such was the strait-jacket in which from eighty to ninety per cent of the cotton growers, proprietors and tenants, black and white, normally found themselves.[2]

Even "Pig-Iron" Kelley, wearing the rosy glasses of the New South, admitted that "apart from the New South," that is, away from the cities and railroads, "the same wretched poverty prevails among the Southern people now, twenty-two years after the close of the war."[3] The situation was even worse, for hope and effort and spirit had been all but exhausted by repeated failure. Finding himself hopelessly entangled, the farmer had almost

[2] M. B. Hammond, *The Cotton Industry*, pp. 122-123, 145-154, 195; R. P. Brooks, *The Agrarian Revolution in Georgia*, pp. 32-36; A. M. Arnett, *Populist Movement in Georgia*, pp. 49-59; J. D. Hicks, *The Populist Revolt*, pp. 40-49; C. H. Otken, *The Ills of the South*, Chapters II and III. Hallie Farmer, "Economic Background of Southern Populism," *South Atlantic Quarterly* (Jan., 1930), pp. 406-427; G. K. Holmes, "The Peons of the South," *Annals of the American Academy of Political and Social Sciences*, Vol. IV (Sept., 1893), pp. 265-274.

[3] W. D Kelley, *The Old South and the New*, p. 121.

ceased to struggle. His land declined in value and washed away, fences disappeared, buildings became propped ruins, machinery fell to pieces. The mortgage was foreclosed, and he moved to a poorer farm, to slide further down the scale of living to the margin of subsistence.

A Southerner of the period, whose sympathy was with the farmer, described the life around him: "Each year the plunge into debt is deeper; each year the burden is heavier. The struggle is woe-begone. Cares are many, smiles are few, and the comforts of life are scantier. . . . Anxious days, sleepless nights, deep wrinkles, gray hairs, wan faces, cheerless old age, and perhaps abject poverty make up in part the melancholy story. . . . Independence! It is gone. Humiliation and dependence bow the head of the proud spirit." [4]

This was a drama that Tom Watson had seen acted out to the bitter end by his own family—from John's bepillared mansion to the "miserable shanty" on the swamp near Augusta. In it he had had some lines to speak himself, playing the part of a plow boy in Screven County—his brother the part of a share-cropper under a planter's lash in McDuffie. There was no part of the story he did not know, and there was no part he would not relate at the hustings, on the stump, in formal debate or address. His opponents found something unanswerable about the story.

You were born in plenty and spent your childhood in plenty. I had it too. Then you lost your houses. The sheriff's red flag was planted at your front gate. You and yours took down the family pictures from the wall, picked some favorite flowers from the grave yard and took your weary march out into a strange, cold world. You walked the roads asking for work. I have done it too. [5]

He knew the proprietor's story and he knew the tenant's:

Here is a tenant—I do not know, or care, whether he is white or black, I know his story. He starts in and pays $25 for a mule, 1,000

[4] C. H. Otken, *The Ills of the South*, pp. 21-22.
[5] T. E W. in *The Cotton Plant* (Orangeburg, S. C.), Oct. 31, 1891.

131

pounds of cotton for rent, and two bales for supplies. By the time he pays for that mule, and the store account, and the guano, he has not enough money left to buy a bottle of laudanum, and not enough cotton to stuff his old lady's ear.

A voice—"How did you find that out?"

I've been through the mill. I have been between the plow handles as well as in office. . . .

The land gets poorer year by year and the landlord has no money to improve it—the tenant has no money to improve it. Thousands of your Georgia homes are going to decay. I have witnessed it, and it makes my heart ache with sadness. It is a bad thing for the landlord in another respect. He cannot command labor. Why? Because by the time he pulls out a pencil to write an order the laborer is mad. Why? He knows what an order to the store means. He knows perfectly well that he cannot get goods as cheap as for cash . . .[6]

Watson knew that the lien system merely provided the shackles of the farmer's economic slavery. It was only the machinery of exploitation. How was it that cotton had fallen from a dollar a pound at the close of the War to an average of twenty cents in the 'seventies, nine cents in the 'eighties, and seven cents in the 'nineties—a level below the cost of production—and had stayed there? He was capable of some shrewd guesses as to what forces placed his class in bondage and kept it bound to their own profit. There were the banks, who refused to lend money on the best farm in the state; Wall Street speculators, who gambled on his crop futures; the railroad owners, who evaded taxes, bought legislatures, and overcharged him with discriminatory rates; the manufacturers, who taxed him with a high tariff; the trusts, that fleeced him with high prices; the middleman, who stole his profit; the city folk generally, with their superior airs, their tax-dodging ways, and their incomprehensible patter about the New South; the government itself, with its iniquitous currency laws and its class favoritism; and finally his own beloved Democratic

[6] *People's Party Paper*, Oct 14, 1892.

132

party of so many fond associations—but now the property, body and soul, of an enemy class. And yet,

We are told in the splendid phraseology of silver-tongued orators from the city that our country is absolutely smothered under the plenteous flow of milk and honey of another Canaan. The city of Atlanta [is] especially noted for that kind of tom-foolery. Listening to the inspired clap-trap of some of its Politicians & Editors one would suppose that throughout the South there was no discomfort in the Present & no apprehension for the future.[7]

Men who do not know the difference between a may pop and a rabbit hunt find a poem in every boll of cotton, a romance in every ear of corn. . . . And yet our newspapers are absolutely crowded with advertisements of sheriffs' sales, and in the county of Richmond alone I noticed from the *Chronicle* that there were some two hundred [farms] for sale on the first Tuesday of November. . . . There is no romance in having landed property excluded from the banks, and in having twenty-five per cent upon our money; no romance in being fleeced by a fifty per cent tariff; no romance in seeing other classes and other properties exempted from taxation, and realizing fabulous dividends upon their investments, when the lands are taxed to their uttermost dollar and farming has paid no dividend since the war.[8]

Another thing Watson understood, a poignant, personal thing, was that essentially the same men or their sons worked the same land now as had worked it in 1860. He had only to look about him and recall his childhood to see what a difference those thirty years had worked. Then the manners, customs, standards, ideas, and ideals of society were fixed by the cotton farmer. His ideas and interests were reflected in pulpit, press, courtroom, legislative halls, classroom—even the cities took their tone from the farm. Never did a class more completely dominate a society than then.

And now—the farmer was ignored even by his own party. Wealth, power, and prestige no longer attached to land but to

[7] MS. notes for a speech, Nov. 7, 1889, Watson MSS.
[8] Clipping, MS Journal 2, pp 433-441

stocks and bonds, banks and factories. Now it was the shibboleths of the city capitalists that the farmer read in every newspaper, heard from every preacher, legislator, and politician. The former lord of a thousand acres and most honored squire in his county could not now ride to town on the back of his mule for a sack of meal without running the risk of being patronized by any urbanite from a banker to a bootblack. The mass of *small* farmers, who once shared the planter's prestige, had become peons.[9] Watson declared:

The contrast between the status of the southern farmer before the war and at the present time is indeed discouraging. Then their [*sic*] influence was felt in every department of business—in commerce, in the legislative halls, in Congress. But now, while every other avocation has its advocates and champions in positions of power and importance, the farmer is practically unrepresented. The entire drift of legislation has been, and is yet, continuously and persistently against him.[10]

Our great trouble has been the carelessness and easy good nature with which we have allowed others to profit by our toils and allowed the legislation of this land to drift into the infamies of the tariff and the banking laws, and the chartered exemptions of special enterprises from the burden of the government which protects them. [11]

If his analysis was correct, an "apathy" had stolen over the energies of his people, "largely the consequence of repeated failure, constant discouragement." This apathy, and not "carelessness and indolence," accounted for the decay Grady described. His people had lost spirit, fight. And yet he felt that these same people came of a richer tradition of rebellion than any in the land. Somehow that deep-lying vein of rebellion must be tapped, must be made to yield its dark riches in this time of need. It was with some such reflections as these, certainly with no pipe-dream

[9] B. B. Kendrick, "Agrarian Discontent in the South: 1880–1900," *Annual Report of the American Historical Association*, 1920, pp. 267-272.

[10] *Constitution*, Sept. 14, 1888.

[11] Clipping, MS. Journal 2, pp. 433-441.

delusions of restoring a feudal slavocracy, that he invoked the "dream of the old-time South"—attributing to the old regime, as he did so, certain virtues that existed only in his imagination:

Fill our souls with thy beauty, our hearts with thy inspiration, till every man of us shall deeply resolve that our laws shall be so framed, our Government so administered that every citizen however rich shall bear an equal share of its burdens & every laborer however poor, an equal share of its blessings. . . .

Let there come once more to Southern heart and Southern brain the Resolve—waste places built up.

In the rude shock of civil war that dream perished.

Like victims of some horrid nightmare, we have moved ever since —powerless—oppressed—shackled—[12]

At least there would appear to exist more than a tenuous connection between these musings and the following appeal made from the stump in the thick of the fight:

To you who grounded your muskets twenty-five years ago I make my appeal. *The fight is upon you—not bloody as then—but as bitter; not with men who come to free your slaves, but who come to make slaves of you.* And to your sons also I call: and I would that the common spirit might thrill every breast throughout this sunny land, till from every cotton field, every hamlet, every village, every city, might come the shout of defiance to these Rob Roys of commerce and to the robber tariff, from whose foul womb they sprang.[13]

The fact was that Watson's call to arms fell upon the ears of men who were already mobilizing—enlisting under the banner of the Farmers' Alliance. The origin of the Alliance, unlike that of the Grange, had been spontaneous and diffuse: in a frontier county of Texas, in a log cabin schoolhouse in backwoods Arkansas, in a rural parish of Louisiana.[14] Finding their purposes the same, these separate societies consolidated under a single

[12] Notes for a speech, Watson MSS
[13] Augusta *Chronicle*, Sept. 14, 1888. Italics mine
[14] W. S Morgan, *History of the Wheel and Alliance*, pp. 62, 281; A. M. Arnett, *op. cit* , pp 76-77; J D. Hicks, *op. cit.*, Chap. IV.

name, and, in one of the most amazing feats of organization in American history, attained a membership of three millions in the South alone by 1890. In March, 1887, two organizers from Texas entered the virgin territory of Georgia, touched a match to the tinder of discontent, and almost immediately the state was aflame. Hundreds of "lodges" sprang into existence, each with its "lecturer"; organizers rode all over the state; dozens of papers and journals were founded, or changed their tone and adopted the new slogans; great quantities of reform literature were distributed. In less than three years 134 out of 137 counties in the state sent delegates to the state convention; well over 2,000 lodges were established with a membership of more than 100,000.[15]

The thing looked innocuous enough at first. Henry Grady gave it his blessings, and many machine politicians were found in surprisingly harmonious accord with Alliance principles. It would doubtless have remained innocuous had some of its most prominent leaders had their way. In 1877 C. W. Macune wrote: "Now to sum up: The Alliance is a strictly white man's non-political, secret business association." [16] But within two years' time not one of these adjectives could be applied to the association qualified by the adverb "strictly." Signs of change were not long in appearing.

The farmers were encouraged by a taste of success in their cooperative schemes. The Georgia exchange, one of the most successful, saved its patrons over $200,000 in fertilizers alone in one year. Coöperatives of many sorts, gins, stores, warehouses, sprang up all over the South. One farmer answered the charge of "socialism" with "a few blood-curdling facts" about the savings on guano, and taunted, "It is a 'socialistic' order and thousands of the best farmers in this and thirteen other states are its

[15] A. W. Ivey, chapter on Georgia in *Hand Book and History of the National Farmers' Alliance and Industrial Union*, pp. 47-49; W. S. Morgan, *op. cit.*, p. 295; C. W. Macune, quoted in *Progressive Farmer*, Sept. 8, 1887; A. M. Arnett, *op. cit.*, p. 100; J. D. Hicks, *op. cit*, Chap. IV.
[16] *Progressive Farmer*, Sept. 8, 1887.

'bomb-throwers.' " [17] The Negro farmer was soon recognized as too costly a sacrifice to "white supremacy" and was organized in a parallel Alliance of one and a quarter millions in the South. Likewise, the Alliancemen were quick to mark out their enemies: excluded from membership were bank cashiers, railroad officials, real estate agents, cotton buyers and sellers, practicing lawyers, and anyone "who buys or sells for gain." [18]

The conflict between town and country was manifest in many ways. The Arkansas Wheel even prohibited the organization of Wheels "within the limits of incorporated towns." [19] The official organ of the Georgia Alliance observed that "it is a well known fact that in many of the Georgia towns there has been manifest secret, but bitter and most vindictive animosity against the Alliance movement, and every scheme possible has been resorted to that would bring it into contempt or ridicule. . . . Now, so long as this spirit of hatred is manifested against this organization of farmers, is it but natural and admirable for them to show a spirit of resentment?" [20]

As for the "non-political" aspect of the Alliance, as early as February, 1888, one of its national leaders, a Southerner, was writing, "We are not to be intimidated or frightened by the cry that 'the farmers are going into politics'. . . . Who in all this broad land has a better right 'to go into politics' than he who clothes and feeds the world?" [21]

This movement, even in its incipient stages, can not be fully described or understood in terms of platforms and statistics. There was too much emotion in it for that, and at the source of that great river of emotion lay something more than crop failures and windy politicians. Two penetrating students of the movement have said that "One must go back to Medieval Europe, on the eve of the First Crusade, for an emotional situation

[17] Letter in *Progressive Farmer*, April 17, 1888.
[18] R. L. Felton, *op. cit.*, p. 115.
[19] W. S. Morgan, *op. cit.*, p. 83.
[20] Clipping from *Southern Alliance Farmer*, Watson Scrapbooks.
[21] L. L. Polk, in *Progressive Farmer*, Feb. 16, 1888.

137

comparable . . ." [22] This emotional-religious element in the movement together with the farmers' habit of dramatizing their enemies in picturesque and pungent epithet—the silver "conspiracy," the railroad "tyrants," "the grasp of the gigantic, cold-blooded money trust"—has been the subject of much rarefied merriment among superior scholarly circles. During the period, even Professor Turner apologized for the farmers' "lax financial integrity" with the remark that "A primitive society can hardly be expected to show the intelligent appreciation of the complexity of business interests in a developed society." [23]

The farmers cared no more for the opinions of the captains of scholarship than for those of the captains of industry, and they knew more about the "complexity of business interests" than some cared to admit. The movement was rural in origin and character, and it was but natural that the powerful feelings it awakened should find expression in religious moods and forms. Thus, the president of the Alliance in Watson's county, himself a preacher, said that "the Alliance was born in heaven"; another member thought "the Alliance next in importance to the church of the living God"; while Senator Peffer believed that "the Alliance is in a great measure taking the place of churches." The first state convention of the Populists in Georgia was opened with "the grand old long meter doxology," and Western meetings were "conducted on the same principle as oldtime religious revival meetings." Of the Populist platform, Watson once wrote: "It is sacred to us because it gives hope to our despair; gives expression to our troubles; gives voice to our wants. Our wives have knelt and prayed for it. Our children have learned to love it. Not a church in all the land, where God's blessing has not been invoked upon it."

Still more danger to the business man's regime, the New South order, lay in the fact that the farmer was beginning to think as well as to throb. A hostile observer commented that

[22] Hacker and Kendrick, *The United States since 1865*, p. 301.
[23] Frederick J. Turner, *The Frontier in American History*, p. 32.

138

"The Alliance came into the State a masterful pedagogue—the Alpha and Omega of all politics, State and National." [24] Thumbed copies of Donnelly's *Caesar's Column*, Bellamy's *Looking Backward*, and numberless pamphlets, tracts, and books were circulated from hand to hand.[25] Those who did not read them heard them quoted by those who had. Country school houses and churches rang with the speeches of farmers who had never debated or read or thought before. Like water from a duck's back the hoary platitudes of professional politicians rolled from heads wrapped in forbidden notions of government ownership, and coöperatives.

Of this bracing intellectual ferment Tom Watson drank thirstily and responded to it as to an intoxicant. "A new era has dawned in Georgia politics," he announced. "The old order of things is passing away. The masses are beginning to arouse themselves, reading for themselves, thinking for themselves. The great currents of thought quicken new impulses. At the bar of public opinion the people are pressing their demands and insisting that they be heard." [26]

Thirty years later, at the age of sixty, as his mind reverted to those stirring days of '89, he wrote:

What radiant visions lured us toward the future! What noble deeds we would achieve! What fame and influence would be our reward!

Were conditions wrong? We would right them. Were laws bad? We would make them good. Were the weak oppressed? We would crush the oppressors. Were righteous principles enchained, like captive maidens in the olden castles of Feudal lands and lords? We would put on the bright armor of chivalry, ride forth to the rescue and smite the dungeon-door with the battle-axe of Lionheart.[27]

[24] Washington *Post*, Aug. 3, 1892.
[25] Watson's personal library, owned by Judge Uly O. Thompson, Miami, Florida, contains many such works.
[26] Atlanta *Journal*, Aug. 31, 1889.
[27] T. E. W., *Political and Economic Handbook*, p. 453.

"Bliss was it in that dawn to be alive"—in 1889, as in 1789, as in the salad days of any revolution—and to be young, to be thirty-three, to be a student of the French Revolution, was, one may surmise, "very heaven."

Watson himself was never a member of the Alliance. He might have qualified for membership when he ceased active law practice, but he preferred not to. "I never did enter any council of theirs," he said. "I did not lead the Alliance; I followed the Alliance, and I am proud that I did follow it." [28]

But Watson followed with works as well as with faith, and it was such "following" as he did and such works as he performed that constituted real leadership in the Alliance. There was the case of the fight against the jute-bagging trust. The official organ of the State Alliance went so far as to state that the farmers' "reason for banding together is fully explained in the recent bagging trust." A *typical* reason rather than *the* reason was probably meant. Ben Terrell, national lecturer from Texas, after visiting 105 Georgia counties, commented upon the fight on the trust that he had "never seen anything like it." He attributed the phenomenal growth of the Alliance to the success of this fight.

In mid-summer, 1888, it was revealed that a trust had been formed in St. Louis to control the price of jute-bagging. Week after week the price was pushed up and up until it was increased more than a hundred per cent. Owing to the Liverpool rules in buying, the bagging was an absolute loss to the farmer, and this doubling of the burden would mean some $2,000,000 loss to the cotton producers. This blow on top of a bad season and low prices was a challenge to fight. Watson pictures the origin of the fight against the trust as spontaneous: a farmer came to his office asking him to write a call for a mass meeting. This done, handbills were printed, and on September 10, 1888, some 800 farmers met in Thomson. Watson himself launched the crusade

[28] MS. of speech delivered in Thomson, Nov. 19, 1904, Watson MSS.

140

in a widely copied speech, said to have been "equal to any that ever fell from the lips of Toombs or Stephens." [29]

It was Watson's wish "to make this jute bagging a symbol of the wrong they put upon us":

Well might outsiders say to the "jute combine," as every Monday morning they raise the price on the Southern farmer, "Hit him again, he's got no friends!" What shall we do? Grin and endure it? I say no! . . . The Southern man who can contemplate this outrage and not get mad hasn't got enough blood to fatten a mosquito. This, as well as all other combinations of the kind, is clearly illegal, and ought to be promptly and effectually crushed by Congress. But we know that it is folly to expect aid from that direction. . . . It is useless to ask Congress to help us, just as it was folly for our forefathers to ask for relief from the tea tax; and as they revolted . . . so should we. . . . The Standard of Revolt is up. Let us keep it up and speed it on.[30]

The plan was to boycott jute and use cotton and pinestraw substitutes. Watson urged the farmers to "Listen to no man who croaks, 'Too late, we must submit!'" Such counselors were plentiful. One paper thought, "It seems impossible to defeat the trust." Another denounced Watson's effort because it would make the farmers "fail to meet their obligations with the merchants" who "carried" them. Watson promptly answered each critic with furious onslaughts. His battle cry was taken up all over the state, and in spite of a multitude of handicaps the farmers won a victory over the trust.[31]

The fight was renewed the following year with more thorough organization and preparation. As the result of an invitation issued by the president of the Georgia State Alliance to a conference on the bagging-trust fight, Macune, the national president, issued an official call for a meeting in Birmingham "To decide

[29] T. E. W., *Political and Economic Handbook*, p. 453; handbill in Watson MSS., Chapel Hill; clippings, Watson Scrapbooks.

[30] Printed in Augusta *Chronicle*, Sept. 14, 1888; also in the Columbia *Sentinel*, Sept. 20, 1888, and widely in the rest of the Georgia papers.

[31] *Constitution*, Aug. 22, 1889; clippings, Watson Scrapbooks.

upon the necessity of all the States' coöperating in this conflict with the jute bagging trust." [32] No lack of fervor was shown in the crusade. L. L. Polk told of talking at the Georgia Alliance convention at Macon to "a regular 'Georgia Cracker,'" dressed out in cotton bagging, who told him that "Three hundred and sixty members in his county have uniform suits of it and they are literally the cotton bagging brigade." On Alliance day at the Piedmont Exposition in Atlanta, in the presence of 20,000 Alliance delegates from South Atlantic states, a double wedding was performed, in which "both brides and both grooms were attired in cotton bagging costumes." That year the jute trust suffered an admitted defeat and came to terms.

Watson's friends held that "he called the first meeting on the jute bagging question and was the first public man in the State to address the people and arouse their indignation and to advise the Boycott." His own claim that he "led the fight in Georgia" met with wide acceptance.[33]

The results of the victory over the jute trust, except in immediate economic terms, are difficult to estimate. A Populist novel written in Georgia expressed the view that the fight had taught Populists "the needed lesson that by uniting they were sufficiently powerful to overthrow all monopolies and bid defiance to every form of imposition." It had given them "confidence in themselves and in each other, and one of the first fruits of this great self-confidence showed itself in a disposition to take a more active part in political affairs and to insist upon nominating men from among themselves for all offices." [34]

Watson echoed that judgment: "New wine of reform is not to be put into old bottles of ring politicians. If nothing else was done by the jute fight I would hail it with delight as the resurrection trump which aroused the dead hopes and courage of the Southern people, and brought forth that splendid purpose to

[32] *Progressive Farmer,* May 7, 1889, and June 4, for report on meeting.
[33] Charleston *News and Courier,* May 19, 1890; *McDuffie Journal,* Aug. 16, 1889; T. E. W , *Life and Speeches,* p. 13; clippings, Watson Scrapbooks.
[34] Charles C. Post, *Congressman Swanson,* pp. 333-335.

protest against wrong and bring to the future equality and right." [35]

In December, 1889, two hundred delegates from the Southern Alliance and seventy-five delegates from the Northern Alliance met in separate sessions in St. Louis, both with the hope of effecting a consolidation of the two orders. The Southern Alliance was much larger than the Northern Alliance; it had more vigorous, effective, and prominent leaders; it was more centralized and better organized. And first and last it was more radical.[36] The history of the Alliance officially adopted at St. Louis had as part of its title *The Impending Revolution*. It was the Arkansas author of this work who wrote, "The spirit of rebellion against the many evils is growing stronger. . . . Thousands of men who have already lost all hope of a peaceable solution of the great question of human rights are calmly waiting the issue." [37] Whenever this note of revolution—bloodless or otherwise—was sounded in the movement—and that was not infrequently—it usually came out of the South. Throughout the history of the movement a large element among the Western farmers was afraid of this tendency of their Southern allies. The Northerners were generally more content with gradual reform. A hostile Kansas editor warning the G. A. R. of the preponderance of the South exhibited more historical perspicacity than he knew when he branded the whole Alliance movement a "rebel yell."

Also present at St. Louis were delegates from the Knights of Labor, the Colored Alliance, and the Farmers' Mutual Benefit Association. For various reasons, and despite numerous concessions on the part of the Southern order, the Northern and Southern alliances were unable to consolidate. The state alliances of Kansas, North Dakota, and South Dakota, however, seceded from the Northern Alliance and joined the Southern Alliance under

[35] Atlanta *Journal*, Aug 31, 1889; same idea in the Atlanta *Journal*, July 31, 1890.
[36] J. D Hicks, *op cit*, pp. 112-127; W. S Morgan, *op. cit*, *passim; Handbook of the Farmers' Alliance and Industrial Union, passim.*
[37] W S Morgan, *op. cit*, p. 769

143

the name, Farmers' Alliance and Industrial Union. The new Southern Alliance then united upon one platform with the Knights of Labor, and to emphasize its friendliness to labor, amended its constitution so as to permit mechanics to join the order.

The platform agreed upon by labor and the Southern farmer, and nearly duplicated by the Northern Alliance, demanded the abolition of national banks, the prevention of speculation in futures of all agricultural and mechanical products, the free and unlimited coinage of silver, reclamation of excessive lands granted or sold to corporations or aliens; decrease of the tax burden on the masses, fractional paper currency, and government ownership and operation of means of transportation and communication.[38] Col. L. L. Polk, of North Carolina was elected president by the St. Louis meeting, and Southern leaders pretty much commanded the national movement all along the line.[39]

When the Georgia Alliance delegates returned from St. Louis, a perceptible sigh of relief went up from the ranks of the New South. The scare of a third party had been laid. It seemed that the farmers had declared war only to lay down their arms. "Everything is serene in Georgia," reported the *Constitution*, a little too brightly, "and yet the alliance men of the state were represented by a number of very prominent men. There is no sign of political revolt here. . . . In the south, whatever may be the condition of affairs, the farmers and the alliance men are compelled by circumstances to carry out their views and reforms through the democratic party. There are some things more important than reforms that merely affect the pocket." [40] Here in this appeal to "white supremacy" was raised the New South's perennial answer to a third party threat.

The *Constitution* took pleasure in quoting the New York *Herald* to the effect that "Northern capital is flowing into the

[38] J. D. Hicks, *op cit*, pp 119-125; A. M. Arnett, *op. cit.*, pp. 82-83.
[39] *Progressive Farmer*, Dec. 10, 1889.
[40] *Constitution*, Jan. 13, 1890.

southern states by the millions . . . It is not extravagant, but the simplest truth to say that the south is just now the most prosperous or the most rapidly and richly developing part of the union." [41] From that observation the editor four days later drew a moral:

Any legislation that would tend to unsettle things and check southern progress is viewed with unfriendly eyes in Northern commercial centers.
After all, business is the biggest thing in this country. When the princes of commerce and industry say to the politicians that they must let dangerous experiments alone they will be heard and obeyed. . . .
Politicians may talk, but business men will act, control and dominate the destinies of this common-sense country . . .

From the urban-industrial South, the New South of all the eleven states of the former Confederacy, came similar news and similar deductions. During the first quarter of 1890 it seems that "The *Tradesman's* reports from all sections of the Southern states indicate the planting of more industries in the South at present than at any previous time in its history." [42] Georgia headed the list.

With such sugar-plum visions dancing in his head, and with a certain willful blindness toward a black horizon, the editor wrote:

The CONSTITUTION spreads this morning the blessed gospel of sunshine!
Its sails are bellying with the rising winds of trade. Its expanded columns carry the news of cheerful and hopeful enterprise. On every side things move well. In politics, in business, the outlook is brightening.

That editorial was written in April, 1890.

[41] *Ibid.*, Jan. 4, 1890.
[42] Macon *Telegraph*, March 30, 1890.

145

CHAPTER X

The Victory of 1890

"Shall the people accept orders from Congress?"
"Who shall rule, the politicians, or the people?"
"Shall we allow these, our servants, to dictate to us, their masters?"
"We are sovereigns of this land and we come to our representatives and not to our lords."
"Shall the agent be allowed to grow too insolent to obey the instructions of his principal?"
"When your congressmen come home and begin their preconcerted attack on your platform, ask them what better plan they have advocated during all these years that they have been enjoying fat salaries."[1]

THESE AND SIMILAR CHALLENGES peppered the columns of the Georgia Alliance papers; they were flung in the faces of Congressional committees; they glared from the letters of constituents. It was in such a mood that the Alliance in 1890 determined to apply its "yardstick," the St. Louis platform. All candidates must "stand up and be measured." Woe to any office holder, of whatever military rank or valor, who confessed doubts as to the subtreasury plan, abolition of the national banks, or government ownership of the means of transportation and communication.

Unlike their Western brethren, who were already resorting to independent political organizations, the Southern Alliancemen believed themselves powerful enough, by boring from within, to take over the old party for their own purposes and thus to work

[1] Clippings, 1889–1890, Watson Scrapbooks.

146

their reforms. Why run the risk of political anarchy and a Negro-Republican victory, it was argued, when by voting solidly the Alliance could *be* the Democratic party. Talk of a third party was frowned down. The farmers had their candidate for every office. Revolution was to come from within.

In January, 1889, twenty-two months before the election, the press had observed that "Watson is actively in the race." But it was a full two years before the election, during the jute trust fight, that, so he writes in his Journal, he determined to run for election to Congress from the Tenth District.

Against him was soon brought the charge that virtually all Alliance candidates met: He was merely "riding the Alliance horse into office." He reminded his critic that the pursuit of his profession would yield him a larger income than the office he sought. As for the sincerity of his belief in the Alliance platform, he had practiced its principles before they were expressed in a platform:

My interest is the same as theirs; my grievance as a farmer the same as theirs; my attacks on the legislation of the day the same as theirs. Then why shouldn't we fight side by side to achieve the common victory?

With characteristic whole-heartedness Watson embraced the entire St. Louis platform. He defended with impartial zeal every plank in it, unequivocally, along with the additional demands of the state Alliance, as well as free trade, and the subtreasury plan. The farmers did not have to be convinced of his loyalty. He was no over-night convert. His record as an independent rebel went back to his revolt against the Grady-Pat Walsh campaign for Colquitt in 1880. He had fought their battles against the convict lease system and the railroads in the Legislature; out of office he had opposed Grady's New Departure candidates. His fame as a leader of the crusade against the jute trust had spread not only over the whole state, but into other states as well.

147

The Alliance papers rallied to his support. "It is the plain and unmistakable duty of every Allianceman, every farmer, every lover of good government to support him," urged one. Another thought that, "The combination which is formed to defeat the Hon. Thos. Watson in the Tenth is shameful." Another that, "Brave Tom Watson, the young man eloquent, is making a fight for you in the Tenth District; against him are all the allied powers of money, with their hirelings, but he will win, for his cause is just and fair and the farmers of the Tenth District are not white slaves."

Watson's opponent, the incumbent from the Tenth running for reëlection, represented about the best the New Departure produced in the way of statesmen. At the same time, except that he was free from any suspicion of corruption, the man and his career in every respect conformed to the dominant politics and philosophy of the 'eighties. The Hon. George T. Barnes, called "the weightiest man in Congress," was a portly gentleman, amiable, mild of manner, and rotund of middle, with a broad expanse of shirt front and an impressive presence. His title of "Major" was honorably won in the service of the Confederacy. He was a resident of the city of Augusta, "a man of comfortable fortune, and president of the Augusta Gas Company," which enjoyed a valuable franchise on street railways.[2]

As long as there had been a Tenth District, Augusta had furnished its representative, and that representative had been Major Barnes. Three successive terms he had served, each time elected without opposition. The Major was said to have "been in office or an applicant for office ever since he was twenty-one years old," and he was now fifty-seven.[3]

A defender of Barnes wrote that "There is really no issue between Mr. Barnes and his opponent except that Mr. Barnes is in and Mr. Watson wishes to be in." As proof of the charge, he

[2] Charleston *News and Courier*, May 19, 1890; *Biographical Dictionary of the American Congress*, *1774–1927*, p. 672.
[3] Augusta *Chronicle*, July 22, 1890.

148

appealed to Barnes' record in Congress, presenting evidence to show him a champion of tariff reform, free silver, moderate inflation, and an enemy of the national bank. Furthermore, he had obtained a federal court building, a liberal appropriation for the Savannah River harbor, and was engaged in securing a Government arsenal—all for Augusta.

For his part, Watson was inclined to take few exceptions to these claims. What's more, he believed that Major Barnes was "as nice a man as ever lived" and that he "probably killed as many Yankees as they did of him." He intended to conduct the campaign upon a dignified and impersonal level. But there were other issues. The trouble with the Major was that his record was entirely "negative." When he addressed his constituency the year before, he "didn't say a word about the great revolution that is taking place among the people," and he had "contributed nothing to the enthusiasm which exists among the people for reform." He did not understand the movement; he had lost touch with the masses and was out of sympathy with them. Furthermore, the Major was closely associated with open enemies of the Alliance. Particularly, there was Pat Walsh, editor of the Augusta *Chronicle*, Barnes' "bosom friend" and supporter, who was bitterly hostile to the Alliance. Nor had the Major stood up publicly to be measured by the Alliance "yardstick." Again, he was a "defeatist," inclined to point to the Republican majority, throw up his hands, and wait for the Democratic innings. That attitude would not do these days, Watson assured Barnes.[4]

Apart from early decisions and unofficial reports, the first formal announcement of Watson's candidacy was not made until August, 1889. Shortly afterward Watson sent an invitation to Major Barnes, then in Augusta, to meet him in a series of debates on the stump. Barnes declined courteously, explaining that it was fourteen months before the election, and that neither he nor the farmers had time for debate now. Watson enjoyed read-

[4] Charleston *News and Courier*, May 19, 1890; George T. Barnes to his constituents, Washington, D. C., June 9, 1890, Watson Scrapbooks.

149

ing the Major's reply to crowds of cheering farmers, who were obviously taking time for debate, whether the Major did or not. With a speech at Thomson, Watson "fired the first shot" of the campaign: "It was loaded with bomb-shells. A crowd from several counties, such as assembles only to a mammoth barbecue, were in range, and the result of the discharge was astonishing. His tones rang out like bell strokes, clear and strong, and left no doubt as to his stand on the political issues of the day. He spoke as one of the people talking to the people. There was no hesitating, no evasion, no concealment. He attacked legislative evils in the boldest style and testified clearly that, were it in his power, he would sound the death knell of monopolies, trusts, and railroad combines." It was the "biggest barbecue ever known in McDuffie county." Three thousand people were present. Farmers in their wagons, some having driven a score of dusty miles, were encamped in and about the village like an invading army.[5]

The campaign thus launched continued intermittently during the early fall, as long as "politicking weather" allowed. The crusade against the jute trust was still in progress. The real battle for election would come the next spring and summer.

In early April of the following spring there drew to its climax an event fraught with a multitude of potentialities, perhaps favorable, as likely unfavorable, to Watson's aspirations.

The McGregor-Cody feud[6] had a bloody history of more than two years. The trouble between the two men was referred to in the stilted phraseology of the day as "the vindication of a virtuous and pious woman." There was talk about "a breath of suspicion upon the fair name of a gentle lady." Further into the Southern adaptation of a feudal code it is not important to go. On the night of December 17, 1887, Jim Cody shot Charley McGregor through the body on the latter's front lawn, and es-

[5] Atlanta *Journal*, Sept. 1, 1889; Augusta *Chronicle*, Sept. 25, 1889.

[6] The sources of this story are: Macon *Telegraph*, April 11-18, 1890; *Constitution*, April 13-21, 1890; clippings, Watson Scrapbooks; MS Journal 2.

150

caped undetected. McGregor slowly recovered, Cody helping to nurse his unsuspecting victim to health. Cody later confessed to the shooting, but remained at large, evading trial. Believing his life constantly threatened, McGregor armed himself and waited. On October 12, 1889, meeting Cody in the streets of Warrenton, McGregor shot him down with a pistol, killing him instantly.

Major Charles E. McGregor was perhaps Watson's closest personal friend. Certainly he later came to be. They had served in the legislature together, and, living in neighboring towns, saw each other frequently. McGregor appealed to his friend at once to defend him in his trial for life, and Watson immediately responded.

Cody and McGregor were two of the most prominent citizens of Warrenton, the county seat of Warren, a county in the heart of Watson's congressional district. Both the McGregor clan and the Cody clan had endless ramifications—a very Southern situation. Of the seventy-nine traverse jurors summoned for the trial, twenty were disqualified for kinship to Cody alone. Local authorities on genealogy were put to task, for sometimes "the juror himself could not explain the kinship in question." Intense feeling between the two clans divided the county and pervaded the district, while the rest of the state watched with intense interest. During the trial, Judge Lumpkin, in handing down a ruling, remarked that, "If I allow every suit that has originated on account of this feud between McGregor and Cody to be investigated, there will be no end to the trial." A news reporter wrote that were the verdict in favor of the defendant, "a number of gentlemen have assured me that the friends of Cody will shoot McGregor down as he shot Cody down." Bulging pockets were observed in the streets.

The trial opened at eight o'clock, April 10. "From sunrise there had been a continuous stream of people poring [*sic*] into town, and even at this early hour there was not even standing room in the court house, and a large crowd had gathered out-

151

side." The Cody clan had provided the best legal talent available in the state, five lawyers in all. Judge H. D. D. Twiggs, the main dependence of the prosecution, was a seasoned veteran of the bar, six feet tall, and still powerful of body and mind. His merciless handling of witnesses, his searing tongue and penetrating power of analysis made him probably the most feared opponent of the state bar. McGregor employed two lawyers, Watson and James Whitehead. The day before the trial, however, Whitehead was called home by illness in his family. Watson was left alone to defend the life of his friend against the most brilliant talent of the state. "It will be a battle between giants when Judge D. D. Twiggs and Col. Tom Watson cross swords," it was predicted. "When Greek meets Greek then comes the tug of war."

It would be the crucial test of his professional career, and Watson realized it. It involved not only his professional career, but something closer to his heart: "Watson went into the case heart and soul. He had been told that to do so would affect his chances for the congressional nomination, which he seeks, but his answer, quick and prompt, was that under any circumstances he would do his duty." Given the set of circumstances described, with Tom Watson in the center of the stage, drama was as sure to follow as night the day. For in dramatizing himself, his personal relations, his struggles, and his aspirations, Tom Watson had few equals.

As an orator, he pulled out all the stops and ran every scale; as a stage director he employed every hoary trick of his trade. He had just begun his argument when—enter grief-stricken wife and children of the defendant, seating themselves at his side. Again Mark Antony's trick was revived, as Watson had employed it before. Major McGregor was stripped to the waist to show the wounds Cody had inflicted. Before Watson finished, each of the twelve jurors had been individually summoned before Saint Peter to answer in imagination (that Watson stimulated into vividness) for a verdict of "Guilty"; each had been

152

turned away from the celestial gates; each was made to writhe at the conjured vision of "poor Charley McGregor" dangling at rope's end before him, neck stretched.

"What can I say of Tom Watson?" pleaded an impressed spectator. "Never did lawyer do braver, bolder, manlier battle for his client. His heart was in his work, for Watson and McGregor are warm personal friends. If the spectacle of this little smooth-faced fellow standing here, seeking with all his power and all his eloquence to save the life of his friend, was worth coming far to see, the speech he made was worth coming further to hear. Weird was that scene at night. Two lamps and two small candles furnished the light that radiated fitfully over judge, jury, and spectators as Watson, with words of wonderful eloquence, presented his case." And no eye was unwet.

The jury was out for five days—lacking only one vote of unanimity, it was later revealed. During the days of waiting the state press swelled the celebrity of Watson's name. But on the fifth day when the jury announced its verdict of "not guilty," his fame fairly soared. The warring clans accepted the jury's verdict and the feud quieted down. Politically, contrary to expectation, Watson seems to have been the gainer. Everyone now clamored to hear "the eloquent Col. Watson," no matter what heresy he uttered.

Not long after the McGregor trial, Judge Twiggs joined two other prominent Augusta lawyers in a campaign of letter writing and speech making in behalf of Major Barnes' and against Watson's candidacy. On June 13, in a speech at Waynesboro, Twiggs made the charge that Watson was the real author of a letter appearing in the Charleston *News and Courier*⁷ over the signature, "J. J. H.," which, according to Twiggs, "painted . . . [Watson] as almost a political prophet and genius, which letter was full of detraction and ridicule of Mr. Barnes." Twiggs also berated the subtreasury plan of the Alliance, adding that Watson had swallowed the scheme just as a "yellow gaping mass" of

⁷ May 19, 1890.

153

fledgeling mocking-birds, with eyes shut and mouth open, swallowed whatever the mother bird brought, nor "did he care whether it was a grub, a caterpillar or an eel worm." Watson promptly replied by means of a "card" in the *Constitution*. He had made no secret of giving a news reporter his side of the campaign when it was requested, he replied. The parts of the letter called offensive to Major Barnes were contained in the headlines and parts of the letter that he had not written. Furthermore, "Judge Twiggs' harangue at Waynesboro was simply the vaporings of a soured outlaw, who is so accustomed to abusing everything and everybody that the restraints of truth have no power over him." Judge Twiggs replied the following day with a letter branding Watson's remarks "offensive" and "intended to convey insult," and requesting an "explanation." [8] According to approved etiquette this was correct procedure in opening negotiations for a duel.

Although the long-standing professional rivalry between the two men had been generally upon a rather friendly basis, relations had doubtless been strained at times. Watson was responsible for the widely circulated epigram on Twiggs' phenomenally keen sense of smell: "he could tell the sex of a hog by smelling of the gravy." In the reports of the clash between the two in the recent McGregor case, it had been said that "it was fight, fight, fight from start to finish." These incidents, however, probably contributed more to whetting the public interest over the prospective duel than they did to the challenge itself.

The code of the duel, once so prevalent, had been outlawed by the Georgia Constitution of 1877, but the practice had not been stopped. In fact there had been a recent recrudescence of dueling in the state. The press had carried accounts of three duels or attempted duels between prominent Georgians in the previous year. One paper had run three and four columns on the front page daily for a week upon one duel.[9] The attitude toward

[8] *Constitution*, June 15-21, 1890.
[9] Macon *Telegraph*, Sept. 7-14, 1889.

this popular crime is partly reflected in an editorial of the *Constitution:* "It was a fine and engaging spectacle—those two dauntless men confronting each other in that gentle and dauntless manner, and it warmed the cockles of the heart to read about it. . . . We must condemn in the abstract, even where we admire in the concrete." The Augusta *Chronicle* claimed to be "the only daily paper in the state which has denounced the practice of dueling in commenting upon the recent meeting in Alabama between two Georgia gentlemen."

The correspondence between prospective duelists—an elaborate knocking of chips from shoulders—was inevitably spread over the press of the state for the edification of the public. On street corners, in barnyards, over cotton rows, shrewd judgments were swapped upon the mettle displayed by the respective chip-knockers and sharp distinctions were drawn over fine points of "honor." Thus might a public man's career be forever blighted. It had happened before. It could happen again.

Watson's reply was delivered to Twiggs by Major McGregor. In it he curtly refused to withdraw his remarks; he gave his reasons for making them, then he concluded: "Let me add further that I am no duelist. Whether this position be taken from principle or from want of courage you can form your own opinion and make such experiments to verify it as your judgment may dictate." Twiggs countered with further justification of his remarks in his speech, denied Watson's interpretation of them, and again requested a retraction of Watson's offensive remarks. In his response Watson merely dismissed Twiggs' letter as "a practical evasion of the issue." Twiggs' reply ended with his final decision upon the matter:

In view of your recent statement that you do not hold yourself amenable to those usages requiring satisfaction among gentlemen, I refrain from indulging in the empty form of sending you a challenge. In your intimation that I may test your courage anywhere except upon the field of honor, you imply willingness to meet an attack I

155

may make upon you on the street or other place of resort where the lives of innocent men and women may be endangered.

This willingness may be safely expressed, for I shall not descend to the level of a street brawler, but will leave you to the contempt which you deserve, and to the judgment of a discriminating public.

Watson's final rejoinder was the most dignified document that graced the exchange. It was devoted largely to a demonstration of Twiggs' lack of candor and fairness in his charges, and contained the following statement about dueling: "I have never intended to spend one moment in studying the code which with refined and formal lawlessness tramples on all the statutes human and divine. I have never yet endeavored to fashion my thought to a belief that deliberate murder was any the less murder because the duelist held a pistol in one hand and a book of etiquette in the other." He added that "The foreboding of what would happen when he and I met is needlessly gloomy. We met in the car shed this morning. And yet it is nevertheless true, that water still has the weakness to run downwards and steam clings to the old tendency to go up." [10]

What would the people think? Public opinion appears to have been solidly lined up behind Watson's position on dueling and on other parts of the controversy. Even the Augusta *Chronicle* approved his stand against the duel. Thus the second ordeal of 1890 ended—again to Watson's credit. Neither episode would merit this much attention were they not both so typical of Watson's public life.

Major Barnes postponed his return from Washington to meet Watson's aggressive campaign until less than a month before the primaries, which came around the last of July. Arriving home ill, he left his bed against the advice of his physician in order to meet Watson, whose invitation he had this time accepted.

It was clear from the start that Major Barnes was uncom-

[10] Letters published in the Augusta *Chronicle*, June 21, 1890.

156

fortable in the new political atmosphere. By his own confession he belonged to the tradition of another day. At Sandersville in his first engagement with Watson, he said that it was the first time he had ever spoken in behalf of his own candidacy: "It was distasteful to him to speak of himself and his own work; he would rather have his friends do that." Although his weight, his health, and his age told against him in a contest with a much younger man (who was also devoid of any inhibitions against speaking in his own behalf), Barnes met Watson several times. The younger man adopted an attitude of indulgent, good-natured respect for his elder. Nevertheless, things went rather badly for the Major from the first. He was no match for Watson in repartee and colloquy, and he was at a disadvantage before these crowds of rejuvenated farmers, Alliancemen most of them, saturated by their lecturers, by debates, and by Alliance reform literature, with facts and figures and queer ideas and heresies of all descriptions, shouting their slogans and singing Alliance songs.

One got to Big Creek, Jefferson County, by a slow train over the narrow gauge railroad to Wrenns, and from there by horseback or wagon for six miles through the open country to Hudson's Ford. Along the dusty road, under a July sun, crawled a broken caravan of wagons and buggies—two thousand people approaching the Big Creek barbecue from half a dozen counties. Under the oak trees it was shady and a little cooler. From the pits along the creek bank drifted a savory smoke arising from more than a hundred "carcasses," spluttering crusty brown under dripping mops plied by the Negro cooks. After dinner on the ground came the speaking. The sun was merciless, and, "with the thermometer about 90 in the shade, it was pathetic to see the perspiration run down the speakers' faces and saturate their clothes."

If the Major so heartily endorsed the candidacy of William J. Northen for governor on the Alliance platform, Watson asked, then why did he oppose Watson's candidacy on the same platform? His position on the subtreasury plan, which Twiggs and Barnes found so dreadful, was the same as Northen's . . .

Barnes, interrupting—"I would not support Northen for Congress on that platform."

Watson—"And yet you do support him for governor on it. . . . A rabbit that is good enough to stew ought to be good enough to fry. (Laughter and applause.)

"They are all for Northen, but they can't swallow me because I have swallowed the 'Alliance worm.' To look at me some persons might think I had been living on that diet for a long time, and that same person looking at Major Barnes would be forced to the conclusion that Major Barnes lived on a very different diet." (Laughter.)

Then Watson rapped to order his famous Alliance schoolroom, that so painfully discomfited the Major:

Watson—"Now I want to ask Major Barnes how much money there is in circulation per capita."

Barnes—"There is a difference of opinion among financiers—some say one amount and some another."

Watson—"But what do you say?"

Barnes—"If you count the money on deposit in banks there is about $22 per capita. . . ."

Watson—"They count the same money twice."

Carroll (Barnes' colleague)—"We do not. How much do you say there is?"

Watson—"I say there is about $4.75 per capita."

A hundred voices—"That's right; you're right; hurrah for Watson." [11]

Then the lesson would proceed with more catechizing of his inept and discomfited pupil. How much silver was coined between 1873 and 1878? How many national bank notes were redeemed? "Wrong again. Wrong again," Watson would reprimand, and the Alliancemen would roar with laughter and

[11] Atlanta *Journal*, July 19, 1890; clippings, Watson Scrapbooks.

shout for Watson, or at his command supply the answer to his question.

At the end of Major Barnes' reply, which in sharp contrast to Watson's speech, was received in silence, he said, a little plaintively, one imagines:

"Six years ago you sent me to Congress and you have reëlected me, and all the time I have served you to the best of my ability. You endorsed me and sent me back before; in what have I changed?"
A voice—"Times have changed and the people have changed."

After a few such unequal engagements Major Barnes ceased to meet Watson on the stump. But Watson ceased not at all: he "made speeches, played with babies, talked crops with the men, discussed fashions with the ladies, and made friends with everybody." When figures were not at hand, he answered the enemies of the Alliance with ridicule or humor. The charge that the farmer needed to "live closer and work harder" was "an insult to the industry of Georgia farmers." Everyone knew that the farmer "skimmed his milk on top and then turned it over and skimmed it on the bottom. (Laughter.) If a fly lit in his sugar he made him thump his legs on the sides of the barrel for fear a grain would stick to his feet. (Laughter.) And they stop their clocks at night to save the wear and tear on the machinery. (Laughter.)"

A loud clap of thunder interrupted his speech at Tenniville. As the reverberations ceased he continued: "Like the thunder that shakes yon sky, the voice of the people has shaken the power from the hands of the political bosses and placed it in the hands of the masses where it belongs." During a speech at Wadley a drunken man created a panic by brandishing a pistol. After he was disarmed several people called, "Watson, he tried to shoot you." His reply was instantaneous: "The man who undertakes to inaugurate reform must stand, not one fire, but a thousand." [12]

[12] Clipping, Watson Scrapbooks; Atlanta *Journal*, July 31, 1890.

The campaign in the Tenth District was the subject of more comment and interest than any in the state. It was said to be "as hot as Nebuchadnezzar's furnace." That was in 1890, before the Populist campaigns had set a new record for torrid politics. Conspicuously missing from this contest with the amiable Major were the night riders, the herds of "liquored" Negro voters, the burning ballot boxes, and the deadly gun play that so lamentably characterized the later elections. Yet the later contests were conducted by essentially the same leaders, for the same votes, upon the same platforms. It is important to understand this difference when those later campaigns are described.

During this campaign Watson was observed to entertain an "irritating confidence and sanguine assurance of every county in the district except Richmond." Richmond, Major Barnes' home county, also the county of the highly industrialized city of Augusta, was not even contested by Watson, who conceded Barnes his home county as a matter of political courtesy. There were eleven counties in the District. Ten were overwhelmingly rural-agricultural, and one urban-industrial. In all they had thirty-four votes at the convention. Of these, eighteen were required to nominate. Watson and the Alliance insisted upon holding primaries in each county. Barnes' only hope lay in capturing Burke, Washington, Johnson, and Warren counties, along with Richmond.

Returns from the primaries beginning in the last days of July quickly dispelled any hope for Barnes. In the whole of McDuffie County he got eleven votes, one only in the Thomson District. In Warren, the county of the McGregor trial, which the Barnes papers counted as "conceded" to Barnes, Watson's victory was four to one; in Washington, strongly contested by Barnes, Watson's majority lacked nine votes of being three to one; in Glascock only twenty-three votes were reported for Barnes. Columbia, Jefferson, and Lincoln fell in line with heavy majorities for Watson, and Johnson County ended the contest by giving him a ten to one majority and enough votes at the convention to nominate him without waiting to hear from the remaining counties. Major Barnes withdrew from the race, formally acknowledging defeat. He carried only one of the eleven counties, Richmond. Even there the county Alliance passed a resolution endorsing Watson's candidacy, and he polled a heavy vote in the working class wards. Watson's victory was unmistakable and complete.[13]

"The election passed off quietly" was a phrase used in describing nearly all the county primaries. The Democratic district convention, held in the village of Harlem upon the insistence of the Alliance, instead of as usual at Augusta, was described as "a quiet body, performing a perfunctory duty," until time came for nominating Watson. "His hands were shaken on all sides and by everybody. He was in smiles all day and when the thing was over the boys went wild." A further endorsement of Watson was registered when the convention, by an overwhelming vote, tabled a resolution condemning his favorite measure, the subtreasury plan. In November his Republican opponent was smothered—as such candidates were usually smothered.[14]

The triumph of the Alliance was state-wide: "In six out of ten Congressional districts, the 'Bourbons' lost their seats; in the other four, they made their peace with the 'embattled farmers,' via the less radical element. The Alliance controlled the state convention, chose the governor, wrote the platform, named three-fourths of the senators and four-fifths of the representatives." [15] All over the South and West the Alliance enjoyed victories of greater or less degree than in Georgia. "Before the Alliance was organized," observed the Macon *Telegraph*, a corporation newspaper, "it was a rare occurrence for a farmer, or a farmer's son to receive honor and recognition. The offices

[13] Augusta *Chronicle*, July 30 to Aug. 3, 1890; *Constitution*, Aug. 3, 1890; Macon *Telegraph*, Aug. 2, 1890; *McDuffie Journal*, July 11, 1890; clippings from county weeklies in the Watson Scrapbooks.
[14] Augusta *Chronicle*, Aug. 29, 1890.
[15] A. M. Arnett, *The Populist Movement in Georgia*, p. 116.

161

all went to the towns and to the lawyers. . . . But now the bottom rail is on top . . ." It was a "Farmers' legislature" that convened in November.

One of the first duties of the new Legislature was to elect a United States Senator to succeed Joseph E. Brown. It had been just ten years since Brown had gone to fill the seat vacated by the sudden resignation of Gordon. Having lately discovered a remarkable identity between his own principles and those of the Alliance, General Gordon now decided that duty called him back to the Senate, and he generously offered his services. Since there was in prospect "a wrestle of giants," he said, ". . . you need to call to your assistance the greatest intellects . . . men self-possessed and prudent, who cannot be shaken." While he was sure he qualified, he urged that "the unity of the Democratic party was essential to the supremacy of the white race in the South," and he could not give his unqualified support to the subtreasury scheme of the Alliance, since it was a threat to party unity.[16]

"First, a railroad lawyer; second, a railroad promoter; third, a railroad president; and fourth, the farmer's best friend. . . . Nothing but your failure to be a railroad president drove you back to Georgia to be the farmer's friend for the same office you threw away when you deserted them to join a railroad." [17] Thus Norwood, himself a candidate, characterized his opponent. The *Chronicle* felt sure that the General's charm was fatal, for the farmers "have been told repeatedly that he is visionary, profligate, unreliable, and unbusinesslike. But they have declared that with all his faults they love him." It would seem so.

It was admitted that an Alliance caucus could elect any candidate agreed upon. It happened, however, that confusion and difference existed among Alliance leaders. "Indeed," said one member of it, "our caucus favored Hammond at breakfast, Hines at dinner, Norwood at supper, and Calhoun just before

[16] Augusta *Chronicle*, Aug. 20 and 30, 1890; Macon *Telegraph*, Aug. 21, 1890.
[17] T. M Norwood to J. B Gordon, in Augusta *Chronicle*, Aug. 29, 1890.

going to bed." [18] For a time it looked very much as if two Alliance "bosses," L. F. Livingston, President of the State Alliance, and C. W. Macune, a prominent national leader, were going to succeed in swinging the Alliance vote to Patrick Calhoun. Calhoun, grandson of the great Carolina statesman, was a wealthy railroad lawyer whose most spectacular accomplishment was the successful combination of a large number of Georgia railroads under the Richmond Terminal Company, a heavy investment of Jay Gould's, with headquarters in Augusta. The Allianceman was not far wrong who said Calhoun was "Wall Street's biggest representative in the South." Livingston and Macune were charged with yielding to corrupt influence in backing him, and some evidence of their guilt was later produced.[19]

Watson, as an Alliance Congressman-elect, was called to Atlanta and given orders by Livingston to "go into our caucus and indorse Calhoun." Watson refused to do so, explaining that Calhoun "is the representative of one of the classes against which the Alliance and the Democratic party are arrayed. I cannot indorse the paid attorney of a great railway monopoly. . . . I will not consent to sell out my constituents." [20] Although Watson had led his county in the fight against Gordon in 1886, he now, apparently as a choice of the lesser evil, lent him his influence, though he did not make a public speech. He later claimed credit for the defeat of Calhoun, though with what justice is doubtful.[21]

General Gordon was elected Senator. The better to consummate the union with his brother farmers he soon joined the Alliance. We are afforded two painful glimpses of the General's initiation ceremony through the secret doors: once hoisted to

[18] A scrapbook in the Watson collection devoted entirely to the Senatorial race of 1890 is the source of this and much other information in this account.
[19] A. M. Arnett, op. cit., p. 119.
[20] Clippings, Watson Scrapbooks and Northern Scrapbooks, especially from the *Southern Alliance Farmer* and Savannah *Morning News*, Nov. 16, 1890.
[21] J. B. Gordon to W. J. Northen (MS.), Sept. 25, 1890, in Northen Scrapbook, Vol. I, pp. 66-67; clippings, Northen Scrapbooks and Watson Scrapbooks.

the roof by the seat of his pants, "dangling in the air, with hands and feet vainly clutching the floor," and once more, stretched across a barrel while the "Supreme Spanker" let fall the "subtreasury plank" full forty times to "convince the new brother that it was not a rotten one."

Now that the farmers began to the test the fruits of their victory, they found it spotted to the core and sour in their mouths. What had become of their class struggle—now that their enemies had taken to celebrating Alliance victories? How was it that the *Constitution* had come to rejoice that "The Farmers' Alliance *is* the Democracy party"; that the Managing Editor of the *Constitution* had been elected Speaker of the farmers' House of Representatives; [22] that Alliance leaders had supported a hireling of Jay Gould for Alliance senator; that General Gordon, of the notorious New Departure triumvirate, had been elected senator by the farmers' legislature? How was it that there were two kinds of Alliancemen—the "wool-hat boys" and the "plug-hat bosses"? How had this come about?

On March 4, 1889, Henry Grady addressed a letter to W. J. Northen marked "Strictly Confidential." He wrote:

Let me give you an idea. Put yourself in line with the movement to bring about peace between the agricultural and commercial interests of the state which is now threatened by the Alliance. The farmers have the sympathy of the commercial community in their efforts to organize and coöperate, but there is a danger that these two interests will find themselves in hopeless opposition unless somebody smooths the friction. The man who does it will be master of the situation. [23]

Being completely in harmony with Northen's conservative temperament and interest, this suggestion of Grady's seems to have been religiously followed. During his campaign, Northen

[22] Clark Howell, son of Captain E. P. Howell, owner of the *Constitution*, and railroad promoter.
[23] MS. of letter in Northen Scrapbooks, Vol. III, p. 264.

repeated many times that he was the friend of all classes and the enemy of none, that he would "faithfully serve all classes." With this understanding he was still able to win the backing of the Alliance, and consequently the governor's chair. Many other conservatives (some not as candid about their conservatism) likewise won office through the Alliance.

On Alliance day at the Piedmont Exposition, Grady, as master of ceremonies, addressed 20,000 Alliancemen. "It gave him the greatest pleasure," he said, "that the Piedmont Exposition had brought together in harmonious council the business men of the chief city of the south Atlantic states and the leaders of and members of the most important farmers' organizations in history. There is no room for divided hearts in the south . . . without regard to class." [24] There were those, said Grady elsewhere, who believed that "the South should divide, the color line be beaten down, and the southern States ranged on economic or moral questions as interest or belief demands." But this was "The worst in my opinion that could happen." The only "hope and assurance of the South" was "The clear and unmistakable domination of the white race. . . . What God hath separated let no man join together. . . . Let not man tinker with the work of the Almighty." [25]

Henry Grady died in Atlanta on December 23, 1889. Considering the history of the year following his death, which has just been reviewed, one might conclude that his creed had triumphed over death. Yet viewed from a longer range, his death might well symbolize the end of an era of Southern history. Grady's creed was the creed of the 'eighties. Briefly summarized, its tenets embraced: industrialization of the South; glorification of the capitalist and his way of life; political, economic, and cultural unity between the South and the East; rigid subordination of class conflict in the South to the maintenance of the *status quo* of a business man's regime identified

[24] *Constitution*, Oct. 25, 1889.
[25] Joel C. Harris, *Henry W. Grady*, pp. 99-101.

165

with white supremacy; and the exclusion of the Negro from political life.

In the way that Henry Grady might be said to have symbolized the 'eighties, Tom Watson might be said to have symbolized the decade that followed. In general, Watson's creed was the reverse of Grady's: agrarianism for the South; a glorification of the farmer and his way of life; war upon the industrial East and alliance with the agrarian West; open and relentless class conflict with the enemy classes both without and within the South; and the enlistment of the Negro in the battle for the farmer equipped with as many political weapons as Watson dared give him.

CHAPTER XI

"*I Mean Business*"

As soon as the fight for the nomination was won—a struggle entirely within the Democratic "white man's party" be it noted —the state press, until then openly hostile or indifferent to his cause, rallied behind Watson, promising him support. The *Constitution* believed "The Tenth could not have elected a better man than the Hon. Thomas E. Watson"; the Atlanta *Journal* discovered that he was preaching "Sound democratic doctrine, sterling common sense"; and the Augusta *Chronicle* promised solemnly to "forward his cause by every possible means and sustain him during his Congressional career by all the power we may possess."

At the same time, curiously enough, these and other papers with greater or less degree of virulence, continued unabated their onslaught upon the platform on which Watson was elected. Patrick Walsh's *Chronicle* was especially noted for this paradoxical conduct. It warned that "the Alliance is becoming a political machine," and that it is "repugnant to free institutions." It asked desperately: "Throughout the length and breadth of the land is there no man sound enough and strong enough to confront the emergency and turn the people from their strange gods?" The Alliance platform advocated "paternalism," "communism," and "downright socialism." The farmers were "running after false gods and following false teachers." Like General Gordon and Henry Grady, Walsh reminded them that

167

"White supremacy is the very foundation of our civilization" and "no mess of pottage in the shape of a sub-treasury sop should induce the people to sell their birthright and forsake the party and principles of their fathers." Besides, in all this talk of the farmer's "miseries" there was "a great deal of clap-trap." The farmer needed to "work harder and manage better."

Not content with belaboring "the credulity and ignorance of the people in believing any such nonsense" and such "transparent humbug" as the subtreasury plan, Walsh, along with other Democratic politicians, did all in his power to discourage the agreement between South and West that Watson and the Alliance planned. "There can be no union of agricultural interests of the South and West," said Walsh. "We have no interest in common with them. Politically they hate the Democratic party and the South. Let us not be deceived. They will continue to vote as they shot during the war." Back to the diplomacy of Henry Grady, was the cry, back to the alliance with the East, to the friendly New York capitalists. "The richest man in America," Jay Gould, "has not only put thousands into the Richmond Terminal. He has put millions into it," argued the *Chronicle*.[1]

In December, after the elections of 1890, a convention of the Southern Alliance Supreme Council, together with invited delegates from other farmer and labor organizations, met in Ocala, Florida. Kansas delegates and others urged immediate formation of a third party. While some were willing to listen, the Southerners were generally disposed to test action through the Democratic party first. A compromise was effected that postponed definite action on the third party. The most advertised result of the convention was the formation of a new platform. In reality, the Ocala convention made only a few changes in the older St. Louis platform to conform more to Southern demands.

[1] *Weekly Chronicle*, Oct 22, 1890; see also the *Chronicle*, July 5-13, Aug 3, 1890, Feb. 8, 1890; Macon *Telegraph*, Mar. 22, July 14, 1890; and clippings, Watson and Northen Scrapbooks.

It emphasized in particular an expanded form of the subtreasury plan. Thereafter the "Ocala platform" became the rallying cry of the embattled farmers, evoking more enthusiasm than any other.[2]

To Patrick Walsh the Ocala declaration was the red flag of revolution. He could not abide for a moment the "reckless financial scheme of the Ocala platform" with "its impracticality and unconstitutionality." It was the "greatest fraud of the age."

How was it that one and the same editor could promise every support to Watson in one breath and damn everything he stood for in the next? This paradox was implicit in the thinking of more men than this editor. How did it arise? The fact seems to have been that the New Departure Democrats relied rather confidently upon the fact that the Alliancemen in the South worked from within, and in loyalty to, the Democratic party. So long as the old shibboleths of race, party, and section could be employed. effectively (and had they not always worked?) the state and national party leaders would be able by means of party caucus, party whip, and Federal patronage to keep the Alliancemen in line. Cheerfully the *Chronicle* wrote of the Alliance-elected state convention of 1890: it was not "a conclave of Alliancemen. It was a meeting of Democrats, pure and simple, and it nominated Democrats upon a Democratic platform and adjourned." Others whistled the same tune to steady shaken nerves. The paradox was resolved in the *Chronicle's* statement that, "The Alliance is a side issue compared with the Democratic party."

Such was the reactionary attitude. The radical attitude, Tom Watson's position, might almost be expressed by reversing this last quotation: The Democratic party was a side issue compared to the Alliance principles. Watson was not long in revealing this position.

Indications pointed to a successful candidacy for Speaker of the next House of Representatives by Charles F. Crisp. Crisp

[2] *Constitution*, Dec. 2-7, 1890; *Progressive Farmer*, Dec. 9, 1890; New York *World*, Dec. 3, 1890; *People's Party Paper*, Feb. 3, 1893.

was one of the four Georgia Congressmen whom the Alliance had not removed in the previous election. A suave politician of the old school, smooth of address and popular with his colleagues, Crisp was a conservative, a representative from a black-belt, large-planter district. His election to the Speakership would greatly enhance the prestige of the Georgia Democratic delegation, and heavy pressure was put upon the new Alliance congressmen to give him their support.[3]

Early in 1891 Watson wrote Crisp an open letter asking his position upon the Alliance demands. Crisp's reply contained much concerning his tariff record, but "nothing as to the Ocala platform." Watson's rejoinder was a ringing challenge to the conservatives and a battle cry to the Alliance:

We reformers have for years been patiently, yet ardently, building up a sentiment which would imperatively demand better laws.

We have succeeded. It makes our hearts thrill with pleasure when we contemplate our work. . . .

There was never a time when the people looked more hopefully to Congress for help. They have turned out old members by the score. They have put in new ones. . . .

Now, gentlemen, how can we explain ourselves to the people if we elect a Speaker of the House who gives us no guarantees? How does Mr. Crisp stand upon these questions? Last summer . . . Mr. Crisp wrote flatly refusing to indorse the subtreasury. Since that time the Ocala convention has met and put forth its platform. It is the best one now before the people. Does Mr. Crisp endorse it? If not shall I vote for him anyhow?

Suppose Mr. Crisp should be antagonized by some Democrat who stands on the Ocala platform; shall I still vote for Mr. Crisp? If so, would I not go back on those who elected me?

He would apply the Ocala yardstick strictly, everywhere, making no exceptions, no allowances for party prestige, none for self-interest. Only by strict consistency of principle and action could the movement hope to succeed.

[3] A M. Arnett, op. cit , p. 129; Watson Scrapbooks.

170

To-day there stands waiting in the South and West as grand an army as ever brought pride to a warrior. It only needs leaders bold and true. Leaders who can't be bought, or duped, or bullied. Leaders who knowing what the enemy is will dash straight against it and take no rest and make no terms until the enemy is routed. Leaders who do not stand aside and shirk dangers and avoid responsibilities, but who will dash to the front; who by example will dispel doubt and remove hesitation and who by their courage will win the right to say, "let the bravest follow me."

Given leaders like that there can be no retreat. We know what we want; let us take nothing else. With this resolution strictly adhered to, we draw all our energies to a focus . . . any other policy breeds divisions, factions, malcontents. Our energies will be scattered. . . .

When I entered this reform movement I meant business.

The people who elected me meant business. I mean it yet. So do they. We never meant to carry the movement a trifling distance and then stop. We meant to go clear through or die trying. We mean it yet![4]

About Watson's seriousness, his conviction, and his consecration to his task there can be no doubt. Profoundly and completely he "meant business." He meant it so thoroughly that his convictions laid hold upon his naturally intense character and quite possessed the man wholly, changed his way of life, as well as his way of looking at life, at past, present, and future.

Shortly after his election Watson announced his intention to give up the practice of law, and not long thereafter he sold his law library and declined new cases. He explained that he wished to devote his entire time to his new duties. When they ended he could "find work more congenial than the practice of law." When the *Constitution* chose to interpret his action as motivated by a belief that his profession was degraded, Watson wrote a hot reprimand:

I am profoundly impressed with the belief that . . . [the people] are the victims of cold blooded, deliberate villainy, and their homes

[4] Clipping from *Southern Alliance Farmer*, April, 1890, Watson Scrapbooks.

are being taken from them through the fraudulent collusion of federal lawmakers; that industrial and political servitude is coming to them as fast as time can bring it.

It may be asking too much to expect you to believe that I have gone into this work with something of the spirit of consecration; that it is a cause which commands my devotion and upon whose altar I cheerfully lay all my time and all my strength. That no crusader ever poised lance or bared a blade with a more implicit belief that the work was holy and must be done.

It may be asking too much to expect you to believe this, but the friends who know me best believe it; my district in its majority believes it; and the time will come, if I live, when the great majority in the state shall believe it.[5]

Along with the consecrated zeal of the crusader went some of the unholy glee of the iconoclast. To an audience in Milledgeville he said: "You will hear much said about the English common law. You will hear it praised as if it were some divinely inspired oracle. Don't believe a word of it. The English common law was the brutal code of half-naked savages. The truth was not in it, and it fell. It deserved to fall. Under it a woman was a serf, and a poor man a slave. Its land tenure was infamous, its methods of trial were heathenish and idiotic, its punishments were revolting in their devilish cruelty."

Even in the modern court the judge tried railroad cases with free passes in his pockets. The lawyer was compelled to exploit human emotion "that my miserable scoundrel of a client may gain where he should lose, and that I may have the credit of winning where I should be defeated." A system of law that "tears a tenant from his family and puts him in chains and stripes because he sells cotton for something to eat and leaves his rent unpaid, and which at the same time cannot punish its railroad kings" was "weak unto rottenness." This system deserved to die, "and it will die just as certainly as there are

[5] *Constitution,* July 11-18, 1891; also Macon *Telegraph,* July 15, 1891.

172

enough brave men left to denounce the system and arouse the people to tear it to pieces." [6]

"Ah, me!" he said in a speech to an audience of Augusta workers on Labor Day, "how alarmed we all grow when frantic laborers, ruin staring them in the face, derail some freight car or thump one of Pinkerton's toughs with a stick. We hold up our delicate hands in feigned horror, and cry, 'Put it down.' Yet we are the same people who exult in the piracy which our ancestors committed on the English tea ships. The same people who acquired this land from its owners by a long series of fraud, murders, and violating treaties; who made a president out of Andrew Jackson, the executioner of prisoners." Workers are eternally hoodwinked, for "History has not been written by the laborer. It has usually been written by his enemy. Therefore we only catch glimpses of the truth from time to time." Rapidly he sketched the history of labor, especially in England, that his audience might be "astonished at the infinite blackness of the tyranny with which capital crushed it and fattened on its sufferings."

He, too, had walked the streets of Augusta with the unemployed: "The horror of that dreadful time I shall never forget. It has left its mark on my mind and on my heart. It has shaped my convictions and controlled my feelings. When the easy owner of inherited wealth or position sneers at the warmth of my utterances upon this subject, I beg to remind him that it is the man who has been burned who can best describe the pain of the fire." [7]

"A great pity swells within me," he once said. And as pity swelled, rage welled up out of the same fountain and flooded his spirit. "Men of the country!" he cried to a throng of Jefferson County farmers, "let the fires of this . . . revolution burn brighter and brighter. Pile on the fuel till the forked flames shall

[6] T. E. W., *Life and Speeches*, pp. 48-52.
[7] *Ibid.*, pp 59-70.

173

leap in wrath around this foul structure of governmental wrong
—shall sweep it from basement to turret, and shall sweep it
from the face of the earth. (Applause.)"

In May, 1891, there convened in Cincinnati delegates from a
number of national farmer, labor, and reform organizations, those
from the Alliance of the Northern and Western states constitut-
ing the largest body of delegates. The South held aloof from
official representation, but unofficial representatives, thought
some Alliance members, "did everything within their power to
prevent, or postpone, the organization of a new political party."
Southern Alliancemen generally felt that such action should be
postponed until election year at least, but at the same time
warned the Democratic leaders to toe the Ocala line, or expect
revolt. The Convention, nevertheless, took steps that assured
the existence of the People's Party. New South Democrats were
divided in opinion: the *Constitution* believed the new party
spelled good fortune for the Democrats, since it would be entirely Western, and "the Republicans will be demoralized." The
Cincinnati platform, it thought, was "in sympathy with the general tendency of the Democratic party." The *Chronicle*, in more
forthright fashion answered, "God help the Democratic party if
the resolutions adopted at Cincinnati are Democratic." [8]

It was about this time that Watson seems to have set his sail
in the third party wind. He made no public commitment, and
executed a good bit of tacking during the next several months,
but any close observer could have predicted his destination, for
his course toward that destination was as straight as a shifting
wind and perverse currents permitted. In April, answering Editor Dana of the New York *Sun*, who requested that he leave the
Democratic party or the Alliance, Watson could write, "I do
not have to leave the one to be put in harmony with the other.
The Democracy is not yet ostracised by the Alliance." [9] That

[8] *Constitution*, May 20-23, 1891; Augusta *Chronicle*, May 26, 1891; clippings,
Watson and Northen Scrapbooks; J. D. Hicks, *op cit*, pp. 211-217.

[9] T E. W. to the *Chronicle*, quoted by J. C. C Black in letter to the *People's Party
Paper*, Sept 9, 1892.

was before the Cincinnati convention; but in June, a few weeks after it, he was in North Carolina conferring with President L. L. Polk, who was openly sympathetic with the third party idea as a final resort. While there Watson said in a public speech, "Our feet are on the Ocala platform and we are not going to wear any man's collar, be it Democratic or Republican by name. This third party talk don't hurt us." The same day he is reported to have admitted in private conversation that he believed "the only hope for reform lay in organizing a Third party." [10]

Two weeks later President Polk appeared in Atlanta for a great Alliance rally at Piedmont Park. Speaking from the same platform were the Western leaders, General James B. Weaver, and Congressman "Sockless" Jerry Simpson, who had recently attended the Cincinnati Convention. The Westerners were making a speaking tour of Georgia. They had promised not to preach the third party revolt, but the idea lay behind their every utterance; the rank and file realized this, and their conservative leaders grew restive under their enthusiasm. The "keynote of the Alliance demonstration" was said to have been President Polk's warning: "If there is a third party established in the south, it will be due to the domineering, proscriptive and intolerant spirit of the so-called democratic leaders." This sentence was said to have been "the essence of all the speeches made, and the enthusiasm which marked its utterance clearly defined the sentiment of his Alliance hearers." [11]

That evening Watson addressed the Georgia Assembly and an audience of Alliancemen. Why all the outcry against the visit of their Western friends? he asked. "What if Jerry Simpson does come down here to make a few speeches . . . I do not care whether he has socks on his feet or not." He welcomed his allies. He also recognized his enemies, in whatever disguise. There was on foot "an attempt to deliver your vote to Davie Hill and

[10] A L Levinson, Goldsboro, N C, in the *Progressive Farmer*, Sept 29, 1896.
[11] *Constitution*, July 16, 1891; also the *Chronicle* and the Macon *Telegraph* and the Atlanta *Journal* of the same date.

Tammany Hall. . . . Dave Hill is a miserable little trickster, a small ward politician," while "Cleveland represents the gold-bugs of Wall Street and we will not take him."

He then defined his position upon the tense question of party loyalty and revolt. "Attention was so close," it was reported, "that the drop of a pin could be heard, and every sentence of Watson's was cheered by the Alliance audience, including nearly all of the Alliance members of the legislature. . . . The effect of his speech was electrical":

> We are in the midst of a great crisis. The war is on. What is the situation? We have before us three or four platforms. We have the republican platform, the democratic platform, and the Ocala plat-form. I say here and now that the Ocala platform is the best of the three. It is the only one that breathes the breath of life. The others are so much alike you can't tell them apart. . . .
>
> Let third party talk take care of itself. I have none of it to do, but my highest duty is to stand by what I think is right. . . . Let the democratic party take warning. We have borne your ridicule long enough, we will bear it no longer. I am going to bear the Ocala plat-form wherever my voice can be heard.[12]

Watson's speech called down upon his head a barrage of impre-cation. The Augusta *Evening Herald* called upon him to resign his seat in Congress. The *Chronicle* declared he was preach-ing "a war of the poor against the rich." The *Constitution* un-dertook "to call him to order in this matter and to protest that he is wronging the very party and people to whom he owes his present position." The *Telegraph* admitted that he was "The most interesting figure perhaps, in Georgia politics today . . . There is no discounting the fact that circumstances and his abili-ties have put him in a position of peculiar importance. Just what he intends doing with it is a matter of general interest. He types the most advanced form of the third party idea in Georgia." [13]

His answer to all critics was the same: Yes, he was elected to

[12] *Telegraph,* July 16, 1891; *Constitution,* July 16, 1891.
[13] July 17, 1891.

176

office as a Democrat, but his support of the Alliance platform was the special reason for his success over Major Barnes, just as it was the reason for the success of the other Alliance congressmen. If he left the Democratic party, he would not break faith with his constituents, but would merely follow his constituents who were true to their principles. The Democrats "treat our principles with hatred and scorn and contempt." [14]

The cry of "demagogue" continued. Watson thought he was "the worst abused, worst disparaged, worst 'cussed' man in Georgia," and he probably was. "My character has been presented to the people of the state in every form of the kaleidoscope, and I am glad of it." He was reported to have said that "he knew he was a demagogue, but he gloried in it." However, that admission might be better understood in connection with his laconic observation a few days earlier:

By some strange necessity, the pure, unselfish patriots have all gone into the bucket shops, brokers' offices, speculative companies, railroad combines, the banks, the warehouses, and the editorial rooms. Outside these charmed circles no patriot can be found. [15]

The Western speakers came in for their share of abuse by the Georgia Democrats. Mrs. Mary Elizabeth Lease, the most spectacular and accomplished of the women campaigners of Kansas, famous for her admonition, "raise less corn and more *Hell*," had recently arrived in Georgia. A woman loose in Georgia politics! Whispers and indignation . . . The farmers cheered and cheered again, but in Atlanta an "indignation meeting" was held when the Alliance condemned a bill to provide a home for disabled and improvident Confederate soldiers. "Did Weaver do it?" "Was it Sockless Jerry?" "Probably 'twas Mrs. Lease," said the speakers. It must have been one of "This trio of communists and south haters." [16]

[14] Atlanta *Journal*, July 18, 1891.
[15] Augusta *Chronicle*, Aug. 5, 1891.
[16] Atlanta *Journal*, Aug. 28, 1891.

Mrs. Lease was unperturbed: "You may call me an anarchist, a socialist or a communist, I care not, but I hold to the theory that if one man has not enough to eat three times a day and another man has $25,000,000, that last man has something that belongs to the first." Addressing the Georgia Assembly, she said: "Georgia and Kansas have clasped hands at last . . . come into the People's party and help defeat that common enemy, the Republican party. . . . Take off your old party collars. What are you afraid of?" [17]

Meanwhile Watson gave alarmists no rest. He was "making a sort of triumphal tour through the State"; he was "going all over the state expressing his convictions." He was explaining why the *Chronicle* cried "communism" and "foamed at the mouth." "Let me show you how communist and paternal it [the Alliance platform] is. We are the people. We have created the corporations. They are our legal off-spring. Shall it be said that the servant is above the master, or the child above the father?" He was asking, "Will you Knights of Labor help the farmers and laborers in the field of their fight on the common enemy?" What of this cry of "class legislation"? "What has this country ever had but class legislation? The second law Congress ever passed was aimed to build up commerce and manufactures at the expense of agriculture. Our statute books are filled with legislation in behalf of capital, at the expense of labor. . . . If we must have class legislation, as we have always had it and always will have it, what class is more entitled to it than the largest class— the working class?" The response of his audiences was generally like that of a Jefferson County crowd: "And then a glad shout of approval from a thousand throats rang through the wood and every eye in the audience flashed with admiration."

The question of drastic railroad legislation was uppermost in the public mind in August. The legislature had a committee investigating the leases and another looking into freight rates. Numerous *cahiers* from the radical county sub-Alliances were

[17] Macon *Telegraph*, Aug 11, 1891; *Constitution*, Aug. 9, 11, 1891.

178

pouring into the legislators' mail demanding rate regulation, government ownership, and laws against combinations. Livingston, president of the state Alliance, was known to frown upon such legislation, particularly laws against railroad combinations, and he had taken that position at the state convention of the Alliance now in session.[18] Watson, on the other hand, was widely known to favor the most radical railroad legislation. This issue, dramatizing as it did the more basic conflict between these two men for ascendency in the movement, lent particular interest to Watson's address to the Georgia legislature while the Alliance convention was in progress.

"How long has it been," he asked, "since Jay Gould came South, peering into every nook and cranny of the railroad systems?" Indeed, it had not been many months since Gould had toured Georgia. The party of millionaires with him controlled "over 40,000 miles of railway lines" and their fortunes "bonded together would make over $250,000,000." The Augusta *Chronicle* hailed the visit as evidence that "Southern development has enlisted the practical support of the richest man in America. Mr. Gould has not only put thousands into the Richmond Terminal. He has put millions into it." [19] The Mayor's council of Atlanta voted Gould and his party "the freedom of the city"; the Chamber of Commerce received him, and a well-advertised reception was given him at the Inman home by Atlanta "society."

"If the devil himself," observed Watson, "were to come to this town in a palace car and propose to haul the balance of the state to his infernal kingdom, and to allow Atlanta capitalists the profits on the transaction, they would cry, 'Hurrah for the devil. He's going to build up Atlanta! . . .'

"Fellow citizens, I believe that the only way we can ever settle this railroad problem is by absolute Government ownership." Cheered to the echo, he then proceeded to enumerate and ex-

[18] Macon *Telegraph*, July 24, 1891; Atlanta *Journal*, Aug. 24, 1891; A. M. Arnett, *op. cit.*, pp. 120-121.
[19] Feb. 8, 1891.

pound sixteen reasons why he believed in government ownership.[20]

The Alliance convention, then sitting in Atlanta, appeared to be under the domination of Livingston, who also controlled the official organ, the *Southern Alliance Farmer*. This man, known as one of the "Big Five" in the National Alliance, occupied a dubious and shifty position in the movement. He was generally thought of as one of the most radical of Alliancemen, given to thunderous imprecations against Cleveland and conservative party leaders. He frequently sounded ominous warnings of revolt. Yet it was Livingston who was involved with Macune in the attempt to deliver the Alliance vote to Patrick Calhoun for senator; it was he who sought to substitute government "control" for "ownership" in the Ocala platform; it was he who at Cincinnati promised to follow the West into the new party, if only they would postpone action till the next year, and yet in Georgia hushed and diverted every demand for revolt; it was he who led in pledging all the Alliance-elected congressmen, *save Watson*, to vote for Crisp for Speaker of the national House of Representatives. For these reasons many Alliancemen put Livingston down in the "Plug-hat" rather than in the "Wool-hat" branch of the Alliance.[21]

Watson had his own suspicions of Livingston's conduct. On the eve of the state convention, before setting out to Atlanta, he was reported to have said to a friend that "the time had come when the people must choose between him and Livingston." Although Livingston seemed practically assured of reëlection as president, Watson set forth to the convention with his own candidate, C. H. Ellington, of Thomson. The *Constitution* was pleased to observe that "the apostle of discord" failed in his effort. His candidate did not even win the vice-presidency; Livingston was elected president; and the resolution of Watson's

[20] Atlanta *Journal*, Aug. 22, 1891.

[21] *People's Party Paper*, Nov. 26, 1891; Augusta *Chronicle*, July 18, 1891; J. C. Manning, *The Fadeout of Populism*, pp. 16-17; Northen and Watson Scrapbooks.

friend C. C. Post, instructing congressmen to vote for no man for Speaker unless he indorsed the Alliance platform, was defeated. Watson did score one point against his rival, however, for, whether as a result of his speech on the railroads or not, the convention rebelled at President Livingston's demand that no action be taken on railroad consolidation.[22]

Watson was still supremely isolated in his position, among officialdom of Alliance and Democracy in Georgia. But it was the inarticulate battalions of rank and file on which he depended, and evidence was not lacking that they looked to him as their leader. There were reports of "an uninterrupted stream of communications for months, all in favor of a third party,"—to Livingston's *Southern Alliance Farmer*.[23]

Much of Watson's time during these months was spent in writing long open letters of rebuttal, correction, or rebuke to the Democratic press. Most of this was necessary to his best interests, for the city dailies were undoubtedly twisting his meaning and misrepresenting and discrediting him in a thousand ways. For example, the *Constitution*, by slightly twisting a sentence he uttered in a debate with Senator Butler of South Carolina made him proclaim himself a "messiah," and printed a ridiculous cartoon of him over the caption, "Sane or Insane? The Last Messiah Crank." [24] His effort to answer such persecution—imaginary as well as real—took much precious time. His continuous speaking campaign over the state seems to have been a rather frantic effort to make his own voice perform the service of a journal of large circulation. Isolated as was his position, he had powerful official antagonists, and an enemy in the editorial room of every Democratic paper. Even the official Alliance organ was in the hands of an avowed enemy. Watson obviously had urgent need of a paper of his own. In the fall of 1891 he took the leading part in the work of establishing one.

[22] *Constitution*, Aug. 20, 21, 22, and 23, 1891; *Journal*, Aug. 20 and 24, 1891.
[23] Macon *Telegraph*, July 24, 1891.
[24] *Constitution*, Sept. 12, 1891; Watson's speech in Orangeburg, S. C. *Cotton Plant*, Oct. 31, 1891.

The first number of the *People's Party Paper* [25] appeared in Atlanta on October 1: Thomas E. Watson, Editor-in-Chief, Charles C. Post, Managing Editor. It was destined to continue to appear weekly for some eight years. A form letter, signed by Watson, announcing the paper's appearance and soliciting subscriptions, stated that "Its purpose is to educate our people upon governmental questions; to assail official corruption, to oppose class-rule, legislative favoritism, and the centralizing tendencies manifest in both old parties." It would champion "the Jeffersonian theory of popular government" and "the common people—their grievances, their hopes, their rights." [26]

C. C. Post, the Populist novelist ("the atheistic, anarchistic, communistic Editor of the *People's Party Paper*," so-called in the Democratic press), deserves more than a casual introduction. Post began his career in Michigan, edited the Chicago *Express* in the middle 'eighties, and, with his wife, moved to Lithia Springs, Georgia, for his health in 1886. He was a young man, described as "tall and slender," resembling "the fellow 'before taking.' " He wore "a lean, hungry look as if in pursuit of something." He was an ardent soul, full of the enthusiasms and the amiable follies of a generous and sympathetic nature—ready to break a lance for any good cause. At Douglasville, where he was known as "Chicago Charlie," he and his wife founded a "School for Mental Healing," which, if his *Metaphysical Essays* [27] is any indication, preached a type of naturalistic Christianity faintly resembling Christian Science and apparently influenced by Darwin. In the West he had been connected with reform movements, and in Georgia he soon took up arms for the Farmers' Alliance. He had attended the Cincinnati convention in May.[28]

Post's first novel, *Driven from Sea to Sea*, published in 1884, after appearing serially in his paper, was said to have been read

[25] Hereafter referred to in footnotes as "*P P. P.*"
[26] Copy of letter in Watson MSS , Chapel Hill
[27] Boston, 1895
[28] *P. P P*, March 10, 1892; Macon *Telegraph*, July 15, 1891; and clippings, Watson Scrapbooks.

by "over a million people," to have had a sale of 50,000 bound copies, and in paper covers to have been still selling at the rate of 2,000 copies a month in 1892.[29] It was an exposure of the doings of Crocker, Stanford, and Huntington in the Southern Pacific Railroad scandal, a picture of "corporate monopoly robbing the people under shelter of the law."[30] The book was forbidden to be sold on the railroads. Post had another novel then on the press, *Congressman Swanson*, the story of a young Southerner, a man of the people, who led a revolt from the old party into the new People's party. It appeared in December, 1891, at the very crisis of Congressman *Watson's* endeavor to perform the same deed. The novelist tells how "the shackles of party fell from their [Alliancemen's] limbs, and when the men of Kansas threw off the yoke of the Republican party and extended a hand in fraternal greeting to their brethren of the South, that hand was grasped with quick and ready sympathy and a new political party . . . redolent of life and eager for action, stepped into the arena, and offered battle to the plutocracy of the world."[31]

Something of the temperament and feelings of Charlie Post is revealed in his statement that "*The thought is in the heart of the people* that violence may have to be resorted to before justice will be granted," and that "Either peacefully or otherwise monopolistic systems are doomed to destruction." Post was one of those who "meant business," and this trait could not but endear him to his editor-in-chief.

The new paper moved off to a slow start. The public, Watson discovered, "was singularly patient and deliberate and made no hurry at all to send in names and cash." At the end of six weeks it was found that the paper had spent $1,500 and received 126 subscriptions, each subscriber costing the owners twelve dollars. Besides, the bookkeeper exhibited postal cards sent in by postmasters stating that addressees refused to accept free sample

[29] *P. P. P.*, March 10, 1892.
[30] *Driven from Sea to Sea, or Just a Campin'* (Chicago, 1884).
[31] C. C. Post, *Congressman Swanson*, p 336.

183

copies and that they "did not like our politics." "Hundreds of such postal cards came in every week." Despite such disheartening experiences, the paper continued, losing about a hundred dollars a week in the summer of 1892. In July of that year Watson became sole owner. "I had no advertising," he wrote, and the paper "had to bear as its own expense the brunt of the campaign in Georgia. It did not ask nor receive a dollar from any candidate. It received no subsidy, directly or indirectly, from any source whatever." [32]

Bravely the first number announced, "This paper is not an experiment, but starts out on a basis which insures its permanency." It was the editor's intention that Southern people "shall have a paper that is not controlled by the politicians and through which they can learn the truth about this mighty movement of the masses." Commenting upon the rise of the Populist press all over the country, the editor said, "The organs of monopoly and plutocracy are now powerless to deceive the masses." The editorials for the first several months emphasized a defense of the Ocala platform, warned against compromise with Democratic half-measures, and appealed for closer alliance with the West.

After the state Alliance convention, Watson's enemies were glad to interpret the failure of his lieutenants to put through their resolution instructing Alliance congressmen not to vote for any candidate for Speaker who did not stand on the Ocala platform as evidence that the third-party revolt was "foredoomed from the first to miserable and inglorious defeat," and that Alliancemen were merely "old-fashioned Democrats." Watson's next hope to gain official sanction for his position upon the Speakership and Democratic caucus control lay with the Georgia assembly. There the effort failed again. The legislators compromised with a resolution "requesting" the Georgia delegation to support legislation that would correct evils complained of by the

[32] Clipping from *P. P. P.*, *circa* Oct. 1, 1893, Watson Scrapbooks Allan Nevins seems to be mistaken in asserting that Watson's paper was a source of riches (*Grover Cleveland*, pp. 594-595)

Ocala platform. Since official sanction from these sources was refused, the last hope for action lay in the convention of the Supreme Council of the National Alliance to be held in Indianapolis in November. Watson appealed to his readers for instructions: "It is time they spoke up and let their congressmen know what they want done." [33]

Behind each successive checkmate of Watson's moves to break the grip of the dead hand of the old party was the skillful strategy of Livingston. Animosity between the two men sharpened as the realization spread abroad that between them lay the most dangerous, the most crucial, political issue that Southerners of that day were capable of envisaging—white solidarity, the Solid South. National interest developed in the struggle between them as it became apparent that they were the leaders of opposing national forces: one seeking to keep the reform movement within the bounds of the two old parties and divided between them; the other attempting to unite the movement in a separate party.

For a long time it was a matter of doubt which flag Livingston was following. But now, with the rank and file of his battalions restive, ripening for revolt, and suspicious of betrayal,[34] Livingston, under the relentless fire of Watson's exposures, was finally revealed in his true colors.

"After all this agitation and the turning out of the old leaders are the new ones going to fall into the old party ruts?" asked Watson. "Then what was the use in turning the old ones out?" [35] He charged Livingston with "trying to ride two horses at once." He was running with the hare and barking with the hounds. When cornered with the question, "Will you vote for Cleveland if he is nominated?" Livingston replied, "I will vote

[33] Lois Gray, "Thomas E. Watson: Leader of Georgia Populism," Master's thesis, Emory University, pp. 40-41.
[34] The air was thick with charges of corruption against Livingston during the summer and fall of 1891. *Vide* Northen Scrapbooks; *Journal*, Aug. 15, 17, and 28, and Sept. 4 and 5, 1891; *Constitution*, June 11 and Aug. 14, and 22-28, 1891.
[35] *P. P. P*, Dec. 3, 1891.

185

for the nominee." Yet in July he had said, "The Democrat who could swallow Cleveland could swallow Harrison." [36] Since it was known that Livingston was pledged to vote for Crisp as Speaker, Watson quoted Crisp as saying, "If the damned Alliance, or the People's Party should carry Kansas this year, all hell can't hold the Alliancemen of the South; therefore it is necessary to break up the People's Party of Kansas, in order to preserve a solid South." [37] At the Cincinnati convention Livingston had asked the Western leaders for only a little more time for "educational" work before he led the Georgia Alliance into the new party.[38] In Georgia, however, he had repeatedly deferred action with the excuse that the time was not ripe. As the day approached for the Indianapolis meeting, it became evident that Livingston would be on hand to block all tendency toward revolt.

With exactly the opposite intention, Watson set out for Indianapolis. It was the first of the National Alliance conventions he had attended; he was not a member, and he had no right to the floor. With him, however, was his friend and lieutenant, M. I. Branch, an accredited delegate from the Georgia Alliance. Branch carried with him for presentation to the convention a resolution that Watson "highly approved of." Upon Watson's advice, Branch showed the resolution to Jerry Simpson, who first agreed to introduce it. This Simpson was unable to do when he failed to be chosen as delegate. Branch then introduced the resolution himself. According to him it "appeared like a clap of thunder in a clear sky." As a matter of fact the sky was by no means clear of third-party thunder clouds. Livingston's "vigorous" opposition was unavailing this time; the resolution was adopted "with enthusiasm." It requested all congressmen elected "by aid of Alliance constituencies . . . to decline to enter into any

[36] Augusta *Chronicle*, July 18, 1891.
[37] *P. P. P*, Nov. 19, 1891, quoting the *Kansas Agitator*
[38] New York *Voice*, May 28, 1891, and a letter from Mrs Lease stating that Livingston pledged his support to the new party, both quoted in clipping from Atlanta *Journal*, undated, Watson Scrapbooks

party caucus called to designate a candidate for Speaker, unless adherence to the principles of the Ocala platform are made a test of admission to said caucus." [39] Watson's views, rejected in his own state under the coercion of Alliance leaders, were now the adopted policy of the National organization.

Livingston was further discredited by the election as president of L. L. Polk, who was strongly in sympathy with the People's party. When his own views against independence became known, Livingston's candidacy, thought by some to have been formidable, collapsed. The convention was, on the whole, a triumph for the People's party. A member of its executive committee was elected vice-president, and there was no longer any doubt that a national ticket would be nominated the next year with Polk at its head.[40] Watson was quoted in Indianapolis as saying he would not enter the Democratic caucus, but that instead the Alliance congressmen would hold a caucus themselves and nominate a candidate for Speaker. "Georgia is ready for a third party," he added, "and will sweep the State with the movement. The great bulk of the Democratic party will pass into the new party lines." [41]

It being only a few weeks until his first session of Congress opened, Watson hurried home. "Realizing the gravity of the Resolution," he later wrote, "I campaigned my District again, *and took a referendum vote,* as to whether I should obey the Resolution. Without one dissenting voice, the people, by a show of hands, instructed me to defy the caucus, and stand firm for the principles." [42] When the Democratic papers sought to discredit his motives by saying that he had written his own instruc-

[39] Letter from M. I. Branch in *P. P. P.,* Sept. 9, 1892, and in the *Constitution,* March 13, 1892; resolution quoted in *P. P. P.,* Nov. 26, 1891; account of convention in *Constitution,* Nov. 17-25, 1891; Ernest D. Stewart in "The Populist Party in Indiana," *Indiana Magazine of History,* Vol. XIV, p. 355, seems to have been in error in asserting that Simpson introduced the resolution in question.

[40] Washington *Post,* Nov. 20 and 26 and Dec. 9, 1891; *P. P. P.,* Nov. 26, 1891; E. D. Stewart, *op. cit.*

[41] Indianapolis *Journal* quoted in the *P. P. P.,* Nov. 26, 1891.

[42] Watson, *Political and Economic Handbook,* p. 454.

tions, since the Indianapolis resolution was virtually his own, Watson replied that it was, with slight change, only a reaffirmation of a similar resolution passed at St. Louis in 1889, upon the basis of which he had made his race.

Upon his return home, Watson was greeted with a hail of abuse that was a hint of what was to come later. Patrick Walsh branded him a "traitor" and read him out of the party. Livingston refused to be bound by the resolution passed at Indianapolis. When his paper complained that "sub-alliances are disbanding, and members are growing luke-warm and discouraged," the membership in some counties falling off twenty-five per cent, Watson observed that it was "not to be wondered at that they grew suspicious" after Livingston's conduct at the convention and his repeated thwarting of their impulse toward revolt.[43]

The radical sub-alliances were becoming articulate against their president. The Howell alliance rather exceeded the bounds of parliamentary decorum in its resolution: "Whereas, one Leonidas F. Benedict Arnold Judas Iscariot Livingston" has committed sundry acts not to their liking, they hereby consign him to his "proper sphere—among the scum and Wall-Street pimps of the so-called Democratic party." [44]

"This is not a political fight," Watson wrote, "and politicians cannot lead or direct it. It is a movement of the masses, an uprising of the people, and they and not the politicians will direct it. The people need spokesmen—not leaders—men in the front who will obey, not command." [45]

With Post as its chairman, the Executive Committee of the People's Party of Georgia was already at work in December setting up the framework of the new party. As commander of the new army, Watson was accepted without question, and a capable general he was. There was also a raw and untried staff of of-

[43] Southern Alliance Farmer, Nov. 24, 1891; P. P. P., Dec. 3, 1891.
[44] Clipping from Atlanta Herald, Northen Scrapbooks, Vol. II, p. 30.
[45] P. P. P , Dec 3, 1891

ficers. The rank and file, however, were still unmobilized, indeed, not even recruited, much less drilled. It yet remained to be seen whether they would spring to arms when Tom Watson raised the banner.

CHAPTER XII

Populism in Congress

WITH APPARENT INTENTION of staying a long while at Washington, Watson bought a house then under construction at 129 Fourth Street, S. E., "a handsome four story brick building," he pronounced it. His family, which now included a son and a daughter, was no sooner moved in than they and he were down with grippe. His reaction to the new situation, like his reaction to his first office ten years before, was one of disappointment. "Being in Congress," he wrote, "does not seem near so big a thing as when I was campaigning for the place." Furthermore, "The speaker [Mr. Crisp] is bitterly hostile to me because I would not support him and will give me no chance to acquit myself with credit." With so much to do, however, there was little time for self-pity. "Am organizing a new political party in Georgia," he noted in his Journal, "because the Democratic Party has drifted away from true Principles and is only seeking office. The newspapers denounce me most bitterly but the people seem to be rallying to me with enthusiasm." [1] "I worked so hard while in Congress," he later testified, "that while I am passionately fond of music, I did not once attend the opera."

Before Congress convened a show-down upon the question of adherence to the Indianapolis resolution and independence was forced upon all Alliance-elected and pledged congressmen. A short while before the Democratic caucus was called, a confer-

[1] MS Journal 2, p. 527; *National Economist*, Jan. 2, 1892.

ence of Alliance congressmen was held in the office of the *National Economist*. To all of them had been sent a letter signed by L. L. Polk, president of the National Alliance, including a copy of the Indianapolis resolution, and reminding them of their obligation in the matter of caucus and Speakership contest. Upon these matters the congressmen were clearly divided into two factions. One, led by Livingston, was made up of eight representatives, all from the South, all agreed upon entering the Democratic caucus. The other faction, led by Watson and Jerry Simpson, was made up of seven congressmen, all from the West with the exception of Watson, all determined to adhere to the Ocala platform no matter where it took them. Here was the issue that had to be settled before this meeting ended. As discussion circled near it, the atmosphere became tense.

For a while, financial questions and policies were discussed. Then Otis of Kansas took the floor and addressed an "earnest talk," to the Southerners. "We are disappointed," he told them. "We came here expecting you to work with us for the Ocala Platform irrespective of Party caucus, and but one of your number has met us on that ground." Jerry Simpson arose and proposed independent action, and at the same time made an uncomplimentary reference to the Democratic party. Livingston was on his feet instantly. "The Democratic party is not opposed to us," he roared. "It is willing and anxious to work for the relief of our people." Furthermore, Simpson had no right to call his party corrupt. But, replied Simpson, he had heard Livingston himself denounce it as corrupt. This rejoinder set the meeting in an "uproar," with several members on the floor at once talking excitedly at the tops of their voices.

Livingston was a powerful man physically, "a most compelling, commanding personage," said an acquaintance, and a "born leader of men." It was not often, nor with impunity, that his will was crossed. Yet he had been compelled to watch a vast organization, which he had all but fathered, slip gradually out of

191

his control and under the spell of a puny orator half his size and several years his junior.

Watson, in spite of the uproar, gained attention by the very fury of his words and manner. The scene that followed is described by an eye-witness:

Tom Watson shouted that it was time to do some plain talking. "You can't choke Simpson in that way," he cried. "He's right. On what platform were we elected? What pledges did we make? Then how is it proposed that we go into the democratic caucus?"

Suddenly Watson turned full on Livingston. "You and I know," he cried, "how we came to be here. We could never have been in Congress but for the reform movement among the farmers of Georgia. These farmers trusted you, and now you want to betray them for your own personal interest."

"Sit down," roared Livingston, jumping to his feet and striding toward Watson, over whom he towered like a giant.

"I'll not sit down," cried Watson, not quailing or budging an inch. "You can't bulldoze me," he cried. "I'd say what was right, no matter if there were a thousand Livingstons here."

Livingston was in a rage. Half a dozen men jumped up to hold him back.

"You needn't hold him," cried Watson. "I guess he's not dangerous."

The men glared at each other, and it took a long time to restore quiet and order.[2]

Simpson was finally allowed to conclude his remarks. Watson followed him to say that there was an "irrepressible conflict between factions; that they were like crossed swords; and there had better be no more meetings." The conference adjourned after a futile effort by Livingston to "pour oil upon the waters."

While the Democratic and Republican caucuses were in progress two senators and eight representatives met at Senator Pef-

[2] Clipping from Washington *Post*, Vol. II, p. 24 of Northen Scrapbooks; cf. Watson's account in *P. P. P.*, Jan. 28, 1892.

fer's house, and the first Populist caucus was called to order. It was unanimously agreed that the Indianapolis Resolution should be respected. The conference also unanimously requested Tom Watson to be their candidate for Speaker. He consented, "knowing of course that it amounted to nothing more than a compliment and a proof of our consistency." He represented a wedge with which the Populists hoped to split the Solid South. "So was formed," declared the *People's Party Paper*, "the first distinctive political body known as the People's party." [3]

After a long deadlock in the Democratic caucus Crisp received the nomination, which, in view of the huge Democratic majority in the House, assured his election. On the day of election, Jerry Simpson rose and nominated Watson for Speaker. He received eight votes.[4] The party of which he was the House leader consisted at this point of Jerry Simpson, John G. Otis, John Davis, Benjamin H. Clover, and William Baker, all from Kansas, O. M. Kem and W. A. McKeighan from Nebraska, and K. Halvorsen from Minnesota.

Hamlin Garland, the young Western novelist, whose *Main-Traveled Roads* had just appeared, had taken part "in meetings of rebellious farmers in bare-walled Kansas school-houses, and watched processions of weather-worn Nebraska Populists as they filed through the shadeless cities of their sun-baked plains." [5] Thrilled by the spirit of revolt among his people, he had now come to Washington in search of material for an article.[6]

He found significance in the seats assigned the Populist members, with Jerry Simpson directly in front of the Speaker's desk, forming the point of a "wedge," his colleagues spread behind him—a wedge that would "symbolize the work of splitting the

[3] Dec. 17, 1891, quoted by John D. Hicks, *The Populist Revolt*, p. 222; clippings in Northen Scrapbooks, Vol. II, p. 25.

[4] *Congressional Record*, 52 Cong., 1 Sess., p. 7.

[5] Hamlin Garland, *Son of the Middle Border*, p. 423.

[6] H. Garland, "The Alliance Wedge in Congress," *Arena*, Vol. V (March, 1892), pp. 447-457.

old parties in pieces." Watson, Kem, and Clover, however, were unable to obtain seats with their colleagues, and were placed on the extreme right of the Republican side of the House.

Garland thought Watson, "next to Simpson, the most striking personality of the group. He speaks with a touch of the dialect of the South, and wears a soft hat in the southern way . . . He is small and active. His face is perfectly beardless and quite thin. His eyes are his most remarkable feature, except possibly the abundance of dark red hair, pushed back from his face. . . . Many remark his resemblance to Alexander Stephens, whose district he has succeeded to. The photographer remarked upon the striking resemblance, which extends to his ability. Simpson calls him the 'coming man,' and has a deep regard for him."

"His life of hard work and suffering has made him a commoner and a radical,—'a dangerous man' to some of the Southern people,—but a very moderate and fair-tempered reformer to me. He is simply one more of the scores of similar young radicals and commoners of my acquaintance. He not only types the best economic thought of the young South,—he leads it . . . He stands for the further extension of the idea of liberty. His faith in man and the forward urge of the human mind never fails him. . . ." Although "one of the youngest members of the House, he will be found to be one of the ablest when any question is being discussed on its merits."

Garland described Jerry Simpson as "about fifty years of age, of slender but powerful build" wearing "old-fashioned glasses, through which his eyes gleam with ever-present humor." He was "full of odd turns of thought, and quaint expressions that make one think of Whitcomb Riley." Simpson had led a hard life—a sailor on Lake Michigan and later a farmer in Kansas. He had no school training. Yet, observed Garland, "he thinks for himself on all subjects religious, economic, and political," is "naturally a studious man," and has "a large fund of common sense and experimental philosophy." Once in debate he referred to Senator Cullom as an "iniquitous railway attorney" and was

194

promptly called out of order. "Well," said Simpson, "I will withdraw that. I beg pardon, I am a new member and do not know your rules. But that is the way we talk in Kansas. We are plain-speaking people." [7]

The other Westerners Garland described in less detail, noting in general their "heavily lined" faces and "a sort of smileless gravity about them that reflects the hard condition of the people from whom they come." There was, for instance, Halvorsen, the Swede, with "long red whiskers, cut away at the chin"—"quiet to the point of reticence." There were doubtless moments when these Westerners looked upon their volatile and irrepressible Southern comrade in wonderment.

This handful of Populist leaders, and those who joined them later, were then, and have been since, the butt of a great deal of misdirected humor. Henry Demarest Lloyd, one of the keenest observers of their generation, pronounced the Populist delegation in Congress "men whom the fierce light of opposition never revealed to be anything but brave, honest, and intelligent."

During his visit to Congress in January, 1891, it seemed to Hamlin Garland that there was "approaching a great periodic popular upheaval similar to that of '61." "Everywhere," he recorded, "as I went through the aisles of the House, I saw it and heard it. The young Democrats were almost in open rebellion against this domineering policy of the old legislators. The Republicans were apprehensive, almost desperate. Placeholders are beginning to tremble." On the whole, he decided, "the House is a smoldering volcano." But the Populists, "the men who are advocating right and justice instead of policy, sat eager, ready for the struggle. They have everything to win and nothing to lose in the vital discussion and re-organization which, in my judgment, is sure to come." [8]

Another young member of the House who came to Washington for his first term was William Jennings Bryan, the only

[7] Clipping, Watson Scrapbooks
[8] H Garland, in *Arena*, Vol V (1892), p. 457.

Democratic member from Nebraska. The other two members of the delegation were Populists. It is said that some 20,000 fraudulent votes were cast against the Populists in Nebraska in the election of 1890.[9] Watson told Bryan "that he would have to abandon his principles or leave the Democratic party." He hoped "this brilliant young man will choose principle—even though he lose office by it. There is such a thing in life as paying too much for office."[10]

* * * * * *

"Poor Tom's a' cold," chanted the Atlanta *Journal* on receiving news that Watson had bolted the Democratic caucus. He was the "lone fisherman." At Thomson, his home, the Democrats celebrated "with bonfires, brass band, fire works, and much enthusiasm" the election of Crisp as Speaker. Watson's own brother was elected secretary of the meeting of Thomson Democrats that demanded his resignation and condemned his stand.[11]

This was a bitter cup to Watson. To his friend Ellington in Thomson he wrote, "As for me, I suffer deeply. I felt very keenly the blow dealt me by my own people at home, but I am here to do certain things, and I mean to do it if it costs me my life." To vindicate their leader, the farmers held a mass meeting in Thomson in answer to the Democratic celebration. The weather was foul and roads all but impassable. "If ever elements conspired against the success of a meeting of men," wrote an unfriendly attendant, "it did today. . . . I dwell thus upon the weather to| . . . emphasize what enthusiasm, and what earnestness of purpose must actuate men who rode from ten to fifteen miles in wagons and open buggies and on horse back through sleet and slush, over bad roads, to come here and declare their

[9] Paxon Hibben, *The Peerless Leader*, p. 124.
[10] *P. P. P.*, Oct. 13, 1893.
[11] Augusta *Chronicle*, Dec. 9, 1891; clipping dated Thomson, Jan. 30, 1892, Watson Scrapbooks.

faith and confidence in Tom Watson. To me there is something pathetic in the spectacle . . . to witness these grayhaired veterans who have borne the Democratic standard to victory in a hundred battles, turning their backs upon the colors for which their sires fought, renouncing and denouncing leaders who stood by them in troublous times that are past, and swearing allegiance to strange gods and untried generals. It indicates how serious is the condition of these farmers at home, how cheerless to them must be the outlook for the future."

Only a few townsmen were present. Ellington remarked, "It is the same old fight between the country and the town." Addressing the farmers, a speaker said, "They say Watson is a dangerous man. It was discontented people who established the Protestant Church, the Magna Charta and which [*sic*] caused France to run with blood. (Applause.) There are a hundred precedents in history. Discontent makes us rebels against these old line parties. If we are united we will win. (Applause.) Let us stand by each other at any cost. (Applause.) Let us wire Watson our action today and let his heart rejoice to know that his people are with him."

The meeting voted "unqualified approval" of Watson, "the only Congressman from Georgia elected on the Ocala demands, who has not compromised the principles on which he was elected." It branded "all such charges as 'traitor to party,' 'Benedict Arnold,' etc., maliciously false." [12]

Scores of similar meetings endorsing Watson were held in sub-alliances all over the state. "At the very mention of his name" the Jonesboro sub-Alliance "arose as one man, making the welkin ring." For two months Watson spread samples of these resolutions endorsing his position over the front page of his paper under the heading, "SPEAKING OUT." [13] It was said by prominent Alliancemen that "Tom Watson is now the recognized leader of the Alliance as an organization political . . . This

[12] Augusta *Chronicle*, Dec. 20, 1891
[13] *P P P*, Dec. 17, 1891–Feb. 11, 1892.

197

meant that the Alliance is already, or will be as soon as plans mature, the third party of Georgia. Livingston was too tame a spirit for the third party emergency. . . . It has been very evident for months past that Livingston had lost his grip. . . . Livingston and Watson are not even on speaking terms." [14] President Polk commended Watson's action,[15] and the *National Economist* thought that the nine Populists with him as leader "immortalized themselves politically, and made traces in American history which will never be obliterated, by refusing to go into the caucus of either party." [16]

For all the notoriety he received before Congress was organized, Watson was still a neophyte and had his place yet to win on the floor of the House. The *Chronicle* admitted that he "especially distinguished himself" in his maiden speech, "not so much by what he said as by his coolness, readiness at repartee and his easy flow of good solid English words." When he got the floor the former "Czar" Reed, who sat across the aisle from him, conspicuously moved a dozen seats away, but returned to his seat before the Populist leader was half through, and "actually smiled graciously" when Watson made some humorous reference to his erstwhile Czardom.

Referring to his committee appointments (the United States Militia, and the Census) Watson remarked that Crisp had placed him "just as low as the law allowed," observing that "A militia which does not exist and a census which has already been taken are not apt to be subjects of very exciting work. Maybe I can get the pages to let me help them bring up stationery, pens, ink, etc. and then keep the rust off. The elevator man seems to be a good natured outcast and possibly he may let me help him pull the cord."

The feud between Watson and Speaker Crisp increased in bitterness. A reporter in Watson's paper doubted if "there ever

[14] Clipping dated Dec. 26, 1891, Northen Scrapbooks, Vol. II, p. 24.
[15] *Progressive Farmer,* quoted in *P. P. P.,* Jan. 14, 1892.
[16] Dec. 12, 1891.

reigned a speaker of the House before this who declined to speak to one of the members or who refused to recognize him in his representative capacity because of personal bias." When Crisp snubbed his effort to get an anti-Pinkerton bill before the House, a labor paper said, "The Speaker's attitude toward Mr. Watson must be considered as a direct slap at every union workingman in the country."

Watson had delivered some ungloved blows at Crisp. During the race for the speakership he had written that Crisp's candidacy was "supported by the Machine politicians, by the boodlers, the subsidy hunters, the protected industries and by Wall Street." From the floor of the House, too, he had attacked the Speaker's "autocratic power," saying he did not "any more want to give it to a man whose name begins with a C, and who comes from Georgia, than one whose name begins with R, and who comes from Maine." [17]

The preceding summer Watson had publicly charged one E. W. Barrett, a correspondent of the Atlanta *Constitution*, with offering him the chairmanship of an important committee for his promise to vote for Crisp.[18] The charge was denied. After his election, Crisp made this same Barrett clerk of the Speaker, a position he held along with that of correspondent to the *Constitution*. In the latter capacity he kept up a running political attack on Watson—an attack that some believed emanated from the Speaker himself. On February 28, he wrote a dispatch that frankly charged Watson with voting against the Democratic contestant and for the Republican contestant in a disputed election case before the House as "an open play to the Republican party," because "he expects financial aid from that party in his next race for congress."

A few days later Watson gained the floor on a question of privilege. First he sent to the desk the Barrett article, which was read by the Clerk. Then he addressed his remarks, "direct, per-

[17] *Cong Record,* 52 Cong, 1 Sess, pp 1682-1683
[18] *Constitution,* Aug. 21-26, 1891.

sonal, and blistering," to the Speaker himself. Since "the Clerk of the Speaker of this House denounces through the public print a gentleman whom he knows to be the political opponent of the gentleman to whom he is clerk" he felt his reply justified:

In my association with the members of this House, I have felt the embarrassment of being in a position open to misconstruction, open to misunderstanding; but I have attempted to establish here a character for openness, manliness, and fairness, which I thought had in some measure won me the confidence of my colleagues upon this floor. Ever since I have been here the clerk of the Speaker has thought it was his duty to deride me, ridicule me, and misrepresent me.

All the members, the Speaker, and the author of the article knew that three Democrats, whose loyalty was unquestioned, had also voted for the Republican contestant, and the inference that the vote had been cast corruptly was no more justified in his case than in theirs. "Mr. Speaker," he concluded, "I denounce that insinuation, cowardly as it is, as a base and infamous falsehood. (Applause.)" [19]

There is no record that relations between the Speaker and the gentleman from Georgia improved after this.

The arch-enemy, however, was still Livingston. The great convention of farmer and labor organizations at St. Louis, to be held on February 22, would settle the fate of the third party as a national movement. Moving swiftly and silently, Livingston early in December appointed handpicked delegates to the convention, who were known to oppose the third party revolt, and elected himself a member and chairman ex-officio of the delegation.[20]

Watson immediately denounced his action as "a usurpation of power," saying he was guilty of "not only appointing delegates to the . . . convention without consulting the people whom those delegates represent, but actually canvassing every name pre-

[19] *Cong. Record,* 52 Cong., 1 Sess., pp. 1682-1683.
[20] *Constitution,* Jan. 2, 1892.

sented for appointment and rejecting every one who was thought to be favorable to views held by a large majority of the Alliancemen of the State." He warned the farmers of their "betrayal" and urged them to renounce Livingston by "a flood of letters." The response to his call must have been gratifying.[21] Livingston and his handpicked delegation, of course, refused to resign as Watson demanded, and set forth to the St. Louis Convention. But another delegation, consisting of Post, Ellington, and Branch, Watson lieutenants, also set forth with no credentials save a conviction that they, instead of Livingston, represented the will of the Georgia masses.

The St. Louis Convention, whose members were mainly grizzled, hard-handed farmers, was immense, somewhat amorphous, and slow to organize due to confusion about credentials. The credentials committee did not report until the second day and then refused to rule upon one contest—that between the two delegations from Georgia. The fight between them was so fierce that the committee referred the decision to the whole Convention. The issue was clearly third party versus anti-third party, and the vote on the Georgia contest would reveal the will of the Convention on this, the most vital issue before it.

Moses, one of the Livingston delegates, took the floor to denounce the contesting delegates and to assure the Convention that whatever the West did, the South would remain solidly Democratic. C. C. Post was on his feet the instant Moses finished. At his revelation of "the whole scheme by which Livingston had sought to betray the Alliance and the reform movement to its death" the audience "broke forth in wildest cheers." Post's excoriation of Livingston, according to the Associated Press reporter was "the fiercest speech made in the Convention." At its close he dramatically unrolled a sheet of paper thirty feet long covered with some four hundred resolutions endorsing Watson, and by its side held up a sheet two feet long endorsing Livingston. With this graphic contrast before them, the Con-

[21] *P. P. P.*, Dec. 17, 1891, Jan. 7, 14, and Feb. 11, 18, 1892.

vention enthusiastically voted to seat the Watson delegation. By that vote the nation knew that this was a third party convention.[22]

Livingston's motion to adopt the proposed *platform* without mention of the radical preamble (a masterpiece of political invective by Ignatius Donnelly) was adopted. But one of the Watson delegates saw through the ruse, and moved the adoption of the preamble also. Of the seven hundred votes, it was said, only three were cast against the motion—and those were cast by the Livingston men from Georgia. After this vote Livingston and one of his lieutenants left the hall. Watson's description of the incident was not entirely free from an attitude of gloating:

The departure of a couple of spectators from the galleries would have attracted as much comment as did the departure of these men, one of whom had once wielded more power over the Alliancemen of the country than perhaps any other man, but who lost it in a mad effort to prove himself greater than the people who trusted him.

Livingston, instead of returning to his duties at Washington (where Watson had remained), hurried immediately to Georgia to raise a hue and cry against the action of the St. Louis Convention. "The Conference," he shouted, "was composed of a lot of cranks and men without character or influence." Ignatius Donnelly said "the New Order of things would wipe out the color line in the South." Would his audience want to eat and sleep with Negroes? The Colonel made other notable observations, all of the same general trend.[23] The Augusta *Chronicle*, only lately wont to refer to Livingston as a "scurvy politician and dirty political trickster," praised his speech hugely. On the other hand, Dr. Felton, the old Independent warhorse who had

[22] Hicks, *The Populist Revolt*, pp. 223-226; clippings in Watson Scrapbooks and Northen Scrapbooks; *P. P. P*, March 3, 1892.
[23] *Constitution*, Feb. 26, 1892; *P. P. P*, March 10, 1892; *National Economist*, March 5, 1892; Northen Scrapbooks, Vol II, pp. 38-39.

fought Watson and the Alliance honestly out of conviction, thought that "Tom Watson's fidelity shines like a star beside Livingston's detestable demagoguery and trickery."

A referendum to the 2,200 sub-Alliances of Georgia upon the action of the St. Louis Convention revealed how clearly Livingston had misrepresented them, and how accurately Watson knew their mood. Issue after issue of the *People's Party Paper* during March and April was filled with hundreds of resolutions under the heading "THE UPRISING: They Will Act with the People's Party." Of 1600 sub-Alliances reporting (their resolutions, "official, signed and stamped"), only three refused to endorse the Convention. All the rest did endorse it. The editor of the official organ of the Alliance reported that "the action of the sub-Alliances means that the Georgia Alliance is almost unanimously committed to the third party." [24] And, instead of complaining of decline in membership as a few months before, the editor reported the "membership rolls are larger than they ever have been, and they are steadily increasing."

* * * * * *

Despite the multiplicity of fronts to his political battle line Watson, unlike some of his enemies, stuck to his post, not leaving Washington during the entire session, and attending every daily session except when he was ill. In the subsequent campaign he once made the statement that he had "introduced bills on nearly every point included in the Ocala platform." This was virtually the case. These included a bill to levy an income tax; a bill to prevent the payment in advance of interest on United States bonds to holders; a bill to abolish duties on jute bagging, iron ties, and binding twine; a bill to recover into the Treasury the $100,000,000 of gold reserve held for redemption of United States notes; a bill to abolish the National Bank; a bill to control the employment of such strike breakers as the

[24] *Southern Alliance Farmer*, March 21, 1892; Macon *Telegraph*, March 22, 1892.

203

Pinkerton Detective Agency provided; and a bill to establish a system of subtreasuries.[25]

Of these bills, only two were ever reported out by the committees to which they were referred. Watson could have had few delusions about them in the first place; he probably introduced some of them mainly as a means of getting them before the public. For the rest, it is true that his record is singularly free from the multitude of petty personal-relief, and pension, logrolling bills that filled the time of the average congressman.

No other plank of the Alliance platform was more discussed, and from none of their schemes for relief did the farmers expect greater things than the subtreasury plan. It was also the subject of more criticism and ridicule, and doubtless the faith of many farmers was that of despair grasping at a panacea. Yet the plan had many substantial and intelligent features and was deserving of a serious consideration that it did not get. Bills to establish the plan had been introduced in both Senate and House of the previous Congress; yet the committees to which they were referred could be induced to make no report, favorable or unfavorable, upon them, despite the flood of petitions from Alliances.[26]

Almost three months had elapsed since he had introduced his bill, without any word from the Committee on Ways and Means, when Watson, determined to force the issue, asked unanimous consent for consideration of a resolution requesting the Committee to report on the subtreasury bill. Whereupon a member demanded the regular order. Watson then adopted the strategy of uncompromisingly objecting to every request for unanimous consent, no matter who asked it. Every morning he arose to make his request, was met with objection, and sat down to await opportunity to block every similar request. Finally the majority yielded, his request was granted, and the Committee

[25] *Cong. Record,* 52 Cong., 1 Sess., p. 126 (H. R. 83, H. R. 84, H. R. 85, H. R. 86), p. 303 (H. R. 3611), p. 993 (H. R. 5680), p. 1164 (H. R. 6000), p. 1578 (H. R. 6660).

[26] T. E. W, *People's Party Campaign Book,* Chap. XVI, "The Sub-Treasury"

was asked to report the bill. This was hailed by the *National Economist* as "The first victory for the People's Party." Another month passed by, however, and still no report. "Give us one hour," pleaded Watson, "two hours, three hours, one day or two days" since "we do claim that you are bound to give us a chance to discuss the bill." When this proved unavailing, he returned to his old tactics, colliding even with his friend Bryan. Still nothing happened, until the very last day of the session when the bill was reported. With not a minute allowed for discussion, it was lost.[27]

Upon other Populist demands Watson was ready to lift his voice. "You take the United States Senate. We demand that its members shall be elected hereafter by a direct vote of the people. Why? . . . We know that the very concentration of power, the concentration of capital, the concentration of privilege which we are fighting is enthroned and intrenched in the Senate of the United States. No man can successfully deny it. Every great corporation of this land has its agents, its attorneys there." [28]

Ever since the 'seventies, a subject of bitter complaint among labor unions had been the gangs of gunmen and strike breakers that the Pinkerton Detective Agency hired out to corporations engaged in struggles with their operatives. The record of their crimes against labor had been a black one; yet no effective measure had been taken against the practice. Watson began an earnest fight upon this "standing body of armed militia which corporations can hire," introducing early in the session a resolution and a bill calling for investigation and control of such agencies.[29] The bill lay in committee for months. No report was made despite Watson's appearance before the committee, and his pleas from the floor of the House. Pinkerton, in what Watson thought "the foulest and most brutal manner," denounced the author of the resolution in the press,[30] which only spurred him to renewed

[27] *Cong. Record,* 52 Cong, 1 Sess, pp. 4432, 4563, 5455-5456, 5665
[28] *Ibid.,* Jan. 27, 1892, pp 598-599
[29] T. E W , *People's Party Campaign Book,* Chap. XV, pp. 127-198.
[30] *Cong. Record,* 52 Cong , 1 Sess , July 7, 1892, p. 5868.

205

activity. Finally the committee reported the resolution favorably, shorn, said the author, "of its strongest features, and restricted merely to the operation of railroad trains." In this form the bill passed, but no action came of it.[31]

A few weeks later, at four o'clock on the morning of July 6, a barge loaded with three hundred armed Pinkerton "detectives" was towed up the Monongahela River to the landing of the Homestead Carnegie Steel plant. The workers met them with arms, and after a pitched battle that lasted all day, captured them, with a loss of half a dozen men on both sides killed, and many wounded. The state militia then moved in, intimidated the strikers and remained for several months. American union-labor had lost one of the most decisive and disastrous battles in its history.

On the day following the Homestead battle, Williams of Massachusetts introduced a resolution calling for an investigation. It received immediate and favorable attention. Watson gave the bill strong support, but he reminded the member that:

As far back as February 9 . . . I introduced a bill which would have made the keeping of such a standing body of men, or their employment illegal, and would then have struck at the source of the trouble, by putting down this body of men . . .

No action whatever has been taken upon that measure. If this Congress meant to do anything to protect the laborers it could have been done . . .

Now I want to say this in conclusion. Look at the difference in the conduct of the committee at that time and on yesterday.

There is a sound of cannon in the air; there is a sound of Winchester rifles abroad; there are barricades and forts; there is a vessel in the river armed and equipped for fight, there is the stain of blood in the street; there are dead men being borne to their homes. So the gentleman from Massachusetts introduces a resolution yesterday and, without hearing him, without compelling him to give them evidence,

[31] *Ibid*, Jan 19, 1892; Feb 9, 1892, p. 993; May 12, 1892, pp 4222-4225; P. P. P, April 14 and May 6, 1892.

206

or any facts, or any law, the committee at once considered his resolution and brought it up here this morning. . . .

But, now that your Presidential election approaches and you want to play to the galleries and to pretend friendship for the working men, you bring in a resolution at this late hour, when the shedding of blood might have been prevented.[32]

The national convention of the People's party, then in session at Omaha, denounced the "hireling standing army, unrecognized by our laws," and passed a resolution demanding the abolition of the system—the first time the demand had appeared in their platform. Five days after the Homestead struggle, a bloody pitched battle was fought between the union miners of the Coeur d'Alene district of Idaho and professional strike breakers. Watson's prompt resolution calling for an investigation of the labor troubles and of the conduct of the Sullivan police therein was refused consideration.[33] The professional strike breaking agencies were to enjoy a long period of prosperity thereafter.

Another piece of labor legislation in which Watson interested himself was the eight-hour labor law. He asserted that he was "the only man in Congress" who consistently supported the measure.[34] Upon military and naval appropriations and questions of foreign relations Watson spoke as if for his party, and his position did conform to the party policy, in so far as it had one. But he also spoke out of personal convictions that were as deeply rooted in him as any he had. Some Quaker subsoil of his background still clung to the roots of those convictions. Those principles remained with him after he seemed to have forgotten many others he now swore by.

When Livingston, shortly before the St. Louis Convention, began to be quoted by the press as favorable to war with Chile, Watson took him to task with ridicule. At the same time he

[32] *Cong Record,* 52 Cong., 1 Sess., July 7, 1892, pp. 5860-5869; *P P. P,* July 15, 1892.
[33] *Cong Record,* 52 Cong., 1 Sess., July 15, 1892, p 6216.
[34] Augusta *Chronicle,* Oct 6, 1892.

207

pointed out what war would mean: In the first place, "it would arouse the military spirit everywhere, and the civil reforms for which we have labored so hard would be subordinated and side-tracked." Secondly, "the battles will be fought by the poor," those "whom heartless Plutocrats fear," "men who will be got rid of by the war." War would also mean oppressive taxes on the poor, and a standing army to threaten their liberties.[35] Speaking generally, he said on the floor of the House: "I believe the time is approaching when wars—those barbarous settlements of disputes by appeal to arms—will be just as much a relic of the past . . . as are now the old, rude ways of trial by combat and dueling or any other method of personal strife."

On the question of increasing the naval appropriation, he was opposed "to any $350,000,000 scheme, to build up an American Navy on a competitive basis with European navies." He believed that "we have nothing to fear from any European nation whatsoever." "Sir, the real truth is that the enemies we have to dread in the future are, not Great Britain, not France, not Germany, not Italy, not Mexico, but our own people. What do I mean by that? I mean bad laws here at home; I mean class legislation at home; I mean overgrown and insolent corporations here at home; I mean the greed of monopolies here at home." He then cited the "thousands of people in the State of Mississippi . . . powerless and homeless, destitute, and suffering for food—holding out their hands and asking the National Assembly to give them relief." He read into the *Record* an account of the horrible destitution in the working class districts of Atlanta, where mill-workers were being paid thirty-six cents a day, and were at the moment dying of pestilence so fast that it was impossible to bury them. No, the "protection" we needed was from corporations and wage slavery.[36]

For diversion, the Populists' dearest delight lay in baiting the old parties and rankling their sore spots. Watson ran in his

---

[35] *P. P. P.*, "Our Washington Letter," Jan. 28, 1892.
[36] *Cong. Record*, 52 Cong , 1 Sess , April 16, 1892, pp. 3360-3362.

paper a weekly column, "Our Washington Letter," almost entirely devoted to this sport. In it he would describe the "Balshazzar tone" of a Jackson Day Banquet of the "democratic nabobs," or give a satirical account of a sham battle between the old parties over tariff or silver.

But the richest thing to us Third Party men [he wrote] was the way the Democrats showed up the Republicans and the Republicans showed up the Democrats.

It was Devil and Witch all the way through; Republican pot and Democratic kettle, and the People's Party members demurely saying "Go it boys. Continue to expose your mutual hypocrisy, fraudulent pretenses, tricks and broken promises—and after a while the people will believe all the bad things you say of one another, and will kick you both out." [37]

In spite of the official party attitude of indifference toward the tariff question, Watson, still an uncompromising free trader, missed no opportunity to break a lance against the protective wall, or ridicule the hypocrisy of the Democrats' policy.

He did not spare "our handsome and brilliant friend from Nebraska, who was put forward as the 'darling' of the Democratic side of the House." Bryan's famous tariff speech was "the sum and substance of the old Democratic position in the tariff, that we will practice what is wrong while we know what is right. (Laughter and applause on the Republican side.)" Judging from platform and campaign speeches one would have thought that "this Democratic majority would crowd over one another in almost indecent haste to tear the McKinley bill off the statute books. (Laughter.)" Yet after six months they had done nothing.[38] He stated the position of the two old parties on tariff thus: "the Republicans come out flatfooted for Protection—with hypocritical reasons; while the Democrats practice Protection under hypocritical declarations against it."

[37] *P. P. P*, Jan. 21, 1892.
[38] *Cong Record*, 52 Cong., 1 Sess., pp. 2338-2339, 4800.

Toward the free-silver demand, even during the high-pitched hysteria over it, Watson always maintained the attitude that it was "a very mild measure of reform," whose benefit would be hardly perceptible. He could not, however, endure seeing the Democrats win hopeful farmers by campaign pledges to silver, only to vote against silver as soon as in office. In March, he announced that "the action in the House on the silver bill is the death knell of the old democratic organization. . . . With a majority of 148 in the House of Representatives it certainly had a chance to pass the free silver bill." Yet eighty-two Democrats voted to table the bill, and it was "only by the help of the nine People's party members and eleven Republicans that the immense Democratic majority was saved from a Waterloo . . . Now, no power on earth can keep Georgia from going into the electoral college with a People's Party delegation." [39] "Speaker Crisp," thought Watson, "as usual, used what some people call 'Diplomacy'; what others call Double-Dealing, and what others call by a still harsher name." [40]

In July, during the last month of the session appeared Watson's *People's Party Campaign Book,* with its sensational subtitle, *Not a Revolt; It is a Revolution.* The New York *Herald* pronounced it "the first heavy literary gun of the third party." It was certainly no polished product. Rather, it was a political handgrenade packed with campaign shrapnel—slogans, excoriations, invective, exposures, denunciation. Watson explained later that "it was addressed to a certain class of voters and written in the style of campaign documents since time began." "While I am prepared to say that no statement in the book is untrue, there is at the same time a certain tone adopted which you will not find in any other style of essay." For its purpose it was extremely effective [41]—too effective for some. For, though there were

[39] *Constitution,* March 31, 1892.
[40] *P. P. P* , March 31, 1892.
[41] Wrote one of Watson's constituents (*P. P. P.,* Dec. 15, 1893): "A serious and prayerful perusal of Tom Watson's book on the Sabbath will make you wiser and better."

bitter chapters on corporations, Pinkerton's strike breakers, and national banks, his most withering fire was turned on the two old parties, especially the Democrats.

"A drop of ink, a few strokes of the pen, and whiz,—Bang, presto, change! We have the showy capitol in mourning and frenzied congressmen asking one another whether the penalty shall be boiling oil, expulsion from the floor, or simply a pained paternal spanking . . ." [42] The journalist exaggerated the detonation of the explosion, but not its suddenness.

On the preceding afternoon Jerry Simpson's little boy had been peddling copies of Watson's book about the floor of the House, doing a flourishing business at a dollar a copy, when the Speaker, in response to an objection raised, ran the young money changer from the temple. [43] The new book was well circulated, however, and the halls were ahum with talk of it.

On the morning of July 29, General Joseph E. Wheeler of Alabama, with whom Watson for several days had been engaging in a series of charges and counter-charges, arose "to a question of the highest privilege, affecting the House of Representatives collectively, affecting its dignity." He sent to the clerk's desk a copy of Watson's book, requesting that a marked passage be read, as follows:

The Congress now sitting is one illustration. Pledged to Reform, they have not reformed. Pledged to Economy, they have not economized. Pledged to Legislate, they have not legislated. Extravagance has been the order of the day. Absenteeism was never so pronounced. Lack of purpose was never so clear. Lack of common business prudence never more glaring. Drunken members have reeled about the aisles—a disgrace to the Republic. Drunken speakers have debated grave issues on the Floor and in the midst of maudlin rumblings have been heard to ask *"Mr. Speaker,* where was I at?" Useless employes crowd every corridor. Useless expenditures pervade every Department.

[42] New York *Herald,* Aug. 1, 1892.
[43] Washington *Post,* July 30, 1892.

211

Wheeler then continued by making, and repeating at considerable length and variety, the assertion that this was "the vilest and most malignant falsehood that has ever been uttered on the American continent." He further said that "There are other untrue statements in this book," and that "the gentleman who wrote the book has so little regard for facts that he is constitutionally unable to distinguish between truth and falsehood. (Applause.)" [44]

Watson began his reply in a dispassionate tone. "If Mr. Watson was in the least flustered when he arose to make his explanation, he did not show it," said a reporter.[45] He attempted futilely to deal first with personal charges of falsehood, and the animus behind Wheeler's attack, but unruly members kept up a shout for his explanation of the charge of drunkenness. Finally he turned to them:

And I stand here to defend every line in the book and will do it against all comers, whether from North or South.

Instantly "the House was in an uproar." A "storm of hisses and derisive yells that went up from the Democratic side" drowned out both Watson's voice and the incessant pounding of the Speaker's gavel. Excited members surrounded the Georgian and filled the space before the Speaker's desk, "howling and gesticulating like so many Comanche Indians." T. V. Powderly, who happened to be in the galleries at the moment, counted thirty-three members on their feet while Watson was attempting to speak, "some with their backs to the presiding officer, others grouped in knots, others shaking their clinched fists at the persons attempting to address the House, others hissing like adders, and all of them talking aloud or muttering as the spirit moved them." [46] During a lull Watson shouted:

[44] *Cong. Record*, 52 Cong., 1 Sess., July 28, 1892, pp. 6931-6940.
[45] Washington *Post*, July 30, 1892.
[46] *P. P. P.*, Aug. 26, 1892; New York *Herald*, July 30, 1892; New York *World*, Aug. 3, 1892.

212

I say that every word in that book is literally true, and all men who have been here keeping their eyes open, and wanting to admit facts, will admit these facts are fairly stated. (A cry of "No!" and hisses on the Democratic side.)

The provocation was at last telling upon Watson's excitable temperament. When Crisp cautioned him that he occupied the floor only "as a matter of grace," he turned sharply on the Speaker, and shaking his fist at the gentleman's face, he exclaimed:

I want no matter of grace from this Democratic majority that seeks to hiss me down when I am defending my character here on the floor of the House. Jeffersonian Democracy grants to a man freedom of speech and freedom of press and if you want to howl me down do it, and I will appeal from your tyranny to the fair sense of justice that abides in the hearts of the American people.

Populist members applauded vigorously. Standing on tiptoe, arms waving and hair flying, he wound up with a "lung-splitting climax": "I scorn your grace! I scorn your mercy!" The sergeant-at-arms, by order of the Speaker, started toward Watson, who took his seat before he was reached. He regained the floor to say that the House might take what action it liked; he would retract nothing.

Boatner, of Louisiana, introduced a resolution, which passed, calling for the appointment of a committee to investigate the charges of drunkenness, and "if untrue, whether the said Watson has violated the privileges of the House." Watson observed that his more serious charges did not seem to trouble the Democratic conscience.

A considerable public interest attended the hearings of the committee on "congressional jags," as the press dubbed it. "Nothing," observed the Washington *Post*, "has so stirred the House for many a day as the publication and repetition of these charges." It was said that "a hundred angry Congressmen" were prepared to endorse Ex-Speaker Tom Reed's statement that "he had never understood the force of the biblical reference to the 'colt of a wild ass' until he witnessed the performance by Congressmen Tom Watson on the floor of the House." [47] The committee listened to much conflicting testimony, including a heated questioning of Watson himself. The main point at issue was the degree of intoxication attained by the Honorable J. E. Cobb, of Alabama, during his speech in a certain debate on the floor of the House.[48]

While the report was awaited there was a good deal of speculation on the probable fate to be dealt out to Watson. Jerry Simpson was quoted as welcoming Watson's expulsion from the House as an opportunity for a triumphant vindication of the approaching election. The report was delayed until the last day of the session. The majority, consisting of three Democrats, recommended a resolution stating that the charges brought by Watson were "not true, and constitute an unwarranted assault upon the honor and dignity of the House, and that such publication has the unqualified disapproval of the House." The Republican member wrote a concurring report, and Jerry Simpson, the Populist member of the committee, wrote a minority report exonerating Watson and upholding his charges.[49] The report was not voted on that session.

That night at eleven o'clock Crisp's gavel rapped the adjournment of the first session of the 52nd Congress. Whereupon, the wags of the press gallery serenaded the departing members with the following song:

"Oh Watson we are truly grieved, sir,
To see you packing your bag;
Won't you tell us before you leave, sir,
What is a Congressional jag?

[47] New York *World*, Aug. 3, 1892.
[48] Hearings and reports published in *House Reports*, 52 Cong., 1 Sess., Vol. 10, Report No. 2132; Washington *Post*, Aug 2 and 3, 1892.
[49] Reports cited above; also *vide* P P. P., Aug. 16, 1892.

What is a Congressional jag?
Is it simply a weakness of knees,
A sip or sup from a bottle or cup,
Or a whoop up and go as you please?"

"And then everybody fled from the great building." [50]

If the intention of the Democratic majority in stirring up the investigation had been to embarrass Watson and cast ridicule upon his party, it is fairly plain that plans went awry. Wrote Mrs. Watson to her husband from Washington: "They [the committee] raised a racket that has recoiled and it's a little hard to shuffle off. They are mad enough with Mr. Wheeler, and," added Mrs. Watson, who had an eye for practical matters, "it will make the book sell." [51] "O," sighed one journalist, "that mine enemy, when I write a book, would advertise it on the floor of Congress." Two New York newspapers devoted a whole page to the affair, and the press of the whole country resounded with it. Observed one of them, "A member comparatively unknown had been advertised from one end of the country to the other. Whether he succeeded in proving his charges or not the Farmers' Alliance people would probably lionize him, and in case he was censured by the House would make a martyr of him." [52]

Realizing the truth of this prediction, the Georgia Democratic press countered with the typical attack: "Perhaps some districts would rather have representatives who sometimes drink too much than to have a cranky, socialistic agitator who never drinks at all." [53]

[50] Washington *Post,* Aug. 6, 1892.
[51] Mrs. Watson to T. E. W., Aug. 4, 1892, Watson MSS.
[52] New York *Herald,* Aug. 1, 1892.
[53] Augusta *Chronicle,* Aug. 6, 1892.

CHAPTER XIII

Race, Class, and Party

When Watson led the people out,
They marched thro' flood and flame;
Old Livingston tried to turn them back,
But they got there all the same.[1]

SPECULATING UPON THE APPROACHING STRUGGLE for reëlection, Watson wondered whether the people understood the nature of the conflict before them. It was, he believed, the same struggle that in the past had been fought "upon the field of battle, behind barricades, in the streets of cities, about the scaffold and guillotine . . . but never at the ballot box, as it will next October and November." It was, in his terms, the struggle between "Democracy and Plutocracy":

We wonder if the people generally understand the full significance of this fact? Do our friends understand it? Do our enemies appreciate its meaning? If so, then the coming contest will be sharp indeed. There will be neither asking nor giving of quarter, for upon both sides there will be the consciousness that the contending forces are not unequally matched, and that as they represent totally different and opposing ideas and theories, there can be but one settlement of the matter at issue, and that it must come through the utter overthrow of the one or the other of the parties to the contest.[2]

[1] *P. P P.*, April 28, 1892.
[2] *Ibid*, March 10, 1892

216

Before proceeding further it might be well to arrive at some understanding of the nature of these combatants who had such "totally different and opposing ideas and theories." Who were the Populists?

Aside from the new factory proletariat of a few cities (themselves of recent rural origin), the Populists were agricultural and rural. But so were the great mass of people of the state and of the South; and that mass was divided by class and race lines. Were they exploiters or the exploited?

In answering such questions the Populists themselves were confusing. In resolving themselves into the People's party, the Oglethorpe County Alliance referred to its members as "the peasantry of America." On the other hand, a Populist of Douglas County said, "Some of our people were once rich, and most all were well to do . . . and it is no fault of theirs that they are reduced to such straights [*sic*]." Tom Watson struck nearer the truth when he said, "You stand for the yearning, upward tendency of the middle and lower classes." Therefore, they were "the sworn foes of monopoly—not monopoly in the narrow sense of the word—but monopoly of power, of place, of privilege, of wealth, of progress." Individualist and middle-class in tradition and aspiration, they accepted the basic capitalistic system. Watson summed up their objectives: "Keep the avenues of honor free. Close no entrance to the poorest, the weakest, the humblest. Say to ambition everywhere, 'the field is clear, the contest fair; come, and win your share if you can!' " [3]

In general, the Southern Populists were mainly the agrarian masses, including tenant, small landowner, and a surprising member of large landowners, together with the industrial proletariat. They were united by their resentment of the crushing oppression of capitalist finance and industrialism. Watson himself recognized the complexity of his ranks. "There is a gradation in servitude," he said. The laborer was the first to feel the lash, the cropper next, the tenant next, and the landlord next—

[3] *Watson's Jeffersonian Magazine*, Vol. V (1910), p. 818.

in Watson's hierarchy of serfdom. "But," he added, "the livery of the serf is there all the same."[4] This livery, he believed, would become the uniform of the army that he led against its oppressors.

Tom Watson was himself one of the largest landowners in the state, with more tenants on his land than his grandfather had slaves.[5] There were other large landowners high in the party ranks, who fought side by side with small farmers and tenants. In this regard a remark of Charles A. Beard upon the battles of Jefferson's day might be recalled: "It is a curious freak of fortune that gives to the slave owning aristocracy the leadership in a democracy of small farmers, but the cause is not far to seek. In a conflict with capitalism, the agrarians rallied around that agrarian class which had the cultural equipment for dominant direction."[6] There is room for doubt whether there was an "aristocracy" of the tidewater sort in Georgia. At any rate, the former slave-owners were divided in the 'nineties. While some became Populists, many of the larger owners became merchants, bankers, and small capitalists, and fought the Populists as bitterly as did the business men of the towns.[7]

It is undoubtedly true that the Populist ideology was dominantly that of the landowning farmer, who was, in many cases, the exploiter of landless tenant labor. But about half of the farms in the state at that time were operated by owners, dirt farmers, and the rank and file of the Populists were of this poverty-ridden small farmer class. They were surely more exploited than exploiting, and the Populist contention that the tenant was in the same boat as the owner had much truth in it.

[4] *P. P. P*, Jan. 27, 1892.
[5] Tenant record and account books, Watson MSS.
[6] Charles A. Beard, *The Economic Origins of Jeffersonian Democracy*, p. 399.
[7] A. M. Arnett, *The Populist Movement in Georgia*, p. 152. The class alignments of the party varied somewhat from state to state in the South. Thus, of Alabama it was said that the movement was "an effort of the masses of the whites to free themselves from the rule of the black belt Democratic party of the old slave-owning type." (Joseph C Manning, *Fadeout of Populism*, p. 60.) Compare maps of Arnett (*op. cit.*, p. 184), showing part of the Georgia black belt as a stronghold of Populism.

218

The southern urban proletariat was yet an embryonic class, largely of immediate agrarian background. They were not yet class-conscious, and thought more as farmers than as industrial workers. Obviously the Populist attack did not strike at the whole system of capitalist exploitation, as did socialism, but in its time and section the Populist party formed the vanguard against the advancing capitalist plutocracy, and its fate was of vital consequence to the future.

That class contradiction was not magically resolved in the Populist-agrarian potpourri is indicated by various signs. Once the Colored Farmers' Alliance proposed to call a general strike of Negro cotton pickers. The *Progressive Farmer*, paper of Colonel L. L. Polk, president of the National Alliance (white), did "not hesitate to advise our farmers to leave their cotton in the field rather than pay more than 50 cents per hundred to have it picked." The Negro brethren were attempting "to better their condition at the expense of their white brethren. Reforms should not be in the interest of one portion of our farmers at the expense of another." [8]

The Populist struggle in the South, moreover, was fought under such peculiar circumstances as to set it apart from the history of the national movement, and to call for special treatment. "Political campaigns in the North," wrote a veteran of Alabama Populism, "even at their highest pitch of contention and strife, were as placid as pink teas in comparison with those years of political combat in the South." [9] Taking into comparative account the violence of the passions unloosed by the conflict, the actual bloodshed and physical strife, one is prepared to give assent to that judgment.

What explained the bitterness and violence that characterized the Populist struggle in the South? To answer in a word— "race." And that is much too simple an answer. But if to race be

[8] Editorial in *Progressive Farmer*, Sept 15, 1891; for same attitude in *National Economist*, Sept 26 and October 10, 1891.

[9] Joseph C. Manning, *The Fadeout of Populism*, pp. 5, 142-144.

219

added the complexities of the class economy growing out of race, the heritage of manumitted slave psychology, and the demagogic uses to which the politician was able to put race prejudice—then "race" may be said to be the core of the explanation.

In later life Watson once wrote a retrospective (and quite candid) comparison of his own career with that of William Jennings Bryan. In it he said: "Consider the advantage of position that Bryan had over me. His field of work was the plastic, restless, and growing West: mine was the hide-bound, rock-ribbed Bourbon South. Besides, Bryan had *no everlasting and overshadowing Negro Question to hamper and handicap his progress:* I HAD." [10] There is no doubt that Watson thought of the Negro problem as the Nemesis of his career. He fled it all his days, and in flight sought every refuge—in attitudes as completely contradictory and extreme as possible. At this stage, however, he faced his problem courageously, honestly, and intelligently. As the official leader of the new party in the House, and its only Southern member in Congress, Watson was the logical man to formulate the Populist policy toward the Negro. This he did in a number of speeches and articles.

The Populist program called for a united front between Negro and white farmers. Watson framed his appeal this way:

Now the People's Party says to these two men, "You are kept apart that you may be separately fleeced of your earnings. You are made to hate each other because upon that hatred is rested the keystone of the arch of financial despotism which enslaves you both. You are deceived and blinded that you may not see how this race antagonism perpetuates a monetary system which beggars both." [11]

This bold program called for a reversal of deeply rooted racial prejudices and firmly fixed traditions as old as Southern history. In place of race hatred, political proscription, lynch law, and terrorism it was necessary to foster tolerance, friendly co-

[10] *Jeffersonian Weekly*, Jan. 20, 1910.
[11] T. E W., "The Negro Question in the South," *Arena*, Vol. VI (1892), p. 548.

operation, justice and political rights for the Negro. This was no small task; yet Watson met each issue squarely.

It should be the object of the Populist party, he said, to "make lynch law odious to the people." [12] Georgia at that time led the world in lynchings. Watson nominated a Negro to a place on the state executive committee of his party, "as a man worthy to be on the executive committee of this or any other party." "Tell me the use of educating these people as citizens if they are never to exercise the rights of citizens." [13] He spoke repeatedly from the same platform with Negro speakers to mixed audiences of Negro and white farmers. He did not advocate "social equality" and said so emphatically, since that was "a thing each citizen decides for himself." But he insisted upon "political equality," holding that "the accident of color can make no difference in the interests of farmers, croppers, and laborers." In the same spirit of racial tolerance he was continually finding accomplishments of the Negro race at home and abroad to praise in articles and speeches. [14]

Tom Watson was perhaps the first native white Southern leader of importance to treat the Negro's aspirations with the seriousness that human strivings deserve. For the first time in his political history the Negro was regarded neither as the incompetent ward of White Supremacy, nor as the ward of military intervention, but as an integral part of Southern society with a place in its economy. The Negro was in the South to stay, insisted Watson, just as much so as the white man. "Why is not the colored tenant open to the conviction that he is in the same boat as the white tenant; the colored laborer with the white laborer?" he asked. With a third party it was now possible for the Negro to escape the dilemma of selling his vote to the Democrats or pledging it blindly to the Republican bosses.

[12] *P P P.,* Nov. 3, 1893.
[13] *Ibid*, May 24, 1894.
[14] For example, the work of a Negro member of the Georgia Legislature (*P P. P.,* Dec. 2, 1892) and a South African king's resistance to Cecil Rhodes (*P. P. P.,* Dec. 29, 1893)

Under Watson's tutelage the Southern white masses were beginning to learn to regard the Negro as a political ally bound to them by economic ties and a common destiny, rather than as a slender prop to injured self-esteem in the shape of "White Supremacy." Here was a foundation of political realism upon which some more enduring structure of economic democracy might be constructed. Never before or since have the two races in the South come so close together as they did during the Populist struggles.

No one was more keenly aware of the overwhelming odds against his social program than Tom Watson. In an article in the *Arena* [15] he wrote:

> You might beseech a Southern white tenant to listen to you upon questions of finance, taxation, and transportation; you might demonstrate with mathematical precision that herein lay his way out of poverty into comfort; you might have him "almost persuaded" to the truth, but if the merchant who furnished his farm supplies (at tremendous usury) or the town politician (who never spoke to him excepting at election times) came along and cried "Negro rule!" the entire fabric of reason and common sense which you had patiently constructed would fall, and the poor tenant would joyously hug the chains of an actual wretchedness rather than do any experimenting on a question of mere sentiment. . . . The Negro has been as valuable a portion of the stock in trade of a Democrat as he was of a Republican.

Henry Grady's statement in 1889 that "The Negro as a political force had dropped out of serious consideration" sounded strange indeed in 1892. The Negro as a political force was the concern of everybody. The Democrats sought industriously to resurrect the scare of the Republican "Force Bill," introduced in the House and defeated in the Senate in 1890. "All agree," said the Augusta *Chronicle*, "that this is the overshadowing issue," and it was obvious that the Populists were "aiding the Republicans in their nefarious schemes." "The old issue of sec-

[15] T E W., "The Negro Question in the South," *Arena*, Vol VI (1892), p. 541.

tionalism is confronting the South," asserted the *Constitution*, and White Supremacy is more important than "all the financial reform in the world." [16]

A Westerner, the most eminent student of Populism, has remarked, "Perhaps only a Southerner can realize how keenly these converts to Populism [in the South] must have felt their grievances." [17] A Southerner might add, "only a Southerner of that period"—which followed close upon Reconstruction. The motives of the most sincere Populists were not above the basest construction by Democrats, many of whom were perfectly honest in their suspicions. It was widely believed that they were in secret alliance with the Republicans, and therefore not only traitors to their section, but to their race as well—enemies of white civilization. The worst slander, however, was the product of editors and politicians who believed that any means was justified by the end they had in view. When a responsible editor wrote that "The South and especially the tenth district is threatened with anarchy and communism" because of "the direful teachings of Thomas E. Watson," there were thousands who believed him literally. Populists were subjected to every type of epithet, scurrility, and insult Democrats could devise. There is record of Populists' being turned out of church, driven from their homes, and refused credit because of their beliefs. Families were split and venomous feuds started. As already noted, one of Tom Watson's brothers was secretary of the mass meeting that pronounced him a traitor; a second brother, a merchant, remained a Democrat, and a third became a Populist. A Southern Populist leader told a Western writer, "The feeling of the Democracy against us is one of murderous hate. I have been shot at many times. Grand juries will not indict our assailants. Courts give us no protection." [18]

[16] Augusta *Chronicle*, July 5, 1892; *Constitution*, quoted in *P. P. P.*, July 15, 1892; Macon *Telegraph*, July 27, 1892.
[17] John D. Hicks, *The Populist Revolt*, p. 243.
[18] Henry D Lloyd, "The Populists at St. Louis," *Review of Reviews*, Vol. XIV (Sept., 1896), p 293.

To overcome the harsh penalties attached to revolt—the compulsions of tradition as well as economic pressure making for conformity—there must have been tremendous forces at work upon the Southern masses. It is furthest from the intention of this work to suggest that adequate cause can be discovered in the eloquence of Thomas E. Watson, or the eloquence of anybody else. More eloquent than any orator in the cause of revolt were the hard times of 1891–1892 that opened the "heart-breaking 'nineties."

After a two weeks' tour of observation in the cotton belt of Georgia in December, 1891, the editor of the *Southern Alliance Farmer* wrote that "the farmer has about reached the end of his row." The crop was selling at "the lowest price that cotton has reached in a third of a century," and "hundreds of men will be turned out of house and home, or forced to become hirelings and tenants in fields that they once owned. . . . The doors of every courthouse in Georgia are placarded with the announcements of such [sheriffs'] sales. Hundreds of farmers will be turned adrift, and thousands of acres of our best land allowed to grow up in weeds through lack of necessary capital to work them. . . . The roads are full of negroes begging homes." There was a veritable "epidemic of distress and foreclosures of mortgages now sweeping over our state." [19] The president of the Burke County Alliance wrote Watson: "Our county is in a terrible, terrible condition. Out of fifteen hundred customers at one store only fourteen paid out; five hundred paid less than 50 cents on the dollar." [20] Mrs. W. H. Felton wrote, "We sold our cotton crop in 1892 for a little over four cents the pound, and it did not pay taxes, guano, and farm supplies." [21]

In the factory slums of the New South, where tenement houses had hardly weathered gray yet, hunger and destitution

[19] Quoted in the *Constitution*, Jan. 3, 1892.
[20] Read into the *Record* by Watson, *Cong. Record*, 52 Cong., 1 Sess., Jan. 27, 1892, p 600.
[21] Mrs. W. H. Felton, *Memoirs of Georgia Politics*, p. 656.

prevailed. The Atlanta *Journal* reported that just outside Atlanta in the workers' district of the Exposition Mills—the mills that occupied the same buildings in which Henry Grady hailed the birth of the New South just ten years before—"famine and pestilence are to-day making worse ravages than among the serfs of Russia." The mill workers are paid "the magnificent sum of 36 cents a day for their labor, and . . . the average wage fund in the factory district is 9 cents a head divided among the members of the family." The bodies of their dead remain unburied. One may see "rooms wherein eight and ten members of one family are stricken down, where pneumonia and fever and measles are attacking their emaciated bodies; where there is no sanitation, no help or protection from the city, no medicine, no food, no fire, no nurses—nothing but torturing hunger and death." [22]

"There is a song in the fields where the plowshare gleams," wrote the heir to Grady's editorial chair, "a song of hope for the harvest ahead, and the man at the plow-handles seems happier than he has been, as the furrows are formed at his feet." "Yes," answered Tom Watson, " 'there is a song in the field'— and it begins, 'Good-by, old party, Good-by,' and ends with a cheer for the St. Louis platform." Patrick Walsh was more forthright in his appeal: "We know the farmers of the South are impoverished and discontented," but "Better, a thousand times better, suffer the ills of the present, suffer poverty, rather than . . . division and separation from the Democratic party."

The farmers felt differently about poverty and the Democratic party. In Watson's district "as well as all over the State . . . the People's party element have been meeting twice a month, on Saturday afternoon, in schoolhouses, for two years, and signal fires are on every hilltop. They are imbued with the spirit of turning things upside down." [23]

The Democratic campaign against Watson's reëlection, and

[22] Quoted in *P. P. P*, April 14, 1892.
[23] Washington *Post*, Aug. 3, 1892.

against Populism in general, had no beginning. It was simply continuous with the battle of 1890. Livingston spent a good part of the spring of 1892 on a speaking campaign throughout Georgia against Watson and Populism. At his home town, however, the local Alliance met before he spoke and endorsed the People's party and the St. Louis platform. The same action was taken in other places where he spoke. At Douglasville the revolt was dramatized by circumstances. A mixed throng was waiting at the courthouse yard to hear Livingston meet a Populist champion in debate, when the president of the county Alliance mounted the steps, announced that the Democratic speaker would not abide by the terms of the debate agreement, and called upon all who counted themselves Populists to adjourn to the Alliance warehouse across the railroad. "Cross over the railroad bridge so everybody can see," yelled someone. "With cheer upon cheer the great crowd swayed and broke—the great majority of those composing it turned their steps toward the warehouse," crossing over the high, arched footbridge into the rebel ranks.[24]

The Democratic State Central Committee met and issued an appeal to the people of the Tenth District. "The chief of the Third Party in Georgia [C. C. Post] is a Republican and an infidel," they proclaimed. "He believes neither in Democracy nor in our God." Populism is the work of "selfish and designing men" who preferred, "like Satan, to rule in hell [rather] than serve in Heaven. . . . Come back, brethren, to the good old Democratic ship. . . . Come back, brethren, come back."[25] An eminent Methodist divine informed the people that a Populist victory would result in "negro supremacy," "mongrelism," and the "destruction of the Saxon womanhood of our wives and daughters."[26] It was reported that merchants were refusing

[24] *P. P. P*, April 21, 1892; *Constitution*, April 21, 1892.
[25] Augusta *Herald*, April 20, 1892
[26] T. Warren Aiken, quoted in Atlanta *Journal*, April 7, 1892.

226

credit to all farmers who did not disavow the intention of voting the Populist ticket.

The old party was shrewd in its selection of a candidate to oppose Watson in his race for reëlection. Major James Conquest Cross Black, an Augusta lawyer, was the very blossom of middle-class respectability and conservatism. He was a deacon in the Baptist Church and for years had conducted an adult Sunday school class. Born in Kentucky in 1842, he had served as a private in the Confederate Army. His title of "Major" was honorary, after the Southern manner.[27]

His path and Watson's had crossed before—once when the Major offered his legal services to the latter in the Tutt shooting scrape; again when Watson seconded his nomination for the United States Senate against Henry Grady's candidate, Colquitt. Since then their paths had diverged sharply. In 1890 Black had publicly denounced the Farmers' Alliance. He summed up his political ideology by saying, "He was a Democrat because he was a Georgian." His eloquence was mentioned in terms of awe. It was reported that "an Augusta lawyer actually and seriously asked for a new trial in a case when a jury had assessed heavy damage" on the ground that Major Black's eloquence "had swept the jury beyond bounds of propriety and practicability." The Superior Court, however, held that "nobody but God Almighty could fix the bounds or limit the influence of human eloquence."

Not content to rely upon Black's God-given eloquence, however, his party rushed its heaviest oratorical artillery to Watson's district. A special election to fill the insignificant office of county ordinary in Glascock brought Senator Gordon, Governor William J. Northen, Patrick Walsh, and Major Black down upon the citizens' heads. Governor Northen informed the voters that C. C. Post was an "infidel," and "anarchist," and, on top

[27] *Biographical Directory of the American Congress, 1774–1927;* Augusta *Chronicle,* Aug. 21, 1892

227

of that, "an infamous cur." His wife was "an atheist herself," who "makes $1,000 a month selling her damnable heresy." It was no breach of the code of Southern chivalry to attack Mrs. Post because "she has unsexed [*sic*] herself." When Mrs. Post denied the charge and Mr. Post resented it, the Democratic press advocated "a sound caning and notice to leave the state," for having "cast the lie in the face of Georgia's chief executive." Mobbing was too good for "the atheistic, anarchistic, communistic editor of the *People's Party Paper*." [28]

A month later the Governor renewed the attack, "setting the crowd wild" when he asked, "Shall they strike down Gordon and uphold Post, the foulest of God's creatures?" At this, it was reported, "Every drop of blood seemed to boil in the veins of the patriotic audience." The Governor then read what he alleged was Jerry Simpson's charge, "that our men sold their honor and our women their virtue." General Gordon interrupted to say, "My God! Hear that, Third Party men. Hear that!" It was said that "A look of solemn thought that could not be mistaken spread over the faces of the Third Party division of the audience." General Gordon, who introduced himself as "a farmer and nothing but a farmer," also spoke in an informing manner of "this preacher of atheism, this sympathizer with bloody-handed anarchy, this shameless defamer of our spotless, pure and peerless Southern womanhood. (Cries of Never, Never, Never.)" Major Black, said the General, "illustrates that lofty and chivalric manhood, which next to the South's peerless womanhood, is her most flawless crown of immortality." In discussing Watson's candidacy, he pointed out that he was "base," "false," "cowardly," and a "self-important little fly." In answer to Watson's searching article on Gordon's fantastic political and business career, the General reviewed his own record in the Confederate Army.[29]

[28] *P. P. P*, May 27, 1892; Macon *Telegraph*, May 28, 1892; clippings, Northen Scrapbooks, Vol. II, pp. 89-90.
[29] Augusta *Chronicle*, June 11 and 15, 1892; *P. P. P.*, May 13 and June 24, 1892.

"Senators left the halls of Congress," wrote Watson from Washington, "and swooped down to the attack; Governors left the State House and flopped down to the attack; chairmen of executive committees, editors" joined them in the strife, and with what result? The Populist candidate for county ordinary was quietly elected by more than a two to one majority. It was the first Populist victory over the Democrats at the polls in Georgia.

An addition to the ranks of the Populist delegation came by the belated conversion of Thomas E. Winn of the Ninth Georgia District. No radical crusader, he explained with lamentable deficiency of humor: "I stand ready to go with my people, and say in the language of Ruth to Naomi, 'Entreat me not to leave thee, or to return from following after thee. For whither thou goest I will go . . .' "

Georgia Democrats were thoroughly alarmed by the prospects, but, because this was presidential election year, they could not—as they did in 1890—make sweeping pledges of radical reform. Bound to their reactionary capitalist allies of the East, they obediently chose Cleveland electors at their state convention. Watson described this meeting: "Protectionists like Pat Walsh and Evan Howell, sweetly smiled as they swallowed the pill on the Tariff Question. And the Cleveland men like Hoke Smith tried to look pretty as they voted for Free Silver, which Cleveland repudiated. And the 'Alliance Democrats' strove to appear happy in a convention which scornfully spat upon their demands." After the national convention nominated Cleveland, Watson rejoiced: "The Harrison and Cleveland wings of Plutocracy have been driven in upon each other, and are open to an aggressive movement. The atmosphere has cleared wonderfully and the battle is now on." [30]

At the national convention of the People's party in Omaha, Watson's lieutenants, Post, Ellington, and Branch, played prom-

[30] *P. P. P*, June 24, May 27, 1892; *National Economist*, May 28, 1892.

229

inent roles.[31] The third party, particularly in the solidarity of the Southern states, suffered an irreparable injury in the death of Colonel L. L. Polk a few weeks before the convention. His nomination for the Presidency was practically agreed upon. Being a Southerner of wide popularity, he would have provided a powerful opponent of Cleveland in the South.[32] The nomination of General James B. Weaver, a Western veteran of many reform battles, was thought unfortunate by some, particularly in the South. C. C. Post, in changing Georgia's vote to Weaver, said his state had been one of the strongest opponents of the nominee. Watson, along with other Southerners, had been mentioned as a possible nominee for Vice President,[33] but the nomination went to General James G. Field of Virginia to balance the Union general on the ticket.

The first state convention of the Populists in Georgia appears to have been a model of harmony. The delegates met unpledged, and nominated candidates (none of whom had spoken in their own behalf) by acclamation, "and without resort to ballot." The main purpose of the delegates, observed a Democratic paper, seemed to have been "to glorify Watson, and they did it elaborately and with unction." Enthusiasm and confidence were boundless.[34]

Through all these events Watson had remained in Washington. The news that he was returning to take personal command in Georgia was greeted by newspaper men with cheers. "It means that whatever the rest of the earth may do, the good old tenth district will furnish its full proportion of news . . . there may be no news at all, but the night editor sitting at his desk may feel no fear; the tenth district will be astir. From one end to the other its political fires will be ablaze and plenty of choice, entertaining news will come in every night. . . . The Colonel [Wat-

[31] E. A. Allen, *Life and Public Services of James Baird Weaver*, pp 52-120.
[32] Joseph C. Manning, *op. cit*, pp. 32-33; Watson in *P P. P.*, June 17, 1892; and Post in *P P. P*, May 27, 1892
[33] *Constitution*, July 19, 1892.
[34] Augusta *Chronicle*, July 28, 1892; *P P P.*, July 27, 1892.

230

son] has in him those picturesque elements that appeal to the newspaper mind. He is not prosaic. He is individual. He illuminates his public career with the brilliance of imagination."

Before the train reached the border of his district it was met at every station by cheering crowds of Populists and boarded by a delegation who accompanied him home. At Thomson between four and five thousand "yeomen" met him, carried him on their shoulders to a gaily decorated carriage, and drew him to a stand erected for his speech. "Proud Caesar," said the *Chronicle,* "never entered the gates of imperial Rome with more pomp and éclat than did Mr. Watson enter Thomson today." He addressed them for two hours and a half, giving a detailed account of his "stewardship," arraigning the Democratic party, and making a plea to "wipe out the color line, and put every man on his citizenship irrespective of color." [35]

It was observed by several that he looked "pale and emaciated" upon his return. At the end of his speech he was seized with a violent fit of vomiting. His greatly increased burden was apparently telling on his strength. C. C. Post had managed party affairs during Watson's absence, but not long after Governor Northen's vicious attack upon him and his wife, a mob at Quitman attacked Peek, the Populist candidate for Governor, and Post, striking Post with a rock. Whether because he believed his life endangered or for some other reason, it was immediately after this—on the day Watson arrived from Washington—that Post announced that he was leaving for Michigan.[36]

Stranded in the midst of a seething battle without an official leader, the party now leaned for leadership upon Watson. On his shoulders also fell the editorship of the *People's Party Paper.* To these burdens was added the handicap the Democrats had devised in 1891 by gerrymandering his district so as to exclude two old counties and add two new ones, Hancock and Wilkin-

[35] Augusta *Chronicle,* Aug. 10, 1892; T. E. W., *Life and Speeches,* p. 13; P. P. P., Aug 12, 1892.

[36] *Constitution,* Aug 10, Sept. 16, 1892: On Post's prominence in the party, prior to this, see the *Constitution,* March 31 and April 15, 1892

son. The new counties, observed Watson in his private Journal, "had not belonged to my District when I was elected and therefore did not understand the issues upon which I had defeated Hon. Geo. T. Barnes." [37] This meant additional campaigning and organization. Watson's victory in Burke County, which was now removed, had been "considered by politicians as the most important victory of his campaign" in 1890.

Along with these discouragements and handicaps there were a few happier experiences. On his return he was greeted with the first number of *The Revolution*, a new Populist paper published in Augusta, bearing under its title the quotation, " 'Not a Revolt; It's a Revolution'—Thomas E. Watson." This along with *The Wool Hat* of Gracewood provided a genuine, if crude, expression of the feelings of the radical farmer element. His own paper reported twenty-two Populist papers published in Georgia in September, 1892. The throngs of cheering rebels that gathered at county seat and cross roads to hear their hero, carried silken banners thirty and forty feet long inscribed with Populist slogans and pictures of Watson. To the tune of "The Bonny Blue Flag" they sang "The Young Wife's Song," written by Watson:

My husband came from town last night
As sad as man could be;
His wagon empty—cotton gone—
And not a dime had he.
He sat down there before the fire,
His eyes were full of tears;
Great God! how debt is crushing down
This strong man—young in years!

Huzza! Huzza! It's queer I do declare!
We make the food for all the world,
Yet live on scanty fare.[38]

[37] MS Journal 2 (under date 1892).
[38] Broadside, copy in Watson MSS

Although Major Black accepted Watson's formal challenge, and several meetings occurred between them, the three months' campaign that followed was far from resembling a formal debate. It was a bitter struggle that raged back and forth across the state, its most intense battles centering in the Tenth District. The "debates" were seldom more than party rallies, where rival generals reviewed their troops and made a show of force.

At Thomson Black repeated some of the usual charges against C. C. Post. C. H. Ellington, president of the State Alliance, leaped up to defend Post. "And we are not ashamed of him!" he shouted. The next moment "pistols and knives were drawn and the adherents of the two parties stood before one another at bay. . . . Bloodshed and wholesale riot was only narrowly averted." One fight broke out after the meeting, and the following day Ellington and a Democrat fought in the streets of Thomson.[39]

In providing special trains to the rallies, the railroads were obliged to set apart separate cars for the two parties. Even then strife was not prevented. As a train pulled out of Thomson, a passenger yelled out, "Hurrah for Col. Black! Watson is a deserter from the Democratic party and sold out!" "You are a God damned liar," asserted Watson. The unfortunate Democrat had not reckoned with the vigilance of his man. Over two passengers Watson leaped, laying his defamer low in the aisles and bruising him considerably before they were separated. When the conductor remonstrated the Congressman would brook "no truckling to petty officials of the Southern Railroad." [40]

The audience at Sparta was predominantly Negro, and on the platform with Watson sat a Negro speaker. On the outskirts of the crowd a brass band from the Democratic barbecue, in progress down in the grove, kept up a din. During Watson's speech a man on horseback pushed his way into the crowd shouting, "A free dinner for everybody; you are all invited down to the bar-

[39] Augusta *Chronicle*, Sept. 22, 23, 1892.
[40] *Ibid*, Sept. 13, 1892; *P. P. P.*, Sept. 16, 1892.

becue—white and colored." "You may have the trees," shouted Watson, "but we have got the men; and these men are not going to be enticed away from free, fair discussion of these great public questions by any amount of barbecued beef!" The dusky ranks held firm though dinnerless—even remaining to escort the speaker to his boarding house.

Major Black's constantly reiterated theme was that "it is un-American and un-Christian, arraigning one class against another," that he was "a friend of all classes," and that the farmer's distress was "exaggerated." Watson's repeated answer was that there was "an irrepressible conflict between the farming interests and Democracy . . . between the laboring classes and the old party." As for exaggeration of the farmer's distress: "when I am addressing people who bend over the cotton rows to pick out six-cent cotton which costs them eight cents, there is no need to dwell on the topic." [41]

For forty-five minutes after Black finished his speech at their joint meeting in Augusta, Watson was unable to make himself heard. He finally had to give up the attempt. At the Capitol in Atlanta the following week he was howled down again by an organized band who kept up the cry of "communism," a charge recently made by Governor Northen. If Northen called the Alliance platform "communism," replied Watson, "he ought to know, for he helped to frame that platform."

The following morning at eight o'clock General Weaver, his wife, and their party arrived in Atlanta to fill a speaking engagement. The Populist candidate for President had received a respectful hearing on his Southern tour until he reached Georgia. There the Democratic press whipped up fury against him by charges of "cruelty and oppression" practiced on the people of Tennessee by Weaver during the War. The day before he arrived in Atlanta a gang of Democrats at Macon had rotten-egged General Weaver while he spoke, striking Mrs. Weaver on the head. When he learned of the treatment dealt Watson

[41] *Constitution*, Aug 26, 29, 1892; *P P P*, Sept. 2, 9, 23, 1892.

234

at the Capitol, Weaver canceled all engagements and abandoned his campaign in Georgia. Explaining to the state chairman of the People's party, he wrote:

I find the spirit of organized rowdyism at some of the points visited within the state so great as to render it unadvisable for me to attempt to fill the engagements at points not already reached. Personal indignity was threatened at Waycross . . . at Albany we were met by a howling mob which refused to accord us a respectful hearing . . . at Macon . . . rotten eggs were thrown prior to the introduction of the speakers, one of which struck Mrs. Weaver upon the head.[42]

Watson's reply to these Democratic tactics was stinging. "Remember," he wrote, "that for the first time in the history of the Republic a Presidential candidate has been driven from the hustings, and his wife found no protection in her sex from the brutal attacks of 'Southern chivalry' as represented by Bourbon Democracy! They call us the ragtag scum of creation. Thank God, we have never yet dreamed we could win our way to public favor by insulting women, and striking them in the face with eggs." [43] State chairman Irwin, in a letter "To the Voters of Georgia," proclaimed that, "The scenes that have been enacted in Georgia during the month of September are only repetitions of Revolutionary France before the crisis came. . . . It is generally believed that plans are being perfected to defraud the People's Party of its vote. Vehement rage prevails wherever People's Party speakers obtain a hearing. . . . The times are ominous. They resemble the days that preceded secession and civil war. There will be bloodshed and death unless there is a change." [44]

To the plea made to Governor Northen by the Populist candidate for Governor, that the Governor assist him in obtaining a fair division of election managers, Northen, after considerable delay, replied that he could "see no reason now to believe that

[42] Fred E. Haynes, *James Baird Weaver*, p. 324; Augusta *Chronicle*, Sept. 24, 1892; *Constitution*, Sept 24-25, 1892; *P. P. P.*, Sept 30, 1892.

[43] *P. P. P*, Oct. 7, 1892; *Chronicle*, Oct. 11, 1892.

[44] *Ibid.*, Sept. 30, 1892.

the proper authorities desire or intend fraud at the coming state election." To the Populists, however, it seemed plain enough that the Democratic machine was bent on employing every device of terror and fraud it had learned and perfected in Reconstruction fights—together with a few new ones.

From Washington, Georgia, was issued a circular addressed "To the Democratic Farmers and Employers of Labor of Wilkes County," and signed by the Democratic chairman of that county. It warned of the impending peril of a Populist victory and advised:

This danger however can be overcome by the absolute control which you yet exercise over your property. It is absolutely necessary that you should bring to bear the power which your situation gives over tenants, laborers and croppers. . . . The success [of the Populists] . . . means regulation of control of rents, wages of labor, regulation of hours of work, and at certain seasons of the year strikes. . . .
The peace, prosperity, and happiness of yourselves and your friends depend on your prompt, vigorous and determined efforts to control those who are to such a large extent dependent upon you.[45]

Other Democratic handbills and circulars flooded Watson's district: one to prove that he had defeated "a Worthy Colored Man's Claim in Congress"; another on "Peek's Slavery Bill," with illustrations depicting Peek and Watson putting chains on tenants, croppers, and Negroes; another on Watson's opposition to the colored contestant's claim upon a seat in the Georgia Legislature in 1882; another to prove him in the pay of Republican bosses.[46]

As the day of the state election approached threats became coercion and coercion turned into bloodshed and open battle. The *Chronicle* reported three homicides in Augusta in a few days preceding the election, which, according to the editor, were "the natural results of paternal, socialistic and communistic utterances of reckless third party leaders." On election day, Dan Bowles,

[45] Circular, dated Sept. 8, 1892, Watson MSS.
[46] Circulars, handbills, and clippings, Northen Scrapbooks, Vol. II.

Democrat, was "marching a line of 50 negro voters to the polls" six miles out of Augusta when he encountered a group of Populists. Isaac Horton, a Negro Populist, sought to disengage one Negro from the line, and a general fight ensued. Bowles shot Horton through the heart. Verdict, "justifiable homicide." On the same day, in Augusta, Henry Head, a Democratic deputy sheriff, was shot through the stomach while attempting to arrest Arthur Glover, secretary of the Populist Campaign Club in the Fifth Ward, a workers' district. Glover escaped to the South Carolina woods, a posse after him.[47]

At Rukersville, Elbert County, a white man, a Populist this time, was on his way to the polls with "a squad of negroes and white men," when encountered by B. H. Head and other Democrats. Head recognized in the Populist "squad" some Negroes "who had once lived with him and who bore the name of Head." Becoming infuriated, Head picked up a wagon standard and struck an old Negro. The Negro's son then struck Head, after which the latter ran across the street to his home, returned with a double-barrelled shot-gun, and "deliberately shot down two Negroes," one of whom died. Another white Democrat drew a pistol and shot three Negroes, after which the Populists were driven from the polls. One estimate had it that fifteen Negroes were killed by Democrats in Georgia during the state election. "If the law cannot protect us," warned a correspondent of Tom Watson, "we will protect ourselves with Winchesters." [48]

Watson professed to be encouraged by the results of the state election. The Populist candidate for Governor was defeated by a two-to-one vote. "But three months have passed," Watson reminded the Democrats, "between the organization of the People's Party and the election, and in the rock-ribbed state of Georgia more than one-third of the hosts assembled at the polls adhered to the People's banner." [49]

[47] Augusta *Chronicle*, Oct. 6, 1892.
[48] *Farmer's Light*, Oct. 20, 1892; *P. P. P.*, Oct. 14, 1892.
[49] *P. P. P*, Oct. 21, 1892.

With the state election out of the way, the Democratic machine could now concentrate its full attention upon the fight on Watson. "So intense is the interest and concern felt in the campaign," said the *Constitution*, "that even here in Atlanta . . . nothing is talked of except the race between Black and Watson. Men declared at the democratic headquarters yesterday that they would much prefer to see Black elected than Cleveland. They viewed it as the supremest issue in Georgia to beat Watson, for they declare that he will endanger the peace and prosperity of the South if his incendiary speeches are not hushed." [50]

The election in the Tenth stirred interest in a wider circle. "The first question asked by everyone when the probabilities of the South are considered is, 'What are Watson's chances?'" "Mr. Watson is now a national character and there is not a single congressional contest going on in the nation that is being looked upon with as much interest as the one in his district." [51] President Cleveland was reported to have remarked to a group of Georgians after the election that "he was almost as much interested in Major Black's campaign in the Tenth district of Georgia as he was in his own election." [52]

Others in the North made more practical manifestations of their interest in the defeat of Tom Watson. Augusta business men made personal appeals to their financial connections, "especially those in New York City," for campaign funds. They argued that Watson was "a sworn enemy of capital, and that his defeat was a matter of importance to every investor in the country." The New York *Tribune* reported that, "Insurance and railroad companies responded liberally, so that $40,000 was in hand for use, in addition to the local funds." [53]

After his experience with his opponents' methods in the state election, Watson could not face the Congressional election with-

[50] *Constitution*, Oct. 23, 1892
[51] *National Watchman*, quoted in *P. P P.*, Nov. 4, 1892
[52] Savannah *Press*, quoted in *P. P. P.*, April 7, 1893
[53] New York *Tribune*, Dec. 20, 1892, quoted in *P. P P*, Dec 30, 1892

out misgivings. "They have intimidated the voter, assaulted the voter, murdered the voter," he wrote. "They have bought votes, forced votes, and stolen votes. They have incited lawless men to a pitch of frenzy which threatens anarchy." To his private Journal he confided: "It was almost a miracle I was not killed in the campaign of 1892. Threats against my life were frequent and there were scores of men who would have done the deed and thousands who would have sanctioned it. Fear of the retaliation which my friends would inflict prevented my assassination— nothing else." [54] Governor Northen was heard to say that "Watson ought to be killed and that it ought to have been done long ago." [55]

"There is no wiping out the fact that this is a revolution," observed a Populist paper, "and it depends upon the enemy whether it shall be a peaceful or a bloody one. To be candid about the matter we believe it will be the latter." [56]

One of the most zealous and effective workers for Watson's cause was H. S. Doyle, a young Negro preacher. In the face of repeated threats upon his life, Doyle made sixty-three speeches during the campaign in behalf of Watson's candidacy. Toward the close of the campaign Doyle met with a threat of lynching (called "imaginary" by the Democratic press) at Thomson, and fled to Watson for protection. Watson installed him on his private grounds and sent out riders on horseback for assistance. All night armed farmers roared into the village. The next morning the streets were "lined with buggies and horses foaming and tired with travel." All that day and the next night they continued to pour in until "fully two thousand" Populists crowded the village—arms stacked on Watson's veranda. Prominent among them was the Populist sheriff of McDuffie County. They marched to the courthouse under arms, where they were addressed by Doyle and Watson. "We are determined," said the

[54] MS Journal 2.
[55] Affidavit of Mrs. Artenia Hall, Warren County, Oct. 31, 1892. Watson MSS.
[56] *Farmer's Light*, quoted in Augusta *Chronicle*, Oct. 23, 1892.

latter, "in this free country that the humblest white or black man that wants to talk our doctrine shall do it, and the man doesn't live who shall touch a hair of his head, without fighting every man in the people's party." The farmers remained on guard for two nights.[57]

"After that," testified Doyle, "Mr. Watson was held almost as a savior by the Negroes. The poor ignorant men and women, who so long had been oppressed, were anxious even to touch Mr. Watson's hand, and were often a source of inconvenience to him in their anxiety to see him and shake hands with him, and even to touch him."

The spectacle of white farmers riding all night to save a Negro from lynchers was rather rare in Georgia. So shocking was the incident to the Democratic press, so clearly subversive of order and tradition, that their indignation knew no bounds. "Watson has gone mad," announced the *Chronicle*, and the *Constitution* gravely agreed. The whole South was "threatened with anarchy and communism" because of "the direful teachings of Thomas E. Watson."

That the danger to Doyle was not imaginary seems indicated by the fact that the following week, when he was speaking at Louisville, a shot intended for the speaker struck a white man in the back and killed him. Two days later when Watson and Doyle spoke at Davisboro they were accompanied by a guard of forty men carrying rifles. The following week another Negro was shot and killed by a white Democrat in the county where the previous murder occurred. At Dalton a Negro man, who had spoken for Populism, was murdered at his home by unknown men.[58]

From Watson's town came the report that "nearly all the ladies whose husbands are democrats have left Thomson, and

---

[57] *Contested Election Case of Thomas E. Watson vs. J. C. C. Black* (Washington, 1896), pp. 669, 683, 717, 781, 793-794; *Constitution*, Oct 25-27, 1892; *Chronicle*, Oct 26, 1892.

[58] *Watson vs. Black*, p. 781; Augusta *Chronicle*, Nov 4, 8 and 10, 1892; *P. P. P.*, Oct. 26, 1892

many democratic families have moved away, as they feared their lives were in danger." The mayor of the city appealed to Governor Northen for "six or eight hundred soldiers" on election day, for fear "the third party people would burn the town and massacre the democrats." A battalion in Atlanta and three companies in Augusta received "orders to march to Thomson at a moment's notice." [59]

A careful scholar's characterization of the Georgia election of 1892 as a "solemn farce" admits of possible error only in the choice of the adjective.[60] That it was a farce is clear enough. Reconstruction practices of terror, fraud, corruption, and trickery were all revived. Democrats found little difficulty in identifying the "cause" of 1892 with the "cause" of 1872, and justified any means by calling the end holy. Populists retaliated in kind to some extent, but they were not nearly so skillful or successful.

Federal supervisors under the direction of United States marshals were in attendance at the polling in Augusta, but against the Democratic local police they were powerless to prevent wholesale repeating, bribery, ballot-box stuffing, voting of minors, and intimidation. Negro plantation hands and laborers were hauled to town in wagon loads, marched to the polls in squads, and voted repeatedly. Negroes were hauled across the Savannah River from South Carolina in four-horse wagon loads and voted in Augusta. Whiskey was dispensed by the barrel in Augusta wagon yards, and cash payment made to voters.[61]

By such methods as these Watson was defeated. At that, he carried by ample majorities all counties within his district before it was gerrymandered, with the exception of Richmond. Of the two new counties, Wilkinson's vote was nearly a tie, and scores of Populist votes were "not allowed," while the irregularities in Hancock were notorious. Most flagrant were the abuses in Rich-

[59] Atlanta *Journal*, Nov. 7, 1892
[60] A. M. Arnett, *op cit.*, pp. 153-155.
[61] *Contested Election Case of Thomas E. Watson vs. J. C. C. Black* (Washington, 1893), *passim*; *Contested Election Case of Thomas E. Watson vs. J C. C. Black* (Washington, 1896), *passim*; P. P. P , Feb. 10, 1893.

mond County, where Black received 10,776 of the total of 17,772 votes he received in the whole district. The total vote in Augusta was about double the number of legal voters.[62]

The attitude of many Democrats in Georgia was much the same as that expressed by those of Alabama over the same election: "Yes, we counted you out. What are you going to do about it?" It even crept into unguarded paragraphs of Democratic editorials. At Augusta the victors celebrated by an elaborate funeral ceremony, in which "Watson was laid out in great state."

"Who believes it?" asked Watson of the result. "Not the Democratic bosses who stole the ballots. Not the managers who threw out returns. Not the newspapers who have to 'cook' their news with such care. Not even the candidates who received the stolen goods. Nobody believes it. Least of all do we of the People's party." In one month, between the state and the national election, the Democratic majority dwindled from 71,000 to 31,000. "So we decided not to die. We unanimously decided to postpone the funeral."[63]

He proclaimed himself undismayed at the result. Considering the fact that not a single daily paper in the state was friendly to the Populists, that "all the machinery was against us; all the power of the 'ins'; all the force of old habit and old thought; all the unseen but terrible cohorts of ignorance and prejudice and sectionalism," as well as "all the money . . . all the concentrated hatred of capital, special privilege," he refused to take too tragic a view of the election returns. The national poll of the third party was truly phenomenal, but its greatest hope—the breakup of the Solid South—was disappointed. Watson's work was still before him.

With spontaneous impulse the defeated hordes of Populists marched on Thomson from all over the district to voice their feelings against the fraudulent election and commiserate with

[62] New York *Tribune*, Dec. 20, 1892; P. P. P., Dec. 30, 1892; MS. Journal 2, p. 524.

[63] *P. P P.*, Dec. 9, 1892

their leader. "Four thousand then," announced Watson. "Six thousand today, and growing stronger and stronger as Democratic methods and frauds become more apparent." At ten in the morning the firing of a small cannon, which they brought with them, announced the arrival of the delegation from Richmond. It had marched from Augusta to Watson's doorstep—a distance of thirty-seven miles! With much heat and enthusiasm resolutions condemning the election methods were adopted, and $877.95 was raised (much of it in small coin) to finance a contest of Black's election before the House.[64]

Before he returned to Washington for the second term, Watson announced that he would "in all possible and proper ways carry on the third party fight. I am determined never to give it up as long as I live." [65]

[64] *P. P. P.*, Dec. 9, 1892.
[65] *Constitution*, Dec. 11, 1892.

243

CHAPTER XIV

Populism on the March

FEW LEGISLATIVE ACTS in the history of Congress have had so many willing claimants upon its authorship as that which established rural free delivery of mails. At least seven public men have expressed anxiety to be known as the "Father of the R. F. D." The heated dispute over the paternity of this measure is to be understood only when the momentous changes it worked in rural life are taken into account, and when the farmer's previous isolation is considered. Not one farmer in three hundred got a daily paper in the 'nineties, and those who lived five miles or more from a post office were fortunate to get their mail once a week. It is not surprising that the rural population of the country has been confronted from time to time with several men to claim their gratitude for initiating the rural free delivery.[1]

When Tom Watson called to witness "every rural free delivery box in Georgia and every other state from the lakes to the gulf, from sea to sea" as evidence of his accomplishment (as he not infrequently did), he could back his claim with proof such as no one of his rival "fathers" could advance. Indisputably, he had introduced the resolution providing for the first appropriation that the United States ever made for rural free delivery.

Credit for starting agitation for rural free delivery belongs to John M. Stahl, an Illinois editor, who began his extensive campaign in 1879. Unable to make any impression upon Congress,

[1] John M. Stahl, *Growing with the West*, pp. 103-104.

though having strong support among farmers, he complained of the opposition from little postmasters, who formed a body of some fifty thousand enemies of a change that would jeopardize their jobs. Friends of free delivery must therefore "overcome the indisposition of the Congressmen to abolish a good part of their political machinery," of which the postmasters were :'ie framework. "In truth," observed Stahl, "those Congressmen first to favor farmer mail delivery were conscientious, courageous men." The notorious star route contractors and the rural merchant who feared competition through the mails were two other vested interests in the opposition.

In the first session of the Fifty-second Congress both Watson and Livingston had introduced resolutions to provide appropriations for rural free delivery, but each had been ruled out of order.[2] Watson asked "whether the delivery of mail matter free to the people who live near the post office, while those who live farther away are obliged to go for their mail, is not a false system?" He pleaded for "one tax system which treats the poor at least as fairly as it treats the rich."[3]

In February of the second session Watson renewed his effort, this time evading the House rules that blocked his way before. His resolution took the form of an amendment to a paragraph of the Post office appropriation bill, reducing the expenditure slightly and directing that $10,000 of the total appropriation be used by the Postmaster-General in "experimental free-delivery in rural communities other than towns and villages."[4] In the galleries when the resolution was read sat John M. Stahl, who had decided that Watson was "the best man to present to the House the proposition." After urging this legislation for thirteen years, he felt this moment was the most exciting of his life.

Objection to the resolution was immediately raised on the ground that its purpose was "already provided for." The objec-

[2] *Cong Record*, 52 Cong , 1 Sess , June 1, 1892, pp. 4927-4928
[3] *Ibid* , May 27, 1892, p 4769; May 28, 1892, pp. 4801-4803; P P. P., June 3, 1893.
[4] *Cong. Record*, 52 Cong , 2 Sess , Feb 17, 1893, p. 1759

tion had reference to a scheme of free delivery sponsored by Postmaster-General Wanamaker and passed by the preceding Congress, which provided for experimental delivery in "rural communities," interpreted to mean small towns and villages. Stahl thought this plan was being used to "throw dust in the eyes of those that really wished to aid the farmers." Watson insisted on his own interpretation. He meant "absolutely rural communities, that is to say, in the country pure and simple, amongst the farmers, in those neighborhoods where they do not get their mail more than once in every two weeks . . ." [5]

The resolution was passed. Having the backing of John Steele Henderson, chairman of the Committee on Post Offices and Post Roads, it was seen safely through the House, escaped debate in the Senate, was signed by the President, and became law.

In spite of the fact that the language of Watson's resolution was mandatory, Cleveland's Postmaster-General Bissell, appointed March 7, 1893, chose to interpret it as "discretionary," and refused to expend the money for the purpose indicated. In this he reflected the opinion of President Cleveland, who regarded rural free delivery as a "craze" that made a preposterous drain upon the Treasury. In his message of December 3, 1894, Cleveland said: "The estimated cost of rural free delivery generally is so very large that it ought not to be considered in the present condition of affairs." The Administration was severely condemned by members of its own party for ignoring the will of Congress, and a second appropriation of $20,000 was added to the first appropriation at the next Congress. It was not, however, until the last quarter of 1896 that either of the two appropriations was used for the experiments indicated. It was out of these experiments, provided for in Watson's earlier resolution, that the modern system of rural free delivery grew. [6]

Along party lines Watson renewed the hopeless program of

[5] *Cong. Record,* 52 Cong., 2 Sess., Feb. 17, 1893, p. 1759.
[6] Archibald Henderson, series of articles on R. F. D., in Raleigh *News and Observer,* Jan. 13 and 28 and Feb 10, 1935; *vide* also John M Stahl, *op cit*, pp. 120-141.

introducing bills to enact the demands of the Populist platform. One was a bill "to prohibit further issue of bonds under the acts of 1875 and 1879"; another sought "to increase the currency and provide for its distribution through homestead land loans"; and still another renewed in modified form the subtreasury bill. None of these bills was ever reported out of the committee room.[7]

On labor legislation he took up the fight with the same zeal he had shown in his attack on the Pinkerton strike breakers. "I will stay here till the ants tote me out of the keyhole before I will give up this fight," he informed the opposition to the bill requiring railroads to install automatic car-couplers and air-brakes as safety devices. He was "tired of this eternal fashion of the railroads bossing this House," he said, referring to lobbyists in the galleries. "Mr. Speaker, I appeal to this majority; let us assert our manhood one time; let us make the corporations retreat one time; let us stand by the people one time, and we will go home having redeemed in some measure the otherwise discreditable record of the Fifty-second Congress."[8]

In the Cutting militia bill Watson discovered what he pronounced a "covert, stealthy" attempt to convert the state militias into a "national guard, a national body." He condemned it as a step in the direction of centralization, done in imitation of "old world militarism." Watson was the most outspoken opponent of the bill in the House. He later claimed credit for defeating this attempt to "centralize the military strength of the laboring people and the farmers of the country under the heel of such men as Grover Cleveland."[9]

* * * * * *

[7] *Cong. Record,* 52 Cong , 2 Sess , Jan 4, 1893, p 324; Jan 9, 1893, p. 460; Feb. 2, 1893, p. 1118; P P. P , May 12, 1893.

[8] *Cong Record,* 52 Cong , 2 Sess., Feb. 21, 1893, p. 1972; P. P. P , March 3, 1893.

[9] *Cong. Record,* 52 Cong , 2 Sess., Jan 14, 1893, pp. 568-569; P. P. P , Sept. 18, 1896.

The adjournment of the Fifty-second Congress ended Tom Watson's career in office for a period that was to last for more than a quarter of a century—though it by no means ended his active political life. If anything, he was politically more important out of office than in. All his energies were now released for a more congenial employment, one for which he was better suited in temperament. It was not in office, but out among the people preaching a crusade that he found his true rôle, and that was the rôle he played until near the end of his life.

Upon his return to Georgia, Watson immediately opened a bombardment against the Cleveland administration that was to continue relentlessly for four years. Personally, he said, he regarded President Cleveland as a man of honor and courage. He also regarded Cleveland as the agent of his sworn enemy, Eastern capitalism, and as a standing menace to every aspiration he entertained for the rehabilitation of agrarian power, economic and political. The task outlined for Watson, as he saw it, lay in winning the Southern Democrat over from his bondage to the enemy. In this regard his instructions to Populist stump speakers are enlightening:

Dwell untiringly upon the fact that the Eastern and Northern Democrat is as much our enemy upon all questions of finance and taxation as the Eastern and Northern Republican.

Explain with all the might that is in you the identity of interests between the South and West; and the antagonism of interest between the South and the East and North;—then ask the country Democrat why he should follow the bosses who allow the South to be plundered in the interest of the Eastern and Northern plutocrats.

Load your guns in this way, men, and you'll hit the bull's eye every crack.[10]

Shortly after his return from Washington, the *Constitution* printed an interview with Watson that clearly showed he was taking a long and deliberate view of the crusade he planned. "I

[10] *P. P. P*, July 21, 1893.

think," said he, "Mr. Cleveland is going to precipitate a conflict between his views and those of the Southern and Western Democrats on that subject [currency]. He is in favor of a bonded debt, national banks, gold standard and all that Wall Street schedule of finance." It was obvious that "Northern and Eastern Democrats do not talk as we do, and their interests are diametrically opposed to our interests . . . and when Mr. Cleveland forces the issue, he will get the worst of it. I think he will draw off into his party all those men up there in the North and East, while the liberal and truly Democratic elements in the South and West will gravitate together with the Populists." [11]

For their part, the Southern Democrats began to view with increasing alarm the first signs of a fulfillment of the Populist leader's prophecy. A large majority of the population, the farmers, had known little but depression since the late 'eighties; but now the panic of 1893 was swiftly spreading its gloom over factory and city. Banks failed, money disappeared, factories closed, unemployed workers returned to the family farm to add burden to its meager larder, and the mortgage foreclosures went forward at an accelerated pace. Families of Negro and white tenants walked the roads seeking relief. At no time since the devastation of Georgia by an invading army was acute poverty, hunger, and misery so widespread among the people.[12] Yet with a Democratic President in the White House—the first since Pierce whose party was in a position to control both Houses—they could get no relief. Cleveland's first, indeed his only concern, seemed to them to be to protect the dollar against the debtor sections' demand for relief and fair treatment.

In vain Southern Democrats pleaded with Cleveland to make good the campaign pledges. "The only way to head off the demagogue, and nip the flaming red flower of populism in the bud," urged the *Constitution*, "is to reform the evils now so galling

[11] Quoted in *P. P P.*, April 7, 1893.

[12] Alex M. Arnett, *Populist Movement in Georgia*, pp. 156-167; Charles H. Otken, *Ills of the South, passim.*

and burdensome. In other words, the speedy action of the new administration in redeeming the pledges of the Democratic platform will leave the Populists no grievances to complain of." Unless silver was remonetized, protection and the whole scheme of Republican legislation was wiped out, and that "without unnecessary delay," discontent would "cause the Hon. Jack Cade to loom up as a controlling factor in our politics."

The allusion to "poor Jack Cade" Watson found "extremely unfortunate." Indeed, considering the pitiful price the farmer was paid for his wheat, "why should not some Jack Cade in every city rise today and demand that the ha-penny loaves be sold for a penny?" What of the pretty promises the Democrats made last fall? he asked:

Campaign pledges? Where are they? The man who made them can't be found.

Financial politics are just as Harrison left them. Even more so.

The volume of money grows smaller every day by comparison.

The McKinley Bill sits on the top rail of the fence and crows defiant self-confidence.

And where is Cleveland? . . .

Cleveland has gone fishing.

Watson reprinted every plaintive appeal the Democratic press made to the deaf ears of the administration. "It's a piercing, ear-splitting, insane howl," he wrote. "Every reverberation bespeaks awful, agonizing anxiety. . . . Oh, how they howl for the free silver act. . . . Oh, how they howl for the income tax law. . . . But why does Democracy foolishly hanker after what she can't get? Because she sees that the people are awake and that her future in this State is in jeopardy. The people are no longer blind, no longer sitting in foolish indifference." [13]

The cordial reception given William Jennings Bryan in Atlanta in June was an important sign of the times. It was not without reason that Populists everywhere viewed the times with

[13] *P. P. P*, April 14, June 9, 16, 1893.

250

some satisfaction. "The political situation," observed the *National Watchman*, "is one that can be viewed with absolute complacency. . . . No change for better or worse can be made from present conditions without furnishing an object lesson for a Populist sermon." [14]

* * * * * *

On July 4, at Douglasville, Georgia, Watson launched a statewide campaign that was to proceed almost without interruption for three and a half months. "No political party," publicly admitted the chairman of the Democratic State Central Committee, "has ever carried on in Georgia so thorough and systematic a campaign in an off year as has been and is now being carried on by Mr. Watson . . ." [15]

This was not so much campaign as crusade, for the people did not listen so much as participate. The contemporary accounts of the enthusiasm evoked by the speeches of Watson border on the incredible. Throngs of three to ten thousand people crowded into cross-roads villages from the countryside of a twenty-mile radius. Riding through the open country from town to town, Watson and his party not infrequently met with such experiences as the following: "When within four miles of Sylvania [at six in the morning] we found the road blocked with vehicles of every description. The rumbling, muffled sound of wheels, ploughing through the sand, sounded like the roar of an army wagon train. The atmosphere loaded with dust and cheers. . . . At least 6,000 people were in hearing of his voice, while at least a thousand more wandered around loosely unable to hear a word."

The Southern masses were on the march, deeply stirred by the conviction that this was *their* fight. Watson's party was stopped by crowds at cross-roads stores, schoolhouses, and churches.

[14] Quoted in *P. P. P.*, May 19, 1893.
[15] *Constitution*, Sept. 7, 1893.

251

Bridges along their road were decorated with flowers. Three times during one speech Watson concluded and begged the crowd to seek shelter from a pouring rain, and each time they urged him to continue. The meetings were generally opened by prayer. Watson's speeches were usually begun with long texts from Jefferson, which he expounded in reference to cotton prices, government ownership of railroads, national banks, financial theories of Cleveland, and political equality for the Negro.[16] He did not neglect to portray the part he played in the movement:

> The work I did, *somebody* had to do. The abuse I took *somebody* had to incur. The losses I have sustained *somebody* had to dare.
> I *did* the work, took the abuse, *risked* the loss, and I am proud of it.
> Proud of my record, proud of my principles, proud of my friends.

Not always was the reception of the Populist crusaders so cordial. At Washington, Georgia, where during his 1892 campaign Watson was insulted and baited by a crowd of Democrats, the rumor arose that the Populists were marching on the town 6,000 strong, wagons loaded with Winchesters, to avenge the insult to their leader. Governor Northen issued orders to hold a battalion of Augusta troops ready for marching at short notice. The mayor of Washington ordered the local militia "to lie on its arms" all the night before, as well as the day of the Populist rally. The meeting was peaceful. "Judging from the Wilkes county meeting of today," observed Major McGregor, "I came to the conclusion if Governor Northen don't put the militia 'under arms,' and then under lock and key, so as to keep them from hearing Tom Watson, he won't have a corporal's guard to rally around his Senatorial banner."

While the campaign was in progress President Cleveland called Congress together in extra session to repeal the Sherman Silver Purchase Act. Watson hailed the extra session as "a God-

[16] *P. P P.*, July 7–Oct. 27, 1893

252

send to us." "Into the clear light, where all honest citizens can see, it will bring the schemes of the bosses." He predicted that, "Democrats who hold Republican doctrines will be driven to the Republican party, and *vice versa*. Members of the two old parties who really hold Populist views, finding no support in either Democrat or Republican ranks, will be driven to the People's Party." He cheerfully printed the silver speeches of those Democrats who were firm in their resistance to Cleveland, and made great sport of the effort of the Southern wing of the party to revive the scare of the force bill: "Anything, ANYTHING, to make the people forget how the Democrats helped the Republicans to carry the plans of Wall Street."

The Atlanta *Journal*, controlled by Hoke Smith, a member of Cleveland's Cabinet, suggested that "Editor Tom Watson, of the *People's Party Paper*, ought to sue the Atlanta *Constitution* for damages for infringing on his patent methods of abuse of President Cleveland and the Democratic administration." "By no means," replied Editor Watson. "Let the boys fall into line."

The President was not without apprehensions of the threat of Watson's growing strength in the South. In the spring a Democratic paper had reported: "Mr. Cleveland has been impressed with the idea that the danger in the Tenth district is almost as great now as last year. . . . The President desires to give the party in the district all the machinery and leverage in his power, and he is evidently willing to have government patronage thrown full and fair against the revival of Watsonism in Georgia." [17]

By fall, however, it was plain that much more than Federal patronage would be necessary to stop Watson and save the old party in the state. Economic collapse menaced the Southern farmer. The appeal of Democratic leaders for redemption of platform pledges became shameless in its desperation. In public interview Governor Northen said that Georgia would demand restoration of silver, despite Cleveland. "How could I believe

[17] Savannah *Press*, quoted in *P. P P* April 7, 1893

otherwise," he asked, "when every democrat who holds office in this Government today was pledged upon that demand and upon his personal pledge to that end? The party must redeem all its pledges and redeem them at once." W. Y. Atkinson, chairman of the Democratic State Central Committee, confessed that he awaited the action of Congress with "great anxiety." "If it had not been for those pledges," he said, "neither the October nor the November elections would have resulted as they did. . . . We induced these men to remain in the democratic party by convincing them that the evils of which they complained were the results of Republican legislation." [18]

In reply to a letter from Major J. C. C. Black, asking about political conditions in the state, Governor Northen, in mid-September wrote: "To be candid with you, I am not only uneasy, I am alarmed. I have reached my conclusions without haste." [19] He enclosed a letter he had written to Cleveland, asking Black to deliver it to the President and emphasizing that no publicity must be given the letter. His letter to the President was written with the advice of the party leaders of the state:

Mr. President: Profoundly impressed with the unusual conditions in this State—political and financial—arising from the long-continued delay in helpful legislation by Congress, I respectfully but earnestly urge upon you the expediency of some public expression, somewhat more comprehensive than your recent message, as to the proper policy to be pursued by Congress upon questions affecting the stringency of the times and the needs of the people.

The conditions of this State are fearful and threatening. The people have confidence in your ability and your leadership, and no one thing, in my candid judgment, would go so far towards restoring quiet as a clear statement made to the public by you.

I agree with you fully in believing that: "It may be true that the embarrassments from which the business of the county is suffering

[18] *Constitution*, Aug 15, Sept 7, 1893.
[19] William J Northen to J C. C Black, Sept. 16, 1893, copy in Northen Scrapbooks, Vol III, p 278.

arise as much from evils apprehended as from those actually existing." The result of such apprehension with us begets a lack of confidence in the party in power, and we are rapidly losing strength in this State. Every election held in this State for the past three (3) months has gone against the Democratic party and in favor of the Populists. Ex-Congressman Watson, the leader of the Populists, has taken advantage of the conditions, and is speaking over the State to assemblies never less than 2,000, and sometimes as many as 5,000 people. . . .

Another reason calling for such a statement from you as I ask affects the sale of our farm products and our business relations. Our cotton is now ready for market. There is not sufficient money to handle it. Farmers are compelled to sell, and the price is necessarily reduced. The cotton must be given in settlement of obligations incurred during the early spring. If the stringency remains until these obligations are canceled, and business improves after the crops have been taken from the control of our farmers and fortunes are made by speculators upon the fruits of their labor, while their poverty continues, there can be no hope of holding them to the Democratic party in the next election. If by any means conditions can be improved, and the farmers receive nine or ten cents for their cotton, the party will get the benefit of the advance, and the farmers will remain Democratic.

I beg to assure you of my sympathy in the responsible position you hold before the people and the obligations put upon you by the political party whose leader you are. You have had my earnest advocacy and enthusiastic support from the beginning of the conflict, because I have had unquestioned confidence in your statesmanship and your courage. I write you now because of what I know to be your power to aid us in this state in perpetuating good government as found in the principles of the Democratic party, and especially in relation to the distressed condition of an unsettled and oppressed people. . . .[20]

With the letter were sent clippings from the state press telling the story of Watson's crusade and the result it was having.

President Cleveland's reply, while attempting a conciliatory tone, carried but cold comfort to Southern Democrats, probably

[20] William J. Northen to Grover Cleveland, Sept. 15, 1893, copy in Northen Scrapbooks, Vol. III, pp. 270-272.

doing more harm than good. "I hardly know how to reply to your letter," he began, and continued at length, merely to restate and defend his well-known desire for "sound money" and "the immediate and unconditional repeal of the purchasing clause of the so-called Sherman law." [21]

Cleveland's letter was immediately released to the press, but Northen's letter to Cleveland was carefully guarded. "I intended it to be a confidential FAMILY communication," explained Northen to Clark Howell. "It is based upon the facts that while they are facts, I fear would be hurtful to the general good of the party if they should be published . . ." [22] Though he never saw the letter, Tom Watson ventured some shrewd guesses about its contents. It was a symptom of the Democratic "Blind Staggers" said his paper. "Cleveland's letter to Northen goes all over America and does not rest its heavy feet till it reaches London. But no man knows what Billy said to Grover." Taunting Northen, he dared him to publish the letter. He candidly wrote, "This Northen letter has done us more good than anything that has happened since our Christian Governor called out the military at Washington, Georgia."

As he brought his campaign to a close in October, with a huge barbecue at Thomson, Watson found much to encourage him. He had visited thirty-seven counties, and addressed crowds estimated to total 150,000 people. After a losing struggle of a year, the *People's Party Paper* now boasted a large subscription list. "We go to every state in the Union," said the paper. "In Kansas, Missouri, and Texas, our list is very large. In Georgia we stand second to only one weekly newspaper, the Atlanta *Constitution*. In the Tenth District we stand first." [23] Thirty-five Populist papers in the state were now listed.

Hardly an issue of the *People's Party Paper* appeared without its specimen of Populist poetry—poems usually in celebration

[21] Grover Cleveland to William J Northen, Sept. 25, 1893; Northen Scrapbooks, Vol. III, p. 272; also *vide, Constitution,* Sept. 30, 1893.
[22] William J. Northen to Clark Howell, copy, Northen Scrapbooks, Vol. III, p 279.
[23] Clipping from *P P P*, about Oct. 1. 1893, Watson Scrapbooks.

256

of the virtues and accomplishments of Thomas E. Watson—scores of them. He mentioned "a hamper-basket full of home-made poetry" among one week's contributions. It seemed to him a "good sign"—for politics, whether for letters or not. "Any party which at the age of four years, shows a capacity to produce plentiful supplies of home-made poetry has gum in it," he wrote. "Bound to stick." It should constitute a warning to the old party: "We have already published some of this poetry, as a warning to the Democrats. If they are wise, they will mend their ways, and not provoke our poets too far." [24]

Such optimism did Watson affect that on Thanksgiving Day he offered a prayer of gratitude: "I am sincerely thankful that the storm of political hatred is abating; that a Populist is now considered a shade better than a pickpocket; and that 'Tom Watson' is no longer regarded as a junior partner to the devil." He suggested to Cleveland that they give Democracy a breathing spell. "She needs time to collect her scattered mind."

It was not until the second session of the Fifty-third Congress that Watson's contest of the election of Black in 1892 was brought before the House. He could expect little, of course, from the Democratic majority, but could he place before the public by means of this case a vivid picture of the injustice done him and his party by corrupt Democratic methods, he would strengthen his position appreciably before the public and bring some restraint to bear upon his opponents when they attempted a repetition of their methods in the next election.

Watson had no friends on the Congressional Committee that heard the case, and its report was a whitewash. It mildly deplored "the excesses of overzealous partisans," but concluded that since it was "utterly unable to determine how many repeaters and illegal voters there were . . . or how many of these votes should be deducted from the majority of the contestee," and since the "Democratic Committee, who had charge of the

[24] *P. P. P.*, Nov. 3, 1893.

257

raising and disbursing of the [campaign] money, were the very first citizens of Augusta, and were representing every business and profession, and were all men of the highest character, none higher"—Watson was not entitled to the seat.[25]

The Democratic majority clamped down the lid tightly upon discussion and protest of the report, so tightly that neither members of his party, nor—for the first time in the history of Congress—the contestant himself, was allowed to speak in his behalf. In vain, Pence, a Populist Congressman from Colorado, pleaded that "from the beginning of the history of this House, this is the first time that an opportunity for a contestant to be heard has been cut off; and your rule here will not only cut him off, but will cut off anybody else from discussing the facts in the case." [26] The report was promptly accepted.

The old parties had not dared to allow him to gain the public ear by presenting his own case, said Watson. "They knew perfectly well that the sworn uncontradicted evidence in that record would have stirred honest men everywhere to intense disgust and indignation and revolt." Yet "here was an election which nine out of every ten democrats in Georgia believe to have been fraudulent. The intention to cheat was boldly proclaimed in advance, and is today a matter of jesting boastfulness after it has been perpetrated." [27]

Already in the midst of another contest by this time, he could see no sign which indicated that the men of "highest character, none higher" intended to mend their ways.

[25] *House Reports*, 53 Cong., 2 Sess., 1893–1894, Vol. III, Report No. 1147.
[26] *Cong. Record*, 53 Cong., 2 Sess., June 30, 1894, pp. 8285-8292.
[27] *The Daily Press*, July 5, 1894.

CHAPTER XV

Année Terrible

THE TWELVE MONTHS THAT BEGAN in the middle of the year 1894 have been well named "the *année terrible* of American history between Reconstruction and the World War." [1] As the national depression reached its nadir, a new record was attained in unemployment, in the intensity of organized labor's struggle for existence, in the brutality of capitalist repression of labor, and in the distress of the agricultural masses. When the paralysis the farming sections had suffered so long finally gripped the vitals of the industrial East, it called forth an expression of new radicalism which, joined to the older agrarian radicalism, formed a flood of discontent, protest, exposure, and some astute analysis of a corrupt capitalist economy.

If his library [2] is any indication, Watson was an enthusiastic and constant reader, particularly of history, but also of current radical reform literature. He was plainly influenced by the novels of Bellamy, and by Henry Demarest Lloyd's superb exposure of the methods of the great capitalist barons of oil, meat, coal, sugar, and tobacco, *Wealth Against Commonwealth*, which appeared in 1894. In his own publications he reflected the new spirit, and revitalized his agrarian radicalism at the same time.

In June he began a long series of articles on "The Railroad

[1] Allan Nevins, *Grover Cleveland*, p. 649.
[2] In the possession of Judge Uly O. Thompson, Miami, Florida.

259

Question." [3] In them he renewed his demand for outright and immediate government ownership and operation. Along with that demand went the intimation that the same remedy might well be applied elsewhere. It seemed to Watson that "Where a business is so clearly of a public nature that the individual can only get fair treatment by having the government to act for all, then individualism ceases to be wise and nationalism [collective action] becomes necessary." It was "perfectly clear that the issue is national, the danger national, the disease national, and that the remedy must be national." [4]

With gusto he struck out at the hypocrisy of reactionaries. Congressmen Crisp and Moses—erstwhile Alliance candidates— opposed an income tax on corporations because they were "not in favor of taxing orphans." [5] Watson was moved by the spectacle of those statesmen "agitating the bowels of their compassion in behalf of the orphans who own the corporations, the motherless and fatherless Hetty Green, Russell Sage, Roswell Flower, W. C. Whitney, Collis P. Huntington, Henry Villard, Andrew Carnegie . . ." [6]

When the anarchist Emma Goldman was jailed for daring (according to Watson) "to denounce the damnable system which makes a God-imaged man of less value to society than a St. Bernard dog," he contrasted her offense with the "immeasurable disaster which stalks behind the anarchy of Grover Cleveland, John Carlisle and John Sherman." A cartoon illustrated the article headed "The Anarchist Who Does the Most Damage," which depicted the President surrounded by Gould, Rockefeller, Vanderbilt, and Carnegie hurling bombs at the crumbling edifice of "Jeffersonian Democracy." The arrest of the leaders of Coxey's Army of protest for treading on the Capitol grass reminded him that "Carnegie stole two hundred thousand dollars from the

[3] *P. P. P.*, June 15 to August 3, 1894.
[4] *Ibid*, July 13, 1894.
[5] *Constitution*, Dec. 4, 1893.
[6] *P. P. P*, Dec. 8, 1893.

government, and Cleveland did not prosecute him as the law requires."

He wished to know why a certain lieutenant was going about from one city in Georgia to another "lecturing the soldiers on the 'Street Riot Drill?' Is Georgia threatened with any riots?" He found evidence of a menacing spirit among the ruling class abroad as well as at home, and printed it prominently in a column headed "How the Plutocrats Talk": " 'The best meal to give a regular tramp is a leaden one'—New York *Herald;* 'Hand grenades should be thrown among those who are striving to obtain higher wages, as by such treatment they would be taught a valuable lesson, and other strikers would take warning by their fate.'—Chicago *Times;* 'He [the tramp] has no more right than the sow that wallows in the gutter.'—*Scribner's Monthly.*" [7]

On July 4, President Cleveland, without consulting Governor Altgeld, sent 2,000 federal troops into Chicago to enforce an injunction obtained against the American Railway Union then on a strike led by Eugene Debs against the Pullman Parlor Car Company. As Secretary Olney explained, it was clear that the blow should be struck at Chicago "because that was the center and headquarters of the strike and that, *if smashed there,* it would collapse everywhere else." [8] The strike did collapse after Debs was jailed, and workers were shot down and killed by United States troops.

To Watson this new labor tragedy was but an added evidence that the administration "has shown by its every word and deed that Cleveland considers but one side of the question (after the election) and that side is capital. If we press closer every day to anarchy and bloodshed, this administration is responsible, for it has repeatedly shown its contempt for law when law stood in Cleveland's way." "If Grover Cleveland possesses lawfully the power he has exercised, then the only difference between our

[7] *P P P*, Feb 23–May 25, 1894.
[8] Allan Nevins, *Cleveland,* footnote p. 616.

president and a European emperor, king, or czar, consists merely in the name." Across the front page of one of his papers was spread a large drawing of federal troops shooting down Debs' strikers, men, women, and children. It was headed, "Government ownership would have prevented this."

With similar denunciations he reviewed step by step, as they occurred, the long series of Cleveland's offenses against popular opinion and his favors to capitalism. The silver-purchase repeal, the first bond issue, the seigniorage veto, the Hawaiian policy, the rabble-rousing chauvinism of the Venezuelan dispute, and the tariff bill were mercilessly caricatured by Watson's cartoonist, and satirized by the editor. They were all "repeated proofs that Cleveland had buncoed the country in a huge confidence game." "Is it never to end?" he asked. "Is it to go forward from bad to worse until the red stain of civil war again splashes our national records?" [9]

On July 4, appeared the first number of Watson's new paper, the *Daily Press*, founded to assist the work of the campaign of that year and overcome the handicap imposed by the weekly paper. Stocked at $25,000, the daily was edited by Watson who owned a tenth of the stock and served as president of the company at a salary of $25.00 a week. The daily proved a financial liability. The *People's Party Paper* continued to appear as usual, though Watson was now the sole owner. "It has a large circulation," he wrote in his private Journal, "& is a financial success—tho it cost me immense labor & much money to make it so." [10] He prayed for "an invention which will enable me to edit a daily paper, manage a State campaign, answer everybody's letter and make a speech in everybody's county—all at the same time. . . . No one man can run the schedule."

Watson was willing to boast continuous gains for his party: "in the county elections since 1892 we have increased our vote in every instance" winning several new counties and losing none of

[9] *Daily Press*, July 7 and 10, 1894; P. P. P., July 13, 1894.
[10] MS. Journal 2.

the old. At the same time he advised against over-confidence. "It is my deliberate opinion," he said, "that unless we make very considerable gains in this campaign it will require almost superhuman efforts to rally the party again." Concerning the rebellion among the Democrats, he warned, "There's a world of difference between cursing Cleveland and voting the Populist ticket. . . . We need candidates who will draw out the full Populist vote, and who at the same time, will draw the disappointed Democrats." He was "willing to mix some common sense with . . . zeal," to attract new recruits. The fact that the Populists possessed "little or no following among business and professional men" had been "a source of great weakness." Other things being equal, his preference was for the veteran Populist, but he wanted "nominees who will reach elements which heretofore we have been utterly unable to reach," and was prepared to sacrifice the old-time dirt-farmer candidate to that end. At the same time these new "respectable" candidates must "have burned their bridges behind them and have fallen into our line of march." [11]

For applying such a policy he was denounced by old Populists for committing dictatorial acts "that the Czar of Russia would be ashamed and tremble to do." He had "relegated the old-timers to the rear and allied himself with new recruits for spoils." [12] It was true that Watson's power over his party was great, and might have appeared "dictatorial" at times. Such a tendency was far from inconsistent with his temperament. He took some pains, however, to prepare his followers for shifts in policy through his papers and speeches so that his "dictatorship" did not seem too highhanded.

One notable example of the new policy of nominating "respectable" candidates was Judge James K. Hines, Watson's choice as a gubernatorial nominee. Hines was an unusual combination of eminent "respectability" and earnest radicalism. One

[11] *P P P.*, May 4, 1894.
[12] L P. Barnes, editor of the Dalton *Economist*, quoted in Augusta *Chronicle*, Aug 20, 1894; Augusta *Chronicle*, Sept. 10, 1894.

of the first professional men to endorse the Ocala platform, he had, as early as 1890, "staggered" the editor of the Augusta *Chronicle* by his public pronouncement in favor of "government ownership of railroads, steamship lines, express companies, telegraph lines, and all other business of a quasi-public nature. Let them be operated by the government as cheaply as possible for the public convenience and general welfare." [13] Yet this man was a highly successful lawyer, trained at Harvard, once Solicitor General, Alliance candidate for the Senate in 1890, now a Superior Court judge, and president of the Board of Trustees of Emory College—a Methodist institution of superlative "respectability."

In nominating Judge Hines at the Convention in Atlanta, the Populist "dictator" assumed a position of self-denial. He knew that many delegates were pledged to nominate him for governor. "But I want to reason with you," he said. "I must not be nominated for the head of your state ticket. We must recognize facts, not fancies. That memorable storm of prejudice and hate that swept over this state two years ago . . . has left me under a cloud of misrepresentation that will not be blown away for several years to come." [14] Hines received the nomination. Watson was again nominated for his old seat by a later convention in the Tenth District. His nomination was proposed by a working man from Augusta, and seconded by a farmer from McDuffie. The latter declared: "I love the Bible. I love Jesus Christ. I love the People's Party, and I love Tommie Watson. I rise to second the nomination."

The keynote of the Populist campaign was sounded in one of Watson's aphorisms at the Convention in May. "We meet under strange conditions," he said. "One year ago this country was being fed on the ambrosia of Democratic expectations. (Laughter.) Today it is gnawing the cobs of Democratic reality. (Great applause and cries of 'The corn is gone'.)"

[13] Augusta *Chronicle*, Sept. 19, 1890.
[14] *P. P. P*, May 25, 1894.

Throughout the campaign Watson's most telling blows were directed at Democratic schism and disunity, and the renunciation of platform pledges. When he was asked to return to the Democratic party, he would first know which competing faction he was to return to. "Shall I become an Evan Howell Democrat, or a Hoke Smith Democrat; a John B. Gordon Democrat, who voted in the Senate to strike down silver, or a Pat Walsh Democrat, who spoke out bravely in its behalf on the floor of the Senate . . . or a Black Democrat, who voted both ways, or a Turner Democrat, who voted four ways." The Populists, on the other hand, all stood squarely on one platform.[15]

Criticizing Democratic principles, he told an old-party audience in Macon, was "like shooting a didapper, you can never draw your aim." "Now in the Democratic meeting house, if the preacher takes a free silver text the house is for free silver; if he takes a gold bug text they are for the single gold standard; if he lines out an income tax hymn they all sing it; if he lines out a high tariff hymn they all sing that; if he prays for monopoly they all say amen; if he prays against monopoly, they all cry amen; if he pronounces the benediction in favor of national banks they all bow their heads and go away happy; if the benediction is against national banks they clap their hands and cry 'Hozzannah!' Just put a Democratic tag on it and it don't make any difference what kind of a dog it is. (Great applause.)"[16]

"You used to think," he said, proselytizing an audience of Atlanta Democrats, "that a northern Democrat was just like you, but that ain't so. (Laughter.) You used to think that an Eastern Democrat was a Siamese twin linked to you, but you know now it ain't so. You know now if you never did before that an Eastern Democrat is as much like an Eastern Republican as a buzzard is like a turkey buzzard. (Loud and prolonged applause.) You were a little slow about finding it out but you got there at last. (Laughter.) You know that the North and East are against you

15 Augusta *Chronicle*, July 22, 1894.
16 *P. P. P*, July 13, 1894; *Constitution*, July 5, 1894.

because theirs is a commercial section and yours is agricultural. Your prosperity is linked to ours; your store has its foundation on my farm." [17]

The Democratic state convention was reported to be a "love feast," and it was said to be "difficult to understand how any man who witnessed the harmony and enthusiasm can contemplate the remote possibility that Democratic supremacy can be jeopardized in Georgia." The state platform contained a demand for free silver, which was said to "satisfy the gold standard Democrats"; at the same time it endorsed Cleveland's administration. The *People's Party Paper* caricatured the "love feast" convention with a cartoon of Howell, the silver editor, and Hoke Smith of Cleveland's Cabinet, engaged in a hair-pulling fist-fight. Watson sat at one side at his editorial desk, saying "Gentlemen, fight as much as you like but please don't spill my ink." The Tenth District Convention, which renominated Black, on the other hand, passed an uncompromising demand for free coinage of silver. "Coming from the Democracy of the Tenth," observed the *Constitution*, "this declaration has the deepest significance. That district is the stronghold of the Populists in Georgia." They were "crying to their brothers of the State for help. Will their cry be ignored?" [18]

The old party managers, in order to meet the devastating Populist attack upon their many vulnerable spots, were forced to adopt an approach to the country voters that was curiously oblique. Their tactics are revealingly illustrated by the experience of a candidate for the state Senate, Nat E. Harris, who was also an autobiographer of guileless candor. He was told by campaign managers that in all his speeches he "must be careful never to say a word in favor of Grover Cleveland or his administration." This advice he "carefully bore in mind." He was interrupted in one of his speeches by the question, "What do you

[17] T. E. W., *Life and Speeches*, p. 141.
[18] Augusta *Chronicle*, Aug. 2, 1894; *Constitution*, Aug. 3, 1894; *P. P. P*, Aug. 3, 1894.

266

think of Grover Cleveland?" "I turned aside the inquiry," he said, "by telling an anecdote, which had in it the suggestion that the sixteen-to-one in the silver dollar meant sixteen negroes to one white man, and that this was the contest that the Populists were waging. Then I started out again on the general questions of the day." Once more he was asked the same question. "I told another anecdote and made the people laugh, with some foolish statement, and then started out on the main questions." [19]

Into the fog of Democratic "hush" tactics, and "anecdotes," John Temple Graves, a prominent and respected Democrat, without warning cast a bomb of candid appraisal and fact. Contemptuously brushing aside "this boastful prophecy of 70,000 democratic majority," as the "mere bravado of politicians who realize the possibility of no majority at all," he frankly admitted that the party was shot through with discord, and had "the most formidable opposition since the war." It would not dare steal another election.

Georgia is ripe today with the spirit of revolt! These are bold words, but they are the truest you have heard since the campaign opened, and I challenge you to refute them in fact, however much your extreme partisan loyalty may lead you to deny in boastful and swelling platitudes. . . .

Will you explain it? If not I will. I will tell you where the trouble lies. It is in the protest of the thinking masses against methods that are objectionable and a drift in our politics that is dangerous and deadly. . . .

Better monarchy than republican infamy like this. Better despotism or populism than corruption masked in the beautiful lineaments of law. Better a king than a prostitute judge! . . .

This is at last a thinking and a reading people. The last four years —the last two campaigns—have been full of education and the people are thinking more freely than they have ever done before. You cannot any longer shake the red flag of negro supremacy in the faces of the masses and make them think that life and death and salvation

[19] N. E. Harris, *Autobiography*, pp. 305-307.

depend upon voting the democratic ticket. They are thinking for themselves now . . .[20]

In line with his policy of more attractive candidates, Watson adopted a conciliatory tone in his speeches. Democratic papers several times remarked upon the fact that his speeches were "free from personalities and bitterness," seeming "moderate and conservative in tone" to those who went "expecting to hear a fiery and vindictive speech in bitter denunciation of the Democratic party." [21]

The appeal had little effect, for there seemed to be no abatement of the proscriptive spirit toward Populism, and there was a wholesale revival of the corruption and terrorism of the previous campaign. A. S. Clay, permanent chairman of the Democratic state convention, advised that the Populist leaders "are anarchists and they must be made odious." As for Watson's daily, "the dirty sheet should be suppressed." A Democratic pamphlet was circulated appealing to Negroes to vote for Atkinson, Democratic candidate for Governor, because "He pardoned Adolphus Duncan, a Negro, who had been twice convicted of rape on a white woman and had been sentenced to hang." When eighteen sharecroppers disobeyed the orders of a Democratic landlord not to attend a Watson speech, his foreman received orders not to issue them their week's rations: they could "go to the People's Party speaking and get their rations." [22]

From a Populist campaign speaker, Watson received a letter that reveals conditions under which the Populists struggled. He planned to speak in a hostile county. "I expect the venture will be fraught with great danger," he wrote. "The bitterest hate [is] aroused, & the chances [are] at least equal for personal violence. . . . I am at a loss to know what to do that day about pistols. If I have one I will almost surely be arrested & it found

[20] John T. Graves, to the *Constitution*, quoted in *P. P. P.*, Aug. 31, 1894.
[21] E.g., the *Constitution*, April 20, 1894; Augusta *Chronicle*, July 22, 1894.
[22] A. A. Elders, to T. E. W., Aug. 8, 1894, quoted in *P. P P.*, Aug. 17, 1894.

on me, & if I don't have it I would be in a terrible fix should they assault me." [23]

The refusal of the Democratic Executive Committee to permit a division of the managers of the polls between Democrats and Populists was held up by the latter as proof that foul work was afoot. From Wilkes County Populists came the hysterical report that "here human life is as valueless as corn cobs. We are in a reign of terror. Free speech is denied us." It was a conservative Democratic estimate that three men were killed and many wounded at the polls of Augusta during the state election. "There were so many shooting, constables and others, that most anybody's bullet may have taken effect." [24]

Even by Democratic count and poll management the new party polled 44.5 per cent of the vote in the state election, more than doubling its vote in the previous election, and reducing the Democratic majority from about 80,000 to about 20,000. The *Chronicle* admitted that "Several of the strongest Democratic counties in the State have been carried by the Populists and with but few exceptions every county in the state shows Populists gains." The returns from some forty counties were suspiciously withheld for several weeks. There is a substantial ground for Watson's claim that a fair election would have resulted in a clear Populist victory. [25]

The old party leaders were thoroughly alarmed at the results of the state election, and said so frankly. Watson proclaimed that "Victory at last is in sight." He felt confident of winning his contest against Black in November, and with reason, for his party had polled a majority in that district in October.

The Democratic machine of Augusta, more desperate than in 1892, determined to win the congressional election in November, 1894, by any means possible. A description of the methods used—the drunken Negro repeaters, the ballot-box stuffing and

[23] J. M. Barnes to T. E. W., Oct. 30, 1894, Watson MSS.
[24] Augusta *Chronicle*, Nov 7, 1894
[25] MS. Journal 2, p. 547; *Constitution*, Oct. 5, 1894; *Chronicle*, Oct. 4, 1894.

burning, intimidation, bloodshed, and bribery—is unnecessary, for the scene was merely a repetition of that of 1892 on a more extensive scale: much more was required to defeat Watson in 1894.[26] A court ruling was obtained that held that registration was unnecessary in congressional elections, and the Populist appeal for an injunction restraining the allowing of unregistered voting was refused.[27]

Watson carried the counties of McDuffie, Columbia, Lincoln, Warren, Taliaferro, Jefferson, Glascock, Washington, and Wilkinson. Black carried only Richmond and Hancock and was declared elected. The nine Watson counties contained a population close to 100,000 and polled some 15,000; the two Black counties, with only 62,000 population, polled over 18,000 votes for Black alone. Since Black's majority in Hancock was only 1,000, the secret of his huge majority lay in the Richmond vote. With only 11,240 possible polls in Richmond, according to the Comptroller General's report, and only 4,100 voting in October, 15,980 votes were cast by that county in November. Of these Watson was allowed only 2,200. Thus out of a possible poll of 11,240, Black received a *majority* of 13,780! [28]

The enormity of this robbery shocked even Democrats of other parts of the state into protest. The machine and officialdom remained unrelenting, however. In reply to protest, Boykin Wright, Major Black's campaign manager, remarked, "Why they [the Populists] would cry fraud if an angel from heaven should come down and run on the Democratic ticket. That's their stock in trade." Another commentator, anonymous but "quite prominent in official life," was quoted as saying, "a democratic newspaper has no right to talk about democratic dishonesty when democrats are elected." [29] The *Chronicle*, taking the

[26] *The Contested Election Case of Watson vs. Black* (1896), *passim*; information on both 1894 and 1895 elections.
[27] Augusta *Chronicle*, Oct. 7 and Nov. 4, 1894.
[28] *Constitution*, Nov. 7, 1894; P. P. P , March 9, 1895; MS. Journal 2, p. 548; *The Contested Election Case of Watson vs Black* (1896), p 5.
[29] *Constitution*, Nov. 8, 10, 1894.

same attitude, thought it "exceedingly unfortunate that so good a cause should have reproach cast upon it at the hands of its friends." "We have no defense to make." [30]

A group of twenty-two Augusta Democrats did sign and publish a denunciation of the dishonest methods. It was "no secret, but a reproach to the very manhood of Augusta" that "the officers of our law stood by and saw worthless negroes vote dozens of times at ten cents each and run outside the crowd in our courthouse yard and sit right down in their very faces and shoot 'craps' . . . for the money that was so nefariously gained." Major Black, however, in a public meeting a few days after this statement appeared said, "I would not parade the frauds that were perpetrated in the past, if frauds they were; I would cover them with a cloak of silence." [31]

As news of the Augusta frauds spread among the Populists of the Tenth District, and resentment swelled with rumor, hatred between the parties grew more and more threatening. When the house of a Democratic party official burned to the ground near a Richmond County factory, the owner immediately attributed the burning to the Populists. Such incidents multiplied.

Pointing out the menacing situation that existed between their followers, Watson, on November 9, proposed to Black through the press that "a commission be appointed by the two opposing candidates to purge the ballot boxes, and to count the legal votes to determine who had been elected." In his reply Black admitted that the election was "shrouded in doubt." He declared himself "in hearty accord with Mr. Watson in his motive for making the proposition for the purpose of putting an end to the terrible state of affairs in the Tenth District." Yet he declined to accept his opponent's proposal to purge the ballot box. He also deplored the prospect of a contest under law, because "that course is tedious." In the same letter he made the counter proposal

[30] Quoted in *The Contested Election Case of Watson vs Black* (1896), p. 675.
[31] *Ibid.*, pp. 675-676; the protest was dated Aug 26, 1895

271

that, provided Watson agreed "within the time allowed by law for notice of contest," he, Black, should take the commission as a member of the Fifty-fourth Congress, but resign it, effective March 4, and "refer the matter back to the people to determine by a new election who shall represent them in the Fifty-fourth Congress." [32]

The apparent magnanimity of this offer is considerably diminished by a little reflection upon its conditions. In order to accept its terms, Watson would have to give up his legal right to submit his case to the House of Representatives, since the limit for filing notice of such contests would expire before the proposed election took place. It is true that his experience in contesting the election of 1892 had been, to say the least, discouraging. But now the tables were turned. Ruling the new House was a Republican majority who would be happy to deprive its rival party of one more seat. Then, too, even making allowance for considerable talent in that direction on the part of Congressional committees, it would seem impossible to whitewash the glaring, palpable dishonesty of this election—as had been done in the previous one. In short, it seems probable that he would have won his contest.

That Watson contemplated making the contest seems evident from the fact that he had already employed counsel to conduct it. Yet he accepted Black's proposal of a new election almost immediately. The only motive he gives for making this questionable decision was an abhorrence of being indebted to the Republican majority for his seat. Such an aversion was certainly in line with his oft-expressed abhorrence of fusion with either old party, and especially of the taint of Republican connivance. Yet there were probably other motives he did not reveal. "Most of my friends think I have made a huge mistake," he wrote in his private Journal shortly after making the decision. "I cannot believe it. The event will, I am sure, prove that I have 'done best' for the party and for myself." [33]

[32] Augusta *Chronicle*, Nov. 20, 1894; also *P. P. P*, Feb. 1, 1895.
[33] Jan. 9, 1895, MS. Journal 2, p. 550.

In accepting Black's counter proposal Watson had attached an additional condition—that the new election be held within thirty days after March 4, 1895, the date his opponent's resignation became effective. He added this condition under the conviction that the state law required its governor to call a new election within that time, anyway. Major Black neither explicitly accepted this attached condition nor rejected it. That Watson was sincere in the assumption that it was accepted seems evident from his repeated reference to the stipulated "within thirty days" in his editorials,[34] and from the entry in his private Journal, dated January 9, 1895, that, "by the terms of our agreement the special election is to be held within thirty days." [35] A dragging postponement of the special election was decidedly to the advantage of Democrats, who relied upon inertia, old habits, and the eventualities of a shifting political and economic scene to dull the disgust of revolting Democrats and dampen the enthusiasm of Populists. On the other hand, the new party had everything to lose and nothing to gain from a postponement that could only fritter away its reserve of zeal and resentment and dissipate the ardor of new recruits.

Major Black resigned according to agreement on March 4, 1895, but as the month progressed it became plain that his party was stalling on the special election, and had no intention of fulfilling the thirty-day agreement. Watson, by open letter, reminded his opponent of their agreement, of the fact that their District was without a representative, of the distraught temper of their respective partisans, and asked him to join in a letter to the governor urging him to order an early election. Black replied briefly that, "We differ so widely as to facts" that "discussion would be useless and a more detailed and extended reply to yours is unnecessary."

In his answer Watson abandoned a tone of remonstrance, habitual with him in addressing opponents, and wrote a stinging

[34] The Augusta *Chronicle*, Jan. 25, 1895, denied the acceptance of the condition, but not Black.
[35] MS. Journal 2, p. 550.

rebuke. He referred to "the disturbance in the Tenth District, caused by the phenomenal capacity of your county to cast 16,000 votes with 12,000 voters," and to dishonesty "of such a colossal type that it almost commanded respect." He continued:

You dreaded the consequences of a fair count of the legal votes. You dreaded the other alternative of an investigation by Congress.

Therefore, to escape both perils, you proposed to me "to resign and submit the matter back to the people". . . .

You were getting me to part with valuable goods. You wanted me to surrender by written renunciation, my legal right to put you on trial before Congress—a Republican Congress at that. . . . Had you objected to the condition I put upon my acceptance, I could have withdrawn my acceptance; I would have gone on with the contest, for which I had already engaged counsel. . . .

I lost my right to contest the election, and to show that I was entitled to the seat. It is too late for you to restore me to the position and to the advantage I held last November and December; but it is not too late for you to loyally stand by your part of the contract— according to its letter, its reason, and its spirit.[36]

Black persisted in his course, however, contending that the Populists had misconstrued the terms of their agreement, that more time should be given for feeling to subside, and that he could not "assume" that he would be the Democratic nominee.[37]

In accepting his renomination as candidate in the special election, Watson hailed the agreement with Black as marking "a distinct epoch in the politics of the South," for "The time has been when any crime committed in the name of the Democratic party was an act of patriotism in the eyes of the majority of the people." But Major Black now "confesses, by his resignation, that a grievous wrong has been done us, and that the time has come for the honest elements of both parties to put the rascals under foot." "Without violence and without crime," he boasted,

[36] *P. P. P.*, March 29, 1895.
[37] *Constitution*, May 29, 1895.

"you have achieved a moral victory which ennobles you and your party." [38]

The Populists were allowed ample time to test the fruits of their "moral victory." Instead of the thirty days stipulated by the agreement, the old party postponed the special election for *seven months* after Black's resignation. Taking advantage of an important political trend in the silver cause (described in the following chapter), the Democrats turned these seven months to rich profit, while the insurgent party chafed at the frustration of its aims.

"Duped again!" was the dismayed cry of the Populists. Their leader pleaded earnestly for patience and peace. "Don't let the politicians of Augusta throw the Tenth District into a turmoil again." Violence would only hurt their cause. "We must have peace, we must have law and order, we must have an end to ballot-box corruption, and to the reign of political anarchists. . . ." In the spring a movement for boycotting all business with Augusta arose among the angry farmers. The *People's Party Paper*, while expressing gratification at "the loyalty which actuates Mr. Watson's friends in this matter," argued that "retaliation as a means of righting a wrong is a bad policy and should only be inaugurated as a last resort."

As the October day of election finally approached, however, and fraudulent use of the new registration law became apparent, Watson turned from the preaching of patience and peace to threaten refusals and boycott. "The unblushing frauds practiced in that city [Augusta]," he wrote, "during the days of registration just closed, evidences that the thieves have not repented. The farmers are tired of chucking grass at the thieves in the apple tree." [39]

The new registration law, passed in December, 1894, shortly after the disgraceful election of that year, set up a powerful registration committee of three in each county. It was given the

[38] Speech reprinted in *Watson's Political and Economic Handbook*, pp. 462-463.
[39] *P. P. P.*, Sept. 20, 1895.

power, from which there was no appeal, to draw up lists of qualified voters. In Watson's district each committee consisted of two Democrats and one Populist. In case of dispute, read the law, the decision of two was final.[40] Bearing some similarity to laws later adopted in all Southern states to disfranchise the Negro, it could be, and was, employed here to forestall more Populist voters—but at the same time to make it possible to use the Negro vote where controlled by Democrats. Thus the registration lists of Richmond revealed the amazing fact that of the 3,431 Negroes registered (almost as many as white) 1,333, or more than a third, were listed as "just attained the age of 21," i.e., since the last year's election. This, as the Populists remarked, was "one of the most remarkable facts in the statistics of population." Of the 3,866 whites registered, only 229, or one-fifteenth, were listed as 21.[41]

The Augusta *Chronicle* expressed surprise that the Populists were "shocked because Richmond County Democrats are paying the taxes of negroes and registering them so they may vote for Major Black," and added cynically that "both parties will employ the usual methods of securing negro votes." [42]

The "usual methods" *were* employed in the special election on October 2, but the new method—the registration law—was a vast improvement over the "usual" ones: its effects were less glaring, more "legal," harder to detect and expose. For the first time there were no deaths reported, and only a minimum of violence. The voting was comparatively peaceful. Thus the total vote of Richmond was reduced from 15,980 in 1894 to 6,435—well within the possible poll—yet giving Black a safe majority of some 5,000, a majority large enough to overcome a Populist majority in all the other counties. For although Watson, as previously, carried nine counties with easy majorities, and Black only two, the Democratic majority piled up in the

[40] The Registration Law is printed as a supplement to the Contestant's Brief, *The Contested Election Case of Watson vs Black* (1896).
[41] *Ibid.*, p. 86; also Contestant's Brief, p. 11.
[42] Augusta *Chronicle*, Aug. 31, 1895.

276

five wards of Augusta alone were sufficient to defeat him. The part played by the Negro vote, the regulation of which was referred to above, may be seen by the returns from the fourth ward, in which Black received 989 to Watson's 9 Negro votes. Watson observed that "Richmond County is so manipulated that no matter whether Populists carried Hancock or not, the city of Augusta arrogates to herself the right to rule the District." [43]

To his followers, crushed by their third defeat, and convinced they had been cheated of their victory the third time, Watson wrote a message:

> Discouraged?
> Bosh! Bosh!! Bosh!!!
> Let the other fellow get discouraged. His troubles are just beginning to commence. . . .
> Comrades! Let the fight of 1896 begin now! [44]

It would be more to the point to know what was really in the writer's mind at this time. He did not, as was his practice, commit his inner reflections upon this election to his private Journal. Yet, unless the very fierceness of his determination had completely closed his mind to facts, he must have realized, after his last three experiences—whatever he said to the contrary—that his was a forlorn cause, that his sacrifice of a successful career in the old party had been in vain—as had most of the prolific energy and effort he had poured into the new movement. He must have realized that his enemies of the old party would stop at nothing whatever to crush him, and that they had not left enough substance in the democratic myth to stir hope in another effort among his followers. He must have entertained these reflections as he entered the fateful year of 1896.

[43] *P. P. P.*, Oct. 11, 1895; Augusta *Chronicle*, Oct. 3, 1895; Augusta *Herald*, Oct. 3, 1895; Atlanta *Journal*, Oct. 3, 1895; *Constitution*, Sept. 13, 1895; *The Contested Election Case of Watson vs. Black*, *passim*.
[44] *P. P P.*, Oct. 11, 1895.

CHAPTER XVI

The Silver Panacea

HENRY DEMAREST LLOYD, like other advanced intellectual leaders of his day, hoped for great things from the Populist movement. He identified himself with it, fought for it passionately and courageously, and suffered at its collapse a despair that was more than the fret of disappointment. Aside from partisanship, however, he viewed his party as analytically and intelligently as he viewed the chaotic capitalism of his time. After a preliminary autopsy upon the defunct Populism, he wrote:

> The free silver movement is a fake. Free silver is the cowbird of the reform movement. It waited until the nest had been built by the sacrifices and labors of others and then it laid its eggs in it, pushing out the others which lie smashed on the ground.[1]

Looking to Populism for genuine, fundamental reform along the lines of extensive government ownership and control, Lloyd deprecated the tendency of right-wing Populists to rely on "spinning-wheel and ox-team remedies" in a dynamo age. He hoped for the nomination of Eugene V. Debs in 1896. He knew that the rank-and-file majority of genuine Populists believed free silver was "only the most trifling installment of reform," or "no reform at all." It was in them, not in the leaders, he placed his faith. If there must be a split between free-silver right and anti-

---

[1] Caro Lloyd, *Henry Demarest Lloyd*, Vol. I, p. 263

monopolist left, he advised in 1895, "let it be a split that will be heard far and wide."[2]

Frank L. McVey, also a contemporary student of Populism, feared the very elements in the party to which Lloyd looked for salvation, and exaggerated those elements to menacing proportions. The silver plank was merely a "screen" that hid the basic "socialism" of the radical majority. But, like Lloyd, he felt that "the presence of the silver faction has obscured the real purpose of the party." Its only honest course, its only hope, lay in "casting aside half measures and following the logic of its underlying tendencies, boldly announcing itself as the socialist party of America, confessing paternalism as its principle of constitutional interpretation, the socialization of industry as its economic one . . ." After all, it was only the leaders of Populism who made up the silver faction, and they could never hold in check the radical mass of followers. Writing on the eve of the debacle of 1896, he thought that the "socialistic" rank and file had gained control.[3]

The genuine Populist of the South, the old-time Allianceman who was educated on the sub-treasury, government ownership, and fiat money under the tutelage of Tom Watson, was never seriously befuddled by the free-silver panacea. Neither the St. Louis platform, the Ocala platform, nor the Omaha platform of 1892 emphasized silver unduly. Each included the demand, but only along with several other proposals for more fundamental reform—all of which the good Populist swore by with more or less impartial fervor. Sometimes one, sometimes another reform in their long creed claimed their especial enthusiasm, but never silver to the exclusion of the others.

The situation in the West was different. There the third party leaders were constantly tempted to cash in on the popular clamor for the silver panacea. It was sometimes easy to purchase cheap victory and office by sacrificing the great body of fundamental

[2] *Ibid.*, Vol. I, p. 256; H. D. Lloyd, "The Populists at St. Louis," *Review of Reviews*, Vol. XIV (Sept., 1896), pp. 293-303.
[3] Frank L. McVey, *The Populist Movement*, pp. 176-177, 190.

Populist reforms. Blocking the application of this policy, however, was the Omaha platform with its wide program of reform and its many radical demands. Various maneuvers were conducted by the silver schemers to discredit and abandon the old platform. It was called wild, hastily adopted, and visionary, and a convention was called to meet at St. Louis early in 1895 to revise it. The radical ranks held firm, however, and defeated the *coup* of the silver propagandists.[4]

Encouraged in their subversive aims by the American Bimetallic League, the silver-Populists of the West continued their maneuvers. As Populist candidate for President in 1892, General James B. Weaver had said: "This movement is a protest against corporate aggression." Yet, in August, 1893, he presided as chairman over the Chicago convention of the Bimetallic League, lending his influence to the purely opportunistic policy of herding together all who would rally to the silver panacea—regardless of party or principles.[5] A plan was under way in Iowa to control the next General Assembly in the interest of General Weaver's candidacy for the United States Senate by a fusion of Populists and Democrats. In 1895 the General announced: "While considering fully and unreservedly the great importance of our other planks, I shall favor going before the people in 1896 with the money question alone, unencumbered with any other contentions whatsoever."[6]

In the summer of the same year, H. E. Taubeneck of Illinois, national chairman of the People's party, advised the members in one state to "keep the money question to the front" for it is "the only living issue before the people." He hoped their platform would make "the 'money question' the great central idea, unencumbered with details or side issues."[7]

Before the People's party was nationally organized, Tom Watson had drawn his line on the free-silver question. Thence-

[4] John D. Hicks, *The Populist Revolt*, Chap. XI, and pp. 240-243.
[5] *P. P. P.*, Aug. 4, 1893.
[6] F. L. Haynes, *James Baird Weaver*, p. 317.
[7] J. D. Hicks, *op. cit.*, p. 344.

forth he hewed to the mark relentlessly, whether the chips flew to the right or to the left. Like many Populists, he subscribed to a "quantitative" or "managed" currency theory, partially exemplified by the sub-treasury plan. Money was purely the creation of the government; its amount should be regulated according to demand, in order to stabilize prices, particularly of agricultural products, and to furnish needed credit. These functions, because they vitally affected public welfare, should be taken out of the hands of national banks and given over entirely to the government.[8] Plainly, free silver was merely tangential to his money doctrine. "Free Silver is right and we ought to have it," he wrote in 1891, "but is a mere drop in the bucket to what we must have if we are ever to save our people from financial ruin." It would mean less than one dollar per capita increase in the currency, whereas "we need at least forty." [9]

He scoffed contemptuously at the Bland silver bill of the Democrats, which, in his eyes, was a mere sop, a thirty-cents-per-capita increase. "With this princely addition to the circulation medium," he said, "they say that we must be satisfied; disband our Reform Army; cease to agitate and educate; cease to ask for $50 per capita; and go back to our drowsy indifference . . ." [10] Examining the free-silver demand in the Omaha platform of his own party, he wrote: "I have never claimed that Free Silver would remedy all our financial ills. It would not do so." However, he supported the plank on the ground that to some extent it "would loosen the grip of the Money kings," and take a step toward a system that was "more just, and liberal, and flexible than the arbitrary, exacting and monopolistic gold standard of today." [11]

Approval of free silver as one plank in an elaborate platform of his own party was one thing; approval of free silver as a

[8] These ideas permeate all his writings on the money question; e.g., vide T. E. W., *Economic and Political Handbooks, passim*.
[9] *P. P. P.*, Dec. 31, 1891.
[10] *Ibid.*, March 17, 1892.
[11] *Ibid.*, July 29, 1892.

panacea employed to destroy the integrity of a movement to which he had dedicated his life was altogether another thing. Once he was convinced that this end was portended in the maneuvers of certain Western Populist leaders, Bimetallic Leaguers, silver-Democrats and Republicans, he struck out boldly and fiercely in a long pronunciamento against the conspirators:

We have known, for some time, that certain wire-pullers in Washington were scheming to side-track the People's Party by having it surrender all of its platform excepting the Free Silver Plank. . . .

If newspaper reports are to be credited, considerable progress has been made with the scheme. . . .

This being the case, we feel that it is time for us to take a position. In doing so we believe that we have the support of every Populist in Georgia.

Gentlemen, the People's Party of Georgia demands that there shall be no cowardly surrender of principles!

We favor Free Silver as much as we favor Fiat money—and no more.

We favor Free Silver as much as we favor Income Tax—and no more.

We hate the greed which strikes down silver in the interest of gold—but we hate just as fiercely the National banks which strike down the right of all people to obtain money from the government upon equal terms; and the High Protective Tariff, under whose shelter Trusts and Combines organize their forces and exploit the public; and the Railroad tyranny which keeps its iron hand laid heavily upon every industry in the Union.

Any political party which ventured to go before the American people with only one plank in its platform would be hissed off the stage, jeered out of existence, kicked into oblivion. . . .

In a party whose only test of membership would be the advocacy of free silver, how could we keep the corporations from coming in and forever checking our advance toward governmental ownership of railways?

282

How could we purge it of these Privileged classes who oppose an income tax?

Viewed from any standpoint, this single-plank party is fatally objectionable.

The scheme is a trap, a pitfall, a snare, a menace, a fraud, a crime against common sense and common honesty.

We are rejoiced to see that Governor Waite, of Colorado, denounces it.

We cannot believe that Taubeneck, and Peffer, and Simpson favor it.

The People's party has nothing to fear so much as unwise leadership.

Our enemies, seeing us sweeping onward with steady growth of members, seek to divide us, confuse us, side-track us. . . .

The rank and file are safe. The people, the *people*, are sound.

The rank and file want to march right on.

The rank and file want no fusion.

The rank and file want no corrupt abandonment of a creed we love, believe in, hope for—a creed in whose sacred keeping is held the longings and prayers of an oppressed people.[12]

Watson's determination to ride the storm without reefing a single sail was put to severe test in the hurricanes of the next two years. Though sailing in the opposite direction, Grover Cleveland likewise ordered all his canvas aloft and likewise suffered from the storm. Others did not hesitate to reef, or to change course.

The most momentous change to which Populism had to adjust itself was the remarkable revolution in the Democratic party. Resulting in the ultimate repudiation of its own administration, this party revolution proceeded in three phases: disintegration, revolt and realignment, and finally the *coup*. Each phase held its peculiar perils for Populism, and each required readjustment.

In the summer of 1895 Watson could write:

[12] *Ibid.*, Dec. 8, 1892.

Never since the "Wonderful One Hoss Shay" went to pieces in one comprehensive, simultaneous and complete smashup—an epic of utter annihilation—has there been such an all-round catastrophe as that which has happened to the democratic party.

It not only managed to do nothing it was pledged to do, but it also continued to do everything its leaders had fought the Republicans for doing.

This judgment was corroborated by A. K. McClure, who, after a tour of the South early in 1896, reported that not a single Southern state was certain to vote for the Democratic candidate for President in the approaching election, that a united South was "quite improbable," and that since "the Populists have rent the Democracy in twain" it was possible that "all the Southern states may be lost to the Democracy." [13]

Some Southern Democratic papers rivaled the Populists in the bitterness of their denunciation of Cleveland's administration. Nothing Watson wrote outdid certain editorials of the *Constitution*. "The people have been taken in and done for," read one. "They have been made the victims of as corrupt a conspiracy as ever disgraced the world's political records. They have been sold out, plastering and furniture, by those whom they selected to protect their interests." [14] There were those who protested that such utterance was dangerous and "not regular." "To the dogs with such false and pretentious democracy!" shouted the rebellious editor. "It is not worth having or holding." [15] While this was going on at one side of the Democratic house, on the other side Hoke Smith, member of Cleveland's Cabinet and a proprietor of the Atlanta *Journal,* was touring the state defending the administration against all comers.

While this confusion of tongues was in progress, and while what Watson called Cleveland's "regular 'Go to hell' administration" pursued its course uninfluenced, Democrats in the South

[13] Quoted in Joseph C. Manning, *Fadeout of Populism,* pp. 38-39.
[14] *Constitution,* Aug. 28, 1895.
[15] *Ibid,* July 5, 1895.

and West were deserting by the thousands to join the Populist ranks. The gain in the Populist vote between 1892 and 1894 had been over one hundred per cent in Georgia and forty-two per cent in the nation. Faced with the glaring probability of a complete rout in the coming election, Democratic politicians in the South and West resorted to strategy.

It is a safe estimate to say that no policy among Cleveland's several unpopular policies made for him more enemies in the Western and Southern branches of his party than his determined stand against silver. His repeated bond sales served to keep resentment fanned to flame. Could politicians in those sections capitalize that resentment, champion silver, win their party to its cause, and outdo the Populists in denouncing Cleveland—instead of dodging and straddling to defend his unpopular administration—they might save themselves. They might win back the Populistic majority of the Democrats, who were either already with the third party or ready to join it, and save the Solid South, along with many profitable offices that had slipped from their grasp. Some of the more optimistic hoped thus to absorb the third party and thereby end the Populist "menace" forever.[16]

This was an ambitious program, but it was adopted by men moved by desperation. There occurred a miraculous mass conversion among Democratic politicians. By the summer of 1895 the *Constitution* could contend that a definition of true Democracy which denounced all who condemned Cleveland's "Republican financial doctrine" as "Populistic" would read out of the party the governor of the state, the chairman of the Democratic state executive committee, both United States senators, a former Democratic speaker of the national House of Representatives, the president of the Democratic state Senate, and the speaker of the Democratic state House of Representatives. "These are the men," boasted the editor, "and this the element that the Cuckoos, goldbugs, and postmaster organs are denouncing as populists." [17]

[16] Alex M Arnett, *Populist Movement in Georgia,* pp 187-188
[17] *Constitution,* July 9, 1895.

285

Watson found the antics of these twelfth-hour converts amusing and lost no opportunity to embarrass them. There was his arch-enemy, Patrick Walsh, editor of the Augusta *Chronicle*, who was now "sorry to say" he could see no hope for the country "until silver is restored to coinage"; and his old opponent, Major Barnes, "with grief in his ample bosom and conciliation in his oily dew-laps." Charles Crisp, who "serenely turns up as the chief mourner at the funeral of Free Silver," had, as speaker of the House, dealt "the two deadliest blows that were ever given to Bi-metallism." "As well," he remarked, "might Iscariot preach the funeral sermon of Christ." The free silver issue was merely a political ball tossed back and forth between the two old parties. "Republicans out of office favor free-silver—to get in on. Once in they take up the gold policy where the Democrats left it; and the free silver issue is tossed back to the Democrats for them to use awhile. . . . A good many of us common every-day dunces need lots of light to show us why it is that the Democratic party loves free-silver and hates the Congressmen who vote for it." [18] "Gold-bugs," "silver-bugs," "straddle-bugs," humbugs—they were all of one species so long as they were Democrats.

Major Black was renominated for the special election of 1895 on a silver platform. The real significance of that platform is attested by the public appeal of a self-styled "gold-bug": "Is it likely that, if elected, he [Watson] will forgive or forget? Fellow 'gold-bugs'—gentlemen so called by those of your brethren who differ from your financial policy—do not let anything that has been or may be said or done prevent your loyal support of Major Black now. . . . We must present a solid front to a wily and insidious foe." [19] The "gold-bugs" were ready to vote for silver to defeat Watson.

In July the state Bimetallic League staged a great convention at Griffin to which were invited all "friends of silver" irrespec-

18 *P. P. P*, Aug 9 and Nov. 22, 1895.
19 Augusta *Chronicle*, Aug 30, 1895.

tive of party affiliation. Patrick Walsh, "acknowledged leader of the bimetallic hosts of the State," presided over the convention and was elected president of the state League. As the Democrats hoped, many Populists attended, and though none of them was appointed on committees they were described as "quiet and deeply interested." All went smoothly until one ardent but innocent Democrat moved, and urged with embarrassing persistence, a resolution that would exclude all Populists from participating in the convention. It was quickly explained that "it would be a breach of propriety to recognize any party or discuss the political issues of any party." The offender was finally silenced by Chairman Walsh. Senator Morgan of Alabama made the principal address. Bitter were the words voiced there against President Cleveland. Sweet were the words spoken there to the Populists.[20] Said Captain Evan Howell, editor of the *Constitution:*

I am an honest bimetallist. I believe in the coinage of silver, free, at 16 to 1. I am willing to join hands with any populist in Georgia, if he will go with me under the democratic banner. I am in favor of granting Tom Watson the privilege of being a democratic leader under the democratic flag. I believe Tom Watson is sincere; I want all populists to come back under the flag.[21]

Realizing the necessity for stiffening the resistance of his ranks to meet these new tactics, Watson clarified his position in regard to Democratic overtures to fusion. Stated in parabolical form his prophecy was, briefly: "The Alliance lamb agreed to lie down in the same pen with the Democratic lion. Result: lamb soon dissolved in the gastric juice of said lion. Does the wily old trickster, Lon Livingston, think he can play that game on *us?*" As for the Bimetallic convention at Griffin:

The Populists who were lured into the meeting went away with the dry grins. It was dinned into their ears that the meeting was a

[20] *Ibid*, July 1, 2, 18, and 19, 1895; *Constitution*, July 19, 1895.
[21] *Constitution*, July 19, 1895.

non-partisan affair, a meeting into which no politics would be admitted. This made the Populists feel good, but when the time came to make up committees, the Populists looked a little foolish, as not a member of their party appeared on the committee on program. . . . It looks as if they might have struck some of the Populists by accident in appointing committees. . . .

But we are glad this convention was held; glad our men went there; glad we showed a willingness to harmonize on principle; glad the meeting failed through the greed and insincerity of professional wire-pullers and not through the fault of the Populists. [22]

Now that the Democratic party was ripe for internal revolution, the problem and the temptation of fusion were more than ever before acute and pressing for Populist leaders. Fusion with one party or the other had, as a matter of fact, been a problem of the third party from the beginning. After all, every Populist recruit had to be won from one or the other of the old parties. In the South the fusion problem presented itself first with regard to the Republican party. After the death of Colonel L. L. Polk, the Populist party of North Carolina had effected a fusion with the Republican under the leadership of Marion Butler, an astute young politician who won a seat in the Senate at the age of thirty-three. Seeking to extend his Populist-Republican fusion throughout the South, Butler attempted in private conference to persuade Watson (as well as other Southern Populist leaders) to adopt the same policy. Watson flatly refused to countenance the plan, contending that it would destroy the integrity of his party.[23] No accusation called forth such angry denial from the Georgia Populist as the suggestion that he was coöperating with the Republicans.

In the West the temptation from the founding of the third party had been fusion with the Democrats, the minority party there as the Republicans were in the South. From the beginning

[22] *P. P. P.*, July 26, 1895, quoted by A. M. Arnett, *op. cit.*, pp. 190-191.
[23] Interview with Marion Butler, Washington, Aug. 7, 1934; Florence Smith, "The Populist Movement and its Influence in North Carolina," Ph.D. dissertation, University of Chicago, *passim*.

288

there had been a certain amount of coalition between the two parties, and in some states outright fusion. As the election year approached it became plain that if prominent Populist leaders of the West, such as Weaver and Taubeneck, had their way, fusion would go the whole way and become complete. The capitulation to the free silver panacea was merely another way of advocating fusion.[24]

On what basis could fusion between Democrats and Populists take place in the South? Henry Demarest Lloyd once observed that "The line between the old Democracy and Populism in the South is largely a line of bloody graves." As hyperbole goes, this strikes near the truth. For six years, during the whole life of Populism, the Democratic party had been recognized as the enemy against whose stubborn, and often treacherous, opposition every gain had to be won. In the bitter struggles of those six years Democrats had slandered, cursed, ostracized, defrauded, and killed Populists, and Populists had fought back with the same weapons. How could enemies be transformed into allies by what Populists suspected was a mere verbal change of heart?

Toward fusion of any kind Tom Watson adopted the policy then known as "the-middle-of-the-road." [25] Far from designating a conservative course, this term had come to signify those radical Populists who refused to compromise any principle in order to coöperate with either of the old parties. The "mid-road" Populists constituted the strictly anti-fusion rank and file of the party. In answer to a Louisiana Populist who wrote asking his advice on fusion with the silver-Democrats of that state, Watson wrote:

In our judgment Populists should keep in the middle of the road, should make no coalition with either old party, and should avoid fusion as they would the devil. To meet Democrats or Republicans,

[24] John D. Hicks, *op. cit*, pp. 344-348
[25] For an explanation of the origin of the term see *Ibid.*, p. 346.

289

acting in their individual capacities, in a free-for-all mass meeting, where a principle upon which we all agree can be discussed, and where no man need be bound by any action which he disapproves, is *one* thing; to make a barter and a trade as Populists with the official managers of either of the old parties to swap a certain number of votes for a stipulated price in Democratic patronage or Republican spoils, is quite *another* thing. . . .

This may be an honest transaction; lots of good men in Kansas, Nebraska, North Carolina and elsewhere have gone into it. . . . It seems to agree very well with the fellows who squat near the flesh pots. But our observation has been that the People's Party never grows a single vote after that flesh pot feast begins . . . but wilts and dwindles away.

We therefore advise our friend to meet and talk with all men—but fuse with no enemy, compromise no principle, surrender no vital conviction.[26]

He continued to warn against the blandishments of the Democratic advocates of fusion. " 'I am willing,' " he quoted Editor Howell of the *Constitution* as saying immediately before the Democratic National Convention of 1896, " 'to advocate every principle of the Populist Platform, if it is necessary, in order to keep the people inside the Democratic party.' " This, according to Watson, was a perfect illustration of the old party's motto: "Anything to keep the offices." It had promised the whole Alliance platform, the sub-treasury excepted, in 1890, and it would not scruple to promise the entire Populist platform, virtually the same, in 1896.[27]

It was this uncompromising rejection of fusion in the face of repeated defeats, when fusion would have won high office, that earned Watson the name of "as extreme a mid-road Populist as ever breathed or wrote." It also earned him the devotion of Southern Populists from Virginia to Texas, as well as the Western rank and file who had resisted silver and fusion. The radical

[26] *P. P. P.*, July 26, 1896, quoted in A. M. Arnett, *op. cit.*, p. 190.
[27] *P. P. P*, June 19, 1896.

Southern Populist, to whom fusion was anathema and silver a "mere drop in the bucket," found his clearest expression in the voice of Tom Watson, and in Watson he placed his faith. From the Middle West, the Lower South, and the Far West Watson received messages commending his stand against fusion.[28]

Upon the maneuvers of Western leaders toward fusion and silver, on the other hand, radical Populists of all sections looked with suspicion and misgivings, not to say hostility. From the West came Senator Peffer's denunciation of the policy of the National Committee of his own party as "treacherous"; [29] from the South came a North Carolina editor's judgment that it was an attempt to "deliver the entire People's party into the lap of Wall Street Democracy at one time." [30] Writing in the Middle West, though speaking for an intelligent element that was non-sectional, Lloyd lamented the curious paradox "that the new party, the Reform party, the People's party, should be more boss-ridden, ring-ruled, gang-gangrened, than the two old parties of monopoly. The party that makes itself the special champion of the Referendum and Initiative tricked out of its very life and soul by a permanent National Chairman—something no other party has!" [31]

Positions of Populist party leadership had passed from the South to the West by the middle 'nineties, largely because Westerners had been more successful in securing national office. It was a Western policy that was adopted as the strategy for 1896. The anti-fusionist South wished to hold the national convention in February, and step boldly forward with its nominees without regard to what the old party conventions did later. Western leaders succeeded in postponing the convention, however, until both old parties had held theirs. The Western argument as-

---

[28] Correspondence in Watson MSS.; letters in *P. P. P.*, 1895–1896.

[29] Quoted in *Progressive Farmer*, June 30, 1896.

[30] Editorial in the *Progressive Farmer*, June 30, 1896.

[31] From a letter written by Lloyd, July 10, 1896, in Caro Lloyd, *op. cit*, Vol. I., p. 259.

sumed that the conventions of both opposing parties would be dominated by their reactionary wings and that the People's party would profit by gathering bolting silverites from both sides.[32]

As time approached for the conventions the fallacy of the Western theory grew more apparent. In June the Republican platform presented an outright stand against silver, a position that pointed more conclusively than ever to a victory for the silver-insurgents at the Democratic convention. Such an eventuality would put an entirely different complexion upon the naïve Western strategy of gathering in bolters. A complete revision of tactics was required without delay. H. E. Taubeneck, national chairman, thrashed about wildly for a new scheme, and at last settled upon the desperate plan of attempting to induce the Democrats to nominate Henry M. Teller, a silver Republican who had bolted the national convention. Teller had never been a Populist and was interested only in silver; yet Taubeneck and his cohorts were prepared to deliver their party to his cause if the Democrats would join them in his nomination.[33] Lloyd thought that Taubeneck had been "flimflammed" by the politicians at Washington, who had persuaded him that free silver was the supreme issue. If the party management had been in capable hands, he thought, instead of in the hands of " 'Glaubenichts' like Taubeneck, the full Omaha platform would easily have been made the issue that would have held us together for a brilliant campaign, but now that cannot be done."

The Chicago convention did go over to silver, as expected, but instead of Teller, it nominated William Jennings Bryan of Nebraska, a man dear to the hearts of Western Populists with whom he had flirted for years.[34] The platform was likewise richly baited for Populists. Besides the expected demand for

[32] Henry D. Lloyd, *op. cit.*, p. 300; J. D. Hicks, *op. cit.*, p. 350.
[33] Editorial in the *Progressive Farmer*, June 30, 1896; J. D. Hicks, *op. cit.*, pp. 352-354.
[34] Jesse E. Boell, "William Jennings Bryan before 1896," master's thesis, University of Nebraska, *passim*.

free silver, it contained denunciation of Cleveland's bond-selling policy and his action in the Pullman strike; it condemned the Supreme Court's decision against income tax legislation; it favored stricter federal control of railroads. It now became the plain duty of Populists and all sincere reformers, the Democrats loudly proclaimed, to rally behind Bryan's cause, to renounce all "selfish" adherence to party in favor of "principle."

This appeal carried weight with the West. General Weaver had been at work for months promoting Bryan's nomination, and now set out for the Populist convention to make the chief nominating speech for him. "I care not for party names," said Watson's friend and former colleague, Jerry Simpson; "it is the substance we are after, and we have it in William J. Bryan." Ex-Governor "Bloody-Bridles" Waite of Colorado capitulated, and even Senator Peffer thought that the West was going for Bryan, no matter what happened. Ignatius Donnelly remained to speak for the more inarticulate mass of anti-fusionist, mid-road Populists of the West.[35]

For the South, Watson voiced the practically unanimous sentiment that to go back to the Democratic party now would be to "return as the hog did to its wallow." He knew his enemies too well to be taken in by them again. "The Democratic party," he wrote, "realizing that it had lost the respect, the confidence and the patience of the people, determined to anticipate the triumph of Populism by a public confession of political guilt, an earnest assertion of change of heart, a devout acceptance of Populist principles, and a modest demand that the People's party should vacate its quarters and surrender its political possessions. A very staggering piece of political impudence was this." [36] With his blessings the Georgia delegation to the National Convention was sent off with strict instructions "to insist upon the original Ocala declaration" and fight fusion.[37] The head of the

[35] St. Louis *Globe-Democrat*, July 20, 1896; F. L. Haynes, *Weaver*, p. 374.
[36] *P. P P*, June 26, Dec. 13, 1896.
[37] *Ibid*, June 19, 1896.

293

delegation wired headquarters at St. Louis: "Tell the boys I am coming—in the middle of the road." [38]

Delegates from virtually all Southern states grimly chose the same route to St. Louis. It proved to be the road to their Waterloo and the Waterloo of Populism.

Declining to comment upon the possibility of his receiving the nomination, and offering no explanation for his failure to attend the Convention, Tom Watson remained quietly at home.

* * * * * *

The fourteen hundred delegates who gathered at Convention Hall in St. Louis on July 22 presented a striking contrast to those who had nominated Mark Hanna's friend in that same hall a month before. City journalists, spotting salable copy, described their rustic manners and quaint doings. A group was found sitting with shoes off. Some took no regular sleeping quarters and fared upon nickel meals at lunch counters. A part of one important delegation was found actually suffering for want of food, as the sessions dragged out longer than planned. An interview with an "eminent physician of Washington" was printed in mock solemnity listing insanity symptoms among the delegates. They were poor men, the majority of them, terribly in earnest, and therefore, one gathers, rather ridiculous.[39]

A sympathetic observer found anxiety written in the face of everyone, no matter to what faction he belonged. Anxiety in the mass of delegates lest they be sold out—and there were both rumors and signs that they would be. Anxiety in the faces of busily caucusing and whispering managers lest the coveted fruits of fusion, finally within their grasp, be snatched from them by the radical middle-of-the-road Southerners. The radicals themselves, distrusting fusion and half measures as they did, feared

[38] A. M. Arnett, *op. cit*, p 197.
[39] St. Louis *Globe-Democrat*, July 21-27, 1896; H. D. Lloyd, "The Populists at St. Louis," *loc. cit.*, p. 293.

at the same time lest their radicalism split the force of opposition to their real enemy—Eastern Capitalism. This might be the last opportunity for a union of reform forces. Edward Bellamy thought that the real issue of 1896—that "between men and money"—was in the back of all minds. "It was in the air that there must be a union," wrote Lloyd. "It was a psychological moment of *rapprochement* against an appalling danger which for thirty years now had been seen rising in the sky. If the radicals made a mistake, it was a patriotic mistake." [40]

The radical mid-roaders were the most distraught and unorganized group of all. Chiefly Southern in membership, they were led by the huge, militant Texas delegation, the largest one present. Their most conspicuous figure was James H. "Cyclone" Davis, a gaunt giant with a bellowing voice. The radicals declared they would not be "swallowed" by the new Democracy, and they were out to nominate a straight Populist ticket. While probably the largest faction present, they were terribly handicapped by want of leadership and a candidate. Their chaotic state was made plain when at their caucus only a day before the Convention opened they were unable to agree upon a candidate. Debs, Donnelly, "Cyclone" Davis, Van Dervoort of Nebraska, and Mimms of Tennessee were all discussed but passed over.[41]

Despite confusion, the mid-roaders were still intent on not being sold out to the Democrats. Said one delegate at the caucus: "They may sell us out here at St. Louis, but before high heaven they can never deliver the goods. I was originally a Democrat. We West Virginia Populists left the Democrats never to return." Another echoed his anxiety: "While we have been shouting the other fellows, with a perfect organization, have been gathering in the stragglers. It makes no difference how many men we may have, if we are not organized we will be swallowed." [42]

[40] *Ibid.*, p. 300.
[41] St. Louis *Globe-Democrat*, July 20-23, 1896; J. D. Hicks, *op. cit.*, pp. 359-362.
[42] St. Louis *Globe-Democrat*, July 22, 1896.

The fusionists were not only well organized; they knew exactly what they wanted. Their object was the endorsement of Bryan and Sewall and the fusion of the two parties into one. General Weaver, in charge of the Bryan headquarters, was industriously working toward this end. Three days before the Convention opened Senator James K. Jones, chairman of the Democratic National Committee, arrived at St. Louis to remain throughout, closeted with Bryan Populists or buzzing in and out of committee room, hotel lobby, and Convention hall. Some 1,000 Missouri Democrats were said to be aiding the plot to steal the Convention. An additional advantage for the West lay in the rule of awarding delegates on a basis of Populist successes in the past three elections. This scheme put a premium upon the fusion victories of Western states, and accordingly penalized the South, which had resisted fusion.[43]

Following the first day's session, at which they showed a strength that shook the confidence of the Bryanites, the midroad radicals of twenty-one states finally agreed, without especial enthusiasm for their choice, to support S. F. Norton of Illinois for President, and Frank Burkett of Mississippi for Vice-President. Their forces greatly rallied, they planned a mighty demonstration for the evening session that would sweep the Convention to the left. That night they found the hall in complete darkness, with no lights obtainable. A futile attempt to hold the demonstration anyway only succeeded in producing scenes "at once weird and picturesque"—the gaunt figure of "Cyclone" Davis gesticulating under the flickering light of a candle he held aloft; Mrs. Lease yelling from the platform; the mob of delegates in the darkness crying out accusations of "ugly work" against the fusionists. Twenty-five minutes after the attempt was abandoned, the lights were burning brightly in the hall. It was not the last time the charge of foul play was made at this Convention, nor the last occasion for the charge.[44]

[43] St. Louis *Globe-Democrat*, July 20 and 21, 1896.
[44] *Ibid*, July 22 and 23, 1896; J. D. Hicks, *op cit.*, pp. 359-362.

The next day the radicals won the first fall in what was considered a test of the anti-Bryan strength. The vote was upon the seating of a contesting mid-road delegation of Eugene V. Debs supporters backed by Clarence Darrow. The margin was narrow, 665 to 642, but the mid-roaders were jubilant. Their hopes were speedily dashed, however, by the election of Senator William V. Allen of Nebraska, an out-and-out fusionist, as permanent chairman of the Convention by a vote of 758 to 564.[45]

With the nomination of Bryan now seemingly assured, the threat of a bolt by the mid-roaders that would split the party in half became more menacing than ever. "Texas is here to hold a Populist convention," exclaimed a delegate, "and we're going to do it before we go home. If some of the delegates nominate Bryan, they, being unpopulistic, will be the bolters." If the naming of Bryan promised a bolt, then the nomination of his running-mate, Arthur Sewall, portended a veritable rebellion. Yet Chairman Allen and his Democratic friends were plotting that as well.

Whatever case the fusionists might make for the Populist leanings of Bryan, they were hard put to it to discover like tendencies in Sewall of Maine. There could hardly have been produced in one figure a more comprehensive challenge to orthodox Populist doctrine. Not only was he the president of one national bank and the director of others, but also a railroad director, as well as the president of one trust and part owner of another. On top of this he was an Easterner, a man of wealth, and he enjoyed an evil name among workers for his labor policies. Scarcely a plank of the Populist platform was left unfouled. No Populist could countenance the nomination of such a man without a ludicrous confession of his party's bankruptcy. Yet the manipulators in control of the Convention demanded Sewall's nomination.

It was obvious that the hope for any compromise between radical mid-roaders and extreme fusionists lay in the nominee for

[45] *Ibid.*, July 24, 1896.

297

Vice-President. Foreseeing this possibility early in the Convention, a group of Southern delegates led by Senator Marion Butler, who had served as temporary chairman of the Convention, agreed upon a plan of compromise that would embrace accepting Bryan for Presidential nominee, but substituting a radical Southern Populist for Sewall as his running mate.[46] As part of the plan members of the Georgia delegation were prevailed upon to obtain the consent of Tom Watson for allowing his name to be used.

Watson had instructed his friends before the Convention not to allow the use of his name. During the course of the Convention, he issued the following statement to the press:

> I am opposed to the nomination of Bryan and Sewall or either of them separately.
>
> The Populist party has good material within its own ranks. I would refuse. I would refuse a nomination.
>
> I say this now, as I do not expect it; and it is my present belief that I shall not change my mind.[47]

The messages he received from the Convention described the chaotic state of affairs and inquired whether he would accept a nomination for the Vice-Presidency on a ticket with Bryan as a means of harmonizing all factions and preventing a split in the party. He was given to understand that an agreement had been reached with the Democratic managers to withdraw Sewall from their ticket. He was told nothing of the caucus of mid-roaders and their candidates, and did not learn of them until after the Convention. Under these conditions he "reluctantly" wired his consent. "Yes, if it will harmonize all factions," was his reply. Later he said that had he known all the circumstances he would never have consented, and the mid-road candidates "would have received my hearty support . . ."[48]

46 Carl Snyder, "Senator Marion Butler," *Review of Reviews*, Vol. XIV, p. 429.
47 New York *World*, July 25, 1896.
48 Interview with J L. Cartledge of Augusta, who wired Watson from St. Louis; New York *World*, July 26 and 27, 1896; editorial in *P. P. P.*, July 21, 1896; Watson's letter of acceptance in *P. P. P*, Dec. 13, 1896; Atlanta *Journal*, July 25, 1896.

Tom Watson's name was a magical one among the disaffected and intransigent radical Populists. It warmed the imagination. He had been the first in the South to cut the old ties and step forward boldly as a Populist. In Congress he had won the admiration of the Western representatives, who elected him their leader in the House and followed him enthusiastically. He had burned his bridges behind him, steadfastly resisted the temptation of fusion, and suffered much for his principles. He was the hero of thousands of Southern Populists who had followed his periodic battles over the past four years against Democratic fraud and violence. The *People's Party Paper* was nationally known and frequently quoted, and its editor stood in the popular mind as the very incarnation of middle-of-the-road Populism, thorough-going, fearless, and uncompromising. He had been mentioned as a possible nominee from time to time since 1892.[49]

Rapid headway was being made at St. Louis with the scheme of compromise. The mid-roaders grasped at the suggestion of resorting to the unusual procedure of nominating the Vice-President before the President. They might at least dispose of Sewall. The report that the Democratic managers had promised that their candidate would withdraw in favor of a Populist nominee if Bryan were nominated for the Presidency was well circulated. Delegates voted with that report in mind. The decision to nominate the Vice-President first was made by a vote of 738 to 637.[50]

Jubilant because of their victory over the determined opposition of fusionists, the radicals expressed their feelings in a flood of nomination oratory. Congressman M. W. Howard of Alabama, "a man of enormous stature, tall and swarthy, with raven black hair that falls to his shoulders," the author of *The American Plutocracy*,[51] nominated Watson. His nominee, said Howard, was "a man who has suffered in the cause; a man who has

[49] Release of the National Reform Press, in *P. P. P.*, Nov. 12, 1891; H. L. Young to T. E. W. in *P. P. P.*, June 24, 1892; Augusta *Chronicle*, Oct. 26, 1894.
[50] St. Louis *Globe-Democrat*, July 25 and 26, 1896; New York *World*, July 25, 1896; *P. P. P.*, July 31, 1896.
[51] Published in New York, 1895.

299

sacrificed his money and his time for its good; a man who has borne the cross and should wear the crown." All speeches in second to Watson's nomination, of which there were many, stressed his unshakable loyalty to principle. A Negro delegate from Georgia expressed gratitude for his courageous defense of Negro political rights. Ignatius Donnelly, representing the compromise idea, said that he was "willing to swallow Democracy gilded with the genius of a Bryan" but he could not "stomach plutocracy in the body of Sewall." He hoped Watson's nomination would be made unanimous. A cautious Texan asked whether Watson, if nominated, would remain on the ticket till the election. "Yes, sir!" came an immediate answer. "Until hell freezes over!" The reply so completely, so accurately, summed up the popular conception of Tom Watson's character, and so well expressed the mid-roaders' feeling in calling upon him in this emergency, that it brought the Convention to its feet in a spontaneous demonstration. On the first ballot he received 539¾ votes against 257 for Sewall, his closest and only serious opponent. It was an impressive proof that Watson's policy was the real will of the Convention. The lights of the hall were again being tampered with, flickering out. Votes were frantically changed to give him a majority, and a motion was passed suspending the rules and nominating Watson unanimously. In pitch darkness the Watson Populists wildly and blindly celebrated their triumph.[52]

The midnight darkness of that hall was symbolic of the conditions in which that whole lamentable Convention groped. The delegates read in the morning papers a telegram from Bryan asking Senator Jones to withdraw his name from consideration if Sewall were not nominated. Chairman Allen had refused to give this information to the Convention. The delegates also read a letter from Senator Jones, which "underwent a remarkable change after it was given to the newspapers," denying that he

[52] St Louis *Globe-Democrat*, July 25 and 26, 1896; *P. P. P.*, July 31 and Dec. 13, 1896; *Constitution*, July 25, 1896.

300

had made any commitment as to the withdrawal of Sewall. The air was again thick with cries of "treachery." "Gagged, clique-ridden, and machine ruled," pronounced delegate Lloyd. What had been anxiety was rapidly souring to disgust.[53]

Relentlessly the steam-roller tactics were continued by the managers, still determined to nominate Bryan. Three times, while the roll call of the states was in progress, Chairman Allen denied point blank when the question was put to him from the floor the existence of a further message from Bryan asking that he not be nominated, despite the fact that he was perfectly aware of the message.[54] Twice during the roll call the Texas delegation hurriedly withdrew to caucus on the proposal of bolting. Once when Bryan stampeders attempted to wrest their banner from them a dozen Texans reached for their guns—and then looked sheepish. Once when the Convention seemed wavering Henry Demarest Lloyd, with a carefully prepared speech in hand designed to rally the delegates back to their principles, stood hes-itating while he was urged to speak. He turned to Clarence Dar-row, who advised against it. Other men of courage and intelli-gence "stood spellbound, fearing to break the union." While they "waited for a protest, a halt," the machine rolled on. Bryan was nominated. Lloyd burst in upon his host late that night "in feverish excitement" and exploded with the exclamation that the party was "buried, hopelessly sold out."[55]

[53] St. Louis *Globe-Democrat*, July 25, 1896; New York *World*, July 25, 1896; Caro Lloyd, *op. cit.*, Vol. I, p. 261.

[54] St. Louis *Globe-Democrat*, July 26, 1896; *P. P. P.*, Nov. 13, 1896; J. D. Hicks, *op. cit.*, p. 366.

[55] St. Louis *Globe-Democrat*, July 26, 1896; Caro Lloyd, *op. cit.*, Vol. I, p. 262.

CHAPTER XVII

The Debacle of 1896

HARDLY ANYONE could be found who expressed satisfaction at the outcome of the St. Louis Convention—least of all the mid-roaders, and certainly not Tom Watson. The question naturally arises: why, of all people, should Tom Watson, the leading advocate of the middle-of-the-road policy, the staunchest opponent of fusion, have lent his name to this weak compromise with fusion? After six years of uncompromising resistance at costly sacrifice, why did he half-way yield at the crucial moment? Before passing judgment upon his own answer it might be well to inquire how other national leaders of radical and reform groups met the test of 1896.

Of the Single Taxers, Henry George himself publicly endorsed Bryan. Edward Bellamy, acknowledged leader of the more radical "Nationalists," proclaimed that the real issue lay "between men and money," and swung his support to the silver champion. W. D. P. Bliss, of the Christian Socialists, took the same attitude. More surprising was the attitude of Eugene V. Debs, a recent convert to Marxian socialism. Debs wired Darrow forbidding the use of his name as a candidate against Bryan at St. Louis, and advised union labor to support the Democratic nominee. Speaking as a Populist, Henry Demarest Lloyd called the Convention "the most discouraging experience of my life"; yet he confessed his own impotence in the face of circumstances at St. Louis. Twelve days before the Convention he stated the

Populist dilemma of 1896 about as accurately as it could be stated: "If we fuse, we are sunk; if we don't fuse, all the silver men we have will leave us for the more powerful Democrats." [1]

All things considered, there is not one of these five men with whose position Watson's course of action does not bear favorable comparison. Being the unanimous nominee of the St. Louis Convention he was naturally under some constraint in expressing his opinion of its work. He did exercise a modicum of restraint until after the election, but it was only a modicum. In the first editorial after his nomination he said:

There will be disappointment throughout the ranks of the People's Party at the failure of our national convention to nominate a "middle-of-the-road" ticket.

The position of this paper upon that subject has not been changed. We thought before the convention met, and we think now, that the welfare of our party, and of the principles it represents, demanded that we nominate our own ticket, and put upon that ticket two Populists, tried and true. [2]

The editorial continued with a justification of his consent to the nomination in view of his earlier decision against it, and in view of his unaltered mid-road position. His comparative isolation and wretched means of communication with the Convention delegates should be taken into account. There was no means of reaching him even from Atlanta during the six hours his name was before the Convention. The Thomson operator went to bed at eight o'clock. Watson was not informed of his nomination until the following morning. [3] His decisions were based upon such information as he received from delegates who were much in the dark themselves. It is interesting (and profitless) to speculate upon the outcome of the Convention if Watson, the only Southern candidate with a wide personal following and the ability to

[1] Caro Lloyd, *Henry Demarest Lloyd*, Vol. I, p. 259.
[2] *P. P. P.*, July 31, 1896.
[3] *Constitution*, July 25, 1896.

direct it, had been at St. Louis to take command of the mid-road forces. One hesitates to pass judgment, yet it seems clear that Watson made a mistake in not attending the Convention himself. Why he failed to do so is not known.

He continues his apology:

> As the hours passed away at St. Louis, it became constantly more evident that our existence as a party hung upon a thread. The West was committed to Bryan beyond recall. . . . With the West gone away from us, how could our party live . . . ?
>
> It was in this chaotic condition of things which I witnessed with keen anxiety, and which caused members of the Georgia delegation to telegraph me to allow my name to be used to restore harmony and save the party.
>
> Upon that express condition, I consented, and the object was obtained. . . .
>
> If now the Democratic managers should refuse to make any concessions at all it would show that our efforts toward unity have all been thrown away. If they continue to demand that the Populists shall go out of existence as a party, they will prove to the world their object in adopting our platform was not so much to get free silver as it was to bury the People's Party.[4]

In a series of articles written at the request of the New York *World* he further elaborated his position. He had consented to the nomination in order "to save [his] party from extinction." "Under no other circumstances would I have agreed to the nomination, and the circumstances under which I did accept were such as I did not dream one week ago would exist." The Democratic party had been driven to the left only because of the pressure exerted by an active Populist party. The dissolution of his party would have removed the pressure and the old party would have swung back to reactionary leadership as it had in 1892 and 1894. "By nominating a ticket of our own," he continued, "and upon a platform of our own, we preserve our identity as a party

[4] *P. P. P*, July 31, 1896.

and we maintain our influence over the Democrats." The Chicago platform did not go so far as the Populists would have liked, but they were willing to march with the Democrats "as far as they do go in our direction." If he and Bryan made the race together, their position would be "that of two men who may differ upon some subjects, but who act together upon those matters about which . . . [they] are agreed. He believed that, "by agreeing to coöperate with them to this extent we [Populists] do not compromise our principles, stultify our record, or disband our organization." He was firmly opposed to "any fusion that would absorb us, annihilate our party and put it in the future entirely in the power of the Democratic organization." [5]

The prospect the new Populist candidate might entertain of having his principles, his personality, his character, or any aspect of his candidacy presented to the nation's voters with accuracy or fairness was slender indeed. The press of the Eastern Republican plutocracy that pictured Bryan as an anarchist, and its pulpit, that denounced him as Antichrist, naturally sought more horrendous adjectives to describe Watson. One of the milder animadversions of the respectable press was the New York *Times'* description of Watson as "a swashbuckling, nagging, vulgar scold, indifferent to the amenities," whose nomination should be treated as "a political joke." [6]

Police Commissioner Theodore Roosevelt of New York City, who rendered valuable (and well rewarded) service to Mark Hanna's campaign for McKinley, had his moments of hysteria. Speaking with "the greatest soberness" he declared that "the sentiment now animating a large proportion of our people can only be suppressed, as the Commune in Paris was suppressed, by taking ten or a dozen of their leaders out, standing . . . them against a wall, and shooting them dead." These leaders are "plotting a social revolution and the subversion of the American

[5] New York *World*, July 25 and 26, 1896; Augusta *Chronicle*, July 26 and 28, 1896.
[6] The New York *Times*, July 26, 1896; quoted by James F. Collins, "Thomas E. Watson: A Study in the New South" (Master's thesis, New York University), p. 67.

Republic." When the dread hour comes, he promised, "I shall be found at the head of my regiment." [7] Once when Roosevelt's brow was somewhat less fevered he wrote an article in which he dealt at length with Watson's candidacy. "He represents the real thing," said Roosevelt, "while Bryan after all is more or less a sham and a compromise." [8]

Mr. Watson really ought to be the first man on the ticket, with Mr. Bryan second; for he is much the superior in boldness, in thorough-going acceptance of his principles according to their logical conclusions, and in sincerity of faith. It is impossible not to regret that the Democrats and Populists should not have put forward in the first place the man who genuinely represents their ideas. . . . He is infinitely more in earnest than is Mr. Bryan. Mr. Watson belongs to that school of southern Populists who honestly believe that the respectable and commonplace people who own banks, railroads, dry goods stores, factories, and the like, are persons of mental and social attributes that unpleasantly distinguish Heliogabalus, Nero, Caligula and other worthies of later Rome. . . .

Altogether Mr. Watson, with his sincerity, his frankness, his extreme suspiciousness, and his uncouth hatred of anything he cannot understand and of all elegancies and decencies of civilized life, is an interesting personage. . . .

Mr. Sewall would make a colorless Vice-President, and were he at any time to succeed Mr. Bryan in the White House would travel Mr. Bryan's path with extreme reluctance and under duress. Mr. Watson would be a more startling, more attractive, and more dangerous figure, for if he got the chance he would lash the nation with a whip of scorpions, while Bryan would be content with the torture of ordinary thongs.

Writing to his friend Lodge, Roosevelt mentioned "a long and really very interesting letter, from, of all persons in the world, Tom Watson," which he promised to show him when they met.[9]

[7] Henry F. Pringle, *Theodore Roosevelt, A Biography*, p. 164.

[8] Theodore Roosevelt in *Review of Reviews*, Vol. XIV (1896), pp. 296-297.

[9] Henry C. Lodge, *Selections from the Correspondence of Theodore Roosevelt and Henry Cabot Lodge, 1884–1918*, Vol I, pp 234, 236, 249.

The letter had reference to Roosevelt's article. "If in Georgia and throughout the South," wrote Watson, "we have conditions as intolerable as those which surround you in New York, can you not realize why I make war upon them? . . . If you could spend an evening with me among my books and amid my family, I feel quite sure you would not again class me with those who make war upon the 'decencies and elegancies of civilized life.' " [10] Roosevelt recanted publicly: "I was in Washington when Mr. Watson was in Congress, and I know how highly he was esteemed personally by his colleagues. . . . He is honest, he is earnest, he is brave, he is disinterested." [11] Their correspondence over this incident marked the beginning of a long and interesting friendship between the two men. Roosevelt's *Autobiography* years later contained a flattering tribute to Watson. Watson's ability to turn animosity into friendship was a gift that he employed too rarely.

His treatment at the hands of less partisan critics was, on the whole, more favorable. James Creelman of the New York *World* thought: "Of the five candidates before the nation he is the most picturesque, the most original, and in some respects the brainiest. He is not afraid of publicity. He is not a sham." Alfred Henry Lewis, later known as a muckraker novelist, wrote for the New York *Herald:* "Altogether, he is a better man than either Hobart or McKinley, thinks less of himself and more of the people, and a syndicate could no more buy Watson or own Watson than it could buy or own a star. No Hannas go with the Horoscopes of such as Watson." Henry Demarest Lloyd called him "a second Alexander H. Stephens in delicacy of physique and robustness of eloquence and loyalty to the people."

His resemblance to Stephens was frequently mentioned. For personal beauty the Populist candidate could ill afford comparison with his running mate, the handsome Bryan. At forty he

[10] T. E. W. to Theodore Roosevelt, Sept. 30, 1896, Roosevelt MSS., Washington, D. C.
[11] Quoted by T. E. W., *Life and Speeches of Thomas E Watson*, pp. 27-28.

possessed the "old-young" appearance he retained until late in life. Creelman described it:

> The mystery about his face is due to the parchment texture of his skin. One moment while he smiles and he shows his loosely set small teeth you think he is a youth of twenty and the next, when he tears up words by their roots, with some of the soil clinging to them, and draws his brows down sharp over his eyes, mouth hard set and little ears standing out on his head, he might be a sage of sixty. His earnestness flames up in a strange old-young face. . . . Mr. Watson's jaw would interest him [Sewall]. It is the jaw of a crusader, the jaw of a martyr.

Another thought him "painfully lean and hungry looking, with a cadaverous, rawboned face and sunken cheeks and dark eyes, alive with the marvelous vitality and the intense earnestness of a man who never tires." It is remarkable that, as intense as was the emotional partisanship he evoked, no one who ever saw him in that era seems to have questioned Watson's sincerity; the common view was that he was "a man of sincerity, tragically earnest in everything." One writer thought he had "no sense of humor," but that "life is a serious struggle with him." [12] Humor he undoubtedly had, but "the jaw of the crusader" completely masked it for the time being.

His manner of speaking was sometimes contrasted to that of Bryan. "Bryan's style of oratory is as far separated from that of Watson as one pole from another," it was said. "Bryan deals in oratorical flowers; Watson discards all efforts at embellishment and cuts to the heart of the subject with keen incisiveness and unrelenting truth." He had a "Dantonian trick" of gesturing with whirling arms, swaying body, and tossing head that loosed a lock of hair which "punctuated his periods with a loppy emphasis." Some noticed a "hawkish tendency" in his manner, and in his "shrill, raspy voice, the power of strong, high flight, the pinion, the talon, the beak, and withal the swoop of the hawk."

[12] James Creelman, New York *World,* Oct. 5, 1896.

The St. Louis Convention's legacy to its nominee and their campaign was a beautiful tangle of problems as knotty and perplexing as could have been devised. Would Bryan be notified of his nomination? Would he accept? How could he accept when the Populist platform in some aspects contradicted the Democratic platform? When acceptance implied approval of Watson? Would Populists support him if he did not accept, or nominate another candidate? Would Sewall withdraw, be withdrawn, or remain on the ticket? If he remained, would Watson be taken down? If both remained, how could the Populist ticket be arranged?

Wildly contradictory answers to these questions flew back and forth after the Convention. Pointing out that his nomination was carried in the face of his disapproval, Bryan said acceptance depended on "what conditions are attached." He would not do "anything unfair to Mr. Sewall." Chairman Jones brusquely declared that Bryan could not accept, and that Sewall would remain on the ticket. Senator Stewart gaily announced that Democrats would have gunmen stationed along the road to shoot the first Populist who attempted to notify Bryan of his nomination. The New York *World*, confidently and repeatedly predicted that Sewall would be withdrawn from the Democratic ticket, after the Maine election, in favor of Watson. The St. Louis *Globe-Democrat* announced as authentic news that the Populist executive committee would withdraw Watson in favor of Sewall. Prominent Democrats declared their party must live up to its contract and withdraw Sewall. A caucus of mid-road Populists issued an ultimatum to the effect that if Bryan did not accept by August 5, his name would be replaced by a Populist candidate.[18] Out of this confusion of tongues and clash of council the crazy pattern of the campaign gradually took shape.

Only a few days after the Convention, Senator Jones, chairman of the Democratic National Committee, set the pace of bit-

---

[18] St. Louis *Globe-Democrat*, July 26, 1896; New York *World*, July 26 and Aug. 3, 1896; clipping, Watson Scrapbooks.

ter recrimination between the allied parties by an onslaught upon Southern Populists. The Western and Northern delegates at St. Louis he had found "broad-minded and patriotic," but, said the Senator:

As a general rule the Southern Delegates were not a creditable class. They practically admitted while at St. Louis that they were out for nothing but spoil. They said that there was "nothing in it" for them to indorse the Democratic nominees, and this same spirit will probably dominate their action in the future. They will do all they can to harass the Democracy and create confusion, and in the end they will do just as they are doing now in Alabama, fuse with the Republicans and vote for McKinley. They will go with the negroes, where they belong. . . .

I suppose that Watson really believes that he can "bluff" us into withdrawing Mr. Sewall. Just as though such a proposition could be considered for a moment by any right thinking man! Mr. Sewall will, of course, remain on the ticket, and Mr. Watson can do what he likes.[14]

Coming from the man who had so assiduously courted the hand of Populism, this was a shocking sentiment indeed. The slur bracketing Populists with Negroes was a fighting word in the South, and the Senator from Arkansas knew it. The loud demand for Jones' resignation by certain Northern Democratic papers suddenly hushed when it was whispered about that his statement was deliberate party strategy: an announcement that nothing would be conceded to Southern Populists.[15]

Anyone who knew Watson's temperament must have been impressed at his victory over his feelings. Without doubt it cost him many a wry face to swallow Jones' insult. The abnegation of his reply is little short of pathetic. Jones' remarks, he said, were "insulting, and were meant to be so. They will arouse resentment, and were meant to arouse it." It was a "clumsy effort

[14] New York *World*, Aug. 3, 1896.
[15] Atlanta *Journal*, Aug. 5, 1896.

to create discord" between Populists of the West and those of the South, and was designed "to invoke a bitter reply." It would fail. He appealed to Southern Populists to "stand by the contract made at St. Louis. Give Bryan every vote you have got and let Senator Jones say what he likes. Let him insult you at his pleasure. Make no angry reply; lift yourselves above it; think of your country; pray for its liberty; work for its best interests; do your duty and let God Almighty take care of you and your party." [16]

To Senator Jones and the Democrats he replied in the columns of the New York *World:*

We have conceded everything short of extinction of our party. To go into the national campaign with no Populist on the national ticket disbands the party. The Democratic managers know this, and they have bent every energy to that end. It is not so much free silver they want as it is the death of the People's Party. . . .

Why should the Democratic managers demand of us a complete and unconditional surrender? They say we must fuse, but their idea of fusion is that we play minnow while they play trout; we play June bug while they play duck; we play Jonah while they play the whale. . . .

We are so heartily anxious to see the people of the South and West come together and act in concert for the good of the country . . . that we yet hope they will do it, in spite of the efforts of the Democratic politicians to prevent it.[17]

The Atlanta *Journal,* a Gold-Democratic paper, confessed that the policy announced by the Democratic managers seemed to indicate that they believed "a fight against the Populists is more welcome than a fight with them."

Three days after Senator Jones' attack upon Southern Populists and their leader, Watson addressed the state convention of his party. It was a trying occasion for him. He was expected to point the way, when he could see no way; to solve problems not

<hr />

[16] Clipping from an Augusta paper, Aug., 1896, Watson Scrapbooks.
[17] New York *World,* Aug. 5, 1896.

within his power to solve. Five thousand people crowded every foot of space in the crude Atlanta "Tabernacle." The day was hot. At the cry of "Off with the calico, boys," coats were shed and shirt-sleeved Populism waited. Watson appeared, looking "pale and frightened." The ovation his appearance evoked is described by a hostile but keenly observant witness: "It had the ring of trust and faith in it, and so quick, so sudden, so spontaneous, so deep was it that it staggered Watson. He tried to speak but could not. He muttered his half tearful thanks and left the stand. . . . An overwhelming sense of all those cheering thousands expected of him seemed to have fallen upon him with crushing weight. Little able to help themselves, they expected all things of him. He was their hope. What could he do?" [18]

Referring to another occasion, he once wrote in his private Journal, "There was a large crowd, and I never fail when there is a large crowd." He was speaking to Democrats as well as Populists. He began with an emphatic reaffirmation of Populist principles. They could not be prettily trimmed down to a free silver slogan. "That is not the whole of our grievance." There was "never a greater unrest than that which stirs the masses today," he said, and "free silver" was too easy an answer. Government ownership of railroads and other public interests, control of trusts, an entirely new system of money and credit, a ballot free from corruption, political rights for Negroes: "That is our case," he said. "Is there anything communistic about it?"

His wish was "to be perfectly honest and make the issue a sectional one." "It is a sectional issue." The East and North were Hamiltonian, "and they always will be." The South must "cut loose from Eastern and Northern connection and make an alliance with the great West," her own kind of people. He had given up an easy berth in the old party in order to "create a common rallying point," the Populist platform, on which to unite the two great sections. "Hasn't time vindicated my course?" he asked. "Southern Democracy is bidding defiance to Wall Street

[18] *Constitution*, Aug 8, 1896.

for the first time in thirty years," and the West has joined hands with the South. But still the Democratic leaders were not free of the East so long as they clung to Sewall. "You can't fight the national banks with any sincerity with a national banker as your leader," he told them. "You can't fight corporations with a corporation king as your leader."

The only honest course for the Democratic leaders was to withdraw Sewall from their ticket. Populists would never vote for him. "They have taken our doctrine, but they don't like our doctors," he said. "They are fond of our physics, but they don't like our physicians. They want to run our ship, but they want to expel our crew. . . . They say they want fusion. So they do. It is the fusion that the earthquake makes with the city it swallows." There was no consistency in calling this campaign a union between the South and the West, if the Southern candidate were ignored. There must be a leader from the South as well as one from the West. "For thirty years the Democratic party has acted as if it was ashamed of the South. You elect Democratic Presidents, and yet you never name any of them. . . . I appeal to Southern pride."

His pledge of loyalty to Bryan despite the bad faith of Democratic managers was the climax of his address: "We did not put up a nominee against Mr. Bryan, and we are going to keep the faith. We are going to vote for Mr. Bryan whether you take Mr. Sewall out or not. I am going to try to so manage this campaign that William J. Bryan shall get the benefit of every silver vote, even if Tom Watson goes to the bottom." [19]

Prefacing their comments with the assurance that "Democratic loyalty remained unshaken," the old-party papers nevertheless admitted that many "came away impressed, disturbed and unsettled." It was "a newer, a stronger, a broader and a more statesmanlike Watson than has ever stood before a Georgia audience." His speech might be called a complete vindication; he had won sympathy by his earnestness, and "thousands

[19] T. E. W., *Life and Speeches of Thomas E. Watson*, pp 144-159

of Georgia Democrats will gladly vote for Watson if Sewall is withdrawn." The demand for Sewall's withdrawal grew louder in the Democratic ranks, and politicians were plainly worried.[20]

Thomas R. R. Cobb, a prominent Democrat of Atlanta, in good standing with the party, was busy in New York organizing Bryan and Watson clubs. Cobb told New York Democrats that the great majority of Georgia Democrats would vote for Bryan and Watson because of Chairman Jones' contract with the Populists at St. Louis. He believed it plain that "morally, legally, and politically, the Democratic party is bound to carry out the deliberate contract of its executive head made before the world and for the valuable consideration of 2,000,000 votes. And I shall stand by the contract even if the agent renigs [*sic*]." Besides, "Sewall is a plutocrat, a national banker, a corporation king; Watson is a statesman and a man of the people." [21]

The journalist John Temple Graves, classified as a Gold Democrat, likewise took a strong position in regard to the "contract, solemn and honorable," which bound the Democrats to support Watson. He went further:

I support Watson because he represents a party that has educated our Democratic party to a due consideration of the welfare of the common people. I say it fearlessly, and it can not be denied, that reforms for which the masses have been clamoring for years—whether it be silver or labor or income tax or popular rights or resistance to government by injunction—had never been written, and might never have been written, into a Democratic platform, until the Populist party, 1,800,000 strong, thundered in the ears of Democratic leaders the announcement that a mighty multitude demanded these reforms. And among the men who have molded, through storm and struggle, the party that has educated ours to popular liberty, Tom Watson of Georgia stands easily first and foremost of them all.[22]

[20] Clippings, Watson Scrapbooks
[21] New York *World*, quoted in *P. P. P*, Aug. 21, 1896.
[22] "Card" in *Constitution*, Aug. 27, 1896.

Secretary Hoke Smith, recently resigned from Cleveland's Cabinet, grudgingly accepted the official decisions of the Democratic managers, but his paper, the Atlanta *Journal,* was openly sympathetic to Watson's cause. The Atlanta *Commercial,* another Democratic paper, frankly denounced the course party managers took against the Populists, and demanded the fulfillment of the St. Louis contract. "We wouldn't give Tom Watson for the whole state of Maine," proclaimed this paper. "Watson is in sympathy with every demand made at Chicago; Sewall is not. Let us be honest with the people. . . . It will not do for Democrats to eat apple dumpling while they give crow pie to the Populists." [23] Watson's organ reported that fifty-two Democratic papers in Georgia had expressed their preference for a Bryan-Watson ticket.

Meanwhile, Watson had locked horns with the chairman of his own Populist Executive Committee over the submissive attitude the latter had taken toward the Democratic managers. During the last confused minutes of the St. Louis Convention, Senator Allen pushed through a resolution bestowing upon the Executive Committee plenary powers to take any action the Convention might take were it in session. It was said that not a hundred delegates heard or understood the remarkable resolution. The charge was made then that its purpose was to pave the way for quietly withdrawing Watson from the ticket later. Senator Marion Butler of North Carolina, head of the compromise movement, became the new chairman of the Executive Committee. Watson regarded Butler with mistrust. The young Senator owed his office to a fusion with Republicans in North Carolina; he had proposed a similar fusion in Georgia to Watson; and now he was directing a national campaign of fusion with Democrats. Furthermore, he enjoyed the name (whether deserved or not) of "getting all that's coming to him," and it had been predicted in the press that he would betray Watson's cause.[24]

[23] Atlanta *Commercial,* quoted in the *Progressive Farmer,* Sept. 29, 1896.
[24] St. Louis *Globe-Democrat,* July 26, 1896; Carl Snyder, "Marion Butler," *Re-*

Senator Butler had issued a statement immediately after the Convention, saying that "The Populist party can not and will not swallow Sewall." Weeks passed, however, and no steps were taken to notify the candidates or to demand the withdrawal of Sewall. After several appeals from mid-roaders, Chairman Butler issued the statement on August 18 that Watson would remain on the ticket with Bryan and that his committee would strive as hard to elect one as the other. Still came no move toward notification. A member of the Notification Committee from Alabama protested to Butler that "we are treating Mr. Watson wrong," and taking a submissive and "humiliating attitude as we bow the knee before the Democratic throne." It was but two months until election, "and we are all at sea—not knowing whether our presidential candidate will accept—afraid to breathe for fear he will not." [25] Butler replied that it was "very probable" that the candidates would be notified in "due time." [26]

Exasperated and fretting in his humiliating position, Watson resorted to the extraordinary expedient of a public attack upon the Committee's submissive attitude. He wrote:

If the National Convention at St. Louis did not mean that Messrs. Bryan and Watson should be notified, why was a committee appointed to notify them? Why does Senator Allen, the chairman of the Committee, refuse to do what the convention instructed him to do? Is he afraid Mr. Bryan will repudiate our support? If so, our party has a right to know that fact. If Mr. Bryan is ashamed of the votes which are necessary to elect him, we ought to know it.[27]

Butler complained bitterly to a member of the Executive Committee of the "great scare headlines as to the lecture that

view of Reviews, Vol. XIV (Oct., 1896), pp. 429-433; Florence Smith, "The Populist Movement and its Influence in North Carolina," Ph.D. dissertation, University of Chicago, pp. 138-155; Atlanta Journal, Aug. 5, 1896.

25 M. W. Howard to Marion Butler, Aug. 21, 1896, quoted in P. P. P., Sept. 4, 1896.

26 Marion Butler to M. W. Howard, Aug. 25, 1896, quoted ibid.

27 New York Tribune, quoted in P. P. P., Sept. 4, 1896.

Mr. Watson is dealing the Committee about not proceeding at once to notify him." He thought it best to defer the notification, and was "inclined to have nothing further to do with it." [28] Nevertheless, Watson's single-handed fight for the mid-road Populist point of view had its effect. The New York *Tribune* commented: "His courageous and persistent efforts to compel a serious recognition of his candidacy at the hands of the Altgeld-Tillman-Bryan managers and their Populist allies are at last to be crowned with deservedly substantial success. . . . These spirited and plain-spoken words have evidently had their effect." [29]

Out of Maine came word from L. C. Bateman, secretary of the Notification Committee and Populist candidate for governor, that he had "positive information" that Sewall would soon be withdrawn. Furthermore, Bryan and Watson would soon receive formal notification. "From one end of the country to the other," he announced, "the Populist war cry is: 'No Watson, no Bryan.' We mean business. This is no child's play with us. Bryan cannot be elected without our help." From the other end of the continent the *Southern Mercury* of Texas contended that it had said, " 'No Watson, no Bryan' first, it will say it last. In fact, a middle-of-the-road ticket is its preference even at this stage of the game." A North Carolina editor predicted that "A million Populists will refuse to support Bryan if Sewall is not taken down."

The mass pressure called forth by Watson's demand for recognition finally stirred the cautious Democrats and the submissive Populist fusionists into action. Official letters of notification were sent to both Bryan and Watson by Senator Butler on September 14, and released to the press. [30] Bryan accepted the Populist nomination in a letter dated October 3, saying that he could

[28] Marion Butler to H. W. Reed, Aug. 27, 1896, Watson MSS.

[29] New York *Tribune*, quoted in *P. P. P*, Sept. 4, 1896.

[30] Marion Butler to T. E. W., Sept. 14, 1896, Watson MSS The letters of notification to both Watson and Bryan are printed in *P. P. P.*, Sept 18, 1896; see also W. J. Bryan, *The First Battle*, p. 430. Mr. Hicks is incorrect in his statement that Bryan did not accept the nomination and that neither he nor Watson was notified. (*The Populist Revolt*, p. 369.)

do so without departing from the Chicago platform.[31] Watson's letter of acceptance, dated October 14, was a scathing denunciation of the bargain-counter fusion policy of the Populist managers, which he considered a degrading swapping of principles for office. Chairman Butler, who bore the brunt of the candidate's wrath, refused to release the letter, and it did not appear until after the election.[32]

It is doubtful whether any candidate ever to appear on a presidential ticket found himself in quite the humiliating position that Tom Watson occupied in 1896. Not only were he and his party publicly insulted by his running-mate's representative, but Bryan himself studiously ignored his Populist running-mate throughout the campaign. He was compelled to ask publicly for his notification, to endure slights from members of his own committee, and to watch state after state desert its own nominee for that of another party. He was publicly denounced by fusionists of his own party for his refusal to withdraw entirely from the race. In short, while acting as its official leader, he was compelled to watch what had been a powerful party disintegrate under his feet. Such an experience could not but leave its permanent effects upon a man.

Before he received his official notification, Watson had left home for a campaign tour of the West. His object, aside from supporting Bryan's candidacy, was to win the Populists of that section back to a straight Bryan-Watson ticket, with no compromise or fusion on Sewall. Watson hoped that by such a policy in all states, the Democrats would be forced to withdraw Sewall. Butler and the Committee at first declared this to be their own policy, but later abandoned it for fusion. Butler explained to Watson that this abandonment was forced by the action of certain Western states which, acting on their own initiative, had made bargains with Democratic managers to support a certain

[31] *P. P P*, Oct 9, 1896
[32] Printed in *P P P*, Nov. 13, 1896.

318

number, and in some cases all, of the Sewall electors in exchange for Democratic support of Populist candidates for state and congressional offices. Such a bargain naturally found great favor in the eyes of local Populist candidates, who were generally also local managers, although the rank and file as a rule frowned upon it. Chairman Butler defended the policy as an expedient of practical politics.[33] Its adoption, however, plainly implied that the Populists no longer took seriously their own demand that the Democrats withdraw Sewall. It also implied that they no longer took seriously their own candidate for Vice-President. So it was that Watson set forth to stamp out the prairie fires of fusion in the West, in spite of the wishes of Chairman Butler and the quite understandable desires of certain Western Populists of prominence.

His first stop was Texas. The great majority of delegates to the Texas state convention had admittedly been in favor of a "no-Watson-no-Bryan" ultimatum to the Democratic managers, but some of the more conservative leaders had, by shrewd management and the simple expedient of out-sitting the majority, blocked the movement and left themselves free to effect a fusion later on, probably with the Republicans and Gold Democrats.[34]

Watson had a powerful personal following in Texas. "Watson is a modern hero," declared the *Southern Mercury*. "The character of the modern politician would look like a mustard seed beside a mountain when compared to Watson." With an impassioned speech he completely won a throng of five thousand at Dallas. "You must burn the bridges if you follow me," he told them. "I am for straight Populism (cheers) and I do not propose to be carried to one side of the road or the other (wild cheering)." He asked their loyal support of Bryan, but reminded the Democrats that if Bryan were elected it would be by "Tom Watson Populists." "This is a movement of the

[33] Marion Butler to T. E. W., Oct. 15, 1896; M. Butler to H. W Reed, Aug. 27, 1896, Watson MSS.
[34] St. Louis *Globe-Democrat*, Aug. 8, 1896; *Appleton's Annual Encyclopedia for 1896*, p 733.

319

masses. Let Bryan speak for the masses and let Watson speak for the masses and let Sewall talk for the banks and railroads." After the speech he received a stream of Populist leaders at his hotel, and before he left the state had won their pledge to stop the movement toward Republican fusion and to put out a straight Bryan-Watson ticket.[35]

The situation in Kansas when Watson arrived was a discouraging one. In front of the Populist state headquarters floated a banner bearing the portraits of Bryan and Sewall. Of Watson there was no sign. The state convention a month before was said to have "degenerated into a genuine quarrel" between the mid-roaders, who wanted a straight Bryan-Watson ticket, and the fusionists who favored Sewall. The Watson men carried their resolution, but later a fusion scheme was entered whereby Populist support of Sewall electors was swapped for Democratic votes for congressional and state candidates of the Populists.[36] There was still much feeling against Chairman Breidenthal's bargain in the state, but he clung to it doggedly. Although he was a member of the National Committee Breidenthal made no arrangements for Watson's campaign of Kansas and had no committee or demonstration to greet him. The candidate's reception was chilling indeed. In long conferences behind closed doors Breidenthal pleaded with the Georgian not to stir up revolt against the bargain, but Watson was adamant. "We are willing to fuse, but we are not willing to be swallowed," he said. H. W. Reed, a Georgia member of the National Committee traveling with the candidate, told reporters that the Kansas deal had "done more to stir up bitterness in the South and to intensify the demand that Mr. Watson shall have fair treatment than any other one act." It showed a disposition among Western politicians to "mislead" and "betray" Southern comrades.[37]

Watson's appeal to the Kansans in several speeches was per-

[35] Dallas *Morning News*, Sept. 8, 1896; *P. P. P.*, Sept. 8, 1896; clippings, Watson Scrapbooks.
[36] St. Louis *Globe-Democrat*, Aug. 8, 1896; Kansas City *Times*, Sept. 11, 1896.
[37] Kansas City *Star*, Sept. 10, 1896; Kansas City *Times*, Sept. 11, 1896.

sonal and extremely effective. He knew that there were those who demanded that he retire from the Populist ticket, but, he said:

Somebody else must be asked to kill that Party; I will not. I sat by its cradle; I have fought its battles; I have supported its principles since organization . . . and don't ask me after all my service with the People's party to kill it now. I am going to stand by it till it dies, and I want no man to say that I was the man who stabbed it to the heart. . . .

No; Sewall has got to come down. He brings no votes to Bryan. He drives votes away from Bryan. . . .

My friends, I took my political life in my hands when I extended the hand of fellowship to your Simpsons, your Peffers, and your Davises in Georgia. The Georgia Democrats murdered me politically for that act. I stood by your men in Congress when others failed. I have some rights at the hands of Kansas. I have counted on your support. Can I get it? [38]

He called for a show of hands, as he used to do in Georgia, and the Westerners swore eternal allegiance. Much pleased, he wrote his wife after one speech: "The audience was colder than in Texas but they gradually warmed up and when I closed they swarmed around my carriage just as the Pops do in Georgia. I voted the crowd as between Sewall and I [sic], and not a Pop voted for Sewall. So it is quite apparent that the rank and file of our party in Kansas are all right and will vote against their leaders if they get the chance. They shall have the chance." [39]

The rebellion against the fusionist leaders was reawakened all over the state. "This Watson crusade in the state," reported a Kansas paper, "has aroused the animals and the menagerie is not sleeping at nights. The straight-out-middle-of-the-road Populists are demanding a Bryan-Watson electoral ticket." A stirring call for a mid-road convention of Watson-Populists was is-

[38] *Ibid* ; also clippings, Watson Scrapbooks.

[39] T. E. W. to Mrs. Watson, Sept. 10, 1896, in possession of Georgia Watson, Thomson, Ga.

sued from Topeka by a former candidate for governor and a former candidate for chief justice. It read, in part:

Brothers:—The trafficking office hunters who have secured control of the People's party organization have entered into a shameless bargain with the Democratic party of Kansas, trading off our principles and our candidate for vice president, Thomas E. Watson . . . for the sake of a chance to capture the state and Congressional offices of Kansas.

It called upon loyal Populists to rally to the cause of principles and Tom Watson "in preference to the traitors and office hunters." [40] The Breidenthal faction refused to give way before the revolt, and Watson left the state with the issue between the two wings still undecided.

Still without a word of recognition from Bryan, Watson entered the Nebraskan's home state to campaign for him. The opening words of his speech at Lincoln brought mid-road Populists to their feet: "I am not here to make a little two by four silver speech. (Applause.) I am a Populist from my head to my heels. (Loud applause and cheering.) I am not ashamed of my cause nor afraid to unfold my banner anywhere and fight under it." He proceeded to reaffirm the important Populist principles omitted from Bryan's Democratic platform, and made an appeal for a sectional alliance between West and South: "Your interests are agricultural just like ours. . . . A community of interest ought to make a community of principle." [41] The speech was printed in full by the New York *World*, which pronounced it Watson's greatest. It was highly praised in Nebraska. The mid-road Populists, who had not been able to carry the state convention for a Bryan-Watson ticket against the fusionists, held a convention of their own after the Georgian's visit and endorsed such a ticket. [42]

[40] Clippings, Watson Scrapbooks.
[41] T. E W , *Life and Speeches of Thomas E. Watson,* pp. 160-172.
[42] *Appleton's Annual Encyclopedia, 1896,* pp. 505-506.

In commenting upon the assistance he gave Bryan in Nebraska in 1896, Watson later remarked that it was the only time that perennial candidate was ever able to carry his own state.[43] Bryan continued to ignore his running-mate, however, without acknowledging his assistance in the West. It was not until ten years had passed that he apologized and explained:

As I did not know that any representation had been made with regard to withdrawing Sewall, I did not of course know of your disappointment and I knew nothing of the pressure brought to bear upon you by the Populists. I appreciated the aid you rendered in the western states and I should have thanked you. . . . The situation which we had to meet in '96 was a very trying one and in looking back upon it I think it is surprising that as few mistakes were made as were.[44]

Although he had invitations to speak in seven Western states, Watson filled only a few more engagements in Nebraska and Colorado before returning to Georgia. He returned with the realization that he had failed to halt the stampede of Western fusionists to board the Bryan bandwagon. He admitted in his editorial columns that his written protests to Chairman Butler against his fusion policy had been ignored, and said that his position had been "humiliating and embarrassing," and that he had "been compelled to submit to policies he did not approve."[45]

Shortly after the Western trip he issued a public statement, widely quoted, which the New York *World* pronounced "the most important political utterance of the campaign." It was, in effect, a warning to the Democratic managers that fusion had failed to "fuse." From county tickets up to the Presidency, he said, "the science of politics has been reduced to the good old business of, 'How much have you got?' and 'What will you take?'" Principles had been flung to the wind. He continued:

[43] T. E. W., *Life and Speeches of Thomas E. Watson*, p. 18.
[44] William J. Bryan to T. E. W., Jan. 24, 1907.
[45] *P. P P*, Oct. 2, 1896.

The menace that endangers Mr. Bryan's success to-day is the profound dissatisfaction which exists among the humble, honest, earnest Populists who have built up the People's party.

Through storms of abuse and ridicule these men have fought the battles of Populism, preached its gospel, paid its expenses and followed its progress with the hopeful devotion of the Israelite who followed the pillar of fire through the nights of dreary trial. Deep down in the hearts of men who want no office and hunger for no pie, is settling the conviction that they have been tricked, sold out, betrayed, misled. . . .

If my statement is true, is it important? To the Democratic "fusionist" it may not appear so. He comforts his patriotic soul with the assurance that the deal has been made, and that the people cannot unmake it. Perhaps so, but the voter can stay at home; and if the Populist voters stay at home, who is to elect Mr. Bryan?

This is not said in any threatening spirit and antagonism.

The Populist voters are dissatisfied and suspicious. . . . They feel that the principles they love are being used as political merchandise and that the Populist vote is being auctioned off to the highest bidder. They suspect that Populism has been bought and paid for, and is now being delivered to those who bought it. . . .

If McKinley is elected the responsibility will forever rest upon those managers who had it in their power to control by fair means 2,000,000 votes and lost them by violating the terms of the compact.[46]

The *World* found his warning "all the more impressive from the fact that he has, in letter, speech and editorial warmly praised and loyally supported Mr. Bryan." It believed that if he was correct, "Mr. Bryan's only chance is gone." James Creelman quoted Watson as declaring in an interview: "I'd lay my head on the block before I'd retire from the race to make way for a plutocrat, a bondholder, a national banker and protectionist like Mr. Sewall. . . . I have been shamefully treated but I am not afraid to do my duty. . . . The whole Populist campaign has been mismanaged. It is outrageous. Georgia and Texas refused

[46] New York *World*, Sept. 28, 1896.

324

fusion. We pointed the way, but North Carolina, Kansas and Colorado failed . . . If they too, had put Bryan and Watson tickets in the field, Mr. Sewall would have had to get out." [47]

It had been repeatedly predicted by relatively disinterested observers that Sewall would be taken off the Democratic ticket after the Maine state election. That event did nothing to discredit the prophets who said he would not carry his own precinct, that his nomination was an "illogical mistake," a "deadweight upon the ticket." Much was made of the report that Sewall's son campaigned against him. It was perhaps not without significance that Watson's letter of notification was dated September 14, the date of the Maine election. There followed a flurry of conciliatory activities among the Democratic managers. Senator Tillman of the Democratic National Committee came straight to Thomson from a New York meeting of Bryan and other committeemen, which Sewall had not attended. Tillman and Watson were closeted together for twelve hours. Watson's "warning" to Senator Jones renewed the cry of "No Watson, no Bryan" among the mid-roaders, and there followed more secret visits of Democratic managers to Thomson. Captain Evan P. Howell, who came with "several telegrams from Chairman Jones," was one of Watson's visitors.[48] Nothing came of these conferences that was announced. The New York *Tribune*, however, quoted a "Prominent Democrat" to the effect that Tillman had offered Watson a cabinet position if he would retire from the race, and that Watson "flatly refused."

Chairman Butler postponed from week to week a formal demand upon the Democratic managers to withdraw Sewall in accordance with the alleged contract at St. Louis, although he admitted that the Democrats had expected the demand to be made earlier.[49] When the demand was finally made, the Democrats knew that it came from men who had already approved several

[47] New York *World*, Oct. 5, 1896.
[48] E. P. Howell to T. E. W., Oct. 17, 1896, Watson MSS.; Atlanta *Commercial*, Oct. 23, 1896; clippings, Watson Scrapbooks.
[49] Marion Butler to H. W. Reed, Aug 15, 1896, Watson MSS

state fusion bargains, whereby Populists had agreed to support Sewall in exchange for local offices. Their demand, therefore, could only be regarded as a formality, and it was not surprising that Chairman Jones, according to Butler's report, "declined absolutely, unqualifiedly and emphatically to consent to the retirement of Mr. Sewall upon any ground." [50] There was considerable room for Watson's complaint of the "outrageous management of his campaign. It is only fair, however, to recall that Chairman Butler was in an extremely difficult position. He was dealing with an uncompromising idealist.

As the election approached, the *People's Party Paper* printed news of the withdrawal of the Bryan-Watson ticket in state after state. Those Southern states that held out against fusion were met with the most adamant refusal of concessions on the part of Democratic machines. Several resorted to fusion with Republicans and Gold Democrats. Alabama and North Carolina achieved the *reductio ad absurdum* of fusion by combining with the Republicans in the state election and with the Democrats in the national ticket.[51] Remarked Watson: "Suppose I were to go into North Carolina to speak. What could I say? I could only repeat the Ten Commandments, say the Lord's Prayer and dismiss the congregation." [52]

The arrangement of the electoral ticket between Populists and Democrats in Georgia long hung fire. The state election in early October, accompanied by as much bitterness, violence, and fraud as any previous election, did not serve to increase the love between the parties. A decline in the Populist vote from that of the previous election served to stiffen the resistance of the old party managers to Populist demand that the entire vote of the state be given to Bryan and Watson. The Watsonites decreased

[50] Marion Butler to T. E. W., Oct. 15, 1896.
[51] Florence Smith, *op. cit.*, pp. 138-155; *Appleton's Annual Encyclopedia*, 1896, pp. 10-11.
[52] Augusta *Chronicle*, Oct. 31, 1896.

326

their demand from seven to six of the thirteen electors, but continued to insist that all thirteen cast their votes for Watson. Watson would not yield another inch. Although there was considerable Democratic sympathy for him as "the worst treated man in America," and several old-party leaders wanted to give him all Georgia's votes, a majority of the committee voted for the resolution that condemned "the unreasonable and unjust ultimatum of the Populist committee, clothed as it is in offensive and unbecoming language." [53] Whereupon, the Populist committee voted to withdraw the Bryan-Watson Presidential ticket entirely. It was denied that Watson actively opposed the withdrawal, but he did resolutely oppose the alternative proposal—fusion with Republicans—declaring that he had "rather lose an arm than see it." At any rate, there was no longer any way in which a Tom-Watson-Georgia-Populist could vote for Tom Watson. And this was the crowning affliction of all the multitudinous afflictions that fell upon the head of the Populist Job.

His last words of advice to his followers before the election were: "I am out of the race in Georgia. There are two tickets you can vote—for Bryan and Sewall, or for McKinley and Hobart; or if you can't stand either you can stay away from the election next Tuesday and not vote at all." Upon the last words of this benediction a solemn voice responded "Amen!" [54]

On October 16 the Washington *Morning Times* carried a cartoon on its front page representing Chairman Jones cavorting with glee as he read the news: "The condition of Mr. Watson's throat will prevent his making any more speeches in this campaign." He was spotted by reporters while passing through Atlanta on his way home and plied with questions. "I have nothing to say," he repeated in a hoarse voice. "I have nothing to say." "If he feels that insult has been heaped upon injury by the ac-

[53] *Ibid.*, Oct. 21, 1896; *P. P. P*, Oct. 30, 1896; Atlanta *Commercial*, Oct. 23, 1896; A. M. Arnett, *op. cit.*, pp. 209-210.
[54] Augusta *Chronicle*, Oct. 31, 1896.

tion of his people in Georgia by withdrawing the electoral ticket against his advice he will not say so," remarked one paper. "He has been deserted by his friends," commented another.[55]

It was in a mood induced by this set of circumstances that Watson sat down to compose his belated letter of acceptance. As a document it is interesting mainly as the obituary of Populism written by its chief mourner, and addressed to one whom he considered a conspirator in its demise. Senator Butler refused to publish it, and it did not appear until after the election. Watson explained briefly that he accepted "solely because of my promise to do so." He stated briefly why he had promised to accept. Then he continued:

To all unprejudiced and manly men, regardless of party, I submit the statement that never before has any party, so badly needed as ours, been so badly treated. Invited to come to the help of the helpless Democracy, we have received no generous recognition from those who appealed to us, and whose appeal we heard. We did not go to them for aid—they came to us. . . . In other words, Populism is allowed to furnish all the campaign principles, all the self-sacrifice and patriotism, and the two million votes which the Democrats need, but they are not to be allowed to furnish a candidate for either place on the ticket . . . it appears the Democratic managers would be willing to make a sacrifice of both Bryan and silver, if they can but destroy Populism. . . .

For this attitude upon the part of the Democratic managers I believe that you, Senator, are largely responsible.

You made no effort to have me recognized. You publicly stated that I would not be notified of my nomination. You went into the fusion policy, over my written protest, with all the zeal of a man who intended to elect the Democratic ticket. . . .

Senator, a reform party has no right to exist if it has no valid complaint to make. Populists cannot denounce the sins of the two old parties, and yet go into political copartnership with them. The moment we make a treaty the war must cease . . . and when we cease our war upon the two old parties, we have no longer any excuse for living.

[55] *Constitution*, Oct. 24, 1896.

328

. . . If we represent nothing but a contest of the "outs" against the "ins," we are a lot of humbugs, parading as reformers, and we deserve the contempt of all good people. . . .

By listening to the overtures of the Democratic managers our party has been torn into factions, our leaders deceived and ensnared, and the cause we represent permanently endangered, if not lost. The labor of many years is swept away, and the hopes of thousands of good people are gone with it.[56]

The election returns provided ample documentation for his letter. The party that two years before had polled close to two million votes gave its candidate for Vice-President some 217,000 votes distributed through seventeen states. He received twenty-seven electoral votes from the following states: Arkansas, 3; Louisiana, 4; Missouri, 4; Montana, 1; Nebraska, 4; North Carolina, 5; South Dakota, 2; Utah, 1; Washington, 2; and Wyoming, 1. A Democratic-Populist fusion for the electoral vote was arranged in twenty-eight states.[57] The figures are of no value whatever as an indication of Watson's strength as a candidate, or of his party's strength in numbers, but they do richly illustrate the ruin that fusion wrought with Populism.

Bryan lost five states west of the Mississippi and four south of Mason and Dixon's Line. It has been computed that a change of 19,436 votes in California, Oregon, Kentucky, North Dakota, West Virginia, and Indiana would have given him the election. Kentucky was lost by 142 votes.[58] In view of these figures, Watson's contention that the Democratic managers "lost the case because they violated the St. Louis compact," that "they sacrificed Bryan in the effort to destroy Populism," is interesting. Kentucky Populists voted 23,500 strong in 1892, and he believed Indiana Populists represented at least 28,000 votes. But in each state, "with true Bourbon bullheadedness the Democrats tried to bulldoze the middle-of-the-roaders, instead of conciliating them,

[56] *P. P. P.,* Nov. 13, 1896.
[57] F. L. Haynes, *Third Party Movements,* p. 300.
[58] Wayne C. Williams, *William Jennings Bryan,* p. 193.

329

and the result was a smash-up—in which Bryan lost the state." [59] Because of the complexity of influences that played upon the election, however, it is impossible to estimate the value of Watson's contention.

In the first issue of his paper to appear after the election, he discussed with utmost frankness the degradation of Populism:

Our party, as a party, does not exist any more. Fusion has well nigh killed it. . . . Fusionists sold the national candidate of the People's Party for the highest price they could get in each state, and the result is that while the fusionists have succeeded in getting some local pie, the national organization is almost dead. . . .

Divided into three factions, in this way, National Populism is almost a dead letter—as a party organization. The sentiment is still there, the votes are still there, but confidence is gone, and the party organization is almost gone. . . . Hence the fusionist had better make the most of his pie, because he will never again have another national nominee to sell. [60]

The loudest mourning that was done in 1896 was over the fallen Silver Knight. Bryan's apparently meteoric rise, the overnight conversion of Democracy to pseudo-Populism, and the fanfare of the campaign had all occupied the brief space of four months. During that time the fate of Populism was forgotten. Its passing was the concern of few; yet in its passing lay the real significance of 1896. Populism, not the falsely regenerate Democracy of Bryan, furnished the backbone of agrarian resurgence, and in 1896 that backbone was broken. Only a Tom Watson Populist could appreciate the irony of Bryan's phrase, "The First Battle." In 1896 agrarian provincialism made its last aggressive stand against capitalist industrialism. In the West the movement renewed its vitality to some extent in Progressivism. It underwent several resurrections in the South—to which the subsequent career of Tom Watson was an important witness—

[59] T. E W., *Political and Economic Handbook*, pp. 458-460.
[60] *P. P. P.*, *Nov.* 13, 1896.

330

but the fantastic shapes it assumed are to be understood mainly by the psychology of frustration.

There is almost enough evidence to indicate that Watson himself grasped the historical meaning of 1896. He could not believe that "any soldier of the Southern Confederacy carried away from Appomattox a heavier heart than I took with me into my enforced retirement." He thought the experience drove him close to insanity. "Politically I was ruined," he later wrote. "Financially I was flat on my back. How near I came to loss of mind only God who made me knows—but I was as near distraction, perhaps, as any mortal could safely be. If ever a poor devil had been outlawed and vilified and persecuted and misrepresented and howled down and mobbed and threatened until he was well nigh mad, I was he." [61]

[61] T. E. W., in *Watson's Jeffersonian Magazine*, Vol. X (Oct, 1910), p. 818; Atlanta *Journal*, Aug. 11, 1906.

CHAPTER XVIII

Of Revolution and Revolutionists

AFTER THE DEBACLE OF 1896, Tom Watson became virtually a political recluse for a period that lasted eight years. Begun when he was barely forty, an age at which the average politician only begins to enjoy the fruits of his apprenticeship, his enforced retirement constitutes a remarkable interlude in an otherwise active career. It was a period about which, although he was wont to expand upon his tribulations, he had little to say in later years. When he did refer to it, he did so briefly and always in the same mood. In 1910 he wrote, "What I suffered in those awful years is known to none but the wife who shared my lot and the God Who gave me strength to endure it."

Partly the period was filled with prolific writing, and partly by a thriving law practice. Six years of unremunerative political agitation had plunged him into debt, and it was to law rather than to letters that he first turned to mend his fortunes.[1] Early in 1897 it was reported that "the lawyers of middle Georgia are very generally complaining that they cannot secure a conviction of a man charged with murder." This was attributed to no general indifference to the value of human life, but to the fact that Watson was again "professionally at large" and stood in the way of prosecuting attorneys.[2]

Toward his party and its leadership he continued to maintain

---

[1] T. E. W. to Dr. John N. Taylor, Aug. 15, 1909; personal account books.
[2] Augusta *Herald*, April 6, 1897.

the position outlined in his remarkable Letter of Acceptance. Asked to say how Populism fared, he insisted upon a division of the question. "If you mean the organization," he said, "I must answer that it is in a bad way." For the price of a few offices the party has been sold to the Democrats, whose possession of it was secure as long as the fusionists who enjoyed those offices retained their grip upon party machinery. "It would be a very contemptible person," he said, "who would accept our national nomination in 1900, knowing from the experience of this campaign [1896] that Butler will trade him off in North Carolina, Breidenthal & Co., in Kansas, Pattison in Colorado, etc." There was only one way to resurrect the People's party: that was to "reorganize from the ground up, and rigidly exclude from control every leader tainted with Fusion." That herculean task, he implied, was not for him.[3]

"If, on the other hand," he continued, "you mean to ask me how goes it with the *Principles* of Populism, I say to you that they never commanded more respect, never met with the approval of a larger proportion of you fellow citizens, than they do to-day [1898]." He was able, even at that time, to list an impressive number of reforms, both state and national, that were clearly Populist in doctrine. That list was to grow as the years passed. It was certainly in a moment of inspired optimism, however, that he put forth the following dubious claims for Populism:

It has smashed party ties right and left. It has broken the idols of the market place in a manner beautiful to behold. It has well nigh abolished the party lash. It has utterly abolished social ostracism for political opinion's sake. No citizen any longer hesitates to take sides with any party he likes, or to vote for any candidate he prefers. The day of political persecution is over—even in the South—and Populism did it![4]

[3] *P. P. P.*, Nov. 13, 1896, and Nov. 19, 1898; *Life and Speeches of Thomas E. Watson*, p. 175.

[4] *Ibid.*, Nov. 20, 1896; *Life and Speeches of T. E. W.*, pp 178-179; T. E. W., in *Watson's Jeffersonian Magazine*, Vol. V (Oct., 1910), pp. 817-819.

He continued to keep a hand in the *People's Party Paper* for some time, and to proclaim himself a life-long Populist, "unrepentant and unreconstructed." Though advocating the overthrow of the fusionist leaders of the party, he took no part in the prolonged and futile four-year struggle of insurgent midroaders to recapture the party machinery from the grasp of fusionists. Ignoring his many protests, the state convention of Georgia Populists named Watson their candidate for governor in the spring of 1898. The nomination was made with splendid enthusiasm and urged upon him with persistence.[5] He could not be persuaded to accept it. National events of that spring completed his discouragement. "The Spanish War finished us," he later wrote. "The blare of the bugle drowned the voice of the Reformer." [6] He not only refused the nomination, but ended his connection with the paper and withdrew from public life entirely.

Perhaps none of his contemporaries, and certainly none of the Populists, read more accurately than Tom Watson the meaning of "the splendid little war" upon Spain. Populist congressmen were vying with Republicans and Democrats in demonstrating their patriotism. "Bryan stuck a feather in his cap," scoffed Watson, "and vowed that he, too, would become a soldier in spite of those vile guns." While the War was still in progress he addressed his party comrades in a speech at his home. Some of his remarks were a repetition of the arguments he used against the armament appropriation in the House six years before. "Who gets the benefit of the war?" he asked. He answered his question at length: the bond-seekers, the capitalists, the railroads, and further:

National bankers will profit by this war. The new bonds give them the basis for new banks, and their power is prolonged.

The privileged classes all profit by this war. It takes the attention

[5] *P. P. P.*, March 18, 1898.
[6] *Watson's Jeffersonian Magazine*, Vol. V (Oct., 1910), p. 817.

of the people off economic issues, and perpetuates the unjust system they have put upon us.

Politicians profit by the war. It buries issues they dare not meet.

What do the people get out of this war? The fighting and the taxes.

What was the United States doing in this war with Spain in the first place, he wished to know. True, Spain was oppressing Cuba. But so was England oppressing Ireland, Egypt, and India; France was oppressing Siam and Madagascar; Turkey was oppressing Armenia. Should we then take up arms against the oppressors of the world? We would more likely end by becoming oppressors ourselves. "The Spaniards and Cubans were bushwhacking one another, and killing from three to five men at a battle. We have gone down there and killed more men in three months than they would have killed in thirteen years. If they were starving before, who feeds them now?" And finally,

What are we going to get out of this war as a nation? Endless trouble, complications, expense. Republics cannot go into the conquering business and remain republics. Militarism leads to military domination, military despotism.

Imperialism smooths the way for the emperor.[7]

"Loathing the war," he said later, "foreseeing many of the evil consequences that it has brought upon us, I quit the active agitation of Populism, and shut myself up in my library to write books."

The retreat to his library, as he saw it, did not represent escape from the task to which he had dedicated his life. There he proposed to advocate "the same eternal principles of human liberty and justice and good government in historical works" that he had preached from the stump. He would, in other words, write populist history. On February 17, 1898, he signed a contract with The Macmillan Company for the publishing of *The*

[7] *Life and Speeches of Thomas E. Watson,* pp. 180-182.

Story of France, to appear in two large volumes.[8] The manuscript of the first volume, of more than seven hundred pages, was completed in November.

The origin of Watson's *Story of France* is to be sought in the columns of the *People's Party Paper,* where, during the battles of the early 'nineties, he printed, when space permitted, sketches of episodes from French and Roman history. These sketches were preëminent examples of "history for a purpose." Yet they were pungent and original and rarely failed to carry home their point. Caesars and Bourbons were dealt with in the same vigorous prose, and in the same irreverent manner in which he dealt with Democrats and plutocrats in the adjacent editorial column. His people should not lack for heroes and villains, past as well as present. These sketches were altered somewhat and published in Atlanta in 1896 in a thin volume bearing the same title as his later work. The larger work, though much more dignified and restrained in style, still bore a family resemblance to the polemic sketches.

His history was written largely from secondary materials together with accessible memoirs and autobiographies. He did all his work at home, purchasing such works as he used for his own library, which at one time contained over 10,000 volumes. He took great pride in his collection, pronouncing it the largest personal library in the South.[9] Such sources as he did use were not used uncritically. On the other hand, his statements that he wrote 6,000 words in one Sunday morning, that frequently the pen proved "all too slow to follow the burning thought," and that "many a time the page was blotted with tears" give an insight into his methods. Passionate history written at such a pace could not be free from blunders. Exploded theories, discredited sources, and exaggerations mar his pages—along with the tears. The Seine was "choked with bodies" and France was "devas-

[8] Watson MSS., Chapel Hill.

[9] Now partly in possession of Judge Uly O. Thomson, Miami, Fla, who kindly permitted the author to use the library.

tated" with appalling frequency; while the villainies of the Church, the iniquities of feudalism, and the darkness of the Dark Ages stagger credulity.

Much criticism is, however, forestalled by a statement in the Preface to *The Story of France*. "To mark the encroachments of absolutism upon popular rights," he explains, "to describe the long-continued struggle of the many to throw off the yoke of the few, to emphasize the corrupting influence of the union between Church and State, to illustrate once more the blighting effects of superstition, ignorance, blind obedience, unjust laws, confiscation under the disguise of unequal taxes, and the systematic plunder, year by year, of the weaker classes by the stronger, have been the motives which led me to undertake this work. May it bear fruit." He thought of his book as "aggressively radical in its plea for oppressed humanity." [10]

It was popular history, history for the common man, history with a purpose. As such it meets admirably the demands made upon it. His style is vivid, crisp, and moves with dramatic power, particularly in the narration of mass movements. He is at his best when writing of a figure or event with which he can identify himself, whether it is Peter the Hermit, Joan of Arc, Voltaire, or Marat. Consciously he strives to keep before himself and his reader the mass life of the nation as his central theme, and a Jacobin passion informs his judgments. Woe to that fame, however heroic and celebrated, which was earned by trampling upon the masses. He belabors the Caesarism of Carlyle, the "hysterical accounts of royalist writers," and the reactionary legislation of William Pitt.

The first volume carries the account to the end of the reign of Louis XV, while the second, to which the first might be said to serve as an introduction, devotes its more than one thousand pages to the Revolution down to the First Consulate. It was the Revolution that absorbed Watson's interest, and for him the key to its complex maze was his radical-republican doctrine. While

[10] T. E. W., *Sketches*, p. 164.

337

he was too near the Confederacy to detect the pseudo-classical posturing of the Men of '89, he had a sharp eye for the rogue and an instinct for the intricacies of class contradiction. It was true that he was prone to express a somewhat indiscriminate enthusiasm for revolutionists, whatever their stripe. Yet he discovered the bourgeois joker in the Girondin program. It was designed "only for the good, the educated, the genteel. They were not in touch with the masses. Their republic was too much of an abstraction." His admiration for Danton, "something of the grand gentleman of the masses," is admitted, but he respects the incorruptible Marat and defends Robespierre. He makes a realistic and penetrating study of the Terror, and eloquently defends the Jacobins in page after page of praise for their legislative accomplishments. Here Populism achieves triumphs in the study that it never attained at the polls. "If they were not statesmen, if they were not mailed knights in the long, hard battle of civilization, who are those who deserve the name?" he asks.[11] Especially he admires the Jacobin Law of the Maximum. It is his conviction that "wherever the valiant soldiers of progress wage battle for humanity's sake, there the better spirit of the Jacobin strives."[12]

Needless to say, many more strictures than have been mentioned could be made upon this work. All things considered, however—its origin, and the unusual circumstances of its creation—it would seem of more importance to underscore its virtues. Moreover, this was a day when the tradition of the statesman as historian flourished. *The Story of France* does not suffer in comparison with other products of that tradition.

The first volume appeared in January, 1899, the second in the latter part of the same year. The publisher complained of a "conspiracy of silence" against the book among the New York reviews. One of the great dailies, he said, announced before the book appeared that it "did not care to review it." Another at

[11] *The Story of France*, Vol. II, pp. 840-849.
[12] *Ibid.*, pp. 955-973.

first refused to print an advertisement of it, and then made its appearance the occasion of a "personal attack upon the author and the publisher." [13] Looking back over the reviews today, however, one is more struck by their generosity, their willingness to make allowances, indeed the extravagant praise of some of them rather than by the partisanship of a few. From the superlatives of the New York *Evening Journal*, which proclaimed it "the best history ever written by an American," to the sober strictures of the learned journals, there seemed to exist a prevalent disposition to judge the work upon the terms suggested in the author's Preface. As one example, the *Dial* admitted that "His aggressive truth-telling makes French history superlatively realistic, and his fertile mind, keen wit, and dramatic power combine to make a story of absorbing interest." It protested, however, against his "working upon the feelings of the reader with the weapons of the emotional evangelist." [14]

The book enjoyed a remarkable popular success. It sold some fifty thousand copies while in the hands of The Macmillan Company, and then went through several editions after it was purchased by the author's press.[15] A posthumous edition was published by a third company in 1926. The book was also well received in London.

At the request of his publishers, Watson laid aside the contract he had signed with them for the preparation of a popular history of the United States in order to exploit the popularity of *The Story of France* with another volume on French history. This was to be done through a biography of Napoleon.[16] Begun

[13] George P. Brett (President of Macmillan Co) to Clark Howell, Feb. 15, 1899, Watson MSS.

[14] *Annals of the American Academy*, XV, pp. 466-477; *American Historical Review*, Vol. IV (1888–1889), pp. 586-587; *Dial*, Vol XXVIII (1916), p. 1167; excerpts from other reviews in W. W. Brewton, *Life of Thomas E. Watson*, pp. 286-287.

[15] Royalty statements from Macmillan to Watson, Watson papers. Watson bought the copyrights in 1911.

[16] For reviews of *Napoleon*, see *Nation*, Vol. LXXIV (1902), p. 490; *Atheneum*, Vol. I (1902), p. 562.

early in 1899, the work was published in February, 1902, under the title, *Napoleon: A Sketch of His Life, Character, Struggles, and Achievements*, a volume of over seven hundred pages.

In style, in method, and in general character, this work differs but little from the previous volumes. In fundamental attitude of author to subject, and in basic ideology, however, there exists a subtle but pervasive difference between the history and the biography. The change is elusive, and the author would have been the first to deny it. It exists, nevertheless, and for the purpose of understanding Tom Watson and Tom-Watson Populism the difference is worth exploring.

In the first place the book was a labor of love. "It seems to me," he once wrote, "that there was never a time when Napoleon was not a part of my life and thought." From the time his grandfather had presented him with the Reverend John S. C. Abbott's *Napoleon* when he was nine that figure had quite possessed his imagination. He "knew no better than to devour that marvelous romance with all a boy's eager delight and unquestioning faith . . . the unalloyed goodness of Napoleon, the unsullied virtue of Josephine, and the unrelieved depravity of Napoleon's foes." The reading of many books gradually dispelled the myth, but "interest never flagged." Identification with his hero was easy enough: the impoverished, under-sized, intensely proud school boy with his overweening patriotism for despised and conquered Corsica. "Always, Napoleon has had a friend in me," he once said. "When the rich boys made fun of him at college, my own little fist would double up, ready to help him fight." [17] From a naïve childhood identification it is no great step to the biographer's attitude:

As long as time shall last, the inspiration of the poor and the ambitious will be the Ajaccio lawyer's son: not Alexander, the born king; not Caesar, the patrician; but Napoleon, the moneyless lad from de-

[17] T. E. W., "How I Came to Write a Life of Napoleon," *Prose Miscellanies*, pp. 75-86.

340

spised Corsica, who stormed the high places of the world, and by his own colossal strength of character, genius, and industry took them![18]

Moreover, that name should inspire "not only the individual, but the masses also." For wherever it was agreed that "monopoly of power, patronage, wealth, or opportunity is wrong, there the name of Napoleon will be spoken with reverence, despot though he became, for in his innermost fibre he was a man of the people, crushing to atoms feudalism, castes, divine rights, and hereditary imposture."

That Napoleons make perilous heroes for Jacobins seemed to be one of the implied lessons of his history of the Revolution. Yet under the spell of the great megalomaniac's history he seemed to have forgotten his own lesson. In the biography one gradually loses sight of the unprincipled tyrant of *The Story of France*, who "devoted Frenchmen to wars of selfish ambition, and swindled them out of the 'Principles of the Revolution.' " [19] One's eye is too much filled with "Napoleon the Great." It is true that Watson readily admits that the Corsican was "a colossal mixture of the good and the bad," that "a more contradictory mortal never lived," and that Napoleon's treatment of Poland presents "a sorry picture." "The anti-Bonaparte biographers," however, provoke in him wrath and heated retorts.[20] For an outspoken opponent of American militarism and imperialism he seems strangely serene in the presence of "bleaching bones on battle-fields," and strangely jubilant over the onward march of Napoleon's eagles. As an outstanding advocate of initiative, referendum, recall, and popular election of all officers, he seems reconciled with remarkable ease to the collapse of a republic, and the rise of an emperor—"the necessary man without whom they might relapse into chaotic conditions." [21] While he gazes, transfixed by the splendor of Napoleon, the money-

[18] *Napoleon*, p. 13.
[19] *The Story of France*, Vol. II, p. 494
[20] *Napoleon*, pp. 215, 373, 407, and 423.
[21] *Ibid.*, p. 331.

341

changers creep into the temple of French democracy, unchallenged, indeed unobserved, by Watson. One has the feeling upon closing the book that an author who can use the term, "the great Democratic despot," without consciousness of paradox is reconciled to a union of Caesarism and democracy.

In a different connection Watson once wrote: "There is not a railway king of the present day, not a single self-made man who has risen from the ranks to become chief in the vast movement of capital and labor, who will not recognize in Napoleon traits of his own character; the same unflagging purpose, tireless persistence, silent plotting, pitiless rush to victory . . ." [22] Precisely. But what was a Populist doing celebrating the virtues of the self-made railway king? What was Tom Watson about in erecting an image of capitalist acquisitiveness for his people to worship? Could it be that the Israelites worshiped the same gods as the Philistines? Could it be that the only quarrel between the two camps was over a singular disparity in the favors won?

* * * * * *

On a fly leaf at the back of a huge ledger he used as a personal journal is to be found an elaborate drawing bearing the subscription, "Model Southern Home." The drawing is dated 1884.[23] There is some evidence of subsequent revision and idle elaboration of detail—for in twenty years even the most cherished dream may expand in magnificence. Yet in essentials the plan remained the same. It was twenty years before it received concrete expression in the home he bought, remodeled nearer to his heart's desire, and named "Hickory Hill."

One recalls the lost mansion of his father, the hapless romantic, John, who built his dream house (with its imposing façade and unplastered interior) on the unsubstantial sands of wishes and credit—and lost it, along with his father's log house which

[22] T. E W, "Some Impressions of Napoleon," MS, Watson papers.
[23] MS Journal 2.

it screened. Here are the same imposing fluted columns, four towering ones with Ionic capitals of plaster, supporting the gable of a portico two-and-a-half stories high. Under it, at the second story, is a balcony, and around almost three sides of the wide girth of the house runs an open veranda, partly balustraded. In style as well as in name, Hickory Hill suggests Jackson's Hermitage rather than Jefferson's Monticello: the grandiloquent pretentiousness of a later Southern tradition, rather than the chaste graciousness of an earlier.

Set upon a knoll, the house dominates a wide plot thickly grown with trees, many of which Watson selected for their variety and transplanted. Up from the road to the pillared portico ascends a broad concrete walk, interrupted midway by the great basin of a fountain (faintly reminiscent of Versailles) lit from each side by ornate wrought-iron electric lamps. Other walks skirt through grape arbor, orchard, and summer house. Nor was expense spared upon the interior, with its imported Italian marbles for the fireplaces. "Every detail bespeaks the culture and refinement of the typical Southern gentleman"—so thought a guest whom Watson was pleased to have write an introduction to one of his books.[24] It seems apparent that he was not unwilling to be thought of in such terms. In one of his many asides in his book on Jefferson he wrote:

A democrat, are you?

Of course you are; and yet, in your heart of hearts, you warm to the old-time Cavalier who chose for his home the loveliest spot he could find, reared a costlier house than he could afford, made it as attractive as he knew how, christened it with some pet name of fond association—and then threw open its wide doors, and said to all the world: "Come sit by my hearth, come eat at my table; my house was not built for myself alone. . . ."

Does such a house speak no word of inspiration to the son? Does it awaken in him no sense of consecration? Does it lift no high standard

[24] Charles Bayne, "Introduction" to Watson's *Sketches*, pp. v-vi.

of conduct before his eyes? Does it impose no solemn obligations . . . ? Has such a house no meaning which thrills the very soul?[25]

The years following 1896 seem to have been prosperous ones for Watson. At the end of 1904 he placed his "financial standing" at the figure $121,000, more than double the estimate he gave for the former date. As a "rough estimate" $70,000 of this was invested in land—rather a low figure for some 9,000 acres of his several plantations. An estimate not his own mentions "$300,000 worth of cotton lands in Georgia," and another held him "the operator of more plows than any individual farm owner in Georgia." His own tenant rolls list forty-four names of men, presumably the heads of families.[26] His Virginia place, "Mountain Top," was quoted at $15,000, and an enthusiastic caretaker believed that his island, Las Olas, on the Atlantic coast of Florida, "could be sold for $50,000" for it was "the prettiest place in all the world—the natural scenery and tropical groth [sic] is simply a dream." [27]

Life at Hickory Hill had about it the spacious freedom of the plantation "big-house," and there was much of the ante-bellum flavor (rather more encouraged than not) in its privileged "family Negroes," its bounteous tables, and its tradition of hospitality. The place took its tone, however, from the master of the manor. That meant a certain amount of decorum. There were well-understood rules about the sanctity of the study in which he spent long hours. The dinner table, virtually the only place the family saw its reclusive head with any regularity, had its particular code—that had better be observed. An uncorseted secretary did not go unreproved, and freedom in manners was not encouraged. However much of a "man of the people" there was about Tom Watson, there was a pretty well-recognized point be-

[25] T. E. W., *The Life and Times of Thomas Jefferson*, pp. 170-172.
[26] Personal account books and tenant rolls, Watson papers; undated clippings, one by James Creelman in 1905.
[27] O. S. Lee to T. E. W., Sept. 7, 1906; unsigned letter, Charlottesville, Va., to T. E. W., Aug. 12, 1907.

yond which familiarity did not venture, even among his intimates. That had always been true, and the grand isolation of Hickory Hill tended to call attention to the trait. A poor relation was heard to remark that "Cud'n Tom has studied about French kings so much that he has taken to acting like them."

His notorious irritation at noises became legendary in the community, and innumerable stories that illustrate it still go the rounds. A pair of mischievous little granddaughters could generally count on a handful of coins flung from the study window to bribe them into silence. A peacock that squawked out of turn was unceremoniously beheaded. Neighbors received fabulous offers for bellowing cows and loud-throated roosters, and aspiring young pianists were encouraged to develop their talents in distant lands. Neighbor West, he swore, bursting out of his study in a rage, was clanging his farm bell with the premeditated purpose of annoying Tom Watson. His love for music, on the other hand, led him to spend much time in the music room, which contained two pianos, a phonograph, and an old music box. He took up his fiddle now and again, and later on spent many patient evenings after dinner teaching his granddaughters to waltz. An evening of music could move him so deeply that it sometimes changed his mood for days.

Besides a graciousness of manner that charmed his guests and a zestful imagination that captured the affections of his family, those who knew him best are eager to explain in him "a certain quality of tenderness." The difficulty in understanding it lay in the equal presence of quite antithetical traits. The very individuals whom he most longed to bind to him, and who were often drawn to him by this quality of tenderness, were as frequently repelled by opposite qualities. The psychological tragedy of his life was just this misfortune. He described it himself earlier: the misfortune of a spirit that, "proud of its own isolation, magnifies its own defects . . . retires within itself and imagines that all others are more fortunate, more deserving and more happy." His letters to his wife are expressions of genuine devotion, even

345

late in her life. He is transfixed by tenderness and remorse at the recollection of the pain he caused her by "an ugly fit of temper" twenty-eight years earlier. "No man," he adds, "has ever been more cruelly punished by his passions." [28] Between the lines of these letters one often reads a pathetic struggle to express a tenderness that his perverse nature was eternally thwarting.

No one who has explored the labyrinths of Tom Watson's mind can be convinced that his creed and his vital motivation were the simple products of intellectual conviction. Somewhere back of the consuming heat of his agrarian doctrine were banked fires of faith. Somewhere in his complex nature was hidden a mystic. One feels that on no very citable evidence. In the search for some tangible evidence the signs point to his agrarianism, but lead past it to something else. A significant clue lies in his writings about nature—simple things about planting, growing, and reaping. Unlike much of his other "literary" writings, these essays are usually free from sentimentality. He spent a remarkable amount of time alone in the woods and fields, afoot and on horseback, and the lore of forest and field at his command was vast. His two granddaughters, who sometimes feared him, never felt any hesitancy in rushing to meet him when he returned from one of these tramps. They swarmed about his legs at their game of racing to see which could first get a trouser leg picked free of beggar-lice and Spanish needles. He was always ready for fun at such times. One of his granddaughters later wrote: "Whenever I sensed peace and harmony in him, it seems to me, it was when he was nearest the earth." This remained true even later, when peace and harmony were extremely rare in him.[29]

After his retirement from public life, "respectable" opinion in the South gradually mellowed, then warmed to Watson. His literary successes commanded considerable awe in a community

[28] T. E W. to Mrs. Watson, Aug. 26, 1908, in possession of Georgia D Watson.
[29] Georgia D. Watson to C. V. W., July 30, 1937.

where a man of letters was a rarity. From a respectful "Colonel" he was overnight—with scarcely a pause at "Major"—promoted to "Sage"—"the Sage of Hickory Hill." It was even said that he became "the toast of the culture and intelligence of the State," and was "often referred to as its most distinguished citizen." [30] There was a wide demand for him as a lecturer. During the first half of 1903 he delivered some fifteen or more, at an average of $150 a lecture. It was said that in Atlanta, Henry Ward Beecher and Robert Ingersoll did not attract such houses as Watson, "either in point of numbers or intellectuality." The Augusta *Chronicle*, which so recently trembled before Watson the "anarchist," now asked: "What is the secret of this wonderful man's fascination, or magnetism, at all times and places. . . . We feel that back of this man's genius and culture is the restless beat of a warm, true, great heart." [31]

His repertory of lectures included a number of subjects that hark back directly to the days of the Populist stump speech and the editorial writing of the 'nineties. For example, in his lecture on "The Mission of Democracy" he denounced militarism, imperialism, corruption in high places, materialistic standards of progress, concentration of wealth, "education prostituted to the gospel of wealth and class rule," and the subsidized press and pulpit. His remedies, too, were much the same, though he would now expand government ownership to include coal fields, and perhaps other natural resources. He believed "absolute free-trade" would make trusts impossible, and the remedy in the meantime was "control." [32]

His most popular lecture, however, was that on "The South," or a similar one, "Is the South Glad It Lost?" It is in these lectures that one first meets an important shift in ideology.

Tom Watson's agrarianism was basic (one might almost say congenital); whatever other ideas and principles he professed

[30] Anonymous, *Forum*, Vol. LVI (Nov., 1916), p. 682.
[31] Augusta *Chronicle*, Nov. 8, 1902.
[32] MS. speeches and notes, Watson MSS.

347

were superstructure, whether they were in part populist, socialist, or fascist. The first expression of his agrarianism, called forth in the 'eighties by the aggressive capitalism of Henry Grady, found utterance in the Confederate creed, and was indistinguishable from the doctrine of Robert Toombs and C. C. Jones.[33] The South was a vanquished section exploited by its capitalist conquerors. Caught on the crest of the wave of the Alliance movement, he abandoned Confederate sectionalism to cement a union with the West. There should be "no South and no North," only a union against a common enemy at large the nation over. In this period he was capable of such dispassionate analysis as that revealed in his commenting: "We of the South are among the politically unhappy, with a great political failure, which, like all failures, does not get that criticism of judgment which success always commands." [34] The West-South alliance collapsed in 1896. Thereafter he reverted for a time to the Confederate creed.

A grievous spell had been put upon his people, he decided. The more he pondered the infamy of it, the more evidences he found of its reality—everywhere between heaven and earth—and the more intolerable it seemed to him. So long and so unanimously had the South been despised that Southerners themselves had been persuaded to bow to the verdict of the majority, to swallow pride, and meekly to accept a status of inferiority. National literature was a conspiracy "to put our section upon the Stool of Repentance," to keep it on "the mourner's bench," in an "attitude of apology." "Rebels and traitors," the historians said, and the South had become the "tolerated black-sheep of the flock," patronized with "much charity and pardon." [35] These things surely were beyond endurance, and while he had pen to write and tongue to speak he would not endure them in silence.

The campaign opened along the whole front of American his-

[33] See above, Chapter VIII.
[34] Augusta *Chronicle*, Aug. 29, 1890.
[35] "The South," "Is the South Glad it Lost?" Watson MSS. The quotations that follow are from these speeches.

tory. No citadel went unstormed, and above every ungarrisoned post he hoisted the rebel flag. Away with the notion "that Plymouth Rock was the cornerstone of our Republic and the Pilgrim father the sire of American Democracy." Jury trial, home rule, representative government, the first legislative assembly, manhood suffrage, religious toleration—he claimed them all for the South, and flourished documents in defense of the South's title. Nor was the Revolution "a tempest in a New England teapot." "Talk about Lexington and Concord!" Their laurels he claimed for the battle of Alamance. The first declaration of independence? Mecklenburg. The first organization as a separate state? South Carolina. He made bold to assert on as good authority that "the lordliest man that ever walked this continent was the Virginia planter, the Southern gentleman . . . the highest type of human grandeur." While the South dominated the Union whoever heard of a food riot, a bread line, a Rockefeller, or a Gould?

The next step was a rehabilitation of the Lost Cause. "We are quite sincere in saying," he asserted, "as we have done before, that it would have been vastly better for the South had the Confederacy succeeded." The South had already paid a greater war indemnity than Germany wrung from France, and half of the South's annual cotton crop was stolen by the Northern tariff. The day will yet come when "the Union will be split into four grand divisions, and this hemisphere will be all the happier for it." "ABHORRENCE at the suggestion of Southern independence?" he asked. "Pluperfect bosh! Sickening servility! The quintessence of apostasy! The high-water mark of truckling self-abasement and lick-log propitiation!" If the truth were known, "at bottom, we don't love the North much better than France loves Germany. How well does Ireland love England? Get that measure of affection, and you will be mighty close to the feeling of the South for the North."

Moreover, the South was as much a subject section of this Union as Ireland was a subject province of the British Empire.

The South's was a colonial status, and her economy was ruled in the same way in which Britain rules India:

Just as the English maintain their conquest of India by taking into co-partnership with themselves a certain percentage of Hindus, so the North holds the South in subjection by enlisting Southern capitalists and politicians. They put their money into our daily newspapers; they subsidize such organs as *The Manufacturer's Record;* they buy up our railroads; they capitalize our mills; they finance our street railways; they supply our banks,—always taking Southern men in with them to a certain extent, and they appoint some of our politicians to good positions. United themselves, the Northern capitalists divide the Southerners, and thus rule and despoil the South.

Watson's most refined contempt was reserved for those Southern apologists of the capitalist masters with their glib editorials, their sleek columns of statistics, and their vaunted boasts of expanding industry, increasing investment, "progress." Those were borrowed standards, not "Southern" standards. "Who wants a soulless Commercialism based upon the Havemeyer gospel of 'I don't care two cents for your ethics'?" he asked. "Is that the gospel to which the future of this Republic is to be dedicated?" For that matter, "Averages are arrant deceivers":

You teach me nothing whatever when you tell me that the people have built more railroads, raised more cotton, manufactured more cloth. To all your bombast upon *that* subject I will answer by the query, who got the increased wealth after it was made?

Your railroad may be a blessing—it may also be a curse. Many a ruined city, many a ruined industry will rise to damn the railroads. *Have* the people more *general* prosperity? *That* depends on the laws of *distribution.*

What *does* indicate the progress of a people? Churches? No. Schoolhouses? No. . . .

The way men and women *live* and *think* and *aspire.* . . . If these are wrong, all is wrong, and the nation will gallop to hell no matter how many railroads and factories they build.

350

So full was he of his message that it overflowed its proper channels and quite flooded his subsequent books, leaving long marshes of unnavigable sermons. In the midst of a biography of an early nineteenth-century American he paused for a picture of a cotton mill running at night. It seemed to him "some hideous monster, with a hundred dull red eyes, indicative of the flames within which were consuming the men, women and children chained to the remorseless wheel of labor." Indeed, "every one of these red-eyed monsters is a Moloch, into which soulless Commercialism is casting human victims—the atrocious sacrifice to an insatiable god!" And there were pictures of Birmingham and Pittsburgh that seemed to him to contain "something more infernal than Dante or Milton could throw into their pictures of hell." Describing an agrarian Eden of ante-bellum days, before the serpent Industrialism entered, he reminded his readers: "Our destitute are numbered by the millions, beggars swarm in big cities, tramps infest the roads; men, women, and children perish of cold and hunger in almost every state in the Union. The size of our proletariat is prodigious; its condition frightful."

In October, 1903, was published his *Life and Times of Thomas Jefferson.*[36] He entered the task with clenched fists in his Preface, and his pen is not infrequently wrenched by spasmodic contractions in the text that follows. So embroiled does he become with dead Federalist historians, as well as "modern outcroppings of the old Federalist vein" (whose number is legion), that the serene sage of Monticello is frequently forgotten. Pages are spent in belaboring the inconsequential biography by William E. Curtis, "which literally swarms with errors." His wrath is most deeply stirred, however, by the writings of "the learned President of Princeton," Woodrow Wilson. "Think of it!" he

[36] D. Appleton and Company. Also *vide* Thomas E. Watson, *Thomas Jefferson* (Beacon Biographies), Boston: Small, Maynard & Co., 1900, pp. xv, 150 Reviewed by George H. Haynes, *American Historical Review*, Vol. VI, p. 842. Reviews of *Life and Times of Thomas Jefferson: Arena*, Vol. XXXI, pp. 325-399 (favorable); *American Historical Review*, Vol. IX, pp. 615-616 (unfavorable).

exclaims in a footnote. "Nearly two thousand pages of alleged history and just one short sentence to the tragic chapter [Alamance] in the story of the South!" Yet he could spare six pages for a "Boston street row." And Wilson was a Southerner! Forsooth! A Georgian could spare a whole chapter to the glory of Carolina, and right gladly. Did a Channing of Harvard "perpetuate sectional prejudice and injustice" by intimating that the South was "easier to conquer than the North"? [37] He would devote *five* chapters to repelling the calumny. Jefferson's fame was secure enough to spare the space. When he does find time to examine the history of the Jeffersonian era, his aggressive independence of view produces some hard truths and upsets a few sacred myths. It is nevertheless a poor book, marred by laxness of style and undisciplined garrulity.

The Dedication of his *Jefferson* contains a paradox more apparent now than then.[38] "Because he is to-day working with splendid ability along the same lines which Mr. Jefferson marked out a hundred years ago," wrote Watson, "I dedicate this book to WILLIAM RANDOLPH HEARST."

The Life and Times of Andrew Jackson [39] is cluttered with the same reckless dogmatism and partisanship. Toward Jackson himself, he maintains a surprising candor, unsparing in its revelation of cold-blooded ruthlessness and cruelty. On the other hand, one meets with a contrast between the endearing generosity and chivalry of the Southern Cavalier, and the "monastic gloom, nasal preachments, kill-joy countenances, lank-haired bigotry, and censorious intermeddling with everybody's business" that characterizes the Northern Puritan.[40] Neither of these biographies approaches the standard achieved in the books on French history.

The contract to write a history of the United States remained

[37] T. E. W., *Life and Times of Thomas Jefferson*, p. 47, 86, 218.
[38] See below, p. 356.
[39] Stated as a serial publication, *Watson's Jeffersonian Magazine*, July, 1906; published by the author, 1911, in book form.
[40] T. E. W., *The Life and Times of Andrew Jackson*, p. 253.

unfulfilled, and a proffered contract for a life of General Lee went unsigned while the historian devoted his energies to an experiment in novel writing—his first and his last. *Bethany: A Story of the Old South* [41] is really a hodge-podge of historical and political essays intermixed with a sentimental love story and some autobiography. "Part First" presents a picture of the feelings, motives, and reasoning of Southern people on the verge of the War; "Part Second" alternates chapters of military history with chapters of a highly episodic romance. It is beside the point to enumerate its failures in construction, its blunders and banalities as a novel, for if it is of significance, it is not as a novel.

Bethany, the author admits, is "frankly Southern in tone," though he hopes "not offensively so." Recalling the way a Southern audience warmed to Henry Ward Beecher when he proclaimed, "I am a Yankee of the Yankees," he writes: "It is upon the same generous instinct of human nature that I rely in frankly putting the Southern case, as though I were 'a Rebel of the Rebels.' " [42] The first sentence is a promise: "Just as the facts were I will relate them to you." He is surprisingly successful in his struggle for intellectual honesty, and scarcely a reviewer fails to pay tribute to his victory over his feelings. Even the *Nation*, of Abolitionist heritage, thought the book "confirmation of the very primer of abolition knowledge of the disposition, habits, standards, and tender mercies of the slave holding section." [43]

Writing as the confessed apologist for a cause and for a discredited way of life, he steadfastly scorns special pleading and begging his case. He will borrow no magnolias and moonlight from Thomas Nelson Page. His grandfather's house did not remotely resemble "a Grecian Temple which had been sent into exile" in a cotton field. It was "just a plain house," and log at that. His mulatto playmate bears an unmistakable resemblance to his Uncle Ralph, the hero of the romance. Robert Toombs,

[41] D. Appleton and Company, 1904.
[42] T. E. W., *Bethany*, p. x.
[43] *Nation*, Vol. LXXIX, p. 506.

his political hero, dashes in and out of his pages roaring drunk. There are no duels at dawn but plenty of eye-gougings, knifings, and drunken brawls. There are "gander-pullings" in place of tournaments, and there are deserters as well as heroes who wear gray. For all that, he feels about the ante-bellum way of life as his family felt about their Baptist creed: "whatever it was, it was ours, and we were for it—strong." And when he thinks of Pittsburgh and Birmingham his faith is born anew in him and warms his blood like old wine and new love, and he writes:

That old Southern homestead was a little kingdom, a complete social and industrial organism, almost wholly sufficient unto itself, asking less of the outer world than it gave. How sound, sane, healthy it appears, even now, when compared to certain phases of certain other systems! [44]

[44] T. E. W., *Bethany*, p. 12.

CHAPTER XIX

From Populism to Muckraking

To ALL WHO HAD EYES to see it was plain that plans for a counter-revolution within the Democratic party were under way for 1904. Weakened by two successive defeats, the leadership of Bryan was open to challenge. The party of Bryan and Tillman, of West and South, of agrarianism and Main Street was likely to become once more the party of capitalism and Wall Street, of Eastern Big Business and Tammany. In their effort to overthrow Bryanism and make Democracy "as respectable as Republicanism," if not a little more so, David B. Hill and August Belmont united in putting forward Grover Cleveland as "a dignified stalking-horse" while they manipulated the nomination of Judge Alton B. Parker. William Randolph Hearst was easily the most serious contender for the nomination in opposition to the conservative combination.[1]

"Were I in politics," Watson began a statement in March, 1904, tentatively subjunctive in mood, "were I in politics, I should heartily approve and support the candidacy of William R. Hearst." Furthermore, Watson thought Cleveland "the most distasteful candidate who could be offered to the South." He admired Roosevelt "the man" very much, but Roosevelt "the politician" stood for those things he most abhorred—"imperialism, extravagance, class legislation, militarism, Hamiltonism, of the rankest sort."[2]

[1] Allan Nevins, *Grover Cleveland*, pp. 754-755; P. Hibben, *The Peerless Leader: William Jennings Bryan*, pp. 245-249.
[2] Atlanta *News*, March 7, 1904.

A conjunction of Watson and Hearst presented no grave problem of doctrinal adjustment. It was a day in which a Herbert Croly could write of Hearst as an expression of "the radical element in the Jeffersonian tradition," to be feared as "revolutionary in spirit," because he was as unfair to capitalists as the abolitionist had been to slaveholders. Croly compared him to Robespierre, and Harry Thurston Peck believed his ambition was to "bring about a socialistic millennium." [3]

After the March statement, Hearst conducted a lively courtship of the Georgia Populist. Letter after letter urged him to come to New York and join the Hearst staff. Arthur Brisbane suggested that he accept the editorship of one of the New York papers at $10,000 to start with, at the same time mentioning his own "very large salary" and suggesting unlimited advancement. Should Watson accept, he believed, "Mr. Hearst would have a far stronger man than myself to help him in his fight." [4] He was finally persuaded to go to New York for an interview with Brisbane. The offer was repeated and urged upon him then and later, but nothing came of it.

Watson nevertheless continued his advocacy of Hearst. In May, Grover Cleveland issued a statement explaining that when leaders "began to experience alarm over the strength this man Hearst was seemingly developing," he joined the Parker supporters, because it "appeared necessary to concentrate upon some available man in order to stifle the Hearst movement." Watson replied with a type of attack new to him then, but typical of his tactics in the future. The attack was based upon alleged instances of Cleveland's violation of the Southern attitude on "social equality" with Negroes. Cleveland denied the charges publicly and Watson repeated them loudly. [5]

As the time for the convention rolled around a conservative

[3] Herbert Croly, *The Promise of American Life*, pp. 163-167; Harry T. Peck, *Twenty Years of the Republic*, p. 711.
[4] Arthur Brisbane to T. E. W., June 23, 1904.
[5] Augusta *Chronicle*, April 11 and 28, 1904; Thomas W. Hardwick to T. E. W., April 12, 1904.

victory seemed inevitable. Even Hearst seemed to give up the fight.

* * * * * *

The history of the People's party since 1896 had fulfilled Watson's blackest prophecies. More amusement than alarm was provoked by the party's part in the election of 1900, for it was split into two quarreling factions. The fusionists, with exemplary self-denial, nominated a Democrat and a Republican; the mid-roaders put forward a ticket dedicated to pure Populism. Neither faction won any victories of consequence. Watson took no part whatever in the campaign, and seemed to manifest no personal interest in the future of the party.

The promise of a return to conservatism by the Democrats in 1904 revived Populist hopes greatly, however, for it was hoped that the Silver Democrats, and perhaps Bryan himself, could be persuaded to bolt their party for the sake of principles.[6] With much optimism a call was issued for a convention in Springfield, Illinois, to meet two days before the Democratic convention opened at St. Louis. Although the call provided for over nine hundred delegates, only about two hundred appeared at Springfield, much to the disappointment of the leaders. The report of the committee on permanent organization made it readily apparent that the mid-road faction controlled the Convention, for all convention officers were of that wing. The Omaha platform of 1892 and subsequent ones were reaffirmed, and the new platform called for government ownership of public utilities and for strict control of corporations doing interstate business.

Three names were placed before the Convention: that of Senator William V. Allen, who was present and spoke in defense of his record at the convention of 1896; that of Judge Samuel W. Williams of Indiana, also present; and that of Thomas E. Wat-

[6] William V. Allen, "A Western Statesman's Reasons for Supporting Hon. Thomas E. Watson," *Arena*, Vol XXXII (Oct, 1904), p 395.

son, who did not attend. John J. Hollaway, a Georgia delegate, made public a letter from Watson saying that he did not want the nomination. Before the balloting there was much discussion of whether Watson would accept were Hearst nominated at St. Louis. The first ballot stood Watson 334, Allen 319, Williams 45. Williams' withdrawal in favor of Watson started the shift of one delegation after another to his column. Finally the withdrawal of Allen's name and a motion by Williams made Watson's nomination unanimous by acclamation.[7] Thomas H. Tibbles of Lincoln, Nebraska, was named for the second place. The final scene, as described to Watson by one of the delegates, recalls some of the religious fervor of the early 'nineties. Men of all sections joined in a "general handshake with tears of joy in their eyes which shows the deep love and esteem you have from the patriotic people of America."[8]

Letters and telegrams poured in upon Watson urging him to accept. "With me," he asserted, "the only question was: Do a sufficient number of old line Populists and free silver Democrats want this fight made. In reaching a conclusion upon that subject, I was guided by the evidence of general discontent with what had been done in the Democratic national convention."[9] The work of the St. Louis Convention, following hard upon the Populist meeting, was a bitter dose for the Bryan Democrats. Senator Tillman was seen "swearing and shedding floods of tears by turns." Judge Parker's famous "gold telegram" reversed the party's monetary doctrine; the platform was silent on silver; the demand for income tax was dropped. Cleveland's name was repeatedly cheered, and it was plain that Eastern Big Business leadership was in control.

In view of the results at St. Louis Watson's nomination received serious attention in some circles. The New York *Tribune* thought it "a mistake for political prophets to class him as a

[7] Illinois *State Register*, July 5 and 6, 1904; New York *Tribune*, July 6, 1904.
[8] John J. Hollaway, to T. E. W., July 8, 1904.
[9] Atlanta *Journal* Aug. 22, 1906.

negligible quantity," since he was "distinctly *persona grata* with the radical Democrats," and therefore likely to attract the many discontented of that party.[10]

Watson seems to have entertained few illusions. "Our papers are dead," he said. Indeed, of the fifteen hundred Populist papers that flourished in 1896, the party secretary could count only twenty-three in 1904. The nominee admitted that his party had "almost nothing to start with in the way of party organization, campaign funds and newspaper support," and there were only four months in which to work.[11]

Much hurried construction was begun in setting up abandoned party machinery in the states. The People's party campaign of 1904, however, consisted almost entirely of the stump speeches of Tom Watson. The field was singularly free from competition in that respect: Roosevelt, being President, did not take the stump; Parker remained at home, speaking only to visiting delegations, and the more voluble and picturesque elements of the Democracy sulked in silence. Watson was a welcome relief in the dullest campaign in years. "Everybody with the least curiosity wants to hear Tom Watson," it was said. "The man who has no show is putting up the best show in this campaign." "He is entertaining; he does funny things with language, laughs himself and gives hilarity to his crowd." He indulged in considerable clowning: "Roosevelt could tie both hands behind him and run Parker clean out of the ring by shining his teeth at him," he said, with appropriate gestures. Laughter punctuated every sentence of some speeches, while in others he employed the uncanny magic he used in the 'nineties to galvanize demoralized farmers into action. "There was no reason for them to be weeping," wrote a puzzled reporter; yet weep they did.

Opening his campaign in Nebraska, he left no section unvisited, from Boston to California. He made three speeches in New York City: his acceptance speech at Cooper Union, another

[10] New York *Daily Tribune,* July 8, 1904.
[11] Dalton (Georgia) *Herald,* Aug. 25, 1904; Atlanta *News,* Nov. 14, 1904.

359

at a huge Union Labor banquet in his honor, and the third at a final rally, where he was introduced by Judge Samuel A. Seabury. Undaunted by the advice of his friends who told him that not a Watson man could be found in Chicago, he insisted on speaking there anyway. Clarence Darrow introduced him as "a beacon light to those in doubt," and he kept a large audience of Democrats doubled in laughter at the stupidities of their own party.[12]

Watson had much to say of the "System," using the word in the way Lincoln Steffens was using it at the time. "The 'system' has gotten its nominees; has captured both parties. No matter which is elected the system stands as it is." What if Morgan was pouring thousands into Roosevelt's campaign chest? Morgan partners were investing their money in Parker. It could make no difference to Wall Street which was elected. Roosevelt and Parker were "two drinks from the same jug," "two eggs from the same nest." A prohibition campaign led by the whiskey trust could be no more preposterous hypocrisy than Parker's "campaign against the corporations, financed and led by the Standard Oil Company, the Sugar Trust, August Belmont and Arthur Gorman." [13]

It seemed to Watson a "colossal piece of effrontery" for the Democratic party to go before the American people and proclaim that "for eight years they have been wrong and the Republicans have been right, and at the same time demand that the crowd which has been wrong shall be substituted for the party that has been right." How could the Democrats pretend to be a party of principle? In 1896 they had stolen his platform, and for eight years he had stepped aside, refusing to fire on his own colors. But at St. Louis they dropped his platform and stole the Republican platform. He picked up his standard where Bryan had dropped it and called upon all Jeffersonian Democrats to

[12] Clarence Darrow to T. E. W., July 17, 1904; T. E W, *Life and Speeches of Thomas E. Watson,* pp. 190-244; clippings, Watson Scrapbooks
[13] T. E. W., *ibid ,* pp. 190-244, especially pp. 195, 229-230, 234-240.

rally to it. Where else was there for them to go? He repeated his cry of the Alliance days: "There is a party for Caesar, a party for Pompey, but no party for Rome." [14]

Watson frankly directed his entire appeal to the Bryan Democrats who were discontented with the reactionary leadership of their party. Exhaustively he campaigned his own section, laying every claim he could to Southern pride and allegiance to principle. It was not from the South, however, but from Illinois that a call was issued for a "convention of true Democrats." It repudiated the St. Louis Convention as a betrayal, "a Wall Street manoeuvre," and declared that "the true issue is that presented by Watson vs. Roosevelt." It commended "that distinguished author, statesman, lawyer, citizen, patriot and true Democrat, Thomas E. Watson, whose speech of acceptance at New York was and is the only Democratic utterance of any candidate for the chief magistracy." Nevertheless, "the only real Democratic convention of 1904" failed to materialize.[15]

Much depended upon the attitude Bryan would take. He had denounced the Parker movement before the convention as harshly as any Populist. Would he eat his words and support Parker for the sake of "regularity"? At St. Louis Watson quoted Bryan's earlier statement that "Mr. Parker stands by the New York platform, which crooked Dave Hill had put together," and swore that if there was any consistency in the man he would support the Populist ticket—even as Watson had supported Bryan in 1896.[16] There was little chance that Bryan would turn Populist, but for some time it seemed that he might refrain from giving Parker active support.

Thomas H. Tibbles, Populist candidate for Vice-President, who lived in Lincoln, Nebraska, informed Watson of a deal he had made with T. S. Allen, Bryan's brother-in-law. Tibbles

[14] *Ibid.*, pp. 210, 234, 238; MS. speeches, Watson MSS ; clippings, Watson Scrapbooks; New York *Tribune*, Aug. 19 and Oct 6 and 25, 1904.
[15] *The Saturday News* (Joliet, Illinois), Sept. 17, 1904.
[16] MS. speech, delivered at St. Louis, Sept. 6, 1904, Watson MSS.

agreed to support a Populist-Democratic fusion on the Nebraska state ticket, while Allen promised that Bryan would go to Arizona "and get sick," and refrain from making speeches for Parker. Bryan was said to be a candidate for the Senate. He did go to Arizona and "get sick." Later, however, when Allen went to New York, Bryan returned and took the stump for Parker.[17] His speeches for the erstwhile minion of Wall Street were not lyrical in their praise—merely contending, for the most part, that where Parker's views were questionable, Roosevelt's were more so. More disastrous to the Populist hopes, however, was his treatment of Watson. Bryan not only denied Watson's allegation that consistency demanded his support of Populism, but told his followers that "Every vote for Watson is a vote for Roosevelt." [18] After a blow like this from a pretended friend, Populist hopes sank low.

The election returns gave Watson a popular vote of 117,183. Bryan took pains to point out in his paper that it was "a vote much smaller than Populists, Democrats, and even Republicans expected him to receive," and drew the moral that it was "more charitable" to assume that "the reformers had personal confidence in Mr. Watson, but did not agree with him as to the best method of securing remedial legislation." [19] As a matter of fact Watson's vote was more than double that received by the Populist candidate in 1900. It was none the less a great disappointment. Also dejected were the new Democrats, who suffered the worst defeat their party had had since 1872, failing to carry a state outside the South—and not all of the South. Discontent was largely expressed by abstention from voting. What defection there was went not to Watson but chiefly to Eugene V. Debs, whose vote leaped from around 90,000 in 1900 to over 400,000.

Watson confided his feelings to a comrade of the early 'nineties, C. C. Post. "If there ever was a time," he wrote, "when a

[17] Thomas H. Tibbles to T. E. W., Nov. 16, 1904.
[18] P. Hibben, *op cit.*, p. 257.
[19] Quoted by Watson, *Tom Watson's Magazine*, Vol. I (March, 1905), pp. 7-8.

Populist had no excuse whatever for voting the Democratic ticket it was this year, and I feel very keenly the defection of those who should have been more courageous." Bitterest of all, however, was the ingratitude of his own South, and of his state. "A great many of my old friends in Georgia went squarely back on me . . ."[20] How could such things be . . . not only a Yankee, but a damned Yankee, a Wall Street Yankee at that . . . He would speak to them, he announced, and they came, as they used to—by the hundreds to his doorstep. He lashed them furiously first for their apostasy, and then remonstrated rather hopelessly:

You did not care to know anything about the platform, you didn't read it, you simply wanted to know if it was labeled "Democratic." Whether Peruna, or apple jack, or champagne, or cider, it did not matter what, you put the dear old jug up to your lips and just drank it down all the same.[21]

*   *   *   *   *   *

Consolation came from an unexpected quarter. During the campaign it was not in the South but in New York City that seven hundred plates were sold to a banquet in his honor. It was the New York headquarters that were "ablaze with electric and forensic lights and enthusiasm." General Weaver had made an unexpectedly good showing in New York in 1892, the peak year of Populism, but Watson had exceeded his mark in 1904. No campaigner had worked harder or more gallantly for a forlorn cause than Watson had that year. His fight, however, won more admiration than votes. There were more banquets and more ovations. At Chicago Elbert Hubbard, the eccentric editor of *The Philistine*, delivered an address entitled, "Thomas E. Watson of Georgia, a Producer of History as Well as a Producer of Literature and the Foremost Man of America." President

[20] T. E. W. to C. C. Post, stenographer's notes undated.
[21] MS. speech, delivered at Thomson, Nov. 19, 1904. Watson MSS.

Roosevelt even invited his erstwhile opponent to the White House for a conference, though Watson was unable to accept on account of illness. "You and I do not agree upon some fundamental points," wrote the President, "but eight years ago I made up my mind that you were fearless, disinterested and incorruptible; and with all Americans who possess these qualities I earnestly hope that I may claim some right of spiritual kin." [22]

Watson found it as easy to pack Cooper Union after the election as during the campaign. Cooper Union was known as "an edifice of protest" in that day, and the crowds that came to hear him illustrated the spirit of the times. One meeting at which he spoke was presided over by James Graham Phelps Stokes, "the millionaire settlement worker," and a contributor to his campaign fund, shortly to marry Rose Pastor, "the working girl poetess of the Ghetto." Mayor-elect Edward F. Dunne of Chicago, advocate of municipal ownership of public utilities, also spoke. Judge Samuel Seabury was present. Single taxers, municipal reformers, socialists, and "suffragettes" joined in cheering a Georgia Populist. [23]

American democracy was in ferment in 1905, and strangely varied elements were thrown together by the fermentation. Municipal reformers, settlement house workers, budget experts, conservationists, advocates of direct legislation, workmen's compensation laws, mothers' assistance, and a thousand other reforms, all became vocal and simultaneously joined in the march. It was spoken of generally as "the reform movement," and its proponents were known as "progressives." They had great faith in what Herbert Croly was pleased to call "the orderly processes of reform." Although the movement was Populistic in ideology and in heritage, its members, unlike the Populists, never for-

22 Theodore Roosevelt to T. E. W., Nov. 30, 1904; T. E. W. to Roosevelt, Dec. 6, 1904, Roosevelt MSS., Washington, D. C.
23 New York *World*, April 9, 1905.

364

mulated a platform. They submitted to no party discipline. They had no recognized leaders.

It was before such a group that Watson analyzed the results of the election of 1904 and made an appeal for unity. "Who gained ground by that contest?" he asked. His answer was, "The radicals."

Suppose Eugene Debs had not made his splendid fight; suppose I had failed to answer the call of the Springfield convention, does anyone believe that Congress would now be so eagerly interested in reform . . . ?

What then is the hope of the country?

The union of all the reformers.

We must draw from the Republican party those who oppose class law and money-bag aristocracy. We must draw from the Democratic party every true hearted man who puts Jeffersonian principle above party dictation. We must gather into one compact, aggressive movement all patriots, no matter what they call themselves, who are broad-minded enough to agree upon essential reforms which are in the reach of this generation.[24]

While he was in New York Watson was approached by W. D. Mann, the promoter of *Smart Set* and *Town Topics*, with the proposal that Watson assume the editorship of a magazine, the launching of which Mann would finance. Presumably Mann was not unaware of the unexploited potentialities of a hundred thousand Populist voters, since Charles Q. DeFrance, secretary of the People's Party Executive Committee, was suggested as circulation manager of the proposed magazine. Watson found the proposal more attractive than Hearst's offer for a number of reasons. The magazine was to bear his own name; its policies, ideas, and politics were to be dominated by his personality. Furthermore, it would be possible for him to edit the magazine from Hickory Hill. With the understanding that he was to re-

[24] T. E. W., *Life and Speeches*, p. 256.

ceive $500 a month and expenses for trips between Georgia and New York, he accepted the offer.[25]

The magazine of exposure, or muckraking, was just attaining its most sensational development in 1905. Ida M. Tarbell's exposé of the Standard Oil Company began to appear in *McClure's* in 1903; Lincoln Steffens' *Shame of the Cities* began in the same magazine in 1904, and Ray Stannard Baker's *Railroads on Trial* in 1905. *Everybody's* presented Thomas W. Lawson's *Frenzied Finance* in 1905. Like the reform movement, of which it was a part, muckraking sprouted from the seeds of Populism. Whereas Populism produced only one first-rate journal of protest, the *Arena* (to which Watson had contributed), the muckrakers had a dozen by 1905. There was another difference. Where the Populist literature framed its criticisms in general abstract terms, the muckrakers called names and exposed specific abuses with documented facts.[26] Nowhere is the nexus between the two movements more concretely illustrated than in their confluence in Watson's periodical.

The first number of *Tom Watson's Magazine* bore the date of March, 1905. The title was boldly printed in large blue letters upon a red cover decorated with a drawing of the Liberty Bell. An edition of 100,000 copies, at ten cents each, was sold out in twenty-four hours, and another had to be printed. In six months the magazine had a list of 10,000 paid subscribers.[27] It was liberally, and sometimes exorbitantly, praised in a surprising variety of quarters. "Tom Watson, in his magazine, writes the best editorials that are published in the United States," said the New York *American*.[28] Judge Ben B. Lindsey wrote Watson: "I find much help in reading your wonderful editorials, in which it seems to me you more clearly present present-day difficulties

[25] *Tom Watson's Magazine*, Vol. VI, pp. 1-2; *Watson's Jeffersonian Magazine*, Vol. I, p. 1.
[26] C. C. Regier, *The Era of the Muckrakers*, p. 49; John Chamberlain, *Farewell to Reform*, pp. 128-129.
[27] Charles Q. DeFrance to T. E. W., Aug. 25, 1905.
[28] New York *American*, Aug. 6, 1905.

than any editorial writer in this country." Lindsey thought Watson's "splendid sincerity and courage and pluck in the fight for decency and right" was an "inspiration for every man in this country." [29] A contemporary Horace Mann was convinced that the editor was "guided by the everlasting stars of Truth and Right." [30]

Theodore Dreiser was a frequent contributor to early numbers, and Edgar Lee Masters, Edwin Markham, and Maxim Gorky found their way into *Tom Watson's Magazine*. For the most part, however, its literary offerings were third-rate and worse. There were occasional articles of exposure by such men as Clarence Darrow and Samuel A. Seabury, but these were not featured, and were of minor importance.

The soul of *Tom Watson's Magazine* plainly resided in the Tom Watson editorials, which monopolized the first thirty pages, or nearly a fourth, of every number. The policy was Populist in creed, of course, but with a hospitable attitude toward "reformers" and "progressives" of many stripes as well as toward their sundry causes. Watson's editorials dealt with the same material that absorbed the attention of muckrakers, but in a different way. Where the muckraker was content to expose, Watson was moved to flay, and ridicule, and denounce, and abuse in a manner marvelous to behold. In castigating the frauds of the Equitable Life Assurance Society, for example, he took occasion to refer to "a sleek old Oily Gammon, named Chauncey Depew," and "Thomas F. Ryan, the very embodiment of commercial greed." He proposed to beard such "shameless, unprincipled, lawbreaking robbers," and say to them, "if you don't drop the stolen goods I will rouse your victims till they rise in the elemental wrath of human nature and string you up to the nearest lamp-post." [31] He served similar notice from time to time upon a host of villains: corporation lobbyists, "the Standard

[29] Ben B. Lindsey to T. E. W., Jan. 23, 1907.
[30] Horace Mann to T. E. W., July 31, 1905; editorial, Buffalo *Progress*, July 27, 1905.
[31] *Tom Watson's Magazine*, Vol. II (Aug., 1905), pp. 135 and 139.

367

Oil crowd," "the Gas Trust thieves," franchise grabbers, Wall Street bankers, "the professional boodler and grafter in both the old parties." Let them quake in their boots before the wrath of an indignant people.

The cartoonist, Gordon Nye, admirably caught the spirit of the editorials, which he illustrated with leering plutocrats (clad uniformly in suits checked with dollar marks and skull-and-bones), all of bulging paunch and money bag.

The temperate reformer and the scholarly muckraker doubtless viewed with alarm some of the vagaries of their Populist recruit. Muckrakers had exposed Sam Spencer of Georgia as the organizer of a systematic scheme of bribing the public press in behalf of Morgan railroad interests, but it remained for Tom Watson to suggest that a continuation of the good work begun by pen and ink might be made with a length of hempen rope:

Sam Spencer calls Rate Regulation by Government LYNCH LAW. *Let Sam Spencer beware* . . . !

Revolutions have been; revolutions may be again.

When crime runs riot and courts are powerless, it may be that the people will rise up in their natural right as a Society, and do swift justice upon criminals taken red-handed . . .[32]

In regard to political developments of the time, Watson was alternately elated by the mighty words, and goaded to distraction by the mild performance of President Roosevelt. "In case of blood poison," he admonished, "shinplasters for surface abrasions never yet saved the patient; and Mr. Roosevelt's plans for another tribunal *to control the railroads* are mere shinplasters."[33] Woodrow Wilson was quoted as saying, "Trusts can never be abolished. We must moralize them." The vials of Watson's wrath, already stirred by Wilson's slight to Southern glory, were quite overturned:

[32] *Tom Watson's Magazine*, Vol. III (Dec., 1905), p. 154.
[33] *Ibid.*, Vol. I (April, 1905), pp. 136-137.

How will you do it, impractical prig?

Mr. Rockefeller is moral, isn't he? Goes to church every Sunday . . .

Go back to thy gerund-grinding, Woodrow—thou insufferable, impractical prig. Among the dead Greeks and the extinct Romans thy labors may, haply, be useful; but when thou comest among the practical men of today seeking to master actual conditions and to take part in the great battle of thought, motive and purpose which rages around us, thou art but "a babby, and a gal babby at that." [34]

Along with other reformers and progressives and muckrakers, however, Watson shared the sanguine faith that "education and agitation" would in no distant future put to rout the evildoers and restore the democracy to its pristine purity. Perhaps he would at times assist Mr. Croly's "orderly processes of reform" with a little lyncher's hemp. For all that, he believed that "The day of the Common People is at hand, for the Masses are being educated as never before." [35]

[34] *Loc. cit.*
[35] *Ibid.*, Vol. II (July, 1905), p. 11.

CHAPTER XX

Reform and Reaction

As HE CAMPAIGNED the South in the forlorn crusade of 1904, Watson was confronted in state after state with a revival of the Democratic dialectic of the 'nineties. It varied not at all. An editor in Houston, Texas, saw behind Populism "the ominous shadow of negro domination," and an editor in Augusta, Georgia, saw the same apparition and described it in exactly the same words. "The argument against the independent political movement in the South," wrote Watson in 1892, "may be boiled down to one word—nigger." [1] If twelve years had worked no change upon his Nemesis, they had had their effect upon Tom Watson.

In Atlanta he threw before the Democrats a challenge and a promise. He was "not at all afraid of any negro domination in the South," and never had been. Furthermore, he believed that "the cry that we are in danger from 'the nigger' is the most hypocritical that unscrupulous leadership could invent." What could the Negro do? He had been disfranchised in nearly every state in the South except Georgia. There he had been "white primaried." If the Democrats were honest in their fears, why did they not write the principle of the white primary into the state constitution, as other states had done? He would tell them: "In Georgia they do not dare to disfranchise him [the Negro], because the men who control the democratic machine in Georgia

[1] *P. P. P.*, Aug. 26, 1892.

know that a majority of the whites are against them. They need the negro to beat us with." The white primary, being nothing more than a party custom, could be shelved at any time the machine needed the Negro vote. He therefore pledged his support, and the support of the Populists, to any anti-machine, Democratic candidate running upon a suitable platform that included a pledge to "a change in our Constitution which will perpetuate white supremacy in Georgia." [2]

How Watson managed to reconcile his radical democratic doctrine with a proposal to disfranchise a million citizens of his native state is not quite clear. When South Carolina, under the leadership of Ben Tillman, changed its constitution in 1895 with the avowed purpose of disfranchising the Negro, Watson wrote an indignant editorial:

All this re-actionary legislation is wrong.

There can be no sound principle, consistent with our democratic theory of government, which says that a negro worth $300 is a better citizen than one worth $200. . . .

The whole scheme of the democrats of South Carolina is to perpetuate the rule of their party. . . .

Old fashioned democracy taught that a man who fought the battles of his country, and paid the taxes of his government, should have a vote in the choosing of rulers and the making of laws.[3]

Watson, nevertheless, repeated and underscored his offer to the Democrats after the 1904 campaign ended. Later he expanded his reasons. "The white people dare not revolt so long as they can be intimidated by the fear of the negro vote," he explained. Once the "bugaboo of negro domination" was removed, however, "every white man would act according to his own conscience and judgment in deciding how he shall vote." [4]

 ` [2] Watson's offer to support a disfranchisement program was printed by none of the papers reporting the speech, but *vide* MS. Speech, Aug. 1, 1904, Watson papers. *Constitution*, Sept. 2, 1904; Atlanta *News*, Sept. 2, 1904.
[3] *P. P. P.*, Nov. 8, 1895.
[4] Atlanta *Journal*, July 27, 1906; *vide* also: *Weekly Jeffersonian*, March 24, 1910.

371

With these words Watson abandoned his old dream of uniting both races against the enemy, and took his first step toward the opposite extreme in racial views. There was another consideration which he did not mention. With the Negro vote eliminated, Watson and the Populists stood in much the same relation toward the two factions of the Democratic party as the Negro had occupied toward Populists and Democrats: they held the balance of power.

Watson's offer did not long go begging.

Since 1898, when the Populists had last put forth a state ticket, a succession of staunchly conservative governors had ruled the state. They belonged to that wing of the party which, since the 'seventies, had been hospitable toward Northern capital, and friendly to corporate interests, especially the railroads. Resistance to the dominance of this wing had reached its lowest ebb in 1904, when the candidate had been reëlected without opposition. In the spring of 1905, more than a year before the next election, Clark Howell announced himself as a candidate for the gubernatorial nomination. A logical successor in the scheme of office rotation, Howell had back of him a long record of party service and the support of the conservative machine. His prospects could hardly have been fairer.

Early in 1905, Thomas W. Hardwick, congressman from Watson's district, and a representative of the opposition to the Howell faction, came to Watson to discuss the proposal concerning disfranchisement. Together they worked out a platform combining that issue with several reform demands for railroad regulation, and agreed upon Pope Brown as a suitable candidate. Then shortly after Watson's support of his candidacy became known, Pope Brown withdrew from the race in favor of Hoke Smith. It later developed that Brown took this step because he received from Hardwick the impression that Watson desired it.[5]

Watson was left in perplexity after this maneuver, and for several months he refused to commit himself. There had been

[5] Pope Brown to T. E. W., Feb. 22, 1908.

372

political enmity between Watson and Hoke Smith ever since the 'nineties, when, as a member of Cleveland's cabinet, Smith had led the gold forces in Georgia. It had not been six months since Watson had written the editor of the Atlanta *Journal*, with which Smith had long been associated, asking that his name be removed from the circulation list. He explained: "In this campaign you have pursued me with such bitter vindictiveness that I can no longer accept any favor at your hands." [6] The editor was doubtless justified in denying the charge. Tom Watson was ever quick in perceiving injury and ever slow in forgiving.

On the other hand, there were certain forces at work to draw Smith and Watson together. Since the subsidence of the silver issue, Howell and Smith had reversed positions with respect to relative conservatism. The critical issue now was government control and ownership, and Hoke Smith, an anti-corporation lawyer, was far in advance of Howell upon this question. In 1902 he had joined Watson in speaking before the Georgia legislature in support of a bill prohibiting child labor.[7] For years he had been fighting the state machine in the columns of the Atlanta *Journal*, a rival of Howell's *Constitution*. He charged that the machine was owned by the railroads and that the state railway commission served the railroads. He pointed out rate discriminations, abuses, and corrupting influences. Smith's platform for 1906 might have been written by a Populist. It contained demands for primaries to nominate by popular vote all officers, including senators; for the abolition of poll-workers and the disfranchisement of vote-buyers; for a stringent corrupt practices act; for making pass-giving and lobbying a crime; for compulsory domestication of Georgia railroads and their submission to state courts and to heavier taxation; for an elective railway commission; and for state ownership of railroads.[8]

It was the heyday of the reform governor—La Follette of

[6] Quoted in the editor's reply: J. R. Gray to T. E. W., Nov. 14, 1904.

[7] T. E. W., *Life and Speeches of Thomas E. Watson*, pp. 184-189.

[8] Augusta *Herald*, June 29, 1905; Herbert Quick, "Hoke Smith and the Revolution in Georgia," *The Reader*, Vol. X (Aug., 1907), pp. 241-247.

Wisconsin, Folk of Missouri, Colby of New Jersey—and Smith of Georgia was hailed by national reformers as one of that number. Herbert Quick said that Smith wrote "the most radical platform ever adopted, with perhaps one exception, by a state convention of either of the two great parties of these times." Smith "has no corporation collar. He is a successful party revolutionist." [9] There was one plank of Smith's platform that struck his Progressive admirers as a bit incongruous. Yet it was the one singled out to appear day after day in bold-faced capital letters on the editorial page of the *Journal:* he favored "THE ELIMINATION OF THE NEGRO FROM POLITICS . . . BY LEGAL AND CONSTITUTIONAL METHODS . . . WITHOUT DISFRANCHISING A SINGLE WHITE MAN."

While Watson hesitated over his decision, James K. Hines, Populist candidate for governor in 1894, urged him to come out for Smith. Hines would go even further. "Let us accept the invitation, often extended by both factions, to come home," he wrote. "Let us take charge of the Democratic Party in Georgia and make it the People's Party." Again he wrote: "You are stronger than any man in Georgia. When Mr. Stephens quit the whigs and joined the democrats he justified himself by saying that the democrats had come to him. Much more true is it, that the democrats have come to you." [10] Hardwick served as a zealous intermediary between Hickory Hill and the Atlanta *Journal.* He begged Watson to tell him "exactly what reparation you think Mr. Smith ought to make" and he would "get Mr. Smith and the *Journal* to do the right thing." [11] It appeared that a number of "reparations" were required, as well as some changes in the platform. They were all eagerly made, however: Smith's in public speeches, the *Journal's* in an editorial actually written by Hardwick. [12]

[9] H. Quick, *op. cit*, p. 241.
[10] James K. Hines to T. E. W , June 8 and Dec. 9, 1905, and July 12, 1906.
[11] Thomas W. Hardwick to T. E. W., June 26, 1905.
[12] *Ibid*, Aug 9, 1905

On September 12 Watson wrote Smith promising his support, and in the October number of his magazine, widely circulated in Georgia at Smith's expense, made public his position. He first reminded his followers that Smith and Howell "were both rock-ribbed, moss-backed, unterrified Democrats" and mortal enemies of Populism back in the 'nineties. "But times have changed," he said. "If . . . [Smith] can do for Georgia what La Follette has done for Wisconsin and Folk has done for Missouri, he will become a heroic figure in the eyes of reformers throughout the land. No matter how faulty his record in the past may have been, he is hitting the bull's-eye *this* time." Cautious in his commitments at first, he refused to say he would vote for Smith. Later he plunged in more wholeheartedly. He was still a Populist, and he refused to commit himself two years in advance to the National Democratic ticket, but he pledged the Populists not to put out a state ticket, and to abide by the result of the white primary. "I am going to vote for Hoke Smith," he finally declared. "And I appeal to every Populist of McDuffie and the surrounding counties, and every Populist throughout the state . . . to follow me now; and if it turns out I am wrong then punish me hereafter by never listening to me with respect upon any issue." [13]

Smith was profuse in his expressions of gratitude. "I cannot tell you how much I appreciate your coöperation," he wrote, and he told of how his campaign had undergone a rejuvenation the moment Watson's support was made public. [14] Continuous correspondence was kept up between the two throughout the campaign, and whole pages of the *Journal* were given over to Watson's opinions. Was it reported that the farmers of north Georgia suspected Negro disfranchisement of being a scheme to disfranchise illiterate whites? Off went Watson to reassure them. Were the Populists in the South rebellious at voting for a former gold bug? Watson was there to tell them that "Hoke Smith is

[13] Atlanta *Journal*, Aug. 7, 1906.
[14] Hoke Smith to T. E. W., Sept. 16, 1905 and Dec. 19, 1905.

trying to do what we want done and cannot do ourselves."

The campaign was the hottest since the 'nineties, and judging from the nature of Howell's attack, one might suppose Watson was the candidate instead of Smith. Smith was declared to be a "demagogue" and a "Muckraker" who was "run by Tom Watson." He had "surrendered his convictions and his democratic allegiance to Tom Watson for the latter's support." In a surprisingly accurate prophecy, the *Constitution* predicted: "The spectacle of Tom Watson controlling the machinery of the Democratic party—and at the same time remaining an open and avowed populist—is one which the Democrats of this state may have to endure." [15] Some of the edge of this attack was taken off when Watson made public a letter from Clark Howell to him begging an interview before Watson had sided with Smith.[16]

As for Smith, he "wouldn't give Tom Watson for the whole crowd."

The executive committee of the Democratic party, under control of the Howell wing, attempted to rule Populists out of the party primary by requiring that all ballots bear the following inscription: "By voting this ticket, I hereby declare that I am an organized Democrat, and I hereby pledge myself to support the organized Democracy, both state and national." [17] The ruling was loudly denounced by Watson and Smith, however, and failed in its purpose.

The foremost issue of the campaign was the question of Negro disfranchisement. None of Howell's objections to the measure was aimed at the principle of disfranchisement, but merely at its effectiveness. It would disfranchise illiterate whites while allowing educated Negroes to vote; it had failed of its purpose in Alabama, and it encouraged Negroes to climb out of their "place" into the ranks of the literate.

The most serious tactical blunder made by Howell and his

[15] *Constitution,* June 24 and Aug. 3 and 5, 1906; Macon *Telegraph,* Aug. 5, 1906.
[16] Clark Howell to T. E. W., Aug. 4, 1905; Atlanta *Journal,* Jan. 13, 1906.
[17] A. M Arnett, *op cit.,* p. 221; *Constitution,* Aug. 3, 1906.

friends was their attempt to defend the corporations and railroads upon whom Watson and Smith made war. Charles R. Pendleton, editor of the Macon *Telegraph*, launched a bitter personal attack on Watson and undertook to answer his editorial onslaughts upon Samuel Spencer, president of the Southern Railroad, a Morgan subsidiary. The attack precipitated a cloudburst of railroad-denunciation from Watson. Wall Street's plundering of Southern railroads—the stock frauds, illegal combinations, extortionate rates, criminal negligence—were already a familiar story.[18] But no one could make these villainies quite so heinous, nor the villains quite so monstrous as Tom Watson. It was a specialty with him. Early in 1905 he had pronounced J. P. Morgan *"the absolute king of the railroads in Georgia."* "He makes the Governor," Watson charged, "controls the legislature, overrides the commission and tramples the Constitution of the State under his feet." Samuel Spencer's crime, moreover, was "unnatural as well as heinous." "He is the Sepoy, the hireling of a foreign master, trained, uniformed, armed and paid to conquer and plunder his own people. A Southern man, he has looted the South; a Georgian, he has robbed Georgia." When Watson read Spencer's report of a 525 per cent increase in net earnings in eleven years his indignation was "deep and hot," and he wrote:

Those eleven years rose up in perspective before me, and the awful MEANS by which Sam Spencer had reached that END stalked by like a procession of spectres. The frightful loss of human life; the bribing of politicians; the corrupting of men in power; the violation of state laws and Federal statutes; the disregard of the rights of shippers and passengers; the discriminations which have ruined whole communities; the extortionate charges which have beggared individuals . . . the defiance of State Commissions and of public opinion; the overwork and underpay of the men who bear the brunt of the toil. . . .

Watson declared that "we lost fewer lives to the invading host of Sherman's army than we have lost to the railroads" during

[18] Lewis Corey, *The House of Morgan*, pp. 381-382.

Spencer's regime. He demonstrated that the railroads owned considerable stock in the Macon *Telegraph*, and turned furiously upon the editor: "you hypocrite, you sneak, you corporation slave . . ." [19]

Joel Chandler Harris's Populist character, "Mr. Billy Sanders," summed up the old guard's response to Watson's campaign: "I'll tell you the honest truth: thar ain't skacely a night passes that I ain't rid by some red-eyed trust or 'nother, an' ef 'tain't a trust, then it's some villainous railroad corporation; an' that's lots wuss'n a trust, bekeze the trains is allers late, an' they've got a habit of switchin' back'erds and forrerds on the pit of my stomach— I reckon they think it's some new kind of a turn-table." [20]

The primary election resulted in an overwhelming victory for Hoke Smith. How much of the credit was due Tom Watson is, of course, difficult to estimate. "To swing 90,000 populists to your candidate [Smith] required the hardest fighting I had done since 1892," wrote Watson, and surely his efforts were not wasted. However the votes were obtained, there is less doubt about the issues, for they were clearly Watson issues. Some of the sweetness of victory was soured for Watson by his failure to carry his own county, after he had made a special effort to do so. In general, however, he was much elated by the turn events were taking. Pointing out that Smith was making "the same fight we used to make," that President Roosevelt had put his hands to "the same work we wanted to do," and that "the Bryan boom for 1908 lashes itself to the most radical plank of the Populist platform," he concluded that "the skies do verily begin to redden . . . for the glorious coming of morning." [21]

There was a tragic sequel to the election—the Atlanta race riot of 1906. Its mention gains pertinence in view of the future

[19] T. E. W., "Clark Howell's Defense of the Corporation," *Tom Watson's Magazine*, Vol. IV (March, 1906), pp. 1-8; "Sam Spencer," *ibid*, Vol. IV (April, 1906), pp. 161-165; Atlanta *Journal*, July 13 and Aug. 11, 1906.

[20] Joel Chandler Harris, "Mr. Billy Sanders," *Uncle Remus Magazine*, Vol. I, No. 4 (Sept., 1907).

[21] Atlanta *Journal*, July 13, 1906.

history of Watson and of Watsonism. "Everybody knew that the Disfranchisement issue was the cause of our success," wrote Watson. During the campaign the papers of Atlanta were almost daily filled with sensational stories of Negro atrocities. Lynching was openly advocated and frequently practiced. A concerted crusade of race bigotry and hatred was preached. Partly it was the result of newspaper rivalry, augmented by the recent intrusion of Hearst into Atlanta, but the political significance was readily apparent. An editorial of the Atlanta *Journal,* one of the milder papers, indicates the trend. It was printed in bold-face capitals:

Political equality being thus preached to the negro in the ring papers and on the stump, what wonder that he makes no distinction between political and social equality. He grows more bumptious on the street. More impudent in his dealings with white men; and then, when he cannot achieve social equality as he wishes, with the instinct of the barbarian to destroy what he cannot attain to, he lies in wait, as that dastardly brute did yesterday near this city, and assaults the fair young girlhood of the south. . . . It is time for those who know the perils of the negro problem to stand together with deep resolve that political power shall never give the negro encouragement in his foul dreams of a mixture of races.[22]

Watson employed the same appeal in his speeches for Smith. A few days after the election the riot broke upon the streets of Atlanta. It raged for four days. Innocent men and women were hunted by packs and shot down in the streets of the city. Destruction, looting, robbery, murder, and unspeakable brutality went unrestrained. A committee of indignant citizens was shocked that "the small minority which constitutes the tough element was allowed to crucify this community in the eyes of the world . . ."[23] The "tough element" expressed no regrets. It wrote no editorials.

*   *   *   *   *   *

[22] Atlanta *Journal,* Aug. 1, 1906.
[23] Glenn W. Rainey, "The Atlanta Race Riot of 1906" (Master's thesis, Emory University), *passim; Constitution,* Dec. 29, 1906.

379

Between the rôle of national reformer and the rôle of defender of White Supremacy stretched an embarrassing hiatus. Faithful readers of *Tom Watson's Magazine* might now find wedged between a defense of the Russian revolutionists and an attack on Wall Street such editorials as one entitled "The Ungrateful Negro." [24] Watson closed an editorial attacking Booker T. Washington with the remark:

> What does Civilization owe to the negro?
> Nothing!
> *Nothing! !*
> NOTHING! ! ! [25]

This editorial was more widely quoted in the South, especially in Georgia, than anything he wrote. The response of the reformers and progressives, on the other hand, ranged from bewilderment to dismay in tone. "It is all so disappointing," wrote a Southern woman. "I thought I'd struck the magazine, the writer, and the reformer after my own heart." [26] A Northern reformer wrote Watson: Your position on the Negro puts you in "the same category with the men you censure," very close, indeed, to "a professed politician merely out for his own advantage." [27] Upton Sinclair wrote a long letter of remonstrance. Thomas H. Tibbles reported that "the Populists are all at sea over the negro question in the South and are writing to me about it." [28]

The tenuous lines that Watson had tied between National Progressivism and Southern Agrarianism—practically the only prospect of a bond between them—had snapped under the tension of the race issue.

[24] *Tom Watson's Magazine*, Vol. IV (April, 1906), pp. 165-174.
[25] *Ibid.*, Vol. I (June, 1905), p. 298.
[26] Mrs. Martin Singer to T. E. W., May 27, 1905.
[27] James F. Morton, Jr. to T. E. W., Jan. 6, 1905.
[28] Upton Sinclair to T. E. W., June 25, 1905; Thomas H. Tibbles to T. E. W., Oct. 8, 1906.

The strained lines between Fifth Avenue and Hickory Hill were burdened with more than ideological tension by this time. Differences between the editor and the New York office of the magazine over matters of management and business were constantly arising, and heated disputes were conducted by mail. Each side had just grievances. Watson was unable to collect $9,000 of salary due him, and he discovered that Mann's business reputation was not what it might have been.[29] He was embarrassed when forced by Clark Howell to admit that Mann's *Town Topics*, a scandal publication, owned a majority of the stock of *Tom Watson's Magazine*. He had endless complaints to make concerning details.[30] Mann and those of the staff who sided with him said that Watson was "too dogmatic, abusive and narrow in his relations with other reformers and radicals." Their more pertinent, as well as more justifiable, complaint, however, was that he was dictatorial, quarrelsome, and "a difficult person to work with." They also resented his proclaiming, *"I am this Magazine."* [31] The upshot of the dispute was Watson's withdrawal from the editorship in October, 1906.

In January appeared the first number of *Watson's Jeffersonian Magazine*. A surfeited public might now choose between two Watson magazines. The New York competitor, however, after two more numbers, gave up the attempt to produce a *Tom Watson Magazine* without Tom Watson. "Hamlet with the Prince of Denmark left out!" jeered Watson. He appealed to all loyal followers to help him "down that brace of rascals in New York." The appeal was significant, for the new magazine took a more sectional, as well as a more personal tone. It was published in Atlanta, and Watson was proclaimed "Editor and Proprietor." The cover was decorated with a drawing of Monticello and an inset portrait of Jefferson. Gradually, national issues and na-

29 Arthur Brisbane to T. E. W., Jan. 12, 1906. Brisbane warned Watson that Mann was unreliable.

30 T. E. W., "Foreword," *Watson's Jeffersonian Magazine*, Vol. I (Jan., 1907), pp. 1-28.

31 "Explanatory," *Watson's Magazine*, Vol. VI (Nov., 1906), p. 1.

tional reforms gave way in the magazine to sectional issues and Southern concerns. No issue, whether national or sectional, however, was given precedence over the burning issue of *Tom Watson*. One number of the magazine contained seven pictures of the Editor and Proprietor (two on horseback), and two pictures of Hickory Hill, to say nothing of a number of pictures of the Watson household of three generations, and several Watson servants.[32] Had there been any possible necessity for it, Watson could now have said without the remotest fear of contradiction, *"I am this Magazine."*

In October, 1906, he had begun the publication of a newspaper, the *Weekly Jeffersonian*. Since it was devoted more to Watson's editorials than to news, its subsequent change in format to a three column journal, and the change in name to *Watson's Jeffersonian Weekly* were not inappropriate.

The use of the mailing lists of the Atlanta *Journal* was doubtless of no little assistance in the launching of two periodicals by one man within two months' time. The lists were obtained through the courtesy of Governor-elect Hoke Smith.[33]

* * * * * *

"You are a hard man to get along with—almost an impossibility," wrote a member of the staff of the original magazine to Watson.[34] He was not the first to find this so—nor the last. The complaint recurs again and again in Watson's correspondence: complaints of "language that was marked by coldness and bluntness," of "the extreme anger displayed in your letter," of "bad humor," of "an unfriendly spirit." The complainants ranged from William Jennings Bryan to the secretary of a college debating society.[35] There was something elemental and inexplica-

[32] *Watson's Jeffersonian Magazine*, Vol. I (Feb., 1907), *passim*.
[33] Thomas W. Hardwick to T. E. W., Sept. 30, 1906; J. R. Gray (Editor of *Journal*) to T. E. W, Aug. 28, 1906.
[34] Charles Q DeFrance to T. E. W., Oct. 15, 1906.
[35] Correspondence, 1895–1908, Watson MSS.

ble about his wrath that in some instances defies analysis. It was most regularly provoked, however, when his will was crossed by one whom he considered under obligation to him. There were times when he showed remarkable restraint, but these instances were fewer now than in the earlier part of his career.

Relations between the governor-elect and his Populist ally continued cordial. Smith acknowledged his obligation and emphasized his gratitude to Watson repeatedly by letter. "Your generous support during this race I can never forget," he wrote. Again: "I appreciate more than I can tell you the broad line upon which you planted your position." [36] He also saw to it that public acknowledgment of Watson's assistance was made in the Atlanta *Journal*.[37] He invited Watson to visit in his home in Atlanta and discuss plans for the coming administration, and he sent his son to visit at Hickory Hill.[38] As plans were shaped for the new legislature they were sent to Thomson with urgent requests for suggestions. "We are trying to have ready a bill covering every provision of the platform adopted at Macon to meet our promises to the people," wrote Smith, enclosing with his letter an important bill.[39]

In both his publications Watson gave the new administration his unstinted endorsement. He heralded Smith's inauguration with enthusiasm:

Last year we fought it out in Georgia, and *we whipped the Yankee corporations*.

In spite of their money, and their venal tools, their Hessians and their Sepoys, their campaign tricks and lies—WE WHIPPED THEM!

And with the passing of Joe Terrell [outgoing executive], ends the era of Yankee corporations' bossism in Georgia.

[36] Hoke Smith to T. E. W., June 29, 1906; July 29, 1906.
[37] Editorial, Atlanta *Journal*, Aug. 23, 1906.
[38] Hoke Smith to T. E. W., Dec. 30, 1906.
[39] *Ibid*, June 17, 1907.

With the term of Hoke Smith *begins Home Rule.* . . .

With Hoke Smith in office, armed with the confidence, and inspired by the hopes of the people, A NEW ERA BEGINS.[40]

Judging from all appearances, Smith the governor was as attentive to the voice from Hickory Hill as Smith the candidate. He was careful to consult Watson over all appointments that might involve the latter's interests; he continued to submit bills for Watson's approval, and to solicit advice. When Watson showed signs of complaining of the slowness of the wheels of reform, the Governor sought to calm him. "As to the other matters about which you have written to me, don't grow impatient," he begged, and he carefully outlined the strategy he was following.[41] Smith's complaint that the legislature was not with him was corroborated by the reports of Congressman Hardwick, who was likewise in close touch with Hickory Hill. "I am now quite sure," wrote Hardwick, "that the administration has not an actual majority in either House that *at heart* supports it. Whatever is obtained from them seems to be literally forced . . ." [42] Leaders of the legislature, some of them ex-Populists, also asked instructions and advice from Watson. Few indeed were the coming events at the Capitol that did not cast their shadows at Hickory Hill.

In spite of persistent obstruction and a large lobby, the reform governor accomplished wonders. Not since the famous "Farmer's Legislature" of 1890 had so many important laws, "reform" and otherwise, been written. The railroad commission was increased in size, in power, and in dignity. A wide range of public utilities, service and power companies, were brought under its supervision, and violators of its rulings were made punishable like other criminals. Moreover, a special state's attorney was created to assist in prosecuting violators of the commission's

[40] *Watson's Jeffersonian Weekly*, July 4, 1907.
[41] Hoke Smith to T E. W., July 30, 1907.
[42] Thomas W. Hardwick to T. E W., Aug 8, 1907.

rulings. To this office Smith appointed James K. Hines, Populist candidate for governor in 1894, and a personal friend of Tom Watson. Under the new dispensation passenger and freight rates were materially reduced and some discriminations eliminated. Free passes were forbidden, except to railroad employees and officials.

After considerable debate, the legislature passed a bill submitting to the people for ratification a constitutional amendment designed to disfranchise Negroes by the indirect means of registration requirements. The governor was satisfied with it, and Hardwick, whose judgment on the measure Watson trusted, assured him that it would disfranchise ninety-five per cent of the Negroes. Caught up on the wave of the reform movement, a bill providing for statewide prohibition of the sale and manufacture of intoxicating liquors was swept through the legislature. Prohibition had not been a dominant issue in Smith's campaign, but it had been the leading issue in the Populist state campaign in 1896, and Populism was now in the saddle.

While looking askance at the disfranchisement amendment, the national reform press nevertheless rang with praise for Smith's accomplishments. "He has done what most of our trust-busting governors have merely been talking about," wrote Herbert Quick. He was "now second only to La Follette, if second to any, as a trust-busting governor." [43]

The question, "What will Watson say?" was an important one for the future of the reform administration. He had had some criticisms to make, but nearly all were made privately. Now, at the end of the first session of the legislature, his verdict was an unqualified endorsement:

Under difficult conditions, Governor Smith has done well. No man could have done better. In spite of lobbyists and obstructionists,

[43] Herbert Quick, *op. cit.*, p. 241; A. F. McKelway, "The Suffrage in Georgia," *Outlook*, Vol. LXXXVII (Sept. 14, 1907), pp. 63-66; editorial, *Outlook*, Vol. LXXXVII (Sept. 7, 1907), p. 2; "Georgia's Example to the Nation," *Independent*, Vol. LXIV (Jan. 16, 1908), p. 162.

he has wrung from the legislature a sweepingly good law which gives the railroad commission the power of the state in dealing with public service corporations. He has also secured the passage of a bill which redeems the main pledge of his campaign—to wit the disfranchisement bill. . . . Governor Smith! The *Jeffersonian* welcomes you to the great class of men who will battle for an idea . . . !

Some day, our proud old state will send you to the senate!

What may not be done by co-operation . . . !

That Governor Smith has done everything in his power to keep his contract with the people no one can doubt.[44]

Then came the case of Arthur Glover.

Glover, a semi-literate factory foreman of Augusta, was convicted of the murder of a woman mill-worker and sentenced to hang. Of his guilt there was no question. He wrote Watson pitiful, illiterate letters imploring his assistance.[45] Watson did not need to be reminded that Glover had been one of his most loyal and formidable apostles in the bloody battles of the Augusta workers' district back in the 'nineties. When last mentioned in these pages he was fleeing to the South Carolina woods a jump ahead of a posse, after a Democratic deputy sheriff had been shot through the stomach at the Augusta polls.[46] When politics reached the shooting stage—as they not infrequently did in the 'nineties—Glover was generally on hand, his trigger-finger a-twitch. In the trial for his life he was prosecuted by Boykin Wright. Wright was the manager of the Democratic campaigns against Watson in Augusta and Richmond County that dashed Populist hopes in three elections in the 'nineties. Watson nursed an intense hatred against Wright and the "Augusta ring" and could always be persuaded to believe the worst of them. Wright was said to have mentioned Watson's name in Glover's trial, and it was easy for Watson to believe that his apostle was a victim of political persecution. Watson promised that after Smith's in-

[44] *Watson's Jeffersonian Magazine*, Vol I (Sept, 1907), p. 847.
[45] Arthur Glover to T. E. W., May 18, 1907.
[46] See above, p 236

auguration he would ask the governor, as a personal favor, to commute the death sentence to one of life imprisonment.

It was characteristic of Watson that, once he had put his hand to the task, the saving of Glover's life became a holy cause, and all who stood in its way stood in the way of righteousness and therefore constituted a sinister force of evil. He brought to bear all the powerful forces at his command. When he heard that Boykin Wright was attempting to persuade the governor against Glover's cause, a new aspect was given to the cause. It was now a test of political power between Watson and his most detested political enemy before a governor whom Watson believed he had made. In August he wrote Hardwick, who still served as an intermediary between Watson and Smith, saying: "Boykin Wright's intense hatred of Glover originated with Glover's fearless partisanship in '92, and his gallantry in coming to my rescue on the night when the Augusta crowd meant to do me up. I would have been killed that night had it not been for a few such devoted friends as Glover." He did not wish the matter presented "in a way that Governor Smith would consider it a threat." Nevertheless, he added significantly: "Governor Smith should weigh these matters well, for it will make a world of difference in the relations between himself and me, if he should fail to measure up to the size of a full grown man in the emergency." [47]

The governor could not reasonably be expected to commit himself before the prison commission made its report on Glover's petition. In the meantime, however, Watson grew impatient. Late in November he published an editorial taking Smith to task for praising the work of the summer legislature. Watson severely criticized its work, some of which he had previously praised. Not long after this appeared, Hardwick arranged a conference between Watson and Smith at the Capitol. Watson later portrayed himself "with one leg thrown across the corner of . . .

[47] T. E. W. to Thomas W. Hardwick, Aug. 6, 1907, published in the Atlanta *Journal*, Aug. 7, 1910.

[Smith's] big working desk," pleading for Glover's life for more than an hour. Pleased with his conference, he wrote Hardwick: "Had a long talk with Gov. Smith and everything lovely. He will stay on the job." [48] A few days later there arrived at Hickory Hill a handsomely bound set of Voltaire's complete works— a present from Governor Smith, who sent his best wishes for the new year.[49] He also invited Watson to accompany him to Roosevelt's White House conference of Governors.

The report of the prison commission was unfavorable to Glover's petition, and the final decision now rested with the governor. James K. Hines, one of Watson's many intercessors with Smith, wrote that he believed the governor was "not influenced by our enemies," and was "sincerely desirous of finding some good reason for reducing the death penalty," but the case was a bad one, and he begged Watson to be reasonable.[50] So did others. The set of Voltaire, however, was promptly ordered removed from Hickory Hill. Governor Smith wrote Watson reviewing at length the facts of Glover's case and the report of the commission. "I am deeply grieved," he concluded, "to see no other alternative in the discharge of my official duty than to leave the sentence placed upon him to take its course." [51]

Such monstrous proportions had Smith's "betrayal" assumed in Watson's mind that he made the mistake of bursting into print with an open letter to the governor full of extravagant contentions. "Pardon me for speaking plainly—" he wrote, "this is a matter of life and death, and my feelings are deeply stirred." He denounced capital punishment, pronounced Glover a "cracked-brained degenerate," and said that his execution would be "murder." He also repeated the charges of political persecution. "Boykin Wright wanted me assassinated and Arthur Glover was one of those who saved my life. I had hoped that

[48] T. E. W. to Thomas W. Hardwick, Dec. 18, 1907, Atlanta *Journal*, Aug. 7, 1910.
[49] Hoke Smith to T. E. W., Dec. 29, 1907.
[50] James K. Hines to T. E. W., Jan. 28, 1908.
[51] Hoke Smith to T. E. W., Jan. 28, 1908.

this would have some weight with you, but it seems that I was wrong." [52] The governor remained unshaken. Glover was executed. "The Governor has chosen and will take the natural consequences," wrote Watson to Hardwick. "No such cold-blooded and selfish politician can ever be friend of mine again." [53]

Watson lost no time in initiating reprisals. Major McGregor was sent to Joseph M. Brown, of Marietta, with the request that he enter the gubernatorial race of 1908 as a candidate against Smith. Watson's promises were not committed to paper, but Brown wrote his friend Pendleton of the Macon *Telegraph* in "strictest confidence" that Watson had assured him of "vigorous support." [54] He also wrote Watson expressing his gratitude for the offer, which, he said, almost persuaded him to enter the race. "But there are two or three considerations of great importance entering into the question," he continued, "which I scarcely feel willing to decide without a personal conference with you." [55] He proposed a meeting between them in Atlanta, suggesting elaborate precautions for secrecy. In less than a month Brown announced his candidacy.

In heritage, training, occupation, and interest Brown was completely identified with corporate interests and their point of view. A son of Joseph E. Brown, the millionaire railroad promoter, he entered a railroad office after college and remained for twenty-five years either an employee or an official of railway companies. He was still financially interested in railroads when he was appointed to the state railroad commission in 1904. As governor and during his subsequent career he became known as a bitter enemy of organized labor, and wrote many pamphlets and articles to prove that unions were dominated by foreigners, affili-

[52] T. E. W. to Hoke Smith, Jan. 26, 1908, in the Atlanta *Georgian*, Jan. 29, 1908; also *Watson's Jeffersonian Weekly*, Feb. 7, 1908.

[53] T. E W to Thomas W Hardwick, Jan. 28, 1908, Atlanta *Journal*, Aug. 7, 1910.

[54] Joseph M. Brown to Charles R. Pendleton, Feb. 29, 1908 (a first draft), Brown MSS

[55] Joseph M. Brown to T. E. W , Feb 29, 1908 (a first draft), Brown MSS.

389

ated with Negroes, and enemies of public welfare generally.[56]

Short of Wall Street, it would have been difficult for Tom Watson to have hit upon a more thorough representative of the forces he had fought since the days of Henry Grady than he found in Joseph M. Brown.

Brown had made himself an issue in the campaign of 1906 by writing articles attacking Smith's platform of railroad reform. The latter retaliated by charging that Brown represented the railroad interests instead of public interests, and he declared that if he were elected governor he would remove Brown from the railroad commission. As commissioner, Brown voted against the governor's rate-reduction measures, and continued to attack in print the governor and the rulings of the commission of which he was a member. For some reason Governor Smith did not suspend Brown until three days after the legislature adjourned, when it was too late for him to defend himself against the charges brought. This seemed unfair to many. The conservative press, the Howell faction, the railroads, and all those who had opposed Smith in 1906 took up the cry that "Little Joe" was a "martyr" and should be "vindicated." [57]

Many powerful interests had been antagonized by the reform legislation. The liquor interest, for one, was in arms. Reaction was in the air. The national panic of 1907, that burst upon the state in the midst of the reform program, offered a convenient argument to reactionaries. Railroads reduced wages and services, and thousands of workers were discharged. It was easy logic to demonstrate that "Hoke Smith caused the panic." The campaign slogan became "Brown and Bread: Hoke and Hunger." [58]

There was little for Brown to do but join in and lead the chorus. Wrote Brown:

[56] Pamphlets, clippings, campaign literature in Brown MSS , e g., *Gov. Brown's Letters on the Labor Unions* (pamphlet, Atlanta, 1914); *Gompers' Thugs* (pamphlet, Atlanta, 1921); Atlanta *Journal*, May 3, 1914.
[57] Lucian L. Knight, *op. cit.*, Vol. II, pp. 1077-1087.
[58] Cf. *ibid.*, pp. 1088-1093; Joseph M. Brown, *Reduction of Passenger Rates* (pamphlet, Atlanta, 1907).

What was the cause of this paralysis of business? Agitation. Agitation which denounced the corporation. . . . This agitation seemed to take no account of the fact that the interests of capital and labor are inseparably interwoven. . . . The proof was absolute that confiscation, not proper control, was the logical result of the crusade which had been waged against capital. . . . Protection of property is the paramount duty of government. . . .

Brown revived some of his older themes. The reduction of freight rates was "an assault by the manufacturers and jobbers, clients of Hoke Smith, upon the owners of railroad property." Such measures would drive capital out of the state, and frighten off Northern capitalists. But always his principal concern was over the lamentable ravages of the reformers among "widows, orphans, hospitals, colleges, and church societies" who owned railroad stock. The "demagogue" had said to "the seamstress, to the blind boy, to the helpless orphan, to the student in college, to the aged and indigent minister and all others whose funds are invested in railroads and like corporations, 'Your income shall not exceed five per cent.' " [59]

There was little Watson could say for his new candidate—as long as Watson was denouncing the governor for not carrying reform *far enough*. There was little he did say. For two months after he had secretly pledged Brown his support, he did not acknowledge a partiality between the two. He was for neither of them, he announced. Gradually his criticisms of Smith became harsher. "Gentle voter, did you ever, *ever*, EVER know of a case of back-sliding equal to that of the Great Reformer whom we elected Governor of Georgia in 1906?" he asked. " *'Fooled again,'* is about the size of it." Hardwick pleaded with him: "If you haven't had enough reform under Hoke's administration— my God, how much less would you have under Brown's." [60]

Watson denied repeatedly that he had turned against Smith because of the Glover incident. No! It was because of his "back-

[59] MS. speeches, 1907-1908, Brown MSS.; Atlanta *Journal*, July 14, 1908.
[60] Thomas W. Hardwick to T. E. W., April 20, 1908.

391

sliding," because of inadequate railroad reforms, broken pledges, compromises. He hurled one anathema after another with little regard for consistency. Some of Smith's measures that he had earlier approved he now damned. He succeeded in making it plain, however, that he had a score to settle with Hoke Smith, and that he expected all Populists to uphold his hand. Smith was a Clevelandite, a bad bargain to begin with, and Watson had only made the most of it. Besides, the governor had proven an ingrate and refused to give Populist vote credit for his election.[61]

Aside from these fulminations there was one issue of more validity between Smith and Watson, which the latter urged with great conviction and effectiveness upon Populists. After the break occurred between the two men, the Democratic Executive Committee, dominated by the Smith faction, adopted a rule that the party nominee for governor would be selected by a majority of all the votes cast in the primary. Heretofore the nomination had been made by a majority of the county delegates elected to the state convention. Under the old "county unit system" the largest county could have no more than three times the number of delegates controlled by the smallest, though it might have a hundred times the number of voters. It was in vain that Smith pointed out that this change had been a part of his platform in 1906, and that he quoted the Populist platform of 1904 as demanding proportional representation and a direct vote for all offices. Watson was convinced that the new rule was made to undermine his power:

My deliberate opinion, after the coolest reflection, is that Hoke Smith, being jealous of me politically, and attributing to me the ambition to go to the senate from Georgia, deliberately devised this scheme for the purpose of preventing the country counties from having their influence in elections.

He knew that my following was mainly composed of country people, and that when he practically disfranchised the country counties he was putting the knife to me.

[61] *Watson's Jeffersonian Weekly*, March 5, April 2 and May 7 and 21, 1908.

Under this new rule a few city bosses, using "corporation influ-ences, the job-lash, money, whiskey and log-rolling," would control the state, while the Populists of the rural counties, where virtue and honor still resided, would be powerless. "*The evil of a pure democracy is that the minority have no protection from the majority . . .*" [62] Brown and his supporters likewise took up the cry against majority rule and used it effectively in the rural counties.[63]

"I would be quite untrue to my sense of propriety," Brown wrote Watson in the midst of the campaign, "were I to fail to write and express to you my high appreciation of the kind editorials you have been writing . . ." He begged advice, which he promised would be "treated and protected as perfectly confidential." "Some work among the Populists is needed in Carroll, Milton, Hart, and Franklin counties," he believed.[64] Watson assured him that his editorials on Smith were "adding to your vote in the country counties steadily." [65] The business manager of the *Jeffersonian* proposed to Brown that, provided enough extra papers were ordered, he would print a "campaign issue" that would be "a document of tremendous force." He added: "In making you this offer we are practically giving you the advantage of a thorough campaign organization." [66] The offer was accepted. The itemized bill presented by the *Jeffersonian* to Brown, presumably covering all services during the campaign, amounted to $2,674.10 in payment for 82,500 extra copies of the paper and fifty-one two-months' subscriptions.[67]

At the primary election in June the Smith landslide of 1906 was reversed, and Joseph M. Brown was nominated by a small majority of 12,000.

[62] *Watson's Jeffersonian Weekly*, April 2 and May 3, 1908 and Jan. 6, 1910; *Constitution*, May 3, 8, and 24, 1908.
[63] Joseph M. Brown, MS. Speeches, 1908, Brown MSS.; Clark Howell to T. E. W., May 14, 1908.
[64] Joseph M. Brown to T. E. W., May 2, 5, and 27, 1908.
[65] T. E. W. to Joseph M. Brown, May 17, 1908, Brown MSS.
[66] James Lanier to Joseph M. Brown, May 15, 1908, Brown MSS.
[67] *Ibid*, May 29, 1908, Brown MSS

It was not in the election returns, but in his daily mail, that Tom Watson read the real meaning of the election of 1908. Bewildered at the stand he had taken, the old Populists spelled out their perplexity in hundreds of letters. "Tom be Plain & don't whip the devil around this way tell us in plain words," wrote a "Vetran Pop." "Tom it [the new majority rule] only makes my vote equal yours and yours equal mine." Another painfully listed Smith's campaign pledges, following each with the comment, "He done it." "Think of it Mr. Watson!" pleaded another, "the Whiskey men, the railroad ring, the Howell ring, and the old bitter Macon *Telegraph* fighting Smith, & you fighting him too! It does look like the rocks will cry out if you don't." Many refused to follow him: "You have lost some of the truest & bravest Populist[s] that ever wallke Gods green Earth. I Personally know of six in my neighborhood that will not vote for you for Prest." [*Sic.*] One signing himself "An Old Friend," wrote: "The charm of your career, the romance of your life, the heroic sacrifices you have made for liberty fade from my view in this mean hour of fate." One of the authors of the Omaha platform, a man who had recently published an admiring sketch of Watson, wrote a genuinely grieved letter resigning a position he held under Watson and ending a long friendship: "I did not dream that the man who so fiercely denounced the alliances made by trading politicians would himself ever descend to their level. . . . I see now that the 25,000 men who follow you blindly turned the scale, and you have therefore become a menace to the state."[68]

Along with letters of this type, however, came much of the adoration to which he had been accustomed: "When you lead in great strides toward the sublime heights of wisdom and justice we can only follow in possibly faltering and feeble steps." Upon the unsubstantial foundation of such faith as this man expressed Watson was now compelled to construct his plans for the future.

[68] Letters to Watson, May–July, 1908. The last quoted is from Bernard Sutler, June 6, 1908.

394

At the Populist convention of July in Atlanta he sought to re-assure his followers:

Boys, it's all right. We've got them by the hair of their heads. We have them in the hollow of our hands. (Laughter.)
All you've got to do is to sit steadily in the boat and trust me.
And if God spares my life, we will dominate this state during the next decade . . .

With the election results he professed to be completely satisfied. The county unit system was now safe. "We hold the balance of power in the country counties," he said, "and the country counties rule the state." [69]

* * * * * *

With Watson, as with many men, a sense of misgiving and a need of reassurance were often expressed in reassuring someone else. "I want to be more with you," he wrote his wife after the campaign. "We cannot expect so very many years of health and strength and we must make the most of the Indian Summer. We have lost far too much already." They would ride, walk, or drive together every afternoon, he assured her. After dinner there would always be music, while studies would be postponed until morning. "In other words, I am going to live more for you, and less for 'the people.' We will be happy, perfectly happy, and no cloud shall come into the sky for us any more." [70]

A turn of life's seasons was upon him, as he clearly foresaw, but his prognostic of the weather of his soul was lamentably far from accurate. The plain fact was that the serene skies of Indian summer, for which he so earnestly yearned, were already men-aced from half the points of the compass.

[69] Atlanta *Journal,* July 9, 1908; *Watson's Jeffersonian Weekly,* Nov. 12, 1908.
[70] T. E. W. to Mrs. Watson, August 26, 1908, in the possession of Georgia Watson.

CHAPTER XXI

"*The World Is Plunging Hellward*"

As THE LEADER of a national party, Tom Watson occupied an anomalous position with relation to three of his rivals in the approaching presidential contest of 1908. In the fall of 1906, while he was dictating from Hickory Hill the reform policies of a Democratic governor, he received a letter from Bryan, then touring the South. Bryan expressed his regrets that he was unable to return the visit that Watson had paid him at his home, and added:

It is gratifying to know from what I have learned that we are going to be able to act together in the coming contest. There has been a remarkable change in public sentiment, so that things that were formerly denounced as radical, are now regarded as not only quite reasonable, but even necessary.[1]

Watson's public answer was: " 'Act together,' William? *Why not—if you take our principles for your creed and reorganize your old party to fit your new faith?*"

In the meanwhile President Roosevelt confirmed the predictions of his bitterest critic that "he would next be going to the noted Populist for advice and inspiration." He invited Watson to dine at the White House. Watson reported that he warned the President against the prostitution of the federal judiciary to

---

[1] William Jennings Bryan to T. E. W., Sept. 22, 1906, *Watson's Jeffersonian Magazine*, Vol. I (Jan., 1907), p. 31.

the corporate interests, and advised the use of greenbacks as a remedy for money panics. When Bryan expressed surprise at the latter suggestion, the Populist put him on notice that if he is "disposed to sidestep the money question" it is likely "the leadership of the Jeffersonian Democrats will slip out of his hands." He found the President "more of a Tom Benton Democrat than he himself is aware of." [2] Joel Chandler Harris' Populist character, "Billy Sanders," regretted that he was not also invited: "I'm mighty sorry we wa'n't all thar together; if we had 'a' been you could 'a' retched out your hands an' tetched the only three ginnywine Democrats in North America, all warranted to be free from saddle-sores an' things like that."

Shortly after he returned from his visit to the White House, Watson wrote Roosevelt a flattering letter, comparing the great power he held over the people with that swayed by Napoleon, the Kaiser, and Andrew Jackson. He strongly urged the President to run for another term:

Mr. Bryan will be compelled to support you; so will Mr. Hearst; so will I. For my part, there will be no compulsion about it; I will do it openly, boldly, aggressively, and to the finish. A victory so won will take its place in history side by side with the triumphs of the administrations of Jackson and of Lincoln. . . .

To change Presidents now would carry with it the idea that your policies had received a set-back, for the simple reason that none of your lien tenants are [sic] identified in the public mind with you; each of them stands in a class apart. Unless you run, I, for instance, would support Mr. Bryan,—though no one else knows this but yourself. If you run, I would throw my open support to you, even though Mr. Bryan himself should be a candidate and should offer me a place in his cabinet. . . . We can whip those rascals [Harriman and Rockefeller] if you hold your position in the White House . . .[3]

[2] New York *World,* Nov. 30 and Dec. 3, 1907; clippings, Watson Scrapbooks.
[3] T. E. W. to Theodore Roosevelt, Dec. 18, 1907, Roosevelt MSS., Washington, D. C.

During that same interval Watson was corresponding with William Randolph Hearst, with whom an intermediary thought "there will be no real trouble in getting together . . ." [4]

These gyrations of Tom Watson were illustrative of the political confusion of the times, as well as of the plight of the Populist party. With Roosevelt continually stealing Bryan's thunder, and each party vying with the other as the true proponent of Populist principles, with no differences between the old parties over which anyone became excited, the old Populist party was hard put to it to find unclaimed territory of its own. As late as January, 1907, Watson was "still hoping that some honorable plan may be hit upon which will enable all true-hearted reformers to 'act together.' " Earlier he had invited Bryan and Hearst to a conference of the three. Bryan was afraid that "a public conference with you might be construed as an attempt to organize a new party." Hearst was more interested, but reticent, and the conference failed to materialize.[5] One after another Watson renounced them: Bryan, when he backed down on government ownership of railroads; Hearst, because he favored the ship subsidy; Roosevelt, when he selected Taft. It was time, he decided, to return to his own house. However barren its comforts and deserted its appearance, it was still his own.

Early in April, 1908, two hundred delegates, grizzled bitter-enders from twenty-three states, gathered at St. Louis to weep on each other's shoulders. It was clear to the most sanguine that it was the last Convention of the Populist party. Jacob Coxey presided as temporary chairman. Bravely the old mid-roaders lifted the cry, "To hell with fusion and Bryan." The old malady, however, was still at work upon the decrepit body of Populism. The Nebraska and Minnesota delegations bolted because the majority would not postpone the nomination till after the Democratic Convention. The Convention nominated Tom Watson for

[4] William R. Hearst to T. E. W., Jan. 17, 1907; C. A. Walsh to T. E. W., Jan. 31, 1907.

[5] W. J. Bryan to T. E. W., Jan. 24, 1907; W. R. Hearst to T. E. W., Jan. 17, 1907.

President and Samuel Williams of Indiana for Vice-President, and tearfully adjourned.[6]

"You ask me what we are to do," wrote Watson after he had received the nomination. "Frankly, I don't know. The Democratic Party is chaotic; the Republican Party is becoming so; the Populist Party is dead, and we are all at sea." He undertook the leadership of what was admittedly another forlorn crusade, only, as he put it, "to the end that Jeffersonian Democracy shall neither lose its identity in Bryanism, be trampled out by Taftism, led astray into socialism, or be gobbled up in the personal selfishness of Hearstism." [7] He was the first candidate in the field.

For several years the most disheartening reports had been coming in from old Populists of all sections; especially from members of the national committee of the party. In the fall of 1905 an enthusiastic secretary undertook the heroic task of "securing 'Old Guard' Populist clubs in each of the 2862 counties of the United States—without one cent of expense money on hand or in sight." [8] He reported religiously to Watson, but it was plain that his ambition greatly outran his accomplishment.

Watson did not even pretend to pitch his campaign upon a national scale, and his rôle in the election was almost entirely a local one. The nature of his appeal frankly precluded any but a sectional response. He was the only candidate, he said, who was "standing squarely for *White Supremacy*." By expressing sympathy for the Negro troops whom Roosevelt had punished in the Brownsville incident, Bryan had proved himself "unworthy of Georgia's vote." Moreover, the Nebraskan believed in and practiced "social equality" and had showed his contempt for the South by saying that he would never vote for a Confederate soldier. Of course, Watson renewed his familiar denunciations

[6] St. Louis *Globe-Democrat*, April 3, 1908; *Watson's Jeffersonian Weekly*, April 9, 1908.

[7] *Watson's Jeffersonian Weekly*, Oct. 8, 1908.

[8] H. L. Bentley to T. E W., Jan. 9, 1906; J. M. Mallet (Treasurer of the National Federation of People's Party Clubs) to T. E. W., Nov. 6, 1906. Jacob S. Coxey to T. E. W., May 17, 1908.

of the "millionaire plunderers and land-grabbing corporations," and "the remorseless greed of capitalism," but somehow they rang a bit hollow this time. His speech of acceptance in Atlanta breathed death and destruction to capitalist industrialism, but it was followed in awkward juxtaposition by Joseph M. Brown's speech in the same city the next day accepting the nomination for governor. Brown deplored the "demagogue's war on legitimate investment," the "crusade against capital," the "agitation which denounced the corporation."

Apparently Watson's only real motive in entering the race of 1908 was to provide some means of rallying his following in Georgia around its own colors. During the four years in which he had shifted them from one Democratic faction to the other as a balance of power, the loyal Populists had not once united on a ticket of their own. Stray sheep are easily lost in a common fold. The only reason Watson had given Populists for voting for Joseph M. Brown—other than as a means of punishing Smith—was that Brown, "a native Georgian, would probably not consider the state disgraced" by honoring Watson with the state's electoral vote, whereas Smith, "*not a native Georgian,*" might feel differently. He made an earnest appeal for this "compliment," even promising to give up the electoral votes to the Democratic candidate should they later prove indispensable to his success. Some color was given to the suspicion of a bargain on this matter when Brown later refused to say that he would support Bryan for president.[9]

The tell-tale election returns very nearly stripped Watson of even the modest pretensions he made before the election. His national popular vote was a pitiful 29,146, while the votes he polled in the state amounted to some 17,000. It was the vote of his native state that he most coveted, and for which he had worked hardest in the campaign. What had happened to the once formidable ranks of 90,000 Georgia Populists he did not

[9] New York *World*, July 10, 1908; *Constitution*, May 14 and July 10, 1908; Atlanta *Journal*, July 11, 1908.

400

attempt to explain. His daily mail was a painful reminder of one explanation. He thanked "the faithful 17,000 who voted for Watson and Williams—from no motive in God's world but a sense of duty," and breathed defiance to his enemies:

Those Hoke Smith editors who are skirt-dancing over my downfall, have done that before. They should know me better. No man is whipped until he gives himself up.

And you know me too well to think that I will ever give up. . . . WE HOLD THE BALANCE OF POWER IN THE COUNTRY COUNTIES, AND THE COUNTRY COUNTIES RULE THE STATE.[10]

As long as Democratic primaries were won by a 12,000 majority his boast had some validity. His was a badly shaken "dictatorship," however, and he knew it.

*   *   *   *   *   *

It was admittedly a time of self-searching for the Populist of Hickory Hill. At frequent intervals he reviewed and reëxamined "Our Creed" in his periodicals. He assured his followers that their principles were the immutable embodiment of justice and right, now and forever, and swore by the ghost of Thomas Jefferson that he was now, and would be forever more, loyal to those principles. Surely his enunciation of them still awoke familiar echoes from the 'nineties. He refused to admit there was any change. He still preached an alliance between West and South—yet he found the cement for the union in their respective race problems. He still denounced the greed of capitalist exploiters—yet they all seemed to be "Yankee capitalists," and "Yankee corporations." He still called for a union of all farmers against the common class enemy, industrial capitalism— yet he disfranchised half his farmers because of their race. He

[10] *Watson's Jeffersonian Weekly*, Nov. 12, 1908.

still called himself the leader of a national party—yet his appeal was almost purely sectional.

Somehow, through the gradual accretion of what seemed to him necessary corollaries, the populism of Tom Watson, perhaps unobserved by himself, had undergone a fundamental transformation since 1896. It might be that, like John C. Calhoun, another renegade apostle of Thomas Jefferson, he had been betrayed by the exigencies of a perverse sectional economy into a complete disavowal of his master's creed. Gradually the Jeffersonian equalitarianism and humanitarianism of the 'nineties had been exchanged for a patchwork of the garments of Calhoun's Greek Democracy: militant sectionalism, fear of majority rule, racial domination, and perceptible overtones of a landed aristocracy. There had been a time when he believed that "the accident of color can make no possible difference in the interests of farmers, croppers, and laborers," and had said to both races: "You are kept apart that you may be separately fleeced of your earnings. . . . You are deceived and blinded that you may not see how this race antagonism perpetuates a monetary system which beggars both." [11] He now advocated the adoption of a policy of repression so severe and so firm that "the great mass of negroes would reconcile themselves to a condition of recognized peasantry—a laboring class . . ." [12] No Southern leader of post-bellum times ever equaled Tom Watson in his scathing ridicule of "Negro domination" as the "stock-in-trade" of the Southern demagogue. Yet few there were who could rival his later asseverations upon *the superiority of the Aryan*," or the "HIDEOUS, OMINOUS, NATIONAL MENACE" of Negro domination. [13]

In an address to a convention of the Farmers' Union, a new organization more middle-class and conservative than the old

[11] *P. P. P.*, Sept. 16, 1892.
[12] T. E. W., "The Negro Question," *Watson's Jeffersonian Magazine*, Vol. I (Nov., 1907), pp. 1032-1040.
[13] T. E. W., "The Hearst Paper, the Egyptian Sphinx, and the Negro," *Watson's Jeffersonian Magazine*, Vol. III (Feb., 1909), p. 97.

Alliance, in which he professed to see "the reincarnation of the Farmers' Alliance," Watson threw out one admonition with especial emphasis: "Your organization *must represent your class interest*." [14] It is made obvious by the context that he was still employing the ideology of the 'eighties and 'nineties, that is, the assumption that the class struggle lay between industrial and finance capitalism on one hand, and an undifferentiated class of "farmers" on the other. When the editor of a Farmers' Union paper ventured to question the simplicity of this picture and to mention the growth of tenancy and the concentration of land ownership in fewer hands, Watson attacked him furiously. He went to considerable pains to prove "how unfounded are the statements that poor men can not acquire landed property in this country." As for the increase in tenancy, some farmers simply "prefer to rent." He concluded:

Consequently when a certain Farmers' Union editor goes to publishing articles demanding that land ownership be restricted to his own narrow notions, I call him
   A Contemptible Little Demagogue.
When a certain Farmers' Union Editor got to printing stuff calculated to sow discord and strife between landlord and tenant, I did not hesitate to call him
   A Contemptible Little Demagogue. [15]

Watson's own experience bore testimony to the significant differences in the cotton economy that marked the contrast between the 'nineties and the first decade of the new century. His own estimate of his "financial standing" in 1908 was placed at the figure of $258,000, or more than double his "standing" in 1904. [16] He still thought of himself as a "farmer," of course. The price of cotton was relatively high throughout the decade, and the value of all farm property in the state increased 154.2 per

[14] *Watson's Jeffersonian Weekly*, Jan. 24, 1907.
[15] *Ibid.*, Feb. 17, 1910.
[16] Personal account books, Watson MSS.

cent, as against an increase of 20.7 per cent in the 'nineties. The average value of farm lands and buildings per acre advanced from $6.95 in 1900 to $17.78 in 1910, while the average value of land alone increased 167.4 per cent. During the same decade, however, the percentage of tenancy increased from 59.9 in 1900 to 65.4 in 1910, and the percentage of owners correspondingly decreased.[17] There was evidently a large group of "farmers"—the majority in fact—who had not shared the new prosperity.

The trend toward increasing tenancy was fraught with fatal implications for the ideology of populist agrarianism. Yet it was a trend that Tom Watson's logic never took into account. Watson persisted to the end in applying to a changed economy the ideology he employed in the 'eighties—when there really was some validity to the populist dichotomy of farmers (the oppressed) and industrialists (the oppressors). The dichotomy between dispossessed farmers and possessing farmers was one he chose to ignore.

There were certain signs of a political as well as an economic rift in Populist ranks that were giving Watson food for reflection at the same time. Reports were continually coming to him of Populist defections to Socialism. A Texas editor wrote Watson: "The old populists are all right, but it is the younger who need looking after. They are sliding into the Socialist party or what they think is such, but which is really an aggravated case of Populism." [18] Similar reports came from Alabama, Missouri, and other Southern and Mid-Western states. The secretary of the Populist executive committee of Georgia wrote him that "Most of the leading Populists of this section are Socialists. They are my friends; but in no way enthusiastic in the work of keeping Populist papers alive." [19] The national organizer of

[17] Robert P. Brooks, *The Agrarian Revolution in Georgia*, pp. 90, 122.
[18] Taylor McRae to T. E. W., Jan. 23, 1907.
[19] J. A. Bodenhamer to T. E. W., May 29, 1905.

People's Party Clubs likewise reported that "some of our late Populist friends have gone over to Socialism." [20]

In the issue of his magazine for October, 1909, Watson began a series of articles entitled "Socialists and Socialism," which he featured for nine consecutive months. The style of the articles was borrowed from stump hustings and the lawyer's brief rather than from the scholar's study. If, as he said, he "bought pretty nearly every Socialist book named in the catalogues," he seems to have contented himself largely with mere possession. His avowed intention was to "disembowel" Bebel, "explode" Marx, and "drive Socialists so completely into the corner that they haven't got room to grunt."

To a confidant of long standing who complained of his tactics he explained his purpose. He believed that Socialism "would sweep the rural districts like a prairie fire if not opposed in time." If he could compel Socialist leaders "to renounce these extreme parts of the Marxian program," he hoped to herd their followers into the Populist fold. "If you will watch the strategy," he advised, "you won't find it so bad . . . you will see that there is 'a method in my madness.' " [21] To the same confidant he later wrote: "I am a State Socialist through and through . . . but the lines of division between public utilities and private property are just as plainly discernible as are the lines between murder and arson." [22]

For a time Watson's "strategy" ran true to form. "Like a sheet of flame from hell," he wrote, "Socialism would devour the Home, and all that is purest and best in Christian civilization,—reducing all women to the same level of sexual depravity . . ." Socialism would never *"make a white woman secure from the lusts of the negro."* Furthermore, "Women have no business to intermeddle in politics," and there is "no equality of races or of sexes." It also appears that Karl Marx favored

[20] N. L. Bentley to T. E. W., Feb 4, 1907
[21] T. E W to Dr. John N. Taylor, April 23, 1910.
[22] *Ibid* , Nov 19, 1919

"the damnable doctrine that gold is the natural and proper standard of value." Besides, Marx was "a Jew." Friedrich Engels, it seems, was "another Jew." [23]

As he warmed to his task, however, convictions began to get the better of "strategy," and his tone changed to one of earnest defense. "I will prove to your complete satisfaction," he promised in February, "that *the origin of private property was not only just but sacred.*" By May he had arrived at the conclusion that "*private property is a law of nature*—as any one who will use his eyes can clearly see . . ." Likewise rooted in sacred and natural law were the institutions of rent, interest, and profit, not to mention tenancy. Because "*competition is inseparable from private ownership*," it followed that "In free competition, the reward goes to the swiftest runner, the victory to the abler man . . ." He held that "every one of the terrible conditions which Marx seeks to relieve by establishing a new order of Society grew out of the abuses of power and privilege, and not out of the system itself." All that was necessary was reform.[24]

Given to frequent autobiographical reference in all cases, Watson drew almost his entire defense of land ownership and tenancy from his personal experience: the long struggle up from poverty, and the fight for land, and still more land. "I toiled and moiled for thirty years to get that land," he said. And he meant to keep it, all the theories of Surplus Value to the contrary notwithstanding. It was a passionate, personal *apologia* for agrarian individualism. Once in the 'nineties he had exclaimed: "I can put forth the strength of my hand in any field of industry, and whatsoever I earn is mine, *mine*—and is not carted up to feed some lazy lout of a robber who calls himself my feudal chief." It was the historic battle-cry of a class, and Tom Watson never lifted a new one.

[23] T. E. W., "Socialists and Socialism," *Watson's Jeffersonian Magazine*, Vol. III (Dec., 1909), p. 914; *ibid.*, Vol. IV (Jan., 1910), p. 4; "Populism vs. Socialism," *ibid*, Vol. IV (July, 1910), p. 537.

[24] *Ibid.*, Vol. IV (Jan., 1910), p. 5; *ibid.*, Vol. IV (Feb, 1910), p. 93; *ibid.*, Vol. IV (April, 1910), pp. 276-277; *ibid.*, Vol. IV (May, 1910), p. 360.

Of the socialist writers who took up Watson's challenge, none devoted more critical attention to his articles than Daniel De Leon, the editor of the *Daily People*, official organ of the Socialist Labor Party. In a series of nineteen articles and "open letters" De Leon subjected almost everything the Populist had to say on the subject to an attack that came to rival Watson's in asperity. In answering the articles of his "effervescent, though oft admired, acquaintance Tom Watson," De Leon proposed to illustrate "the pitiable wreckage" that a "liberal education in heels-over-head populistic economics will work even in so bright an intellect as Tom Watson's." [25] Needless to add, De Leon found no difficulty in running dialectic rings around his opponent in a combat over Marxian theory. He read "our Georgia Don Quixote" elementary lessons in surplus value and class contradictions, illustrated by such homely examples as the observation that "Mr. Watson and his 'Niggers' have their hands in each other's wool." He finally put the Georgian down as a "feudal junker." "Hit the junker," he said, "and the capitalist will yell—we are seeing the spectacle in Great Britain in the matter of the House of Lords; hit the capitalist, and the junker will shriek—we are seeing the spectacle in Mr. Watson's deportment." De Leon's *coup de grâce* was administered when Watson innocently quoted a remark *literally* that Marx intended ironically. In so doing Watson "immortalized himself as an unconscious humorist." [26]

Watson showed a disposition to strike back for a time, and once went so far as to include De Leon by name in a public challenge to a number of Socialists to come into his magazine and debate with him. "I just dare any and all of you to come," he announced. "I am rubbing my fist right under your noses, you know." De Leon promptly shipped him his articles from the *Daily People* and in an open letter dared him to publish them.

[25] Daniel De Leon, *Watson on the Gridiron*, p. 4. De Leon's articles on Watson were published posthumously under this title.
[26] *Ibid*, pp. 20, 31, and 39.

407

Watson recanted. He had discovered that De Leon did not "represent the true Socialist doctrine." In reprinting the challenge, he neglected to withdraw De Leon's name. Such conduct, concluded De Leon, was "something worse than the bluster of the cross between the feudal junker and the bourgeois which you typify." [27]

In concluding his series of articles, Watson called down a plague upon both houses, industrial capitalism as well as socialism. As for him and his household, they would return to a Golden Age of their fathers. "With a resolution which nothing can shake," he announced, "*I take my stand for the ideals of the Old South. . . . Here*, I choose my ground; *here*, I form my line of battle: *here*, I fly the flag of revolt . . ." He was never very definite about his ideals or his line of battle, but they all had something to do with eighteenth-century England: "The old Whig ideals of England—that's what it was—the democracy of Charles Fox, of Samuel Romilly, of Henry Vane, of Algernon Sidney, of Pym and Hampden." He disposed of the socialists, finally as "Goths, Huns, Vandals, who lust for loot," and who are patently beyond the reach of argument. "These men cannot be driven back by arguments," he concluded. "The only method of dealing with such barbarians is to have the guns ready and the powder dry. And the men behind the guns must be American-born; for the time is surely coming when he who is in command must issue the order, 'Put none but Americans on guard tonight.' " [28]

* * * * * *

The year of 1910 was pivotal in Tom Watson's career, and on it more than one issue turned. His announcement of a return to the Democratic party, though it put a formal period to twenty

[27] Daniel De Leon to T. E. W., May 3, 1910, "An Open Letter," in De Leon, *op. cit.*, pp. 42-43.

[28] T. E. W., "Socialists and Socialism," *Watson's Jeffersonian Magazine*, Vol. IV (June, 1910), pp. 451-452; "Populism vs. Socialism," *ibid.*, Vol. IV (July, 1910), pp. 539-540.

years of rebellion, was of more symbolic than real significance. In May he wrote the national chairman of the People's party that he had decided it was "impossible to do anything in the South outside of the Democratic party," and that he would not join in the effort to reorganize the third party. "I am going to devote the balance of my life to driving out of the Democratic party its deserters and do-nothings, and I am going to take command of the Democratic party myself," he announced publicly in July. There had been a time when such a proclamation would have created more of a sensation than it did now. Since he disclaimed all ambition for office, his rôle in state politics was little altered by his return to the old party. He still posed as the foreman of a jury before which the two evenly matched factions of Democrats must plead their cases. It was true that he had elected his governor in 1906 and spectacularly defeated him two years later, but there were those who held that the latter *tour de force* had been a costly one. There were even those who held his power in contempt. Consciously, then, he faced a showdown in the contests of 1910.

If he must needs grapple with the Browns and Smiths and Joneses of an office-greedy world for the restoration of the Golden Age, he was ready to do it. If scruples, and dignity, and what some considered honor stood in the way of the necessary votes, they might have to be doffed, like a frock coat in a combat of catch-as-catch-can. It was a regrettable concession, to be sure, and there were those (estimable gentlemen, no doubt) who might not approve, but he stood ready to be judged in the light of the Golden Age. "A great uplifting faith wells within me," he wrote that year, "and sustains me in the fight that I am making." Such a faith once converted windmills into giants, and it still commands a sort of respect.

The gubernatorial contest again lay between Brown and Smith, with the latter as the aggressor this time. The issues were much the same as in the previous election. Watson promised Smith he would not oppose him, and let that contest run its own course without interference [29] in order to mend fences in his own district. Thomas W. Hardwick, congressman from that district, had virtually served as Watson's lieutenant for eight years, during which they had been in constant correspondence and on the friendliest terms. In 1908 Hardwick refused to break with Governor Smith when Watson did, though he continued to conciliate his patron in every way possible. The following year, however, he begged to be excused from giving a petty appointment to a friend of Watson's on the ground that the man was an enemy of Hardwick's. On the margin of Hardwick's letter making this announcement Watson wrote "Why we parted ways." [30] Such insubordination could never be tolerated. He had made Hardwick, he announced, and would most certainly break him. Hardwick proceeded to treat the threat with contempt, contending that Watson had discredited himself with Populists, that he "stood convicted of outrageous falsehoods and that he should be dealt with as a leper, a man unclean, morally and mentally." The struggle rapidly assumed the dignity of fish-mongers' repartee: each man held a rival rally in the same town, screaming imprecations at the other to the edification of the multitude. According to the "Sage," Hardwick "went to bed drunk in Hotel Lanier in Macon, with a cigar in his mouth, and set the bed on fire." The appeal he made to his followers was frankly personal:

I never was more conscious in my life of having reached a crisis. It must be evident to you, as it is to me, that unless I leave these grounds today victorious I might as well be laid in my grave. . . .

Now, he [Hardwick] says I have lost out with the old Pops in the Tenth district and that they are going with him against me. . . . Now, boys, will you stand by me? I appeal to you. If Hardwick is reëlected I will be considered in disgrace. Don't put that cup to my lips. Stand by me . . .

[29] Hoke Smith to James J. Green, Aug. 8, 1910, Watson MSS.

[30] Thomas W. Hardwick to T. E W, Jan. 1, 1910; also Oct. 16, 19, and 23, and Nov. 23, 1909.

Somehow everything went awry. The "boys" did not stand by him. Hardwick was elected, and Watson by his own admission was "in disgrace." Not only that, but a fickle state electorate again changed its mind: Brown was defeated, and Hoke Smith won the nomination by less than a two-thousand popular majority. At the state convention in Atlanta a week later the victorious Smith-Hardwick forces dominated the entire proceedings, and by "steam-roller" and "gag-rule" methods prevented the Brown minority delegates from offering the slightest resistance to the platform or any resolutions offered.[31]

Watson, in the meantime, had announced that he would deliver an address in Atlanta to which he broadcasted invitations far and wide. He promised that the speech would be pitched upon a nonpartisan plane and would rise above personalities. "Night and day it monopolized his thoughts," he wrote of the speech. "The occasion was to be the turning point of his life." He rented the largest auditorium in the city, and, according to one estimate, eight thousand people were attracted to hear him. His opening sentence, one might suppose, was sufficient to strike home the gravity of the occasion to the most frivolous. "The world," said the Sage, "is plunging hellward." He continued:

For nearly twenty years I have been in the Valley of the Shadow, politically, enduring with what patience and dignity I could the insults and slanders heaped upon me by my enemies. To-night I have come to drink with you, if you will let me, the rich, pure wine of reconciliation. I beg of you a fair hearing and nothing else. . . .

If something isn't done to check the rising tide of discontent in this country, there will be the bloodiest struggle between the rich and poor that ever drenched a continent with human blood.

My mission is to tell you what you must do to be saved—to that high and holy purpose will be devoted the remaining years of my life. I beg you to listen . . .[32]

[31] *Constitution*, Sept. 1, 2, 1910; *Watson's Jeffersonian Weekly*, Sept. 22, 1910; L. L. Knight, *op. cit*, Vol II, p 1108.
[32] *Constitution*, Sept. 3, 1910; *Watson's Jeffersonian Weekly*, Sept. 8, 1910.

But they would not listen—however high and holy his purpose. So long as his jeremiad remained abstract they were quiet. But Watson had reached the belated conclusion that the registration law he had sponsored in 1906 was now being used by Smith and Hardwick to vote Negroes as a balance of power to overthrow his influence. When he touched upon that subject, a pandemonium of hissing and heckling broke loose in one section of the balcony. The interference appeared to be organized. Wheeling upon the hecklers "like a tiger at bay," he launched a furious tirade at them:

Listen to me, I say! You may not hear me now, but you will later. I am seeking no office. I am representing the thinking masses of the people of Georgia, and if you do not hear me tonight you will hear me in my magazine and through the columns of my weekly papers.

The "wine of reconciliation" was badly spilled by this time. In the momentary inspiration of his rage he hurled one threat after another. He would "make this insult tonight ring from Rabun to Tybee and from the Savannah to the Chattahoochee." They would see. An outraged people would turn upon them. He would organize an independent ticket, bolt the primary, and defeat Smith in the general election in October. Abruptly he stopped speaking, turned about, and quit the stage. Later he said that he had had a premonition of assassination.

"Poor old Jeremiah!" commented the *Constitution* patronizingly. "Compressing in his lamentations the woe, the pessimism of all sacred and profane history, he occupied the shining eminence of typifying the One Great Grouch of humanity's story. Mr. Watson has him 'lashed to the mast' and 'faded to a finish.'" Instead of "plunging hellward" the world was "getting purer, better, brighter . . . every hour and every day." Clark Howell asked: "Is it not a thousand pities that these magnificent gifts should be diverted to the sordid, picayunish, indescribably petty arena of billingsgate and fish-mongering politics?" [33]

[33] Clark Howell, editorial in the *Constitution*, Sept. 3, 1910.

412

Smith's organ, the Atlanta *Journal*, commented condescendingly: "It may have been a threat; it may have been a prophecy. Upon the strength of the following remaining to the old sage of McDuffie—an uncertain quantity of recent years—depends the answer." [34]

Far from forgetting the threats hurled during his temper tantrum in Atlanta, Watson plunged seriously into the task of fulfilling them. He obtained Joseph M. Brown's promise to oppose Smith in the state election, and urged his followers to "set aside" the defeat of Brown in the state convention and vote for him anyway since "frauds annul everything—including rotten nominations." More "premonitions" haunted his waking hours. Returning to Atlanta to "finish" his speech, he announced: "If James R. Gray, Hoke Smith and Tom Hardwick kill me they will find enough of my friends left to kill them. A man who does not protect himself is a fool."

His desire to bring disgrace upon Hoke Smith became a blinding obsession. He informed Smith that he held him individually responsible for breaking up his address in Atlanta and charged him with a long list of political perfidies, which he published.[35] Not content with this, he unearthed a long discredited scandal against Smith's name and set to work upon it. All was grist for his mill: anonymous letters, third-handed stories, stale rumors, anything. His serious attempt to substantiate the charges he made revealed what had happened to an astute mind trained in criminal law. "Most of my information came to me originally by anonymous letters," he admitted, but he had corroborated it amply. There was a letter from a friend who had the story from a man who heard it first hand, "or was told of it by a man who did hear it." If one of his informants turned out to be "an inmate of a house of prostitution in Columbus," it only proved her ingenuousness.[36]

[34] Editorial in the Atlanta *Journal*, Sept. 3, 1910.

[35] T. E. W. to Hoke Smith, Sept. 4, 1910 (copy), Watson MSS.; *Watson's Jeffersonian Weekly*, Sept. 22, 1910.

[36] T. E. W. to F. L. Seely, Nov. 12, 1910 (copy), Watson MSS.

On September 27 he wired Smith: "It is closing in on you. I give you one more chance to save your wife and son. Resign by two o'clock today, or your crimes will be known to all the world." [37] In the issue of his weekly for September 29, only a few days before the state election, he published the sensational scandal: "Hoke Smith has ruined more than one pure girl, more than one pure wife." Details were furnished in an anonymous letter, also printed.

Smith ignored the charges. A few days later he was overwhelmingly elected. Watson's own county, which had turned against Smith in 1906, when Watson supported him, now went for Smith. As compared with Smith's poll of 95,000, Watson's candidate Brown received 17,000 votes—"the faithful 17,000."

Instead of dropping the charges of immorality against Smith after the election, Watson renewed them with colorful elaborations, and repeated the demand that Smith resign or refute the charges.[38] In the meanwhile, F. L. Seely, editor of the Atlanta *Georgian*, offered Watson his assistance in exposing Smith and asked to be directed to the evidence that would substantiate the charges. Watson sent such flimsy evidence as he had, saying there was no doubt in his mind of the correctness of the charges.[39] Rejecting this evidence, Seely printed an authentic repudiation of the scandal from its source, thereby completely discrediting Watson. Undaunted, Watson renewed his charges and viciously attacked Seely. "WHAT IS THE MATTER WITH THOMAS E. WATSON?" inquired the *Georgian* in a streamer across its front page. "Like a hydrophobic animal . . . he is snapping and biting at nearly everything nowadays." The editor believed that if Watson was in a sane condition of mind, he was "the basest, most depraved, most poisonous man in Georgia today." [40]

[37] T. E. W. to Hoke Smith, Sept. 27, 1910 (copy of telegram marked "paid."), Watson MSS.
[38] *Watson's Jeffersonian Weekly*, Oct. 13 and Dec. 29, 1910.
[39] T. E. W. to F. L. Seely, Nov. 12, 1910 (copy), Watson MSS.
[40] Atlanta *Georgian*, Dec. 3, 1910.

The sequel to the exposure of Watson's irresponsible charges against Smith was a ludicrous hoax, of which Watson was the unmistakable victim. Provided with an insight into Watson's methods in the Smith case, Seely saw to it that an invented story of his own complicity in a land swindle fell into the Sage's hands. Completely duped, Watson rushed into print with the whole story, only to have Seely expose the hoax upon him before the *Jeffersonian* reached the news stands.[41] The state rocked with laughter. It was the lowest ebb for the Sage of Hickory Hill.

The following June Watson put forth all the strength at his command in an attempt to defeat Governor Smith for the Senate. The response to his call, "Meet Me in Atlanta, Boys," was so feeble that it provoked ridicule. Smith was elected to the Senate shortly after his inauguration as Governor. Calmly ignoring Watson's loud outcry, he continued to occupy the governor's chair for four and a half months after his election to the Senate.

[41] W. W. Brewton, *Life of Thomas E. Watson*, pp. 354-357; *Watson's Jeffersonian Weekly*, Dec. 29, 1910.

CHAPTER XXII

The Shadow of the Pope

A NEW SPIRIT seems to have taken possession of Hickory Hill in the fall of 1910, most clearly manifesting itself in the master of the house. He confronted the critics who said that he was sinking into a morbid and misanthropic dotage with a denial that was disarming in its candor. If he were as bitter and vindictive as they said, how was it that his writings enjoyed "such an enormous circulation," or that there was "such a tremendous demand" for him as a public speaker? He now spoke, he assured them, "as easily as the birds sing—and there are no failures." As usual, when his self-esteem was called in question, he thought of Bryan. He was a better lawyer than Bryan, a better writer, a legislator of more enduring works, he asserted. "I can now draw larger crowds than Bryan can, and no man's gospel is more enthusiastically cheered. His sun is setting, and mine is rapidly rising." There had been a time when he bowed to discouragement. "But of late a new spirit has taken possession of me," he wrote, "and I have to obey it. Nothing tires me; nothing discourages; nothing intimidates." He was convinced, he said, that the people were "beginning to believe that I am one of the men whom God Himself raises up and inspires." [1] Thus everyone was reassured—including himself.

The process begun with his break with the New York maga-

[1] T. E. W., "And Mr. Clark Howell Also Asks Mr. Watson to Change the Law of His Nature," *Watson's Jeffersonian Magazine*, Vol. V (Oct., 1910), p. 810.

zine was completed in 1910 when he concentrated his entire publishing business at Hickory Hill. There he erected what he pronounced "one of the best equipped printing plants in the South." The new plant, said to represent an investment of $100,000, was fitted with machinery for the rapid production of newspapers, magazines, pamphlets, and books. Drawing the skirts of his estate still more tightly about him, he bought up the copyrights of his books (selling better than when published, he reported) and prepared to print them himself.[2]

No unimportant part in the new regime was that taken by Mrs. Alice Louise Lytle. Attracted by her work on a small-town paper, Watson employed her in his Atlanta office where she proved of such value that he made her managing editor of both periodicals in the new organization. A large, vigorous young woman of Irish extraction, Mrs. Lytle was possessed of great capabilities and an ingratiating fund of sympathy. She was separated from her husband. In the eyes of his new employee, Watson was a great man of letters, a genius, and her admiration of him was unbounded. Moreover, she had a ready Irish wit, a fund of stories that put guests at ease, and a certain facility with drinks. She was at home in talk of politics, and was not incapable of using, in off-hand fashion, the language of the mind. Mrs. Watson had never been a source of much intellectual comradeship for her husband, and now that she was aging rapidly he sought compensation elsewhere. Mrs. Lytle soon moved from the near-by cottage where she was first installed to quarters at Hickory Hill. There were later times in that tragically distraught household when her robust nature seemed the only anchor of sanity that held. Watson's dependence upon her grew steadily greater as time passed. Their relationship does not appear to have been what many suspected. At any rate her affections were centered elsewhere. Her influence upon him, nevertheless, seems to have been strong. Although she was born in Philadelphia of non-native parents, she was the greater "profes-

[2] *Watson's Jeffersonian Weekly*, Dec. 29, 1910, and Jan. 5, 1911.

417

sional Southerner" of the two, and was given to strong expressions about "niggers" and Catholics. Though Watson was often repelled by her laxness of manner, dress, and expression, it is likely that her influence fostered certain traits and prejudices already present in him. Of an intensely practical turn of mind, with an eye for profits and a managerial assertiveness, she made her personality felt in a pervasive way in the *Jeffersonians*. To Watson's readers she became known as "our Mrs. Lytle," and he as "the Chief"—appellations of her own invention.[3]

Honored guests at the "House Warming" Watson gave at Hickory Hill and the new plant for the "*Jeffs*" were "Old Man Peepul" and "Aunt Sarah Jane" (names he had recently bestowed upon his readers), who attended by hundreds. Their host reported proudly the presence of "more Thomas Watson Everythings and little girl Tom Watson Everythings and Georgia Watsons with every known surname, than anyone but the census enumerators knew about." He launched the Jeffersonian Publishing Company in a speech, and welcomed purchasers of the company's stock. The liquor and wine bill (no small item in Hickory Hill's budget thenceforth) for this occasion amounted to $232.31.[4]

The change that took place in the character of Watson's publications did not occur overnight. Tendencies already manifested, however, quickly grew more exaggerated. Italics and capitals and bold-faced type came to sprinkle virtually every paragraph, and the red-inked headline soon made its appearance. Attacks upon political personalities were reduced to a fine art of scandal and slander. Articles on the plutocracy, corporate privilege, and capitalist legislation dropped out of the *Jeffersonian* almost completely, only to be replaced by crusades of a more exciting type.

Frustrated in their age-long, and eternally losing struggle against a hostile industrial economy, the farmers, together with a large depressed urban element, eagerly welcomed exciting cru-

[3] From sources that do not wish to be named.
[4] Check stubs, Watson MSS.

418

sades against more vulnerable antagonists: against anything strange, and therefore evil. Vicarious as were such easy victories, they offered some tangible compensations to a people hungry for satisfactions. A frustrated man and a frustrated class found that their desires and needs were complementary.

In his magazine for August, 1910, Watson published the first chapter of the series entitled, "The Roman Catholic Hierarchy: The Deadliest Menace to Our Liberties and Our Civilization." It was not the first time he had boxed with the shadow of the Pope, but this article marked the beginning of a deliberately planned crusade. Thereafter no issue of the monthly or the weekly was complete without its exposure of the "Deadliest Menace." The series on the "Hierarchy" ran for twenty-seven months, to be followed immediately by "The History of the Papacy and the Popes," which was followed and overlapped by others and still others. Upon the completion of each series, it was published in book or pamphlet form. For seven years, until his publications were excluded from the mail during the World War, the crusade continued, sometimes swelling, sometimes subsiding in its fury. During those seven years Tom Watson became almost as closely identified in the public mind with the anti-Catholic crusade as he had once been with the Populist movement.

The question of personal motivation is rather beside the point. It was true that in the battles of the 'nineties a small, but solid and strategically important block of Catholic votes in Augusta under the control of Patrick Walsh had been repeatedly used against Watson. It also appears that a local organization of the American Protestant Association made some effort on Watson's behalf because of his Catholic enemies. Nevertheless, Watson himself publicly deprecated the exploitation of religious prejudice at that time.[5] Later, in writing his *Story of France*, he was frankly Protestant, but not exceptionally unfair to the

[5] Atlanta *Journal*, Oct. 3, 1895; *Constitution*, Sept. 13, 1895; Augusta *Chronicle*, July 22, 1894.

419

Church. Still later he placed his daughter in a Catholic school for a short period.[6] In any case, the personal motivation of a Martin Luther would not be sufficient to explain Tom Watson's onslaught upon the Pope.

From first to last the Catholic articles were a curious mixture of erudition and sensationalism bordering upon the pathological. Watson was able to persuade himself that he was "emulating the glorious example of Erasmus," and he undoubtedly lavished considerable work on the articles. "Really I am devoting as much research and study to the epochal era of Henry VIII as I gave to the *Story of France*," he wrote a friend. Indeed, I have just "slaughtered a long line of Popes for my May installment." [7] Standards of accuracy, and moderation, and fairness that he at one time undoubtedly cherished as a historian seemed to disintegrate and quite lose their sway over him. New standards prevailed. He admitted privately that the boorish cartoons illustrating his articles were "too crude to appeal to the scholarly taste, but they seem to be effective with many of our readers." Furthermore, the "Hierarchy" series was "making a tenstrike," and the publications were making "handsome clear profits." A year before he had complained to the same correspondent that he was "in the hole $20,000" on his publications.[8]

At the head of each installment of his first series of anti-Catholic articles Watson placed an italicized note proclaiming that the sole object of his attack was the Church organization, and deploring any offense that might be given to the individual believer, whose faith he promised to respect. Whatever his intentions were, the performance speaks for itself. His series of open letters to Cardinal Gibbons was matchless in its insulting offensiveness. "And there is no discoverable vocabulary which would adequately express the profoundity [*sic*] of my loathing and contempt for that stupid, degrading faith of yours, Cardi-

[6] T. E. W., in *Watson's Jeffersonian Weekly*, Aug. 11, 1910.
[7] T. E. W. to Dr. John N. Taylor, April 10, 1917.
[8] T. E. W. to Dr. John N. Taylor, Oct. 5, 1910; also Jan. 1, 1910, and July 15, 1909.

nal," he wrote.[9] A favorite diversion (presumably another "tenstrike," since it was so frequently employed) lay in printing pictures of Church dignitaries accompanied by elucidating comment. "Look at that nose!" he wrote. "Such a proboscis *always* marks the sensual man. It is thick, and I shouldn't wonder if it is red. . . . It being so manifest that O'Connell eats and drinks deep, how does he control his *other and* STRONGER passions?" Indeed, "How does he keep from it—when so many of the fair sex are held behind the bars of convent dungeons, where they are at the mercy of priests?" For the priesthood he evolved an inexhaustible number of epithets: "chemise-wearing bachelors," "bull-necked convent keepers," "shad-bellies," "foot-kissers." Theirs was a "jackassical faith."

If half his readers had never set eyes on monk or nun, they were none the less absorbed by lurid revelations of convent, confessional, and "convenient sacristy," not to mention a hundred other sinister wonders undreamed of in the rural imagination. The titles themselves were irresistible: "The Murder of Babes," "The Sinister Portent of Negro Priests," "How the Confessional Is Used by Priests to Ruin Women," "One of the Priests Who Raped a Catholic Woman in a Catholic Church," "What Happens in Convents." One example of their contents is perhaps sufficient:

Through his questions, the priest learns which of his fair penitents are tempted to indulge in sexual inclinations. Remember that the priest is often a powerfully sexed man, who lives on rich food, drinks red wine, and does no manual labor. He is alone with a beautiful, well-shaped young woman who tells him that she is tormented by carnal desire. Her low voice is in his ear; the rustle of her skirts and the scent of her hair kindle flames. She will never tell what he says or does. She believes that he cannot sin. She believes that *he* can forgive *her* sin. She has been taught that in obeying *him*, she is serving God.[10]

[9] T. E W , "Cardinal Gibbons and 'The Guardians of Liberty,'" *Watson's Jeffersonian Magazine*, Vol. XIV (April, 1912), p. 1000.

[10] *Watson's Jeffersonian Weekly*, Jan. 25, 1912; *vide* also issues of *ibid*, April 16, 1914, and Dec. 23, 1915.

Should the reader like to see for himself "those nasty questions" of the confessional, they might be obtained in pamphlet form for twenty-five cents.

If Watson had any legitimate grievance against the Catholic church, it was a political one. It was true that the Church had shifted its allegiance to the Republican party in the crucial battle of 1896. He did advance several valid criticisms and exposures, but they were all drowned in the wild hue and cry he kept up over imaginary menaces of incredibly horrendous proportions. "Protestants!" he shouted to a complacent, Taft-ruled nation. "Your Government is in the control of Rome. Your White House is little more than a Vatican annex." The "Hierarchy" was busily "laying in guns and ammunition; buying control of papers and magazines," and in fact "working day and night, spending money like water to *'Make America Catholic.'*" They had already made one dreadnought of the navy *"a completely popish ship,"* and had even "bought the strategic positions, from which batteries would hold Washington city at their mercy." [11]

In 1911, Watson, together with the Civil and Indian War veterans, Lieutenant-General Nelson A. Miles, ex-Congressman Charles D. Haines, and Charles B. Skinner, organized The Guardians of Liberty. General principles were announced, such as immigrant restriction and prevention of interference from foreign ecclesiastical authority. The society did not assume a predominantly anti-Catholic complexion until 1912, and then largely through the influence of Watson, who persuaded General Miles to his way of thinking. Miles toured the country making speeches on such subjects as "America's Danger," while Watson's services to the order were given largely through his publications. Cardinal Gibbons denounced the new organization as "nothing more than an attempt to revive the bigotry of the A. P. A., which was presumed to have died of inanition. Surely

[11] *Ibid.*, Dec. 16, 1909, and Oct. 21, 1915; T. E. W., "Cardinal Gibbons and 'The Guardians of Liberty,'" *Watson's Jeffersonian Magazine*, Vol. XIV (April, 1912), p. 996; T. E. W., editorial, *ibid.*, Vol. XVIII (March, 1914), p. 225.

no sensible man will be misled by the thin and thread-bare arguments of such people." [12] The Guardians of Liberty nevertheless took root in fertile soil and flourished at least until the World War. Watson used the organization effectively in state politics as late as 1916. According to him it was a "movement requiring nerve, and the robust American spirit." It seems that "American Americans" were preferred as members. "The fight is on!" announced Watson to Cardinal Gibbons. "Your foreign ruled crowd were the aggressors. You made the first threats." [13]

From the beginning of the anti-Catholic crusade the tranquillity of Hickory Hill was constantly menaced by "premonitions," "plots," and "assassins." Footprints of snoopers and peepers were reported; anonymous letters threatened or revealed plots. Guards were placed about the house for a time, and Watson became virtually a recluse in his own home. When he went to Atlanta he was protected by detectives. Readers of the *Jeffersonian* were kept posted on the nefarious doings of the "assassins." "Those persistently daring assassins are not very far off," he told them, "nor have they abandoned their murderous purpose. If the same merciful Providence does not continue to throw its shield over me, you may never see in this paper another editorial of mine." Once he received a letter from an unknown man who proposed to save his life from assassins. Watson wired him to come, paid his expenses, bought him a suit of clothes, and gave him his own revolver. He then suddenly decided that his would-be protector was himself not above suspicion. He declared that, had the man made a false move, he would have "shot him without a moment's hesitation, *because of those eyes.*" That same night he doubled the guard around his house and had his "protector" arrested. [14]

The pathological, almost maniacal, conduct to which his obsession led him was illustrated by an incident that occurred in

[12] Michael Williams, *The Shadow of the Pope*, p. 114.
[13] T. E W, "Cardinal Gibbons and 'The Guardians of Liberty,' " *Watson's Jeffersonian Magazine*, Vol. XIV (April, 1912), p. 1000.
[14] *Jeffersonian Weekly*, June 22, 1911.

1912. In the lobby of the Kimball House in Atlanta he happened to notice a man from Savannah whom he knew to be a member of the Knights of Columbus. "The sight of him was good to my eyes—as that of a red rag to a maddened bull," he recounted. Deliberately he bumped into the man, then stood aside expecting a demand for an apology. "I meant to refuse it," he explained, "and then I hoped that we should have a perfectly beautiful fight. I was simply spoiling for one." The man showed no resentment, however, and Watson's friends "dragged" him out of the hotel. At the railway station he broke away from his friends and returned to the hotel in a vain search for the Catholic. Watson proudly related the whole incident in his paper.[15] He was a man fifty-six years of age at that time.

Catholic organizations undoubtedly undertook measures of reprisal against Watson. The national secretary of the American Federation of Catholic Societies circulated letters to firms advertising in his publications, threatening a boycott against those who did not withdraw their advertisements, and the American News Company cut into his news-stand circulation in certain cities.[16] Watson's advertising patronage did decline for some time, and he privately estimated his loss due to this cause at "about $50,-000." [17] At the same time, however, an advertisement of his magazine boasted that he had "gained thousands of new readers by the publication of these articles on the Roman Catholic Hierarchy." Every reprisal by the Catholics, real or imaginary, was dramatically paraded by Watson. "Remember! I am up against 263,000 Knights of Columbus who have sworn to put me out of business," he wrote, appealing to three hundred Protestants to send him one hundred dollars each to help "in this great fight."

None of the persecutions to which he was subject, however, was so much publicized and dramatized as the case of the United

[15] *Ibid*, Aug. 22, 1912.
[16] *Vide* Anthony Matre, National Secretary, American Federation of Catholic Societies, to an advertiser who patronized Watson, in *Watson's Jeffersonian Magazine*, Vol. XIII (Aug., 1911), p. 290; *Jeffersonian Weekly*, Nov. 4, 1915.
[17] T. E. W. to Dr. John N. Taylor, July 14, 1914.

States against Thomas E. Watson based on the charge of his violating the postal law against sending obscene literature through the mails. The offensive matter in question was contained in certain excerpts in Latin quoted in his magazine articles on the "Catholic Hierarchy." Watson assumed that the prosecution was inspired by Catholics: "The Romanists are trying to put me in the penitentiary, *because I quoted* FROM ONE OF THEIR DIABOLICAL BOOKS." He was arrested on June 3, 1912, but the case was not called until October of 1913. He won a tactical victory by a motion to quash the indictment. However, the prosecution was renewed, and, in all, the case was prolonged over a period of four and a half years. The second attempt of the prosecution resulted in a mistrial, and it was not until the third trial, in November, 1916, that he was finally acquitted.[18] Expertly handling his own defense, Watson proclaimed it his ambition to make this "one of the celebrated cases of history." Whole issues of his magazine were devoted to his speeches of defense, and the proceedings of the trial crowded the columns of his weekly. Each trial was thoroughly advertised in advance.[19] A hint that his life was imperiled would throng Augusta with armed followers. "One blast from Watson's horn would put 50,000 men in the field at any central point as quick as the iron horse could carry them," wrote a loyal Watsonian.[20]

* * * * * *

"I have forced the popery issue into Georgia politics, where it is now cutting a wide swath to the consternation of the old-line politicians," wrote Watson to a friend in 1914.[21] Since his defeat at the hands of Smith in 1910, he had been almost constantly at work seeking to regain his dominance over state politics. In the

[18] Atlanta *Journal,* May 31, 1912; *Watson's Jeffersonian Weekly,* June 6, 1912; Jan. 2, Feb. 27, and Oct. 30, 1913; Dec. 2 and 9, 1915; and Nov. 30, 1916; Augusta *Herald,* Nov. 28, 1916.
[19] E.g., the entire issues of *Watson's Jeffersonian Magazine,* Jan., 1916 (55 pages), and Jan., 1917 (101 pages), were devoted to the trial.
[20] Letter published in *Watson's Jeffersonian Weekly,* Oct. 28, 1915.
[21] T. E. W. to Dr. John N. Taylor, July 14, 1914.

fall of 1911 he canvassed almost the whole state, making several speeches a week. He found that "men who had been cussing Tom Watson for years were seen laughing, crying and cheering before I was half-way done with my message."

As early as January, 1912, Watson announced that he had undertaken to defeat the Wilson-for-President movement in Georgia. In doing so he had to face the opposition of the dominant Smith faction, which supported Wilson, and to overcome Wilson's primary advantage with Georgians because he had lived in Georgia during his youth, and had taken his wife from the state. Aside from the hated Smith faction's support of Wilson's cause, the main personal motive that seems to have actuated Watson's fight against the candidate was the bitter distaste he had conceived for the man some ten years before when he had read his five-volume history of the United States. Watson never forgot that impression, and his anger flamed out against Wilson several times before he was thought of as a candidate for President. That history *"showed the Tory* all the way through," he thought, and revealed *"a* cold cynicism toward popular movements, a deference to wealth and social power." Besides, although he was a Southerner, the Virginian had glorified New England and neglected the cause of the South.[22] Such an offense Watson deemed intolerable.

Complaints of a less academic nature were not wanting in the case he made against Wilson—the sort of complaint he launched against anyone who dared cross his path in these days. Governor Wilson, he charged, had "kow-towed to the Roman hierarchy," and even employed "a Romanist, *as private secretary."* Moreover he was *"ravenously fond of the negro,"* and had "SENT BOOKER WASHINGTON A MESSAGE OF CONDOLENCE AND CONFIDENCE WHEN THAT COON

[22] *Watson's Jeffersonian Weekly,* Jan. 25, April 11 and 25, and Dec. 21, 1912; *Constitution,* May 12, 1912; T. E. W. to W. J. Jelks, Dec. 21, 1912, copy in Watson MSS.

426

WAS CAUGHT AT A WHITE WOMAN'S BEDROOM
DOOR, AND WAS DESERVEDLY BEATEN FOR IT."
Wilson's conversion from the Cleveland school to Bryanism was
all too recent to be convincing, he thought. "FARMERS! LIS-
TEN TO ME!" he commanded. "Let Woodrow Wilson alone.
He's another Bill Taft. VOTE FOR UNDERWOOD!" [23]
Watson's support of Oscar W. Underwood of Alabama rested
chiefly upon the contention that he was more of a Southerner
than Wilson.

The presidential primary resulted in an Underwood victory,
with a majority of some 15,000. Immediately a movement was
put under way by the national party leaders to rid themselves of
Watson. Charles E. Murphy, the head of Tammany, Norman
E. Mack, chairman of the National Democratic Committee,
Thomas Taggart, secretary of that committee, and even Senator J. H. Bankhead, Underwood's campaign manager, all sent
word that Watson would be distinctly *persona non grata* at the
Baltimore Convention, that he would create "far-reaching dissension and strife." A conference of Underwood leaders and
national party managers was called in Atlanta to plan the overthrow of Watson at the state convention. Leaders of the "regular" Democracy declared it unthinkable that "the Red-headed
Person" should head the state delegation, as he promised. "We
will beat him, beat him, BEAT him," declared Thomas B.
Felder, leader of the regulars.

Watson's response to this turn of affairs was an article of im-
perious tone under the familiar heading, "Meet Me in Atlanta,
Boys!" The "city politicians" who were "hogging all the credit
for the Underwood victory" were courting a fight with him, and
they should have it. That victory was "the country man's triumph," he maintained, and he promised that the state convention would be "a red-headed affair." All delegates friendly to
him were ordered to be present at his caucus the night before the

[23] *Watson's Jeffersonian Weekly*, April 11, 1912.

convention. "I mean to head the Georgia delegation to Baltimore, or know the reason why," he announced.[24]

The arrival of "the red-headed person" in Atlanta was said to have suggested the return of some Roman conqueror. So dense was the throng at the station waiting to meet him that police had to form a lane for him to pass to his carriage. This initial ovation astounded and all but silenced opposition. It was a day of delirious triumphs for an outcast, and, as an enemy of his observed, he enjoyed it "with all the bluster and arrogance of a Tartar chief." At his personal caucus that night, overflowing with delegates, he was cheered to the echo when he announced with utmost assurance: "I propose to snatch from the hands of William J. Bryan the leadership of the national Democratic party. I mean to lock horns with him at Baltimore, and I don't care who knows it." After the caucus had obediently passed his resolutions, he said:

We've got 'em, boys.
(Voice in the crowd:) Us country fellows?
Yes, we've got 'em. It has taken us six long years of hard work, but we've done it.
Old man Peepul is on top. Aunt Sarah Jane is on top. We country folks are on top, and everybody is going to be happy.[25]

At the convention the following day his appearance was the signal for a third and greater ovation. He was continuously on his feet, offering resolutions, dominating the opposition, and showing in every way possible that he was the master. The platform adopted was liberally seasoned with Watson principles of the newer, as well as the older, sort. It advocated disfranchisement of the Negro and other non-Caucasian races, discontinuance of foreign immigration, as well as more stringent regulation of child labor, and tariff reduction. He was obliged to agree to a compromise on the naming of the delegation to Baltimore

[24] *Watson's Jeffersonian Weekly*, May 9, 1912.
[25] *Constitution*, May 29, 1912; *Watson's Jeffersonian Weekly*, June 6, 1912.

and share the honors with some of his enemies. This he could do with good grace, however, after his vanity had been thoroughly appeased in other ways.[26]

One after another the proudest of the opposition trooped to his headquarters to make their peace and pay obeisance. The governor, the ex-governor and present candidate for the chair, John M. Slaton, the aspirant for national committeeman from Georgia, Clark Howell, and the Underwood campaign manager, who now gave Watson credit for the Underwood victory, were all reported to have made their visit to Watson's rooms. "Beyond any doubt," admitted a Smith paper, "Mr. Watson held the whip hand." [27] A more neutral observer remarked that "He has now succeeded in making both wings of his old enemy, the Democratic party of Georgia, walk up and eat out of his hands." [28]

The *Constitution* and the *Journal*, each speaking for its wing of the party, conducted a penitent colloquy over the state of affairs. The latter paper lamented: "Thomas E. Watson, receiving the obeisance of the heads of the now dominant faction of Georgia Democracy—Thomas E. Watson, a Georgia delegate to a national Democratic convention! It is almost incredible, we repeat, that such a disgrace has befallen the state." The *Constitution* reminded its rival that it had been only a few years since that paper had wanted its candidate's picture "hung in the same frame with Watson's," and observed: "It's the same old story of whose ox is gored!" The *Journal* responded: "We had as well be frank. Both factions of Georgia Democracy have lain down with the dog and got up with fleas. Both have had the experience of falling into the hands of this political pirate. . . . Henceforth the alliance of Watson with any faction should be considered, as it truly must be, a badge of disgrace to the cause that has sought his support." [29]

[26] Lucian L. Knight, *loc. cit.*; Atlanta *Journal*, May 29, 1912.
[27] Atlanta *Journal*, quoted in *Watson's Jeffersonian Weekly*, June 6, 1912.
[28] Augusta *Chronicle*, May 31, 1912.
[29] Editorials, Atlanta *Journal*, May 30, 1912; *Constitution*, May 31, 1912.

After enjoying his triumph in Atlanta to the fullest, Watson seems to have lost interest in the high and mighty purpose he meant to fulfill in Baltimore. He did not even attend the national Convention. Illness was the excuse he offered for remaining at home, although he later mentioned that he got wind of a Catholic plot against him should he attend the convention at Baltimore.[30] From his home he poured telegrams into the Georgia delegation urging them to give up Underwood and support Champ Clark. After the Convention he wavered for some time, made a few half-hearted gestures in Wilson's behalf, and then flatly repudiated his nomination in an article, "Why I cannot Vote for Woodrow Wilson." [31]

In the end he did exactly what the prophets of the regular Democracy had predicted: he bolted his party's ticket. This time he turned to Roosevelt and the Progressives. "My correspondence," he reported in August, "indicates a strong disposition on the part of the old Pops to vote the Bull thing ticket." He swung his personal support to the new party too late to be of much influence, but in the issue of his paper immediately before the election he printed a full page of ballots for the Progressive National ticket. After the election he opened correspondence with Roosevelt upon the question of organizing the Progressive party in the South.[32]

[30] *Watson's Jeffersonian Weekly*, June 27, July 11, and Aug. 22, 1912. Watson was arrested on the charge of violating the postal law against sending obscene literature through the mails only four days after the Convention

[31] *Ibid.*, Aug. 15 and Oct. 24, 1912.

[32] Theodore Roosevelt to T. E. W., Jan. 13, 1913, Watson MSS.

CHAPTER XXIII

The Lecherous Jew

IT WAS A NONDESCRIPT ARMY that Tom Watson commanded after 1910. That army was no longer a party: it was a "following," and a "following" is a very different thing from a party. In place of a platform and officers it has prejudices and a master. It is amorphous, mercurial, and unstable. The "faithful 17,000" still formed an important nucleus of Watson's power, but its populist character was diluted and lost in the anonymity of the "following." Besides the residual third party, there were other organizations of indeterminate strength subject to his control. He had succeeded in placing a loyal lieutenant at the head of the powerful Farmer's Union, and the Guardians of Liberty looked to him to direct their struggle against the sinister machinations of the Pope. An important lever in his machine lay in the "county-unit system" maintained at his pleasure by the state Democratic party. The maintenance of his renovated power, however, depended largely upon the ephemeral recruits attracted by the crusades conducted in his publications—his "following." They were the "boys"; they were "Old Man Peepul" and "Aunt Sarah Jane" to whom he was wont to address himself as "Your Uncle T. E. W."

A journalist visiting the state was perplexed at the character of Watson's weekly now called the *Jeffersonian*. He could never discover what the editor was "for," and decided that he was "violently against" everything. "The thistles of chaos are

431

sweet in him, and order in any department of life is a chestnut burr under his tail," he concluded.[1] Indeed, the turmoil in the Sage's soul was reflected in some unaccountable eccentricities. Concomitant with the anti-Catholic crusade was a prolonged attack upon Protestant foreign missions. At the root of his attack on missions was his hatred of imperialism and his "isolationist" doctrine, which were also the basis of his opposition to the Spanish-American War, and later the World War intervention and the League of Nations. Part of his attack was grounded on firm economic and political realism. The missionary was the advance agent of the capitalist and imperialist. Besides, the whole idea was an outrage to reason: "This idea that missionaries can go to China, undress it of its civilization, and re-clothe it with ours, *is as crazy a notion as ever found lodgment in the human brain,*" he declared. Another feature of the polemic arose out of his old anti-clericalism. It found fullest expression in his series entitled "Teasing the Preachers," in which he clearly took unfair advantage of the parsons. He ran definite risk of antagonizing all the powerful evangelical denominations of the country by this attack.[2]

Most of his fulminations ran no such risk: that against the Negro, for example. Negroes, he observed, "simply have no comprehension of virtue, honesty, truth, gratitude and principle." "In the South, we have to lynch him [the Negro] occasionally, and flog him, now and then, to keep him from blaspheming the Almighty, by his conduct, on account of his smell and his color." He defended lynching both in principle and in specific instances. "This country has nothing to fear from its rural communities," he wrote. *"Lynch law is a good sign: it shows that a sense of justice yet lives among the people."* As for himself, he would no more hesitate to lynch a Negro rapist than

[1] Julian Street, *American Adventures*, p. 383.
[2] T. E. W , "The Foreign Missions Craze," *Watson's Jeffersonian Magazine*, Vol. V (Aug , 1910), pp. 629-632; also, e g., *Watson's Jeffersonian Weekly*, June 17, 1909, May 25, 1911, and Jan. 11, 1912.

to shoot a mad dog.[3] There was a peculiar malignity that pervaded his tirades against the Negro ... A friend betrayed is the enemy most despised.

Prominently characteristic of the *Jeffersonian* were the vituperative attacks upon personalities. Some were shrewd and comic, others vicious, and all irresponsible. A prominent bishop was a "Coca Cola lobbyist"; "Professor Woodpile" Wilson was an "arrant liar"; Bryan was a "cheap political· comedian, whose pose is that of a typical Pharisee." To his crimes of "seduction, kidnapping, adultery, violation of the oath of office, and rape, this vilest of rascals [Senator Smith] is seeking to add murder." Christopher Columbus was a "rapacious and inhuman monster" whose only object in discovering the New World was in adding another hemisphere to the dominion of the Pope. The Pope himself, "Jimmie Cheesy," was a "fat old dago" who lived with "voluptuous women." State politicians, of no matter what moral rectitude, lived in constant danger of being revealed in the *Jeffersonian* as keepers of Negro concubines or minions of Rome.

As a political boss of his kind Tom Watson was unique. Standing virtually outside the party he bossed, he manipulated it through its own machinery. This was what galled the pride of Democratic politicians who were, or had been, obligated to him for favors. They knew him for a party outlaw, openly contemptuous of their party, cynically playing one faction against the other, and committed to none of the restraints of party discipline, rule, or traditions. He had bolted their primaries, deserted their nominees, and openly supported a rival national party. And they knew he would do so again. When they lectured him on political morality, he replied with instances of Democratic morality in the 'nineties, and continued to fly his pirate's flag unabashed. Yet Democrats of both factions kept a beaten path to Hickory Hill, and news of Watson's favor or disfavor made or unmade many a candidate. As a boss his power was not abso-

[3] *Jeffersonian*, May 15, 1913, Jan. 4, 1917, and Feb. 12, 1914; T. E. W., *Sketches*, pp. 39-40.

433

lute: the power of no boss is absolute. His influence waxed and waned. Yet there was no governor of the state between 1906 and the time of Watson's death, a period of sixteen years, who did not owe at least one of his terms, in a greater or less degree, to Tom Watson's support. Some of the men whom he elected he as surely defeated; in fact, that was the rule rather than the exception, for rarely did he support the same man twice. From those who were obligated to him he expected a high degree of subservience.[4]

The state contests of 1914 were typical of this era of personal politics; and Watson played his usual rôle. The gubernatorial race being three-cornered, Watson's candidate, Nat E. Harris, an old Confederate veteran, easily won. In his *Autobiography* Harris acknowledges his indebtedness to Watson as naïvely as he complains of the defeat at his hands two years later.[5] The senatorial contest, a revival of the perennial feud between Hoke Smith and Joseph M. Brown, had a different result. An assiduous understudy of Watson, and a convinced believer in his methods, Brown launched a series of anti-Catholic articles during the campaign that, it was remarked, might have been dictated by Tom Watson. As bitter as ever against Smith, Watson attacked him as a Negrophile, an enemy of "White Supremacy," and a truckler to Rome. "If you want to strengthen the Protestant religion and American liberties against Italian popery and the advancement of a priesthood which believes the church of Rome should rule all States," he wrote, "you will vote for BROWN *in the race against Hoke Smith.*"[6] The method failed this time, however. Smith was elected, receiving twice the number of popular votes polled by Brown.

One of the charges Watson brought against Smith during the campaign was that the Senator was a subsidized supporter of the cause of Leo Frank, the Jew. This campaign marks the introduc-

[4] For discussions of Watson as a political boss see editorial, *Nation*, Vol. CIII (Nov. 9, 1916), pp. 440-441.

[5] Nat E. Harris, *Autobiography*, pp. 239-240.

[6] *Jeffersonian*, July 30, 1914.

tion of the celebrated Frank case into Georgia politics. The case has a long and sordid history, a history that is inextricably a part of the history of Tom Watson.

* * * * * *

At 3:30 on the morning of April 27, 1913, the body of Mary Phagan, a fourteen-year-old girl, was discovered in the basement of an Atlanta pencil factory. She had been horribly murdered. The young superintendent of the factory, Leo M. Frank, who admitted paying the girl her wages when she came to the factory alone during the holiday on which the murder took place, was at once arrested. A fateful weight of irrelevant but prejudicial fact dogged Frank's case to the end. He was a Jew, a Northerner, an employer of underpaid female labor. Mary Phagan was a Gentile, pretty, popular, and a working girl. The Atlanta press immediately assumed the guilt of Frank, and rival papers vied with each other in exploiting the sensational details of the story. Irresponsible gossip of sexual perversion and gross immorality on the part of Frank was printed as "scoops" in bold headlines of "extras." Whispered rumor supplied unprinted details. The city police, publicly committed to the theory of Frank's guilt, and hounded by the demand for his conviction, resorted to the basest methods in collecting evidence. A Negro suspect, later implicated by evidence overwhelmingly more incriminating than any produced against Frank, was thrust aside by the cry for the blood of the "Jew pervert." [7]

The trial lasted thirty days, attended throughout by manifestations of mob spirit. On the final day the howl of the mob, packed for many blocks about the courthouse, was continually in the ears of the jurors. The crowd in the courtroom repeatedly jeered, laughed, and applauded. Editors of city papers joined

[7] Christopher P. Connolly, *The Truth About the Frank Case, passim*; Files of Herbert J. Haas & Co. (attorney for Frank) relating to Frank case, in the possession of Rabbi David Marx, Atlanta, Ga.; Hugh M. Dorsey, *The Argument of Hugh M. Dorsey at the Trial of Leo M. Frank, passim.*

in a petition to the presiding judge to adjourn the case for the day, because an acquittal would "cause a riot such as would shock the country and cause Atlanta's streets to run with innocent blood." The judge advised Frank and his lawyers not to attend the reading of the verdict for fear of their lives. Threatening messages were received by court officials: "Hang the Jew or we will hang you." Under such circumstances Frank was found guilty and sentenced to die. It was in his dissenting opinion on this case that Mr. Justice Holmes said: "Mob law does not become due process of law by securing the assent of a terrorized jury." Doubt as to Frank's guilt was expressed by every tribunal before which the case was reviewed: the state Supreme Court, the federal District Court, the United States Supreme Court, and the Georgia prison commission were all divided. Even the judge who presided at the trial expressed doubt, but at the same time refused to grant a motion for a new trial. Officials of justice and organs of public opinion seemed cowed before the mob. The victorious solicitor-general, Hugh M. Dorsey, was made a popular hero.[8]

The Frank case for a time rivaled the European war as a subject of national attention. Outside the state the conviction was general that Frank was the victim of a gross injustice, if not completely innocent. He presented his own case so eloquently and so ingenuously, and the circumstances of the trial were such a glaring indication of a miscarriage of justice, that thousands of people enlisted in his cause. The case became a *cause célèbre* in liberal circles the nation over. Such people as Jane Addams were outspoken against Georgia justice, and ex-Governor Eugene Foss of Massachusetts was among the petitioners who came to Georgia in person in Frank's behalf. The movement was not sectional, for the legislatures of both Texas and Tennessee passed resolutions asking that his life be saved.[9] A moving

[8] L. L. Knight, *op. cit.*, Vol. II, p. 1166; review of the case, Supplement to Augusta *Chronicle*, Nov. 25, 1915.
[9] N. E. Harris, *op. cit.*, p. 352.

picture was made and exhibited to present his cause to the public. The zealous defense committee and the wealthy connections of Frank in the North made tactical blunders, however, that fanned the flame of resentment in Georgia against "outside interference." The bringing of William J. Burns, the detective, to Georgia was especially resented. He narrowly escaped being lynched at Marietta (Mary Phagan's former home), and resentment broke out anew.[10]

For almost a year after Frank was arrested Tom Watson remained silent on the case. He later admitted that he declined an offer of $5,000 to defend Frank, and said that overtures were made to him to assist the prosecution.[11] In the early stages of the case he was heard to express surprise that the defense counsel did not demand a change of venue, since in Atlanta Frank had "about as much chance for his life as a snowball in hell." "It would be like trying a rat before the old cat and a litter of her kittens," he said.[12]

In March, 1914, the Atlanta *Journal* dared to break the spell of cowed silence that had fallen on the state press by printing an editorial asking a new trial for Frank and contending that his execution without it would amount to "judicial murder." Watson immediately leaped upon the editorial as evidence that Smith was dragging the Frank case into politics, and promised to *"see to it that the case is taken care of."* "If the Atlanta politicians and editors are crazy enough to make war on Dorsey, *because he did his duty in the Frank case,* LET THE WAR BEGIN."[13] At that time Dorsey, who led the prosecution of

[10] The files of Herbert J. Haas & Co., in the possession of Rabbi David Marx, Atlanta Ga , contain letters of Leo Frank as well as hundreds of letters, written by the committees working in his defense, giving a fairly complete picture of the efforts made in his behalf. Also *vide* private papers of Rabbi David Marx, Atlanta, in regard to the Frank case. Also *vide*, New York *Times*, Aug 20, 1915

[11] *Jeffersonian*, Jan. 11, 1917.

[12] This according to a sworn statement by James T. Hudson, who was visiting in Watson's home when he heard Watson make the remark: *vide*, Augusta *Chronicle*, Sept. 22, 1915.

[13] *Jeffersonian*, March 19, 1914, and June 11, 1914.

437

Frank, seemed a possible candidate for governor; he withdrew, however, and Watson supported Harris. The *Journal* suffered a loss in circulation and quickly dropped its efforts for Frank. Watson continued to use the Frank case against Smith in the senatorial race. When that ended, however, Watson's exploitation of the case had only begun.[14]

In the first place he assured his readers that there was a "gigantic conspiracy of Big money" organized to corrupt the state's courts, its governor, its papers in order to save the life of a wealthy murderer. "Frank belonged to the Jewish aristocracy, and it was determined by the rich Jews that no aristocrat of their race should die for the death of a working-class Gentile." As for Mary Phagan: "Yes, she was only a factory girl: there was no glamor of wealth and fashion about her. She had no millionaire uncle; she had no Athens kinsmen ready to raise fifty thousand dollars for her: no mighty connections . . ." So it was that, "while the Sodomite who took her sweet young life basks in the warmth of Today, the poor child's dainty flesh has fed the worms." [15] Was it not notoriously true that rich Jewish business men corrupted the daughters of Gentiles who worked for them? "Here we have the typical young libertine Jew who is dreaded and detested by the city authorities of the North for the very reason that Jews of this type have an utter contempt for law, and a ravenous appetite for the forbidden fruit—a lustful eagerness enhanced by the racial novelty of the girl of the uncircumcised." Anyone could tell that Frank was "a lascivious pervert, guilty of the crime that caused the Almighty to blast the Cities of the plain," by a study of the accompanying picture; "those bulging, satyr eyes . . . the protruding fearfully sensual lips; and also the animal jaw." [16]

There was scarcely an issue of his publications for more than a

[14] T. E. W., "The Celebrated Case of Leo Frank vs. the State of Georgia," *Watson's Magazine*, Vol XXI (Aug , 1915), p 222; "The Leo Frank Case," *ibid* , Vol. XX (Jan., 1915), p. 156.
[15] *Jeffersonian*, Oct 15 and Dec 3, 1914.
[16] *Ibid* , April 14 and May 27, 1915.

year without its article on the Frank case. Hundreds of pages were devoted to it, whole issues of his magazine, page after page of the weekly. Over and over he reviewed the evidence in the case: the torn garment, "spotted with virginal blood," the tuft of hair, the crumpled white form. Rumors, half-truths, special pleading, merciless slander, every device known to the skilled criminal lawyer—he employed. He pulled all the stops: Southern chivalry, sectional animus, race prejudice, class consciousness, agrarian resentment, state pride. Aside from these resources there were the sociological constants of human cupidity, ignorance, and gullibility. He was convinced, he said, that Frank had had as fair a trial as a man could possibly have had.[17]

As the months passed and the date for Frank's execution was successively postponed the tone of Watson's exhortations rose in a crescendo of threats and alarms. *"How much longer is the innocent blood of little Mary Phagan to cry in vain to Heaven for vengeance?"* he asked. With less provocation, he reminded them, New Orleans had lynched her Italian murderers. *"Now is the time to have a Vigilance Committee* APPOINT ITS OWN SENTRIES TO WATCH THAT DESPERATE CRIMINAL—whose money and whose resources seem *so insolently determined that his crime shall go unpunished."* Later he warned: "If Frank's rich connections keep on lying about this case, SOMETHING BAD WILL HAPPEN." A rumor that the governor might commute Frank's sentence called forth the headline: "RISE! PEOPLE OF GEORGIA." [18]

The final date for Frank's execution was fixed at June 22, 1915. All eyes were concentrated upon Governor John M. Slaton with the question, would he commute Frank's sentence? His term expired the day before the execution was to take place, and he would be succeeded by Harris, a "Watson man." Governor Slaton had himself sought and received the support of Wat-

[17] E.g., the space devoted to the Frank case in *Watson's Magazine* during three months: August, 1915, 53 pages; Sept., 45 pages; Oct., 42 pages.
[18] *Jeffersonian,* Nov. 19, 1914, and March 25 and June 3, 1915.

son in his race for office in 1912. While the hearings of the petition to commute were in progress Watson sent a friend to the governor with the promise that if Slaton allowed Frank to hang, Watson would be his "friend," which would result in his "becoming United States senator and the master of Georgia politics for twenty years to come." [19] The governor recalled, he said, that Watson dated his enmity to Hoke Smith from that governor's action upon a commutation petition—though in the former case it was a *refusal* to save the life of a man who had unquestionably murdered a working woman that caused the break. Slaton had received requests from more than 10,000 Georgians, including a recommendation from the presiding judge at Frank's trial, that he commute sentence. In the face of Watson's threat and the palpable menace of mob violence Slaton signed the commutation on the day before his term ended.

Governor Slaton had been elected by one of the largest majorities ever given for the office, and had been regarded as an exceptionally popular executive. On the day of his retirement it was necessary to declare martial law for his protection. A heavy military guard surrounded his house, and one conducted him to the capitol, where, after the inaugural ceremony, an attempt was made upon his life. By night a mob estimated to number 5,000 people gathered and marched on the ex-governor's home armed with "old fashioned pepper-box revolvers—revolvers with cap and lock—knives and dirks, saws and hatchets, with some modern guns and pistols," not to mention "a large basket of dynamite sticks." Before it was dispersed, the mob wounded and disabled sixteen of the soldiers protecting Slaton. The new governor found that the news of the commutation and Watson's incendiary articles had "caused the gathering of mobs in almost every part of the country and brought about such a state of affairs that no persuasion or remonstrance could control the situa-

[19] John M. Slaton to Thomas W. Loyless, Aug. 27, 1915, printed in Augusta *Chronicle*, Nov. 25, 1915. (Watson admitted this, but said that Slaton had made advances to him first for support, *Watson's Magazine*, Oct., 1915.)

tion." Slaton left for an extended trip—virtually exiled from his native state by the mob.[20]

The first issue of Watson's *Jeffersonian* after the commutation of Frank's sentence amounted to one enraged exclamation after another:

Our grand old Empire State HAS BEEN RAPED!
We have been violated, AND WE ARE ASHAMED! . . .
The great Seal of State has gone, LIKE A THIEF IN THE NIGHT, *to do for an unscrupulous law firm, a deed of darkness which dared not bask in the light of the sun.* . . .
We have been betrayed! the breath of some leprous monster has passed over us, and we feel like crying out, in horror and despair, *"Unclean!* UNCLEAN!"[21]

He defended the Atlanta mobs under the headline, "When 'Mobs' Are No Longer Possible, Liberty Will Be Dead." "You can close your eyes, and see it now," he wrote, picturing a scene from the early days of the American Revolution. "The 'mobs' were Liberty Boys in those days—the old days before we became lolly-pops, vegetarians, grape-juicers, and sissy-boys . . ."

It is undoubtedly a tax upon credulity, but it is still possible to understand how the old Populist—nearing sixty now—could fancy, for the moment, at least, that he saw in the howling ruffians of Atlanta as noble an army of Jacobins as ever marched to the strains of the *Marseillaise*. It appears in his personal letters. "It cost $5000," he wrote, "to save him from the 'mob'— as fully a respectable mob as those that took the tea from the British ship in Boston. Slaton had better not come back. 90% of our people are with us in this Frank case."[22] He could sit at Hickory Hill, "close his eyes," and see himself as Voltaire, as Mirabeau, as Danton. It was the degeneration of the dream that had given form to his chaotic soul.

Addressing himself to the Jewish lawyers defending Frank,

[20] N. E. Harris, *op. cit*, pp. 355-362.
[21] *Jeffersonian,* June 24, 1915.
[22] T. E. W to Dr. John N. Taylor, July 2, 1915.

Watson wrote: *"You have blown the breath of life into the monster of Race Hatred: AND THIS FRANKENSTEIN, whom you created at such enormous expense, WILL HUNT YOU DOWN!"* Proportionally there were in 1920 almost four times as many Jews to the population of Georgia, as there were in North Carolina, South Carolina, Alabama, and Mississippi. Every little town had its "Jew store." An editor of the state reported that since the commutation of Frank's sentence, "Georgia has been, we greatly regret to have to admit, a veritable hot-bed of anti-Jewish feeling." [23] Handbills were distributed on the streets presenting the question, "Can't you buy Clothing from an AMERICAN?" Or shall your money go "To buy Governors"? [24] An editor observed that in the whole state, "an unthinking, unreasoning passion has almost completely obsessed, not merely the worst but some of the best of her citizens, until for weeks and months past this matter [the Frank case] has occupied the public mind almost to the exclusion of all else." [25] Broadside doggerel on the case found a ready market, and the ballad of Little Mary Phagan, still heard in the South, was recorded for the phonograph.

After an important development in the case, on the streets of Atlanta, Augusta, Savannah, and Columbus, great stacks of the *Jeffersonian* "melted like snow-flakes." Eager crowds in small towns met the incoming trains to buy their *"Jeffs"* as soon as they arrived. The circulation of Watson's weekly leaped from around 25,000 at the beginning of the Frank crusade to 87,000 copies for the week ending September 4, 1915. The price per copy to dealers increased from one to one-and-a-half and then to two cents. At this rate a convincing itemized estimate shows that at its maximum circulation the paper made a profit of $1,123.75 per week.[26]

[23] Thomas W. Loyless, editorial, Augusta *Chronicle*, Aug. 1, 1915.
[24] Copies in the files of Herbert J. Haas & Co
[25] Augusta *Chronicle*, Aug. 1, 1915.
[26] Thomas W. Loyless, in the Augusta *Chronicle*, Sept. 12, 1915.

The commutation of Frank's death sentence marked the opening of Watson's campaign of abuse against ex-Governor Slaton. The slander he did not offer directly for the truth, he implied so artfully that it was widely accepted as the truth. The law firm of which Slaton was a member had effected a consolidation with the firm that defended Frank. It was specifically agreed that Slaton's firm should have nothing to do with the Frank case, and that Slaton was not to have any interest in the fees of the consolidated firm while he was governor.[27] Watson charged that Slaton was actually a part of Frank's counsel when he commuted the sentence, and that he secretly received fabulous fees for that action. He freely used Mrs. Slaton's name in his charges, dubbing her "Chief Justice Sally." He argued that the commutation was a "nullity" and should be set aside.

Threats of lynching, half-veiled or unveiled, continued to appear in the *Jeffersonian*. When a demented convict named Creen made an attempt upon Frank's life at the state penitentiary, slashing a jugular vein while the victim slept, Watson urged that a petition be circulated "even into South Carolina, asking for clemency for Creen."[28] In his paper for August 12 Watson wrote: *"The next Leo Frank case in Georgia will never reach the Courthouse.* THE NEXT JEW WHO DOES WHAT FRANK DID, IS GOING TO GET EXACTLY THE SAME THING THAT WE GIVE TO NEGRO RAPISTS."

On the night of August 16 twenty-five armed men, only two of them masked, entered the state penitentiary, took Leo Frank out, boldly drove one hundred and seventy-five miles across the state in eight automobiles, and hanged him on a tree near Marietta. The lynching was faultlessly planned, and executed without a hitch. For audacity and efficiency it was unparalleled in Southern history. It was after the lynchers had done their work that the spirit of the Roman holiday prevailed. A heel was repeatedly ground into the flesh of the dead man's face, and bits

[27] Judge Samuel B. Adams quoted in the Augusta *Chronicle*, Sept. 5, 1915.
[28] *Jeffersonian*, July 29, 1915.

443

of his clothing and of the rope were distributed as souvenirs. "Fiddling John" Carson played the Mary Phagan ballad all day on the courthouse steps in Marietta to crowds gathered from miles around. It was estimated that 15,000 people, women and children among them, filed past the body of Frank in an Atlanta morgue, after compelling authorities by threats to display it.[29]

At Hickory Hill Watson was waiting for word from the lynchers with his wife, his son, and Mrs. Lytle at two o'clock in the morning. The news came that Frank had been taken by the lynchers. He did not say anything.[30]

One feels back of many of his wild utterances on the Frank case the same pathological state of mind that prevailed in parts of his anti-Catholic crusade. "I wish it were possible for me to consult you professionally," he wrote a medical friend in the midst of his activity on this case. "A baffling nervous trouble returns on me about once a month & for several days I am so despondent & distressed, *about nothing*, that it is difficult to live." [31] Whether his psychological condition was more a cause, or a result, of his political preoccupations—or whether it was either—it is, of course, impossible to say. There may have been times, many times, in the study at Hickory Hill, when even Tom Watson—as prone as he was to fall under the spell of his own hypnotic devices—was unable any longer to identify his howling mobs and masked lynchers with his Jacobins and "Liberty Boys." But unless one chooses to interpret the above quotation in such a light, there is no evidence to support this speculation. So far as one can judge on the strict basis of what Watson said and wrote, there is no reason to reject the idea that he looked upon his work and called it good—all of it.

After an investigation, Governor Harris reported: "The penitentiary was not built to keep people out, but to keep them in

[29] *Constitution*, Aug. 17 and 18, 1915; Atlanta *Journal*, Aug. 17, 1915.
[30] Interview with Mrs. Lytle, Baltimore, Aug. 8, 1934.
[31] T. E. W. to Dr. John N. Taylor, Jan. 7, 1915.

when put there. So the attacking party had little difficulty . . ."
He was flooded with letters threatening his life when he announced that an effort would be made to apprehend the lynchers.[32] As the New York *Times* observed, it would have been no more possible to convict them than it would have been "to convict Wendell Phillips in Massachusetts under the fugitive slave law for aiding slaves to escape." The mass of the people were in sympathy with the lynchers, and those who were not seemed completely cowed. The mayor of Atlanta, speaking before the California Mayors' Association at the time of the lynching, defended it, saying that seventy-five per cent of the people believed that the judgment of the courts had been "set aside by one man, and the people felt that it was up to them to take the law into their hands." [33]

Intelligent men were seen to fight their way to news boys to pay twenty-five and fifty cents for the first issue of Watson's paper after the lynching. The event came too late to allow more than a brief comment in a "box" on the front page. "In putting the sodomite murderer to death," he wrote, "the Vigilance Committee has done what the Sheriff would have done, if Slaton had not been of the same mould as Benedict Arnold. Let Jew libertines take notice. Georgia is not for sale to rich criminals." In the next issue Watson devoted eight pages to the case. He wrote a long defense of lynch law based upon the text, "THE VOICE OF THE PEOPLE IS THE VOICE OF GOD." "If Democracy does not mean just that, let us abandon our Republican form of Government, kiss the Pope's foot, and ask him to appoint a 'divine right' king to rule over us." He was sure that "all over this broad land there are millions of good people, not doped by Jew money, and lies, that enthusiastically greet the triumph of law in Georgia. *Womanhood is made safer, everywhere.*"

The state of Georgia stood indicted the nation over because

[32] N. E. Harris, *op. cit*, p. 368.
[33] New York *Times*, Aug. 20-23, 1915; *Constitution*, Aug. 19, 1915.

445

of the Frank lynching. The crime was compared freely with the atrocities in "bleeding Belgium." A Boston paper suggested a boycott on all Georgia products. The *New Republic* placed the state "in the category of communities like Haiti, communities which have to be supervised and protected by more civilized powers." It deplored the fact that "we are in part composed of a people as cowardly, as incompetent, as barbarous as so many people in Georgia have shown themselves to be." [34] The mass of Georgians could no more understand such an attitude than the mass of Germans could understand Allied talk of the "Hun." They believed what they were told. Watson himself printed at great length the worst of the condemnation of Georgia from the national press, along with many cartoons denouncing the lynching. "The North can rail itself hoarse, if it chooses to do so," he wrote. "We've already stood as much vilification and abuse as we intend to put up with; and we will meet the 'Leo Frank League' with a Gentile League, *if they provoke us much further* . . ." He intimated that "another Ku Klux Klan may be organized to restore HOME RULE." [35]

From California ex-Governor Slaton denounced the lynching as "a consummate outrage." He proposed the prosecution of Tom Watson under the section of the criminal code that makes felonious the publication of literature tending to incite riot. The mob that attacked him in Atlanta were "recruited from the dives and gutters of Atlanta." Of course he was not afraid to return to Georgia. He intended to return within a few weeks.[36] "Oh you gutter snipes of Atlanta! Oh you denizens of the dives!" jeered Watson. "Get back to your gutters, and your dives, before Straus, and Haas and Montag fetch John Slaton home!" He published a letter from Columbia County admirers addressed to Frank friends: *"If you don't want to raise H— in Georgia, you and your Slaton crowd had better keep quiet, for there is no*

---

[34] *New Republic*, Vol. III, p. 300.
[35] *Jeffersonian*, Aug. 26 and Sept. 2, 1915.
[36] *Constitution*, Aug. 19, 1915.

limit fixed to which the sons of Georgia will not go to protect her fair women and Watson." Watson suggested more than once that "It might seriously impair his [Slaton's] health, if he were to return to Georgia." [37] Slaton's friends implored him not to return. The ex-governor departed for the Hawaiian Islands.

In January Watson learned that United States Attorney-General Gregory had plans under way for the Department of Justice to take action against him for his articles on the Frank case. The intention was to try his case in a jurisdiction outside of Georgia, on the ground that the government could not get an impartial trial of Watson in that state. The government had already met two defeats at Watson's hands in its prosecution of its case against him involving the charge of obscene matter in his Catholic articles.

Watson called a mass meeting of his followers at Thomson to tell them of the government's intention. "And I tell the Attorney-General to his teeth," he said, "—*you cannot* remove me from the Southern District of Georgia. . . . If I have to give up my life for having incurred the savage hatred of the Roman priests and the rich Jews, it will be given up right here in the same region where my ancestors gave up theirs. . . . I don't intend to budge an inch: the cause is yours as well as mine, and I will die on my threshold, before any officer, State or Federal, shall take me outside of the legal jurisdiction under whose constitutional protection my home was made." A resolution was passed condemning the Department of Justice.[38]

About the same time a "prominent gentleman" came to Governor Harris with the request that he petition Attorney-General Gregory to drop the proceedings against Watson. "The gentleman stated to me," writes the governor with his infallible candor, "that he had just come from Mr. Watson and had been directed to say to me that if I would prevent such a step being taken he would give me his earnest support as well for my re-

[37] *Jeffersonian*, Aug. 19, Sept. 9, and Oct. 7, 1915.
[38] MS. of speech, Watson MS.; also *vide Jeffersonian*, Feb. 17, 1916.

447

election as for any office that I might seek." Harris agreed to do all in his power. The "prominent gentleman" then telephoned Hickory Hill in the presence of the Governor. "I could hear through the phone Mr. Watson's reply . . ." he said. "Mr. Watson expressed his gratification that I took the view that I had outlined." A few days later Harris made a special trip to Washington to see the Attorney-General. Later a meeting of the Georgia delegation was called to discuss the same matter. Said one of its members: "Our old Governor has already gone down to see the Attorney-General and I am sure the rest of us can afford to do so." The entire delegation, with the exception of Hardwick, appeared before Attorney-General Gregory in Watson's behalf. The case was dropped.

"What kind of politicians have you got in Georgia?" demanded the Attorney-General of Governor Harris at their interview. "When you come to me you always denounce Mr. Watson in unmeasured terms, and yet when I propose to silence him or punish him for his misdemeanors, you come here and take his part and urge me to let him alone. Why is this?"

"I did not answer him according to the inquiry," wrote the governor in his account of the interview, "but contented myself with telling him that I wanted him to let Mr. Watson alone for the sake of the honor of my own state and people." [39]

More than a year elapsed between the time of the Frank lynching and the next state election. Watson saw to it, however, that the case was kept in the public eye until the election. Solicitor-General Hugh M. Dorsey paid Watson a visit at Hickory Hill after he had disposed of the Frank case, and later announced his candidacy for the governorship.[40] Forgetting the promise he had made, Watson turned upon Governor Harris, who was a candidate for reëlection, and denounced him as a Slaton man. He then came out for Dorsey, whom he recom-

[39] Nat E. Harris, *Autobiography*, pp. 240-241.
[40] Interview with Judge Hugh M. Dorsey, Atlanta, Sept. 2, 1934.

mended as "the fearless, incorruptible Solicitor-General who won the great fight for LAW AND ORDER, and the PROTECTION OF WOMANHOOD, in the Leo Frank case. . . . *The Jeffersonian is for him tooth and nail.*" Watson also announced his candidate for prison commissioner: *"He is* THE JUROR *who was so outrageously* DENOUNCED BY LUTHER ROSSER IN THE FRANK CASE! *Henslee stood firm and true,* for LAW, for JUSTICE, for WOMANHOOD." [41] Watson also had his candidates for comptroller-general, for state superintendent of education, and for commissioner of agriculture.

The state campaign was fought out largely on the issue of the Frank case. Watson's candidates were victorious all along the line. The strategic post of commissioner of agriculture, which controlled more patronage than any office in the state, was filled by the vice-president of Watson's publishing company. The chairmanship of the Democratic Executive Committee was filled by a personal friend of Watson's. The governor-elect came to Hickory Hill to discuss the matter of appointments. The Democratic state platform contained a plank condemning all efforts on the part of the Federal Government to extradite citizens of the state for trial. That same summer the state legislature, at Watson's demand, passed a law providing for the strict inspection of Catholic convents. Even Watson's power was unequal to the task of forcing a Democratic state convention to denounce its own party's candidate for president—as he attempted to do. He forthwith came out as a "Progressive," in favor of the candidacy of Charles E. Hughes. [42]

* * * * * *

On a summer night in 1915, while the hysteria over the Frank case was at its peak, a strange ceremony was conducted on the

[41] *Jeffersonian,* June 8, 15, 1916; editorial in the New York *Times,* Sept. 14, 1916.
[42] *Jeffersonian,* Aug. 3, 17, and 24, Oct. 26, 1916; New York *Times,* Sept. 27, 1916.

bald top of Stone Mountain, ten miles from Atlanta. That ceremony inaugurated the new Ku Klux Klan—of illustrious history during the next decade. If Watson had any hand in launching the new organization, no record has been found that reveals it. Yet if any mortal man may be credited (as no one man may rightly be) with releasing the forces of human malice and ignorance and prejudice, which the Klan merely mobilized, that man was Thomas E. Watson.

CHAPTER XXIV

Peter and the Armies of Islam

IT WAS AXIOMATIC in Watson's politics that Woodrow Wilson could do no right. More deeply imbedded in his mind than axioms was a hatred of militarism. By the dictates of these two antipathies, more than any other influences, was shaped the tortuous attitude he took toward the nation's part in the World War.

Ever since he led the victory over the Wilson party in the Georgia primary of 1912 Watson had been unremitting in his attack upon the President. Nothing seemed to please him. Had Wilson given a death blow to Dollar Diplomacy? "Then what's our navy doing in Nicaragua?" asked Watson. Had the President secured the passage of anti-trust laws? "Yes; with all their teeth extracted," he replied. Had not eighteen peace treaties been negotiated? They were "eighteen lame jokes." Had not Neutrality been maintained? "Could the administration have done anything else?" His bitterest attack was reserved for Wilson's Mexican policy. The capture of Vera Cruz was a "wanton piece of criminal stupidity," for which he could see no possible justification. For sending the "punitive expedition" after Villa the President "richly deserved impeachment." Intervention meant that Wilson sought "to complete the bloody work of Mora, Diaz, Huerta, and Henry Lane Wilson." [1] Like everything else he wrote in this period, the criticisms of Wilson were

[1] *Jeffersonian*, Sept. 24, 1914; April 20, July 13, 1916.

451

highly spiced with the papal menace. The President was the "pusillanimous tool of a foreign potentate" with "a papal spy" as private secretary, he assured his readers. It was sometimes difficult to tell where the anti-Catholic crusade left off and the anti-Wilson crusade began.

For more than a year after the opening of the World War Watson was so much absorbed in one "menace" or another that he had time for little else. He took pains, however, to assert a strong position of neutrality. "It is the most stupendous tragedy in history," he wrote of the War. "But *you* have nothing to do with it. The quarrel is not yours. It is your duty to hands off [*sic*]." He complained of the sham neutrality that lay in the government's policy of permitting financial intervention on behalf of the Allies. "What sort of consistency is it that prohibits a harmless piece of music [a British war song], and then feeds the titanic fight with food, clothing, guns, ammunition and horses?" he asked. He demanded commercial as well as military neutrality. "Come Ahead, Now, and Let Us All Go Crazy about the Belgians," ran the headline over his editorial on the atrocity propaganda.[2]

Partly because he thought the administration was taking the side of the shipping interests against Great Britain and her blockade and partly because of his sympathies, Watson had, by the end of the first year of war, abandoned his neutrality for a frankly pro-Allies position. "LET ENGLAND ALONE!" he demanded, referring to the blockade of Germany. He had two hundred bales of cotton that he would burn "rather than do a single thing to hamper France and England while they are fighting for the rights of humanity." He urged the farmers to "TELL THAT ATLANTA CHAMBER OF COMMERCE TO GO TO H-LL" when that body demanded an end to the blockade. On the side he advised his crusaders that "the Pope and the Kaiser are in co-hoot on the war." Yet at the end of 1916 he still ridiculed the idea of American intervention. Com-

[2] *Ibid.*, Jan. 7, 1915; *vide* also Aug. 27, 1914, and Jan. 14, 1915.

menting on the slogan, "He kept us out of war," Watson wrote: *"What war?* Where did we have a chance to get into one? What did he do to keep us 'out?' . . . *We had no cause to go in."* Wilson's preparedness program called forth a denunciation of "the insane notion that belligerence of mind, belligerence of preparation, and belligerence of attitude and conduct *lead to peace* . . ." It was Watson's idea that *"big armaments, instead of insuring* PEACE, *insure* WAR." He denounced compulsory military training as an effort to have the republic *"transformed into a German military camp."* [3]

Only two weeks before the President delivered his war message, Watson doubled on his tracks and called for intervention. "If a single vessel of ours is sunk in violation of the Law of Nations," he urged, *"join the Entente,* send money, men and munitions *to France,* and bend every energy of this greatest of Republics to aid those who are trying to crush the Prussian idea, *that the only law* is MILITARY NECESSITY, to be judged of by Prussian militarists." [4] Immediately war was declared, however, he recoiled to his former position. If the government had been, "from the start, *absolutely neutral,* as in sound morals it should have been," there would have been no occasion for intervention. He pronounced the war a result of "the most ravenous *commercialism* that ever cursed a nation." He renounced the war and all its works, and declared he would have nothing to do with it. [5]

His silence was not of long endurance. The dictatorial powers demanded by the President, the inquisitorial espionage and sedition laws, the universal militarism and regimentation—all received treatment at his hands. He seemed to assume single-handedly the task of turning back the tide of war. As he got his feet planted on the road to this new crusade, he seemed to experience a reborn sense of responsibility, and something of his

[3] *Ibid.,* Nov 30 and Dec. 21, 1916; Jan. 4, 1917.
[4] *Ibid.,* March 15, 1917.
[5] *Ibid.,* April 12, 1917.

old spirit of courage in the face of overwhelming odds. In June his paper was refused delivery at Savannah under provision of the Espionage Act pending a decision of the Post Office Department.[6] Early in July he received a notice from the Post Office Department requiring him to show cause why his mailing privileges should not be revoked. This action merely seemed to intensify Watson's attack.

His first reaction was one of amazement at the universality of the war madness. "Men who are ordinarily cool and level-headed are acting like inebriates," he wrote. "A strange intoxication exalts them, sweeps them off their feet, fastens them and leads them on, *and on*, AND ON, until they are mere echoes of slogans which are sounded in Washington." He attacked the Espionage Act with the earnestness of a man defending his own life. It would, he said, "establish the same kind of autocracy in this country that the *lese majestie* [*sic*] laws create in Germany"; yet it was "Jefferson's Democratic Party proposing this, mind you!" "Must we begin our war upon European autocracy *by creating one*, here at home?" he demanded. *"Don't abuse me —ANSWER ME!"* It was his opinion that *"no king that ever lived wielded more autocratic control than President Wilson* has demanded," and he was using that power to "systematize universal goose-stepping." [7]

Treating the "flowers of Wilson's rhetoric" with contempt, Watson kept asking with embarrassing frequency, "Why are we fighting?" and "How is it that we got balled up in this Armageddon?" The answers he made to his own questions were not those that one saw upon the great war posters, or read in the "Loyalty Leaflets," or the "Red, White, and Blue Books," or heard from the Four-Minute Men. For example:

Morgan and his associates banked upon the success of England, France, Italy, and Russia: they have put thousands of millions of dol-

[6] New York *Times*, June 29, 1917.
[7] *Jeffersonian*, April 26, May 17 and 24, 1917.

lars on that side: *they now compel the United States to put up billions of treasure and millions of lives,* ON THE SAME SIDE, *for fear that Germany will win, and reduce their war paper to the status of Confederate money.*

The Russian collapse had taken place; and American lives by the million, must be devoted to the Russian task, *else the billions of dollars which our Morgan banks and Steel Trust combinations had staked on England's success* WOULD BE REDUCED TO WASTE PAPER.

"The World must be made safe for democracy," said our sweetly sincere President; what he meant was, that the huge investment, which our Blood-gorged Capitalists had made in French, Italian, Russian, and English *paper,* must be made safe.

Where Morgan's money went, your boy's blood must go, ELSE MORGAN WILL LOSE HIS MONEY!

That's all there is to it.[8]

At the time he wrote this article Watson was conducting a drive against conscription and openly encouraging resistance to enlistment of troops for foreign service. Draft resistance was wide-spread over the country but poorly organized. While Watson's movement was in progress, the "Green Corn Rebellion," a pitifully ill-conceived attempt of poor white tenant farmers in Oklahoma to march on Washington, was crushed by local authorities who made three hundred arrests. Reports of arrests, indictments, and trials for draft resistance came from Texas, North Carolina, Oregon, Iowa, Ohio, and from Chicago, Philadelphia, and Cambridge, Massachusetts.[9] Disregarding these many evidences of the War Department's determination to silence and punish all resistance, Watson pushed his drive well into the fifth month of the War.

He not only continued his attack upon the war administration and his aspersions upon the holiness of America's cause, but suggested an interstate convention to meet and consider "*the recent*

[8] *Ibid.,* Aug. 16, 1917.

[9] Charles C. Bush, "The Green Corn Rebellion," (Master's thesis, University of Oklahoma) *passim;* New York *Times,* Aug. 5, 1917.

455

unconstitutional and revolutionary acts of Congress." The response "from all parts of Georgia and the adjoining states" was so favorable to the suggestion that he set a date for the convention to meet in Macon. "WE ARE THE MASTERS!" read his call. *"By the living God, we must again make that understood."* [10]

Meanwhile, he announced that he intended to fight the constitutionality of the Conscription Act of May 18, 1917, in the federal courts, and appeal for contributions to assist in the contest. Checks poured in from all parts of the country, small amounts most of them, but totaling in the end about $100,000.[11] Every week he published the names of new contributors, a list usually several columns long. The case selected to bring the law to test was that of two Negro men jailed in Augusta for failure to register as required by the Conscription Act. The hearing, on August 18, attracted such a large crowd that Judge Emory Speer held court in the open air. Watson's argument was based upon four main contentions: (1) that the acts of Congress and the President's proclamation abolished the independent state militia and ignored state-rights; (2) that they contravened the clause of the Constitution that prohibits Congress from making appropriations of this character for a longer term than two years; (3) that they destroyed the English common law principle of *ne exeat,* providing that the subject could not be sent out of the realm without his consent; (4) that they violated the Thirteenth Amendment.[12] Based upon the old creed of strict-construction and state-rights, it was the same sort of argument that Alexander Stephens would have used. The speech was one of the most impressive Watson ever made. The constitutionality of the Conscription Act was, of course, upheld by the Court.

Local patriots as well as federal authorities busied themselves

[10] *Jeffersonian,* Aug. 16, 1917.

[11] Interview with C. F. Hunt, Thomson, Georgia, who was cashier of McDuffie Bank, of which Watson was president, at the time this money was subscribed. His estimate of the total amount received was $100,000 "or over."

[12] *Jeffersonian,* Aug. 23, 1917.

with efforts to forestall the Macon convention. Watson found it impossible to obtain a place of meeting, and on receiving threats of military violence should the meeting be held, he took the responsibility of calling it off altogether in order to avoid bloodshed. "The world must be made safe for democracy, even though none is left in these United States," he remarked in making the announcement.[13]

From his own writings it is clear that Watson was well informed on the ruthlessness with which the Espionage Act and other coercive measures were being enforced by the Administration. Lesser offenders than he fell victim to the law. A candidate for Congress in Iowa was sentenced to ten years in the Federal Penitentiary in Atlanta for violating the Espionage Act. His offense consisted of publishing and distributing excerpts from an address against conscription delivered by Watson at Thomson on June 23, 1917. It had been less than a year since Watson was cleared of the charge of sending obscene literature through the mails—the end of four years' proceedings against him by the Government. He was well aware that he was *persona non grata* to the Attorney-General and that a decision was pending on the suppression of his paper. In spite of all this, he continued to court disaster, progressively intensifying his attack instead of mitigating it. With lance deliberately leveled he charged full gallop against the inexorable.

"I feel sure that Jefferson would have taken the same position . . ." he assured a friend. "Shall I, at my time of life, become an opportunist, a conformist, in order to avoid harsh criticism? The masses—especially the rural masses—are with me." The Farmers' Union, in which his influence was strong, had passed resolutions against Wilson's price-fixing program.[14] In the course of an interview upon a different occasion Watson once remarked: "Freedom of speech, within your limitations, as I have said—I have had a good deal of it. Sometimes I have not

[13] *Ibid.*
[14] T. E. W. to Dr. John N. Taylor, May 8, 1917.

had quite as much as I would like to have had. It takes a good deal of freedom of speech and press for me, I assure you."

In August Postmaster-General Burleson sent a communication to the Senate complaining of certain publications that were "daily accomplishing results clearly in violation of the espionage law." "Common among these publications," he said, "stand *The Masses* and *The Jeffersonian.* Their respective editors are leaders in this movement." [15] That same month the Post Office Department denied the use of the mails to the socialist monthly and to Watson's publications. The same judge who heard his argument against conscription denied his application for an injunction restraining the post office from refusing to accept his publications. There was no other recourse. His parting observation in the last number of the *Jeffersonian* summed up his feelings:

> Without specification of alleged wrong-doing, and without trial by jury, and without knowing why it is done, a publisher's business is outlawed and his property scrapheaped, and his presses stopped: still, this is not press-censorship.
> What is it then?
> Evidently, it is a part of "The New Freedom" which Father-in-law Wilson advocates in his book; which Son-in-law McAdoo employs in his sales of Liberty Bonds; which the Germans are suffering so badly from the want of; and which we are spending blood and treasure to establish throughout the universe.[16]

* * * * * *

The months that followed were full of tragedy at Hickory Hill. The loss of his publications drove in upon him a sense of frustration and defeat. He was reminded that his first paper in the 'nineties "was killed by the Spanish War of 1898, just as the war of 1917—our date—killed my *Jeffersonian*." [17] A week after

[15] *Constitution,* Aug. 23, 1917.
[16] *Jeffersonian,* Aug. 23, 1917.
[17] T. E W. to Robert L. Rodgers, Oct. 6, 1919, Georgia Department of Archives and History.

the government clamped down upon his paper, his remaining daughter died. That blow was "like the crash of an avalanche," he wrote. He found it difficult to readjust himself. "It is hard to feel the same old interest in the same old things," he complained. "You seem to stand upon one bank of a great stream, and they upon the other, while a deep, wide current flows between. To the things on the opposite side, you seem strangely removed and aloof, as if you had parted from them long years ago." [18] He sought relief in drugs and in an increased amount of drinking. His health declined and nervous prostration threatened. Toward the last of January he left Hickory Hill and moved to Florida.

In April his last child, John Durham, died while visiting him. Turning back to the pages of his Journal where he had written of the death of an infant daughter and his second daughter he described the death of his son. He mentioned an experience of his son shortly before the end which was "so full of tragedy that I cannot describe it." Death followed unexpectedly. "Monday afternoon convulsions set in. At just before sundown he fell out of my arms—dead. This ends it all!" [19] A little while later a Negro servant discovered him wandering on the beach out of his mind. For nine hours he talked incessantly, for the most part repeating old speeches he had made in the 'nineties. He soon regained control of his mind, but it was not until July that he began to recover physically. Those who knew him best dated a decided change from this experience. He drank more heavily, had less control of his temper, and was never again capable of the sustained mental exertion he had been accustomed to.[20]

Grief unnerved him as it did few men, and this was grief multiplied by a double calamity that almost at one stroke robbed him of what was dearer to him, he said, than life. He had faced death himself once in a serious illness, and the only observation about the encounter he found worth recording was that he "sim-

[18] T. E. W. in *The Guard*, Sept. 13, 1917.
[19] MS. Journal 2, p. 447.
[20] Interview with Mrs. Alice L Lytle, Baltimore, Aug. 8, 1934; also Mrs. Lytle to Robert L. Rodgers, Jan. 15, 1918, Georgia Department of Archives and History.

ply didn't care." This present stroke, however, was another confirmation of the suspicion he had long held. Providence, or whatever the parsons wished to name this Force—and he frankly entertained his doubts concerning Its friendliness—had always reserved a special malevolence for his head. It was plain enough to see. What other ingenuity could have fashioned the demonic combination that snatched his children from his arms and stopped his printing presses with one malign gesture?

One thing he knew—and his rusting presses bore the realization in upon him once more—that somehow he had been eternally thwarted in his dearest desires. He felt, and he said, that he was "one of those men with whom Fortune deals grudgingly, one of those whom Hope deceives and Success laughs at; one of those who always has wind and wave against him, and who never by any sort of chance finds himself in league with Luck." Frustration, "like a dark thread," to borrow one of his similes, seemed "woven between the warp and woof" of his life, and it never seemed to tire of repeating the same pattern. Born under the star of a declining agrarian society he had received at the start a heritage of defeat. This, along with sundry talents, he had boldly invested in the adventure of agrarian resurgence in the 'nineties and eventually attained leadership of the movement —in the very year of its bankruptcy. He had been the heaviest personal loser in the adventure, and his experience epitomized the frustration suffered then, as well as later, by the cause for which he fought—but more especially by Southern agrarianism. Those struggles of the 'nineties were fought over again and again in his mind in later years. Even such tangible victories as he had won for his farmers—rural free delivery, for example—had eventually been turned to account by his enemies to poison the minds of his people. His very platforms were bandied among them after he was all but forgotten. All the while perverse economic forces, or perhaps another Force, had widened the rift that yawned between the possessing and the dispossessed in his own ranks until it could no longer be bridged by his old platforms and principles. He had resorted to other devices—devices that contrasted strangely with old principles, and could not possibly have gained his consent at one time. At what dire cost to the harmony of his soul that consent was purchased may only be surmised. New recruits in droves took up his cry against the "menaces." But no sooner had he leveled a lance against a flesh-and-blood menace than his tatterdemalion army deserted him, and now they were treading the muck of foreign trenches or marching in goose-step to the rhythm of Wilson's rhetoric. Such reflections led back to the beach, where his endless pacings might too easily become dim wanderings again. Unless he could in some way speak his mind—at least have his say . . .

In a foolhardy attempt to evade the Government's ban Watson brought out a new paper, *The Guard,* soon after the *Jeffersonian* was silenced, but it too was suppressed. In June Eugene V. Debs was arrested and indicted for violation of the Espionage Act, and later sentenced to ten years' imprisonment in Atlanta. Upon learning that the Attorney-General was about to take proceedings against him, Watson wrote that official recounting the loss of his children, telling of his physical condition, and promising to make no further criticism of the administration if he were not molested. The Attorney-General dropped the proceedings.[21]

In August Watson decided to oppose Carl Vinson, candidate for reëlection as Congressman from the tenth district, in the primary of 1918. He had no paper now, and his physical condition prevented him from making more than a few speeches. His campaign was left largely in the hands of his friends. At his first public appearance, a speech at the home of Alexander Stephens, the scene of some of the most heated battles of the 'nineties, it was noticed that his hair was silvered, his eyes sunken, and his face deeply lined. There was none of the old fiery invective that set crowds mad. His voice was seldom raised above a conversa-

[21] Nat E. Harris, *Autobiography,* p. 242. Harris was told of the incident by Secretary of War Baker.

461

tional tone. He said the campaign might "help divert his mind from morbidness and melancholy." [22]

The nation-wide crusade against the Hun was at its highest pitch during the fall of this campaign. A regimen of meatless and wheatless days, Liberty Bond drives, spy-hunts, and Hun-hating held absolute sway. Carl Vinson, who had distinguished himself as a super-patriot, launched his campaign upon patriotic war issues. He charged that Watson had "never bought a Liberty bond, nor a war savings stamp and has never given a dollar to the Red Cross or Y. M. C. A." Furthermore, he had printed "seditious utterances," and "un-American writings" in his "disloyal incendiary publications" until an outraged administration had silenced him. In large advertisements Vinson printed excerpts from Watson's bitterest attacks upon Wilson, the war, and the Conscription Act.[23] Watson said that he had not changed his views on the righteousness of the War, but recognized that it must now be fought to a successful finish. As for the Liberty Bonds, he could see no reason why he should "borrow money at 12 per cent to loan to the richest government on earth at about 4 per cent." He was more interested in the coming work of reconstruction after the War. He promised, if elected, that he would "work for free speech; reëstablishment of the press; reguarantee and make stronger individual liberty and personal rights; all of which must be built up again."

The election was surprisingly close. According to official returns each candidate carried six counties. Watson's victories were won in the old Populist counties and in the Fifth Ward workers' district of Augusta. According to the county-unit system, Vinson had sixteen and Watson fourteen votes in the party convention. Convinced that he was the victim of fraudulent practices such as were used in the 'nineties, Watson contested the election in three counties at the state convention. He charged that local officials made a bonfire of ballots cast in one county to prevent a

[22] *Constitution*, Aug. 25, 1918.
[23] Augusta *Chronicle*, Aug. 27, 1918; *Constitution*, Aug. 22, 1918.

verification of the published returns.[24] Under the sway of patriotic appeal, the state convention refused to consider the contests Watson brought. He was denounced as "the miserable creature whose every word is against his country," and his "political death" was widely proclaimed.

* * * * * *

As soon after the Armistice as seemed reasonably safe, Watson acquired a small weekly paper, the *Columbia Sentinel*, and began to edit it on the plan of the *Jeffersonian*—all columns appropriated for his editorials. Still under governmental ban, he was compelled to post his papers in a neighboring town. Casting aside other precaution, and ridiculing the outcry of "our '100 per cent' idiots," he launched a running attack on "Wilsonism" and all its works, foreign and domestic. This new crusade presents some curious paradoxes, and only against the crazy pattern of the post-War America of 1919–1920 does it make sense.

In domestic affairs Watson demanded immediate repeal of all coercive legislation passed during the War. This included the Espionage and Sedition Acts, as well as the Conscription Act and compulsory military training. He called for the restoration of freedom of speech, assembly, and press and all civil liberties that Wilson had abridged, as well as amnesty for all political prisoners. There was Eugene Debs, "one of the greatest, truest, purest Americans now alive," sentenced to ten years in Atlanta by a "stone-headed Federal Judge." He encouraged Victor Berger, the Socialist representative from Milwaukee who was denied his seat in the House by Congress, to "keep up his fight for the time-honored principle of free choice of Representatives." "*If Milwaukee wants Berger, she has* A RIGHT TO HIS SERVICES." [25]

[24] T. E. W. to J. J. Flynt, Chairman of Democratic Executive Committee of Georgia, Sept 14, 1918, Watson MSS. (copy).
[25] *Columbia Sentinel*, Sept. 12, 1919, and Jan. 2 and Feb 9, 1920.

His strictures on Wilson's foreign policy were equally thorough-going. "What sort of peace was imposed upon the German *people*—whom Wilson said he 'loved?' " he asked. Instead of a "peace without victory," the peace of Versailles was an iniquitous bondage forced on a helpless people by bayonet, and an American blockade still imposed starvation upon German citizens. The League of Nations he regarded as an unholy alliance of the victors to enforce the peace of Versailles, to protect their ill-gotten plunder, and to impose imperial exploitation upon the subject nations. Under it, he thought, the United States would be "made security for every bankrupt nation, and pledged to interfere with every squabble on God's earth." "The Irish war is in bloody progress; the Russian war is a vast welter of blood . . . Germany rocks and reels under revolution after revolution; Turks still slaughter Armenians; and Great Britain is using the gun, the bayonet, and the bomb in every one of her held-down dominions." He proposed that the United States "get out of Europe and stay out." [26]

What were American troops doing in Russia? he asked. "Woodrow Wilson cabled his May-I-not congratulations to Kerensky, when the Czar was deposed; and then, when Lenine took the place of Kerensky, Wilson *himself*, sent an army of American boys to aid the Japs crush Russian Democracy." It looked to him like a conspiracy "to prevent Russia from showing the world how a democracy may be established—thus setting a bad example that may 'infect' other submerged masses." "Morality!" he exclaimed. "Woodrow Wilson preaching morality! *He*, the man who personally made war on Russian Democrats, and starved their wives and children with a most cruel and unlawful blockade." [27]

Shortly after President Wilson's breakdown in September, 1919, Attorney-General A. Mitchell Palmer, being groomed as a candidate for President, captured the public eye by taking the

[26] *Ibid*, July 11 and Aug. 8, 1919, and Jan. 2, 1920; *Constitution*, April 18, 1920.
[27] *Columbia Sentinel*, Jan. 2 and 23 and May 10, 1920.

lead in a crusade against organized labor and radicalism. In his "war on the Reds" the powers of the Espionage and Sedition acts were invoked to sanction a ruthless purge of dissenters. All over the nation meetings were broken up, audiences clubbed and jailed; houses were broken open, desks ransacked; fathers were torn from their families and shipped around the world without so much as an explanation. In December, 249 foreigners were herded aboard a boat and shipped to Soviet Russia. As if this were not enough, Palmer asked Congress for still more repressive powers. The cry of "Ship them, or shoot them," was taken up far and wide. Watson commented:

What sort of language is this we hear, roaring at religious conventions, at peaceable assemblages of Army Hofficers [*sic*], at quiet sessions of City Aldermen, at the afternoon meetings of the Eminently Respectable, and in the confidential conferences of the Better Element?

Colonel Roosevelt raucously imitates his father, and yells, "SMASH UM!"

In the Maryland Conference, Brother Samples tore loose and yelled, "SHOOT UM, OR SHIP UM!"

In the peaceable assemblage of New York Aldermen, Father Kenneally volcanoed, "SHIP UM, OR SHOOT UM!"

Dear me! this kind of conversation sets me to wondering which one of us went crazy *first*.

Of course, we are all crazy *now;* but the question is, who started it? Who was the aggressor? [28]

He begged to remind his betters that, "Under these same arbitrary, autocratic measures the Czars filled Siberia with noble men and women . . ."

Watson's favorite reply to "the '100 per cent' idiots," as he called Palmer and the Red-baiters, was to remind them of the revolutionary heritage of America. What would they have thought of their hero, La Fayette (to whom they were so anxious to pay their debt), had they seen him "at the head of a

[28] *Columbia Sentinel,* Jan. 2, 1920.

huge mob of Parisian Radicals" in the march on Versailles? When the British officers shouted "Shoot um!" at Lexington Bridge, "the farmers all ran to their houses, along the road, *came out with their guns*, AND SHOT BACK!" He reminded Palmer of the misadventures of a certain Stuart King who " 'visualized' an imminent danger from another invasion of Danes, Germans, Bolsheviki, and Emma Goldmans," and levied "Ship Money." The British Parliament had abolished general warrants, but "it remained for Attorney-General Palmer to find a legal way to throw a spreadnet over a mining community, and to imprison, starve, and force freemen back into involuntary servitude."

The gospel Watson was now preaching met with a wide popular response in the general reaction against Wilsonism. Between seven and eight thousand people crowded into Thomson to hear him speak on his birthday, in September, 1919. There were delegations from six Southern states other than Georgia. Three hundred visitors slept in the printing plant, and many could not find a place to sleep at all. Watson spoke for three hours, and afterward resolutions were passed denouncing Palmerism and the League of Nations and demanding the withdrawal of American troops from Europe and Russia.[29] "Our circulation has taken a great rise recently," reported Watson shortly after the speech.[30] Mrs. Lytle said that his health was "splendid," that he slept normally now, "from 7 to 8 hours at night, and doesn't find it difficult to relax as used to be the case." [31] All his regained physical strength he was now bending to the task of rebuilding his political strength.

Early in 1920 Attorney-General Palmer entered his name as a candidate in the Democratic presidential primary of Georgia.

[29] *Ibid*, Sept. 12, 1919; Mrs. Alice L. Lytle to Dr. M. M. Yates, Sept. 18, 1919, Watson MSS.
[30] T. E. W. to R. L. Rodgers, Sept. 10, 1919 (Georgia Department of Archives and History).
[31] Mrs. Alice L. Lytle to Dr. M. M. Yates, Sept. 18, 1919.

He stood as the "Administration candidate," endorsing the League of Nations, and Wilson's administration "in every phrase." His candidacy also involved a defense of his crusade against the "Red menace." "Should we repeal our espionage and sedition laws and thus voluntarily forgo all protection for the institutions and the people of this country?" it was asked in his behalf. "Should we open the country to every red and radical the world over whose fanatical mind may plot against our liberties, our democracy, and our prosperity?" [32]

Watson endorsed the candidacy of Senator James A. Reed of Missouri, who ran as a strictly anti-Wilson, anti-League man. On the eve of the deadline for the entrance of candidates, however, Reed withdrew from the race in Georgia in favor of Senator Hoke Smith. Besides being a political enemy of long standing, whom Watson had fought for twelve years, Senator Smith fell short of the out-spoken opposition to the Versailles Treaty that had characterized Reed's platform. He took a rather indeterminate, mid-way position, neither favoring the League of Nations wholly nor condemning it wholly. He claimed to have assisted in the composition of the Lodge reservations; yet at the same time he represented himself as a friend to the Wilson Administration. [33] With Smith a candidate, the race became another struggle between the two traditional factions of the party, since Palmer was supported by the old Howell faction.

At the last minute Watson entered the race. It was a new rôle he took, for this time he was not playing one faction against the other, but running as his own candidate against both factions. It was the first time he had attempted this, and politicians generally thought that he had little chance of victory. His presidential platform included demands for popular election of federal judges, and for recall. The real issue of the campaign, however, was that of "Wilsonism." He announced himself the only out-and-out anti-Wilson candidate, the only thorough-going

[32] *Constitution*, April–May, 1920, especially May 19, 1920.
[33] Atlanta *Journal*, April–May, 1920.

opponent of the League, and the only defender of civil liberties. "I am utterly opposed to any conscription law, any compulsory military training, any sedition law, any espionage act, or any legislation giving those in power the authority to banish from this country any citizen who is not first given a fair, legal trial," he said.[34]

He ridiculed Smith for his timidity in failing to take a positive position: he was "Straddle-bug Smith" who was neither one thing nor the other. "He wants the League, and yet he does not want it." Watson's chief attack was launched against Palmer, along the same lines he took before the Attorney-General entered the race in Georgia:

Is this the same Palmer who clamored at Congress, demanding a Sedition law which would have criminalized this cheerful editorial? . . .

Palmer would have had me clawed out of bed, at midnight; and I would have been aboard a steamer, off Brunswick, before my wife would have known that I was a Red bound for Russia. . . .

Is this the Palmer who prevailed upon a Federal Judge to decide that, if twenty workers become dissatisfied, and quit, *at the same time*, they are criminals? . . .

Is this the Palmer who virtually said that 60 cents a ton was enough for the miners, and that $10 a ton was reasonable for the owners? . . .

Is he the same man who tyrannically used the irresistible force of the Federal Government to obliterate all newspapers, all preachers, all speakers, all writers, who stood for American rights and American Independence. . . .

With these despotic ideas in his head Mr. Palmer, as President, would out-Wilson Wilson.[35]

Though Palmer, a Pennsylvanian, was little known in the state, and made but three speeches during the campaign, he had the endorsement of the President and the national party or-

[34] *Constitution*, April 18, 1920; *Columbia Sentinel*, April 19, 1920.
[35] *Columbia Sentinel*, April 19, 1920.

ganization, as well as the backing of the powerful Howell faction in the state. Smith brought to bear all the force of his own political organization, which had twice elected him to the Senate. He was said to have "engaged in the most arduous campaign of his life, speaking in every section of the state." By contrast, Watson had no tangible political organization, and no campaign headquarters. He made no speeches. He was opposed by all the daily papers in the state. Great was the astonishment, then, at "the amazing vote of Mr. Watson," who received a plurality of both counties and popular votes: [86]

Palmer	48,460 popular votes,	55 counties,	148 convention votes
Watson	51,977 " "	56 "	132 " "
Smith	45,568 " "	43 "	104 " "

Palmer, however, received a plurality of county-unit votes, and the state Democratic executive committee ruled that he was, according to the party rules, entitled to the nomination and all delegates from the state. At the state convention in May, the Watson forces, through an alliance with the Smith delegates, repudiated the ruling of the committee, and dominated the entire proceedings. Palmer speakers were shouted down, and a resolution endorsing Wilson's administration "was hissed to its overwhelming doom." On the other hand, a series of resolutions was passed declaring "unalterable opposition to the League of Nations" and to the Espionage, Sedition, and Conscription acts, and instructing the delegates to the national convention to support "no candidate for president of the United States who is not in thorough accord with the principles announced by this convention." When a Palmer delegate protested against one resolution as "a veiled attack on the administration," Watson quietly arose and said: "Let there be no mistake about this resolution. It is mine. Its avowed purpose is to criticize the administration." It was promptly passed. The Palmer delegates were not allowed

[86] *Constitution*, April 21 and May 12, 1920; *Columbia Sentinel*, May 3, 1920; New York *Times*, April 22, 1930.

a single place on the credentials committee. "The shame of it!" lamented the *Constitution*, a Palmer supporter. "Watson's mastery was complete. Smith dared not speak."

After the convention adjourned, the Palmer delegates organized to go to the national convention and contest the seats of the delegation named by the state convention. Both the Palmer delegation and the Watson-Smith delegations appeared at the San Francisco Convention. Since the Convention was dominated by the Wilson administration forces, the Palmer men had little difficulty in convincing the credentials committee that they were the rightful representatives of Georgia. Watson's offer (sent from Georgia) to give the contesting delegates one-third of the seats was refused, and the entire Palmer delegation was seated by a vote of forty-three to four on the part of the committee.[37]

* * * * * *

Although several months elapsed between them, the presidential primary of the spring and the regular state primary of the summer were virtually continuous campaigns fought upon virtually the same issues. Like the former race the latter was three cornered—two of the contending forces being led by the same men as formerly. Smith and Watson were this time rival candidates for the Senate. The Wilson administration and the League of Nations did not have a champion until Governor Hugh M. Dorsey also announced his candidacy for the Senate.

Smith's position was obviously weakened by continual trimming. Watson was near the truth when he charged that: "Hoke has been on every side of this question. He's been for reservations, and he's been against them. He's been against the whole d—— thing [the League] and he's been for it. He *admitted*, modestly enough, that he wrote the Lodge Reservations, but he denied that he was supporting the said reservations." Moreover,

[37] *Constitution*, June 27–29, 1920.

470

Smith's delegates at the May convention had solidly voted for Watson's resolutions condemning the Wilson administration, and when the Senator later proclaimed his harmony with the national platform of the party, Watson was ready to remind him of those resolutions.[38]

Following the pattern set by his several predecessors in the same office, Governor Dorsey had broken with Watson after being elected with assistance from Hickory Hill in 1916. The familiar complaint was that Watson demanded too much subservience. In his race for the Senate he was an advocate of Wilsonism and the League. Standing in much the same place Palmer had occupied in the previous race, he received the support of the Howell faction, the national party, and a large number of state newspapers.[39]

A new factor in this race was the participation of the recently organized American Legion, then in the midst of a membership drive. The Legion paid Governor Dorsey's entrance fee, as a candidate in the primary, and supported him as the representative of the cause of "100 per cent Americanism." It also waged an organized campaign against Tom Watson, who was denounced as an exponent of all slackerdom, pro-Germanism, disloyalty, and un-Americanism. Legionnaires appeared in groups at Watson rallies to heckle speakers and create disturbance. Watson was said to have "affiliations with the Bolshevist representatives to America." [40]

The Legion soon discovered to its dismay that it had captured a wild Tartar. Instead of hedging, Watson embraced the opposition of the Legion and artfully converted it into the main issue of his campaign. He assured the public that the Legion was "a gilded brigade of rich young officers who want to tell you whom to elect to office, and what laws to make in building up, in this country, the brutal militarism *which they practiced on your sons*

[38] *Columbia Sentinel*, Sept. 6, 1920; Aug. 9, 1920.
[39] *Constitution* Aug. 1–Sept. 9, 1920, *vide* especially editorial Aug. 30, 1920.
[40] Atlanta *Journal*, Sept. 3, 1920; Atlanta *Georgian*, Sept. 3, 1920.

in the Great War." He was the only candidate to champion the cause of the private against this clique of officers, he said. It was just such autocratic officers as these who murdered Rosa Luxemburg in Germany when she exposed the brutalities which they practiced upon privates. Nevertheless he promised to expose the atrocities of these ex-officers, which had "excited the horror of the world." There was no lack of returned private soldiers to supply him with evidence against their erstwhile officers. Great was the outcry against the Legion, when Watson related the grievances of ex-privates at his speeches. "Many mothers wept," it was said. "Old fathers . . . were moved to the greatest emotion when the speaker described the soldier boy dragged from the fireside, hurriedly transformed into a cog in a vast war machine, hurled across the ocean and landed in a foreign country, to meet the fate of death by gallows by orders of the brutal officers put over them." [41]

This time he did not depend upon an editorial campaign, but traversed the state three times by automobile to speak to great throngs who gathered to hear him. Weekly he wrote dramatic accounts of the campaign for his paper. "We stayed a few minutes among the Bolsheviki at these crossroads," he reported, and were off to meet the next delegation of "Reds." He was not molested by Legionnaires at Warm Springs—"there being so many coyotes and Bolsheviki on hand."

Losing his temper when his sleep was disturbed at a hotel in Buford, Watson appeared in underclothes upon the mezzanine and hurled a book down at a table of noisy card-players, following it with "every possible form of profanity." An officer appeared unceremoniously and without warrant to arrest him, and Watson put up a violent resistance. "They acted as though the Reds were upon them," he reported. His underclothes were torn off; he was roughly handled and bruised. He admitted that he "became so blind with fury at the outrage" that he could not recall "just what happened afterwards." At any rate he spent the

[41] *Columbia Sentinel*, Aug. 9 and 16, and Sept. 6, 1920.

night in jail, and remained locked up until a rescuing party arrived from Atlanta the next morning. He related the occurrence in his paper and in speeches, pronouncing it "as barbarous a specimen of Wilsonism as ever occurred in the mine-slave regions of Pennsylvania." [42]

While scoffing at the Red menace that was played up by the American Legion, and the element which he called "our '100 per cent' idiots," Watson revived the tested and proved Catholic issue as a competing "menace." In effect, Watson was virtually mobilizing the Klan to put to rout the Legion. At the same time, this strange champion of civil liberties was conducting as plain-spoken a fight for freedom of speech and press as was being made anywhere. It was clear before the election that he had won the mass of people to his cause. The paper of a rival candidate admitted that his speech in Atlanta attracted the largest crowd ever to gather there. Ten thousand people were turned away, and the doors closed an hour before the meeting began. A delegation of ex-soldiers sat in front with a banner reading, "We buck-privates and non-coms are with you, Uncle Tom."

In September Watson was elected by a decisive majority. With him his candidate for Governor, Thomas W. Hardwick, allied with Watson again after ten years of enmity between the two, was also swept into office. The returns showed that Watson had more than doubled his popular vote since the April ballot: [43]

Watson	102 counties,	247 county-unit votes,	111,723 popular votes
Dorsey	38 "	103 "	" 72,885 " "
Smith	14 "	34 "	" 61,729 " "

The triumph of Tom Watson was variously interpreted and appraised. To a writer in the *Nation* it appeared to be "essentially the victory of the Fifth Estate, of the sinister forces of intolerance, superstition, prejudice, religious jingoism, and mobbism." "Never before," continued this writer, "has so conspic-

[42] *Ibid.*, Aug. 16, 30, 1920; *Constitution*, Aug. 20, 1920.
[43] Atlanta *Journal*, Sept. 10, 11, 1920.

uous, so violent, so flaming an apostle of every variety of race hatred been invested with the power and dignity of the Senatorial Toga." [44] The chairman of the Democratic National Committee considered his election "something of a blow to the Democratic party." Watson himself said that his victory was "won against the attempted dictation of officers of the American Legion, and for the great English principles of free speech, free press, free assemblage, and complete separation of church and state." [45] To the old Populists, the faithful old guard, it meant that Tom Watson had "come back," and that right had been vindicated after thirty years of defeat. His victory could have meant still other things, doubtless, for its fund of paradoxes was illimitable.

[44] C. P. Sweeney, "Bigotry in the South," *Nation*, Vol. CXI (Nov. 24, 1920), pp. 585-586.

[45] Atlanta *Journal*, Sept. 11, 1920; *vide* also "Seven Reasons Why We Won in Georgia," *Columbia Sentinel*, Sept. 13, 1920.

CHAPTER XXV

The Tertium Quid

WATSON'S RETURN TO WASHINGTON after thirty years was like the emergence of a hermit, already a little legendary. Although those thirty years had been filled with intense activity, Watson himself had been virtually immured at Hickory Hill for a generation—flashing out with comet-like regularity at intervals, but quickly retiring again. He was regarded as a curious anachronism from the 'nineties, with "a good deal of the temperament of a French Revolutionist." Amidst the reactionary element swept into Washington with Harding he was indeed an oddity.

He and his wife had few connections in the city, and they found social honors empty after the death of the children. To prevent his going to a White House reception in street clothes, Mrs. Lytle bought him a dress suit. There was no "small talk" in him. A complimentary pleasantry from Mrs. Harding caught him quite without reply. The old note of disillusionment with attainment recurs. He made known his disgust with Harding's inaugural: "replete with oracles, maxims, proverbs, safe generalities and orthodox truisms." He was never quite reconciled to finding no Websters in the Senate with whom to match wits. Moody spells accompanied by morbid drinking and attacks of asthma interrupted his work, and he was heard to say he was "ready to die." [1]

[1] Interview with Mrs. A. L. Lytle, Aug. 8, 1934; *Columbia Sentinel*, March 14, 1921.

Without observing the probationary period of silence expected of new members, Watson made himself felt from the start. Precious little time there was to set aright a world that was conspicuously awry. He was heard often and at length on a variety of subjects. Great deference was paid to his reputation for erudition, and he not infrequently demonstrated his amazing mastery of historical lore. His performances were once compared by the New York *Times* with the harangues of John Randolph. They did, in fact, seem governed by the eccentric Virginian's maxim, "Let there be justice though the heavens fall." According to mood, he was truculent, gallant, irascible, whimsical, or downright ferocious; and always he was guided by impulse. Few there have been who could more naturally assume the mantle of the *Tertium Quid*. He was usually to be seen grinning sardonically behind his desk piled high with literature. The Senate librarian said there was never such a voracious reader.[2]

His committee appointments were unimportant, and the bills and resolutions he introduced extremely few. He argued eloquently in behalf of his resolution requesting the President to free all political prisoners convicted upon charges of alleged violation of the espionage laws, and to restore their political and civil rights. He also introduced a resolution specifically requesting the pardon of David T. Blodgett, the citizen of Iowa then serving a ten-year sentence in Atlanta for printing excerpts from one of Watson's own speeches. "Should he be in the Senate and I in the penitentiary?" he asked. "He did not say any more in Iowa than I have said here in the Senate, and I think I am in somewhat better company than he. That is only an opinion of mine. (Laughter)" These resolutions, like all his others, failed to be reported out of the committees to which they were referred.[3]

The first subject on which the new Senator delivered himself

[2] New York *Times*, Sept. 20, 1922; Brooklyn *Daily Eagle*, quoted in the *Columbia Sentinel*, July 17, 1922.
[3] *Cong. Records*, 67 Cong., 1 Sess., Oct. 26, 1921, p. 6780; Aug. 23, 1921, p. 5580.

at any length was the proposed treaty with Colombia, intended to conciliate that country for the Panama affair by the payment of $25,000,000. Republican senators, rallying to the defense of Roosevelt, had opposed the treaty as proposed by the Wilson administration. Now that Roosevelt was dead, and certain new factors had entered the picture, even Lodge reversed himself to support the treaty. Much verbiage was perpetrated, but Senator Lodge let the cat out of the bag by his statement: "We must not only enlarge our trade, but we must enlarge our source of supply of oil wherever it is possible to do so, and we can not do it if we take the position that it is a sin for Americans to make money and that those who are engaged in foreign investment and foreign commerce are to be punished instead of sustained." [4]

"Mr. President, are we the agents for the Standard Oil Company—that and nothing more?" asked Watson. "When did that infant, protected in all its roots and branches, need our assistance in securing access to foreign oil fields?" He intimated that all the fine talk about Pan-American brotherhood turned his stomach. "Let us confess what we are doing—that we are here to buy property for the Standard Oil Company." If the country was in such need of oil, why did we voluntarily cut ourselves off from the richest oil fields in the world—those of Soviet Russia? "Because we will not trade with the Russian government, because we do not like their form of government." Did the senators like the form of government in Colombia any better? "What is it, by the way? 'Despotism tempered by assassination.' " [5]

Watson early constituted himself chief defender of the Soviet Government, and continued to be an outspoken proponent of recognition. The stinging rebuffs that Secretaries Hughes and Hoover administered the Communist government moved him to indignation, and senators who professed to be horrified at Red atrocities met with his ridicule. He roundly denounced Ameri-

[4] *Ibid.*, April 12, 1921, p. 162.
[5] *Ibid*, April 15, 1921, p. 313.

477

can intervention in Siberia, and the blockade, and joined with Borah in an attack upon Boris Bakmeteff, the Kerensky government's ambassador, whom the United States continued to recognize. "Where is the consistency," he asked, "of staying in a state of war, or at least of nonintercourse, with a great nation which has always been our friend and at the same time handing out food to them as objects of charity? We first destroy their commerce and then try to replace it by gifts, by doles of food." We had no more right to dictate Russia's form of government than we had to dictate Germany's. Non-recognition was more "Wilsonism," and the Republicans seemed to him "residuary legatees of the political will of Woodrow Wilson." He pounced upon one unfortunate member who ventured a historical analogy with the French Revolution and lectured him at length on that event, asserting that the Russians went to no greater extremes than did the French. Yet President Washington, himself a revolutionist, Watson reminded them, "not only recognized the French republic, whose garments dripped with blood, but he put up to Congress in a respectful way an application for a loan." He quoted a speech of Webster's advocating recognition of the revolutionary government of Greece. "Let us not affect too much saintliness," he admonished. "Are our skirts entirely clear of wrong doing in Hawaii, the Philippines, and in Santo Domingo?" [6] In a different connection, but in the same trend, he said: "We are hereditary revolutionists. We are so from instinct, history, and tradition. We are so by sentiment." Whence, then, all this outcry against revolutionists? [7]

On other questions of foreign policy Watson outdid Senator Lodge in his opposition to anything that remotely smacked of the League of Nations, which, he said, was as much like the Holy Alliance of the nineteenth century "as two black cats are

[6] *Ibid.*, Sept. 29, 1921, p. 5580; *ibid.*, 67 Cong., 2 Sess., May 15, 1922, p. 6949; *ibid.*, May 23, 1922, pp. 7460-7462; *vide* also, *Columbia Sentinel*, June 26, 1922.

[7] *Cong. Record*, 67 Cong., 1 Sess., April 15, 1921, p. 313.

like one another." His most conspicuous fight was waged against the ratification of the Four-Power Treaty upon insular affairs in the Pacific. He denounced it as in reality an alliance with the dominant imperialistic powers, designed to promote imperialism, and to draw the United States into the web of foreign rivalries, if not into the League itself. He chided Lodge for "clothing his thoughts in the classic verbiage of Woodrow Wilson." "Break the heart of the world! Will it break the heart of Germany if we do not go into this alliance with France?" Or the heart of Russia by not entering an alliance with Japan? He thought President Harding "childlike and bland" in his advocacy of the treaty as a harbinger of "a millennium of brotherly love." [8]

A considerable portion of the Senator's time was devoted to relieving his pent-up feelings. This exercise was doubtless of great cathartic value to his emotional life, and a source of diversion to spectators, but it resulted in little substantial accomplishment and much waste of time. He spoke frequently and eloquently on behalf of the soldier's bonus, directing his remarks against the American Legion. He finally refused, however, to vote for the bill unless it could be "stripped of any feature which imposes additional taxation [!]" He championed the cause of Truman Newberry, in the Michigan contested election case, apparently because he disliked Ford's "Wilsonism." But after speaking frequently along that line, he did not take sides when the question came to a vote. The police powers for federal enforcement of prohibition, demanded by the Anti-Saloon League, drew from him fulminations against both prohibition and the unconstitutional infringement of personal liberties and rights, as well as against federal policing of states. Other subjects upon which he took occasion to relieve his feelings included the United States Steel Corporation, the American Legion, Pennsyl-

[8] *Ibid*, 67 Cong. 2 Sess., Feb. 23, 1922, pp. 2940-2942; *vide* also *ibid.*, March 8-15, 1922, pp. 3561, 3852, 3786, 4180-4186.

vania coal mine operators, and all tariff duties of any description or amount.[9]

Any question involving an encroachment of militarism found Watson bristling with hostility—just as it always had. He battled against proposals of increase in naval and military appropriation, and against an attempt to increase the standing army. He admitted that "possibly two or three of our admirals ought to have ships in which to sail around," but that was enough. A standing army of 25,000 men he thought sufficient. He attacked the proponents of an increased army as savagely as he had in 1892. Which among the nations did they fear? he asked, naming them, and rejecting each as an absurd suggestion. "Whom, then, do you fear?" he asked:

You are afraid of your own proletariat. That is what you are afraid of. You are afraid of the dissatisfied workman, thrown out of employment by these soulless, these heartless, these insatiable trusts and combinations of capital; you are afraid of the millions of men and women and children who do not have enough to eat in this land of bounteous harvests; not enough to wear in the very cotton fields where their hands bring forth the staple that clothes the world.

I wonder if they think that a hundred million people will meekly starve while such men as Mellon, and Hoover, and Elbert Gary, and J. P. Morgan lord it over the earth? The American people will not submit. Therefore, these vast combinations of capital want a standing army in order to beat down the dissatisfied, who have a right to be discontented.[10]

In the course of his attack on the "officer castes," which he said was "building up in this country . . . a militarism just like that of the Kaiser and his staff," Watson alluded to the charges of cruel treatment of privates during the War, which he had made in the previous campaign in Georgia. Warming to his subject, he

[9] *Ibid.*, July 8, 1921, p. 3417, on the American Legion; *ibid.*, 67 Cong., 2 Sess., June 28, 1922, pp. 9545-9546, on the tariff generally; *ibid*, Sept. 15, 1922, p. 12668, on coal mine operators.

[10] *Ibid.*, May 25, 1922, p. 7623.

said that "private soldiers were frequently shot by their officers because of some complaint against officers' insolence," and he had a picture of gallows on which men were hanged "day after day, without court martial or any other form of trial." Senator Borah interrupted to say that he had received such a picture, but had been unable to substantiate the charges. Senator Wadsworth of New York demanded that Watson appear before the Committee on Military Affairs to prove his charges. Flaring up excitedly at the challenge, Watson answered:

I am not going to be bottled up in any committee room and have the evidence entombed in some report that nobody will read. When I get through . . . what I say to the Senator from New York will be read by millions of people of this country; the newspapers will have to carry it, because it will be good reading matter. I assure you it will. It will be good copy. You need not doubt that.[11]

The whole incident of the brutality charges recalls the investigation of his charges of drunkenness on the floor of the House in 1892. The same belligerence and exaggeration characterized his conduct in both episodes. His language and bearing as he made the charges were said to have "involved the proprieties of the Senate." "The dignity of the Senate was aspersed at the same time that the honor of the army was called into question," said the New York *Times*. Since he refused to appear before the Committee on Military Affairs, a special committee, headed by Senator Brandegee, was appointed to investigate his charges. Watson was correct in his prediction that the accusations would create a sensation in the press. Letters poured in to him from ex-soldiers promising to substantiate his charges, and he read them into the *Record*.[12] Hearings before the special committee, dragging out over three months, were a disappointment to Watson. Witnesses modified or retracted statements made by letter when they appeared to testify, and little convincing evi-

[11] *Ibid.*, 67 Cong., 1 Sess., Oct. 31–Nov. 5, 1921, pp. 7021, 7069, 7172.
[12] *Cong. Record*, 67 Cong., 1 Sess., Nov. 1, 1921, p. 7070; Nov. 7, pp. 7464-7471.

dence was produced. Watson's temper grew shorter and more violent. Without his knowledge, Mrs. Lytle went to Vice-President Coolidge and asked that the investigation be stopped.[13] In spite of the demand in the press that the conclusions of the committee be announced, no report was made until after Watson's death, and more than a year after the hearings. It was found that the charges were not sustained by the testimony.[14]

The "Watson Temperament" became a problem of increasing difficulty as the months passed. Though sixty-six years of age, and physically perhaps the smallest man in the Senate, he was easily conceded to be the most belligerent member of that body. Within a period of six months he was known to have challenged three men to physical combat or threatened them with assault and battery. One of these was Senator Phipps of Colorado, eight years his junior, who incurred his displeasure by going over his head to make inquiries concerning Georgia post office appointments to which Watson had objected. Another was a young and vigorous major of the United States Army, who crossed the Senator's path in the investigation of the charges of brutality on the part of army officers. In an editorial headed "More Watson Temperament," the New York *Times* suggested that if the Senator from Georgia continued to "run amuck among the proprieties and threaten his colleagues with personal violence, something will have to be done about it." [15] A third such case arose out of his attack upon Secretary of Commerce Herbert Hoover.

Watson plainly disliked the Cabinet appointments of President Harding, and resented the President's personal appearance before the Senate to request their confirmation. It was not in him, however, to undertake such patient and painstaking investigation as Senator Thomas J. Walsh of Montana used to expose the oil scandals in the Harding Cabinet. Instead, he launched a series of attacks against members of the Cabinet, based upon

13 Interview with Mrs. A. L. Lytle, Aug. 8, 1934.
14 New York *Times*, Sept. 26, 1922.
15 Editorial, *ibid* , June 2, 1922.

whatever evidence came to hand. There was "Morgan's partner," Andrew Mellon, "richer perhaps than Rockefeller, holding his office in violation of one of the first laws ever passed by the first Congress of this Republic." He attacked Attorney-General Daugherty for defending the millionaire Morse, and men guilty of frauds against the government during the War. Secretary Fall, he said, was "oiled over with Standard Oil in Mexico and in Colorado, reeking and dripping with Standard Oil scandals . . ." [16]

Secretary Hoover came in for the major share of his attention. "Who is Hoover, anyway?" asked Watson several times, calling him an "Englishman." "What was the secret influence which suddenly put him at the head of things in this country. Who sent him here? Who appointed him? What credentials did he bear?" he asked. The only specific charge he brought against the Secretary was that he had never published any "accounts or vouchers" regarding the hundreds of millions of dollars spent under his direction by the American Relief Administration. [17] This charge called forth a letter of denial from Hoover citing certain reports published by the Relief Administration. The letter was read on the floor by Senator Lenroot of Wisconsin, who had previously crossed swords with Watson on the charges against army officers. Watson was on his feet immediately, breathing defiance:

This is about the third time that the insolent junior Senator from Wisconsin . . . has risen and personally attacked the junior Senator from Georgia.

On one occasion that Senator in his arrogance demanded that the junior Senator from Georgia be compelled by the Senate to answer elsewhere than on this floor to what he had said here in this chamber. I defied him then. I defy him now. I defy him on the floor of the Senate and I defy him outside. I am not in the least afraid of him

[16] *Cong. Record,* 67 Cong., 2 Sess., May 25, 1922; p. 7622; May 31, p. 7913-7914.
[17] *Ibid.,* May 31, 1922, p. 7913.

483

here or elsewhere, and the sooner the arrogant Senator learns that the better it will be for him and for me.[18]

Presiding officer Coolidge called him to order for "using words derogatory to another Senator."

On receiving from Senator Lenroot copies of the reports of the American Relief Administration Watson promised that if he were wrong he would admit it. Several days later, however, he renewed the attack. Referring to statements from the White House defending Hoover, he asked if the Secretary was above criticism. Hoover's published reports did not satisfy him, and he had several pages of one report printed in the *Record* to support his contention that there was indication of wanton squandering of huge sums of money. On top of this he charged that Hoover was an "active member" in the intrigue that equipped Kolchak and Youdenitch with arms and supplies to overthrow the Soviet government in Russia, and that he had converted part of the children's relief fund to this purpose. "How will the great American public feel when they realize that Herbert Hoover was trying to restore in Russia a system in which a few grand dukes and vast landed estate owners were ruling the peasants and grinding the faces of the poor?" he exclaimed.[19] What evidence he possessed for these sensational charges does not appear. No official notice was taken of them by the Administration.

*   *   *   *   *   *

The triumph of 1920 that was hailed by his followers as his long-belated vindication had somehow failed to measure up to that description. Regardless of what he said to the contrary, one feels that Watson himself did not really share the conviction of his followers about his "vindication." In the first flush of victory,

[18] New York *Times*, June 1 and 2, 1922.
[19] *Cong. Record*, 67 Cong., 2 Sess., June 6, 1922, p. 8251; New York *Times*, June 7, 1922.

perhaps, yes, but after that the old pattern took up where it had left off. Replete with the paradoxes of his nature, this brief interlude seemed but a recapitulation—an ironic epilogue, added for no better purpose, apparently, than to assure an ending on the true theme. There were times in Washington, to be sure, when he seemed more at harmony with himself than usual. At picnics with his two granddaughters in Rock Creek Park, or after long walks there by himself, or again while rummaging in the book shops in the city. "On such occasions he was actually a dear," recalled one of the granddaughters. More characteristic of those months, however, were spells of black melancholy and morbid drinking. What victory, after all, would someone say, could "vindicate" the implacable insolence of Fortune?

The summer of 1922 was a particularly hard one on Watson's health. Suffering from the heat and tortured by chronic attacks of asthma, he and his household left the hotel life of the city for a residence in Chevy Chase, Maryland. He was taken ill and remained in such a condition as to require the constant attendance of a nurse for eight weeks. While convalescing he insisted, much against his doctor's advice, on going daily to his office and attending all sessions. On the morning of September 17 he suffered a painful attack of asthma accompanied by severe struggles for breath. After examining him, his doctor insisted that he remain in bed for a week. September 22, however, was the last day of the session, and he was determined to be on hand at the adjournment.[20] He requested that several letters he had received from the striking miners around Brownsville, Pennsylvania, where hundreds of families of workers had been evicted from their homes, be printed in the *Record*. That request and his remarks on the evicted miners closed the Second Session of the Sixty-seventh Congress.[21]

Plans had been made to leave Chevy Chase for Hickory Hill

[20] Mrs. Lytle (who was with him at his death) in the *Columbia Sentinel*, Oct. 2, 1922.

[21] *Cong. Record*, 67 Cong., 2 Sess., Sept. 22, 1922, p. 13141.

on the twenty-sixth. Mrs. Watson had returned home six weeks before. On the night of the twenty-fifth he suffered a hard attack of bronchitis and asthma. "It's my finish," he said at the beginning of the attack. "I am not afraid of death." He repeated the last sentence once. After a cerebral hemorrhage he died the next morning at two-forty.[22]

"A strange and vivid public character, that already seems almost legendary or fabulous," remarked the New York *Times*. Writers of obituaries, with the last years of his career fresh in mind, uniformly expressed puzzlement upon reviewing his earlier career, and were frankly baffled when they attempted an estimate of his life. It is likely that Tom Watson would have cherished above many tributes that of a man he had admired since the 'nineties. Eugene Debs, recently released from the penitentiary, wrote in a letter to Mrs. Watson: "He was a great man, a heroic soul who fought the power of evil his whole life long in the interest of the common people, and they loved and honored him." [23]

Between seven and ten thousand people were said to have attended the funeral services at Hickory Hill. They were mainly the sort of people who had thronged the little town to hear him speak on his birthday, or rallied at his call during one of his crusades. Most conspicuous among the floral tributes was a cross of roses eight feet high, sent by the Ku Klux Klan. A white-haired farmer on a street corner swore he would not part with the copy of the *Columbia Sentinel* he held in his hand for fifty dollars. "It's Tom Watson's last word," he said.

In backwoods Georgia it is still possible, on occasion, to hear a mournful country ballad called "The Thomas E. Watson Song." It tells in endless numbers of "a man of mighty power," and of "how he fought and struggled," and, in the end, failed.

[22] Interview with Dr. Grant S. Barnhart, Watson's physician in his last illness.
[23] Eugene V. Debs to Mrs Thomas E. Watson, Sept. 26, 1922.

Bibliography

COLLECTIONS OF PRIVATE PAPERS AND MANUSCRIPTS

The Watson Papers in the Library of the University of North Carolina at Chapel Hill constitute the largest and most valuable source of biographical materials. These papers are merely deposited with the Library, and, though catalogued, they are as yet available only by permission of the family. Ranging from childhood diaries of the late 'sixties to letters written shortly before Watson's death, the collection includes personal business records, check stubs, lawyer's case books, tenant rolls, memorandum- and note-books, personal journals, manuscripts of speeches, business and personal letters to and from Watson, and some twenty scrapbooks of various sizes, as well as miscellaneous pamphlets, handbills, and campaign literature. The scrapbooks contain material only to 1897, but are valuable for the study of the background, origins, and history of Populism up to that date. Few of the clippings, unfortunately, are dated. There are several serious deficiencies in the collection. Watson did not keep copies of his own letters until the last three years of his life. There are wide gaps in the correspondence addressed to him, notably in that of the 'nineties, when little except letters of a business nature was preserved, and in that of the period from 1910 to 1920. The correspondence from 1900 to 1910 and from 1920 through September, 1922, is especially full and valuable.

Miss Georgia D. Watson, Thomson, Georgia, possesses a collection of the Watson family letters, including letters from Thomas E. Watson to his wife, and also letters to him from Roosevelt, Debs, and others. A diary that Watson kept in 1878 is an important item in this collection. Mr. Walter J. Brown, of Washington, D. C., grandson-in-law of Thomas E. Watson, has in his possession a number of family letters, the letters of Watson to his granddaughters being the most valuable of the collection. Judge Uly O. Thompson, of Miami, Florida, purchased the bulk of Watson's private library, some seven thousand items, which the author has

487

examined. The Georgia Department of Archives and History has on file a small collection of letters from Watson to Robert L. Rodgers, written during the last decade of his life.

The large and carefully preserved scrapbooks of Governor William J. Northen, in the possession of Miss Annie Bell Northen of Atlanta (recently deceased), contain clippings from a variety of agricultural journals and state newspapers, generally identified but usually undated. MS. letters from Henry W. Grady, J. C. C. Black, and President Cleveland are among the items included. Giving detailed information on agricultural societies of the 'eighties, the politics of the Alliance, and particularly on the campaigns of 1890, 1892, and 1894, these scrapbooks proved to be of incalculable value.

A trunk full of unsorted letters and papers of Governor Joseph M. Brown remains in the possession of his son, Charles M. Brown, of Marietta, Georgia. Though it contains but a few letters from Watson himself, there are a number of letters from his business manager and political associates that give a fairly complete picture of the relations between Brown and Watson during 1908 and following years. A large amount of campaign literature written by Brown and others is contained in the collection.

The files of Herbert J. Haas & Company on the Leo M. Frank case, in the possession of Rabbi David Marx, Atlanta, contain letters from Frank as well as hundreds of letters written by the committees and lawyers working in his defense, together with samples of anti-Semitic literature published during the period. This firm defended Frank, and was careful to collect all material pertaining to the case. The papers of Rabbi David Marx, of Atlanta, who took a leading part in the work of the defense committees, are deposited with this collection.

The letters of Watson among the Theodore Roosevelt Manuscripts in the Library of Congress were made available through the kindness of Professor Howard K. Beale and the permission of Mr. Thomas P. Martin.

NEWSPAPERS AND JOURNALS

Of Georgia papers, undoubtedly the most useful throughout the whole period, 1880–1922, were the Atlanta *Constitution* and the Atlanta *Journal*. The former led in the movement for industrialization, and both were usually mouthpieces for rival factions of the Democratic party. The Augusta *Chronicle*, generally conservative, furnishes a more local view of Watson's district, as does the Augusta *Herald*. The Macon *Telegraph* was a consistent spokesman for the industrialist and the capitalist investor. The Atlanta *News*, later the Atlanta *Georgian*, edited by John Temple Graves over a long period, was among the most friendly toward Watson. Occasional use was made of the Savannah *Press* and the Columbus *Daily Times*. Of the Populist papers and journals, the more valuable were the *National Economist*, published at Washington (incomplete files at the Library of Congress); the *Progressive Farmer*, published at Raleigh, and edited for a time by Col. L. L. Polk. Others used were the *Southern Alliance Farmer*, *The Wool Hat*, and *The Revolution*, though only scattered copies were found. Watson's newspapers are listed below. Especially useful during the periods indexed were the New York *Times* and the New York *Tribune*. Also useful for such events as conventions covered by them were the St. Louis *Globe-Democrat* and the Illinois *State Register*. The New York *World* and the Hearst papers, especially the New York *American*, were exceptionally hospitable to Watson's articles and interested in his movements.

WRITINGS AND PUBLICATIONS OF THOMAS E. WATSON

(No attempt has been made to collect all the numerous pamphlets and booklets, on such subjects as anti-Catholicism, that Watson reprinted from his *Magazine*, since that material is more readily available now in the files of the periodical.)

Bethany: A Story of the Old South. New York: D. Appleton & Co., 1904.
    A novel reviewed in the text.
Foreign Missions Exposed. Atlanta: Press of the Jeffersonians, 1910. 2d
    ed. A polemic.
History of Southern Oratory, T. E. W. editor. *South in the Building of*
    the Nation, volume IX. Richmond, Va., 1909. Watson also contrib-
    uted a sketch of oratory in the colonial period, and included one of
    his orations in the collection.
"Jerome Montomar, or In the Days of Napoleon," *The Sunny South* (At-
    lanta), Nov. 18, 1876. A youthful venture in short story writing.
The Life and Speeches of Thomas E. Watson. Nashville, Tenn., 1908.
    A campaign autobiography and collection.
The Life and Times of Andrew Jackson. Thomson, Ga.: Press of the Jef-
    fersonian Publishing Co., 1912. Reviewed in the text.
The Life and Times of Thomas Jefferson. New York: D. Appleton & Co.,
    1903. Reviewed in the text.
Napoleon: A Sketch of His Life, Character, Struggles, and Achievements.
    New York, London: Macmillan Co., 1902. Reviewed in the text.
"The Negro Question in the South," *Arena*, Vol. VI (Oct., 1892), pp.
    540-550. A discussion of the problem of racial coöperation among
    farmers.

"The People's Party Appeal," *Independent*, Vol. LVIII (Oct. 13, 1904), p. 829.

People's Party Campaign Book, 1892. Not a Revolt; It is a Revolution. Washington: National Watchman Publishing Co., 1892. Campaign tract.

Political and Economic Handbook. Atlanta: Telegram Publishing Co., 1908. Party histories and personal beliefs.

Prose Miscellanies. Thomson, Ga.: Jeffersonian Publishing Co., 1917. A collection of literary and personal essays and sketches.

The Railroad Question. Atlanta: Our Publishing Co., 1894. A pamphlet advocating government ownership of railroads.

Sketches: Biographical, Historical, Literary. Thomson, Ga.: Jeffersonian Publishing Co., 1912. A collection of essays.

Sketches from Roman History. Atlanta: the Author, 1908. Rome from the agrarian point of view.

Speech Against the Conscription Act . . . at Thomson, Ga., June 27, 1917. Thomson, Ga.: Jeffersonian Publishing Co., 1917.

The Story of France; from the Earliest Times to the Consulate of Napoleon Bonaparte. New York: Macmillan Co., 1899. 2 vols. Reviewed in the text.

A Tariff Primer. Thomson, Ga.: Jeffersonian Publishing Co., 1911.

Thomas Jefferson. (*The Beacon Biographies of Eminent Americans.*) New York: Small, Maynard & Co., 1900.

Waterloo. New York and Washington: The Neale Publishing Co., 1908. 2d ed., 1910.

Mr. Watson's Editorials on the War Issues. Thomson, Ga.: Jeffersonian Publishing Co., 1917.

What Are Your Constitutional Rights? Thomson, Ga.: Jeffersonian Publishing Co., 1917.

"Why I Am Still A Populist," *Review of Reviews*, Vol. XXXVIII (Sept., 1908), pp. 303-305.

"Why the People's Party Should Elect the Next President," *Arena*, Vol. VI (July, 1892), pp. 201-204.

NEWSPAPERS AND PERIODICALS EDITED BY WATSON

The *People's Party Paper*, founded on October 1, 1891, in Atlanta, was published until 1898. The *Daily Press*, also published in Atlanta, was founded in July, 1894, but was discontinued in less than a year. *Tom Watson's Magazine* was founded in New York in March, 1905; its name was changed to *Watson's Magazine* with the issue of March, 1906, and the magazine was discontinued shortly after Watson resigned the editorship in

October, 1906. He then founded *Watson's Jeffersonian Magazine* in Atlanta in January, 1907, which became *Watson's Magazine* in March, 1912. The *Weekly Jeffersonian* was founded in October, 1906. Both publications were discontinued when the mails were closed to them in August, 1917. *The Guard* was also banned when founded during the War. The *Columbia Sentinel*, his last paper, continued from shortly after the War until after Watson's death.

AUTOBIOGRAPHIES, MEMOIRS, REMINISCENCES, AND PUBLISHED CORRESPONDENCE

BALL, WILLIAM W., *The State That Forgot; South Carolina's Surrender to Democracy.* Indianapolis, 1932. A skeptical review of Tillmanism by a salty Tory.

BRYAN, WILLIAM JENNINGS, *The First Battle.* Chicago, 1897. The Populist alliance of 1896 is merely mentioned.

FELTON, REBECCA LATIMER, *Country Life in Georgia in the Days of My Youth.* Atlanta, 1919.

——, *Memoirs of Georgia Politics.* Atlanta, 1911. A rich source on the Independent movement, but partisan and rambling.

GARLAND, HAMLIN, *A Son of the Middle Border.* New York, 1917. Recollections of Western life during Populist days.

GORDON, GENERAL JOHN B., *Reminiscences of the Civil War.* New York, 1903. An insight into the General's romantic mind.

HARRIS, NATHANIEL EDWIN, *Autobiography; the Story of an Old Man's Life, with Reminiscences of Seventy-five Years.* Macon, 1925. One of the most remarkable books ever written: an autobiography that tells the truth—transparently. It is extremely valuable, for the author knew Watson from his youth until his death.

KNIGHT, LUCIAN LAMAR, *Reminiscences of Famous Georgians*, Atlanta, 1907. 2 vols.

LA FOLLETTE, ROBERT M., *Autobiography.* Madison, Wisconsin, 1913.

LODGE, HENRY CABOT, *Selections from the Correspondence of Theodore Roosevelt and Henry Cabot Lodge, 1884–1918* . . . New York, 1925. It contains several references to Watson.

MANNING, JOSEPH C., *The Fadeout of Populism.* New York, 1928. The reminiscences of an Alabama Populist.

MILLER, STEPHEN F., *Bench and Bar of Georgia.* Philadelphia, 1858. 2 vols.

PHILLIPS, ULRICH B., "Correspondence of Robert Toombs, Alexander H. Stephens, Howell Cobb," *Annual Report of the American Historical Association*, 1911. Washington, 1913.

ROOSEVELT, THEODORE, *Autobiography*. New York, 1913. It contains a tribute to Watson.

STAHL, JOHN M., *Growing with the West; the Story of a Busy, Quiet Life*. Toronto, 1930. The autobiography of an agitator for rural free delivery.

BIOGRAPHIES AND BIOGRAPHICAL ARTICLES

ALLEN, EMORY A., *Life and Public Services of James Baird Weaver*. Cincinnati, 1892. A campaign tract.

BAKER, RAY S., *Woodrow Wilson; Life and Letters*. New York, 1927–1935. 5 vols. The best biography.

BARNES, JAMES A., *John G. Carlisle, Financial Statesman*. New York, 1931. Scholarly work.

BREWTON, WILLIAM W., *The Life of Thomas E. Watson*. Atlanta, 1926. A vindication by a follower.

BROWNE, WALDO RALPH, *Altgeld of Illinois: A Record of His Life and Work*. New York, 1924. A sympathetic portrait.

CROLY, HERBERT D., *Marcus Alonzo Hanna: His Life and Work*. New York, 1912. Thorough and competent.

FIELDER, HERBERT, *Life and Times of Joseph E. Brown*. Springfield, Mass., 1883. A defense, valuable chiefly for speeches quoted.

HARRIS, JOEL CHANDLER, *Henry W. Grady: His Life, Writings and Speeches*. New York, 1890. A labor of love, sketchy and faulty.

HARRIS, JULIA COLLIER, *Joel Chandler Harris*. Boston, 1918. The best biography.

———, *Joel Chandler Harris, Editor and Essayist; Miscellaneous Literary Political and Social Writings*. Chapel Hill, N. C., 1931.

HAYNES, FRED E., *James Baird Weaver*. Iowa City, Iowa, 1919. A political biography.

HENDRICK, B. J., *Life and Letters of Walter Hines Page*. New York, 1924 and 1927. 2 vols.

———, *The Training of an American*. New York, 1928. The early years of Walter Hines Page's life.

HICKS, JOHN D., "The Political Career of Ignatius Donnelly," *Mississippi Valley Historical Review*, Vol. VIII (June–Sept., 1928), pp. 80-132. The work of an authority.

HILL, BENJAMIN H., JR., *Senator Benjamin H. Hill: His Life, Writings and Speeches*. Atlanta, 1893. Valuable for speeches quoted.

JOHNSTON, RICHARD M. and W. H. BROWN, *Life of Alexander H. Stephens*. Philadelphia, 1878. Incomplete and unsatisfactory.

KNIGHT, LUCIAN LAMAR, *A Standard History of Georgia and Georgians.* Chicago, 1917. 6 vols. Chiefly biographical, though the first two volumes contain the most complete history of the state during the Watson period yet written.

LLOYD, CARO, *Henry Demarest Lloyd.* New York, 1912. 2 vols. It contains valuable letters of Lloyd's during Populist battles.

McELROY, ROBERT McNUTT, *Grover Cleveland, the Man and the Statesman; an Authorized Biography.* New York, 1923.

NEVINS, ALLAN, *Grover Cleveland: A Study in Courage.* New York, 1932. The best biography.

PEARCE, HAYWOOD J., *Benjamin H. Hill, Secession and Reconstruction.* Chicago, 1928. A valuable study of the politics of the period.

PENDLETON, LOUIS, *Alexander H. Stephens.* Philadelphia, 1907.

PHILLIPS, ULRICH B., *Life of Robert Toombs.* New York, 1913. Scholarly political analysis.

PRINGLE, HENRY F., *Theodore Roosevelt: A Biography.* New York, 1931. The best book on the subject.

ROBINSON, WILLIAM A., *Thomas B. Reed: Parliamentarian.* New York, 1930.

SHAW, ALBERT, "William V. Allen: Populist," *Review of Reviews,* Vol. X (July, 1894), pp. 30-42. A sympathetic study.

SNYDER, CARL, "Marion Butler," *Review of Reviews,* Vol. XIV (Oct., 1896), pp. 429-433. Chiefly on Butler's part in the St. Louis Convention.

STOVALL, PLEASANT A., *Life of Robert Toombs.* New York, 1892.

WADE, JOHN DONALD, *Augustus Baldwin Longstreet, A Study of the Development of Culture in the South.* New York, 1924. An excellent work.

———, "Jefferson: New Style," *American Mercury,* Vol. XVIII (Nov., 1929), pp. 293-301. An appraisal of Watson by a latter-day agrarian.

WERNER, M. R., *Bryan.* New York, 1929.

WILLIAMS, WAYNE C., *William Jennings Bryan.* New York, 1936. This is the most complete study yet made, but it lacks detachment.

CONTROVERSIAL AND POLITICAL WRITINGS OF CONTEMPORARIES

ALEXANDER, HENRY A., *Some Facts About the Murder Notes in the Frank Case.* Undated pamphlet, c. 1915.

ALLEN, WILLIAM V., "The Populist Program," *Independent,* Vol. LII (Feb. 22, 1900), pp. 475-576.

———, "A Western Statesman's Reasons for Supporting Hon. Thomas E. Watson," *Arena,* Vol. XXXII (Oct., 1904), p. 395.

ATKINSON, EDWARD, *The Future Situs of the Principle Iron Production of the World.* Baltimore, 1890. The author was a Northern proponent of Southern industrialization.

AVERY, ISAAC W., *History of Georgia, 1850–1881.* New York, 1881. Biased in favor of Brown, but valuable.

BENSON, BENY, *Five Arguments in the Frank Case.* Augusta, c. 1915.

BLAND, T. A., *People's Party Shot and Shell.* Chicago, 1892. A campaign pamphlet.

BUTLER, MARION, "The People's Party," *Forum,* Vol. XXVIII (Feb., 1900), pp. 658-662. The author was chairman of the party's national committee at the time.

CONNOLLY, CHRISTOPHER P., *The Truth About the Frank Case.* New York, 1915. A convincing indictment of the processes of justice in the case.

COWLAN, GEORGE B., *The Undeveloped South.* Louisville, Ky., 1887. A pamphlet in behalf of industrial exploitation.

DE LEON, DANIEL, *Ultramontanism, The Roman Catholic Political Machine in Action.* New York, 1928. A Marxian view of the Church in politics.

———, *Watson on the Gridiron, Bourgeois Theories Dissected and Hung Up to Dry.* New York, 1926. A critical bombardment of Watson's articles on Socialism collected from the *Weekly People.*

DIGGS, MRS. ANNIE L., "The Farmers' Alliance and Some of its Leaders," *Arena,* Vol. V (April, 1892), pp. 590-604.

———, "The Women in the Alliance Movement," *Arena,* Vol. VI (July, 1892), pp. 161-179.

DORSEY, HUGH M., *The Argument of Hugh M. Dorsey at the Trial of Leo M. Frank.* Macon, Ga., 1914.

EDMONDS, RICHARD H., *The South's Redemption.* Baltimore, 1890. An optimistic view of industrialization of the South.

GARLAND, HAMLIN, "The Alliance Wedge in Congress," *Arena,* Vol. V (March, 1892), pp. 447-457. Sympathetic sketches.

GRADY, HENRY WOODFIN, *The New South, and Other Addresses.* New York, 1904.

Hand Book and History of the National Farmers' Alliance and Industrial Union. Washington, D. C., 1893. A popular work for the World's Fair.

HILLYARD, M. B., *The New South.* Baltimore, 1887. Published by the Manufacturers' Record Company, this book presents the industrialist's cause along with much statistical information.

HOWARD, WILLIAM H., *The American Plutocracy*. New York, 1895. A polemic by an Alabama Populist.

HUTCHINGS, JAMES KEY, *The Sage of Hickory Hill, A Story of Thomas E. Watson*. No date. In blank verse.

JONES, COL. CHARLES C., and GENERAL JOHN B. GORDON, *The Old South: Addresses before the Confederate Survivors Association* . . . Augusta, 1887.

KELLEY, WILLIAM D., *The Old South and the New*. New York, 1888. The South in terms of potential profits.

LLOYD, HENRY DEMAREST, *Wealth Against Commonwealth*. New York, 1894. A powerful indictment of corporate wealth.

McCLURE, A. K., *The South; Industrial, Financial, Political*. Philadelphia, 1886.

McKISSICK, E. P., *A Story of Spartan Push. The Greatest Manufacturing Center in the South*. Charleston, c. 1890.

MORGAN, W. SCOTT, *History of the Wheel and Alliance, and the Impending Revolution*. Fort Scott, Kan., 1891. The official history of the Southern Alliance.

NEWTON, J. C. C., *The New South and the Methodist Episcopal Church South*. Baltimore, 1887. The Church's attempt to readjust itself.

NORWOOD, THOMAS M., *Plutocracy, or American White Slavery, a Politico-Social Novel*. New York, 1888. A diatribe by a leader of the Independents in Georgia.

PEFFER, WILLIAM A., "The Mission of the Populist Party," *North American Review*, Vol. CLVII (Dec., 1893), pp. 665-678.

————, "The Passing of the People's Party," *North American Review*, Vol. CLXVI (Jan., 1898), pp. 12-23. He admits that the party is done for.

People's Party Campaign Hand Book, 1898. Issued by the Kansas State Central Committee. Hiawatha, Kan., 1898. 3d ed.

POLK, LEONIDAS L., "The Farmer's Discontent," *North American Review*, Vol. CLIII (July, 1891), pp. 5-12.

POST, CHARLES C., *Congressman Swanson*. Chicago, 1891. This is a political propaganda novel with a Populist hero, written by Watson's associate on the *People's Party Paper*.

————, *Driven from Sea to Sea, or Just a Campin'*. Chicago, 1884. This novel pictures the Western farmer's struggle against the railroads. It was widely read.

————, *Metaphysical Essays*. Boston, 1895. Populist theology.

————, "The Sub-Treasury Plan," *Arena*, Vol. V (Feb., 1892), pp. 342-353. A defense.

PUBLIC MAN OF GEORGIA, A, "Why Frank Was Lynched," *Forum*, Vol. LVI (Nov., 1916), pp. 677-693. The author apologizes for the State's disgrace, lauds Governor Slaton, and severely condemns Watson.

Review of Reviews, see for caricatures of Watson, Vol. XIV (Sept.–Nov., 1896), pp. 282, 287, 295, 297, 411, 415, 417, 418.

South Carolina in 1884 . . . A Brilliant Showing. Charleston, 1884. Advertising industrial progress and opportunity.

STREETER, JOHN J., *Populist National Organization United States of America: Populist Rules and Articles of Agreement*. Vineland, N. J., 1907. Proposing a reorganization of the party.

"TATTLER," "Thomas E. Watson; Knight Errant," *Nation*, Vol. CIII (Nov. 9, 1916), pp. 440-441. A satirical review of his career.

THOMPSON, W. E., *A Short Review of the Frank Case*. Atlanta, 1914.

TILLETT, W. F., "The White Man of the New South," *Century Magazine*, Vol. XXXIII (March, 1887), pp. 769-776. The South may also have millionaires.

TOURGEE, A. W., "Shall White Minorities Rule?" *Forum*, Vol. VII (April, 1889), pp. 143-155.

TRACY, FRANK B., "Menacing Socialism in the Western States," *Forum*, Vol. XV (May, 1893), pp. 332-342. An early Red scare.

————, "Rise and Doom of the Populist Party," *Forum*, Vol. XVI (Oct., 1893), pp. 240-250.

TRAIN, ARTHUR, "Did Leo Frank Get Justice," *Everybody's Magazine*, March, 1915.

TRAMMELL, WILLIAM DUGAS, *Ça Ira, A Novel*. New York, 1874. An autobiographical novel of a quixotic Georgian who sheds blood on the barricades for the Paris Commune, returns home to organize the Ku Klux Klan, then joins the crusade for industrialization.

WASHBURN, GEORGE F., "A Boston Business-Man's View of Roosevelt, Parker and Watson, and the Ideals they Represent," *Arena*, Vol. XXXII (Oct., 1904), pp. 396-397. In support of Watson.

WATTERSON, HENRY, "The Solid South," *North American Review*, Vol. CXXVIII (Jan., 1879), p. 47.

WEAVER, JAMES BAIRD, *A Call to Action, An Interpretation of the Great Uprising, its Sources and Cause*. Des Moines, Iowa, 1892. A campaign tract.

WISE, STEPHEN S., "The Case of Leo Frank, A Last Appeal," *Free Synagogue Pulpit*, Vol. III (May, 1915), No. 5.

ARNETT, ALEX MATHEWS, *The Populist Movement in Georgia.* New York, 1922. An excellent pioneer study.

BANKS, ENOCH M., *The Economics of Land Tenure in Georgia.* New York, 1905.

BECKER, CARL, "Kansas," in *Essays in American History Dedicated to Frederick Jackson Turner.* New York, 1910.

BROOKS, ROBERT P., *The Agrarian Revolution in Georgia, 1865–1912.* Madison, Wisconsin, 1914. A competent study of changing land tenure.

BUCK, SOLON J., *The Granger Movement: A Study of Agricultural Organization and its Political, Economic, and Social Manifestations, 1870–1880.* Cambridge, Mass., 1913.

CAFFEY, F. G., "Suffrage Limitations at the South," *Political Science Quarterly,* Vol. XX (March, 1905), pp. 53-67.

CLARK, JOHN B., *Populism in Alabama.* Auburn, Ala., 1927.

CLARKE, GEORGE HERBERT, "Georgia and the Chaingang," *Outlook,* Vol. LXXXII (Jan. 13, 1906), p. 73.

"Coming of Industry to the South," *Annals of the American Academy,* Vol. CLIII (Jan., 1931).

Dial, Review of Thomas E. Watson's *Story of France,* Vol. XXVIII (Feb., 1916), pp. 116-117.

GRADY, HENRY W., "Cotton and Its Kingdom," *Harper's New Monthly Magazine,* Vol. LXIII (Oct., 1881), pp. 719-734.

FARMER, HALLIE, "The Economic Background of Frontier Populism," *Mississippi Historical Review,* Vol. X (March, 1924), pp. 406-427.

"First Presidential Candidate in the Field," *Current Literature,* Vol. XIVL (May, 1908), pp. 492-494.

FLOWER, B. C., Review of Thomas E. Watson's *Life and Times of Thomas Jefferson, Arena,* Vol. XXXI (March, 1904), pp. 325-329.

HAMMOND, MATTHEW B., *The Cotton Industry: An Essay in American Economic History.* Ithaca, New York, 1897. The standard work.

HAYES, ARTHUR GARFIELD, *Trial by Prejudice.* New York, 1933. It contains a chapter on the Frank case.

HAYNES, FRED E., *Third Party Movements Since the Civil War, with Special Reference to Iowa.* Iowa City, 1916.

HICKS, JOHN D., "The Birth of the Populist Party," *Minnesota History,* Vol. IX (Sept., 1928), pp. 219-247.

———, *The Populist Revolt.* Minneapolis, Minn., 1931. The most comprehensive work on the field.

497

————, "The Sub-Treasury: A Forgotten Plan for the Relief of Agriculture," *Mississippi Valley Historical Review*, Vol. XV (Dec., 1928), pp. 355-373.

HOLMES, GEORGE K., "The Peons of the South," *Annals of the American Academy of Political and Social Science*, Vol. IV (Sept., 1893), pp. 265-274.

Independent, "The Election in Georgia," Vol. LXI (Aug. 30, 1906), p. 526.

————, "Georgia's Example to the Nation," Vol. LXIV (Jan. 16, 1908), p. 162.

————, Review of Thomas E. Watson's *Story of France*, Vol. LII (Oct. 18, 1900), pp. 2517-2518.

KENDRICK, BENJAMIN B., "Agrarian Discontent in the South: 1880–1900," *Annual Report of the American Historical Association*, 1920, pp. 267-272. Washington, 1925. A provocative and stimulating essay.

LEWINSON, PAUL, *Race, Class, and Party: A History of Negro Suffrage and White Politics in the South*. London, New York, 1932.

Literary Digest, "Senator Watson's Serious Charges," Vol. LXXXI (Nov. 26, 1921), p. 16. Cruelty of officers during the War.

LLOYD, HENRY DEMAREST, "The Populists at St. Louis," *Review of Reviews*, Vol. XIV (Sept., 1896), pp. 293-303. Lloyd participated in the convention.

McKELWAY, A. J., "State Prohibition in Georgia and the South," *Outlook*, Vol. LXXXVI (Aug. 31, 1907), p. 947.

————, "The Convict Lease System in Georgia," *Outlook*, Vol. XC (Sept. 12, 1908), pp. 67-72.

————, "Suffrage in Georgia," *Outlook*, Vol. LXXXVII (Sept. 14, 1907), pp. 63-66.

McVEY, FRANK L., *The Populist Movement*. New York, 1896. Strongly prejudiced.

MALIN, JAMES C., "Notes on the Literature of Populism," *Kansas Historical Quarterly*, Vol. I (Feb., 1932), pp. 160-164.

MARTIN, ROSCOE C., *The People's Party in Texas*. (The University of Texas Bulletin No. 3308.) Austin, 1933. A political scientist's view.

MITCHELL, BROADUS, *The Rise of the Cotton Mills in the South*. Baltimore, 1921.

MOORE, FREDERICK W., "The Condition of the Southern Farmer," *Yale Review*, Vol. III (May, 1894), pp. 56-67.

Nation, "Georgia Disfranchisement," Vol. LXXXV (Aug. 8, 1907), p. 113.

————, Review of Thomas E. Watson's *Bethany*, Vol. LXXIX (Dec. 22, 1904), p. 506.

————, Review of Thomas E. Watson's *Napoleon*, Vol. LXXIV (June 19, 1902), p. 490.

NIXON, HERMAN C., "The Cleavage within the Farmers' Alliance Movement," *Mississippi Valley Historical Review*, Vol. XV (June, 1928), pp. 22-33. The South versus the Midwest.

OTKEN, CHARLES H., *The Ills of the South*. New York, 1894. This is an objective analysis of economic evils with no attention to politics.

Outlook, "Government by Commission in Georgia," Vol. LXXXVII (Sept. 7, 1907), p. 2.

————, "The End of the Convict Lease System in Georgia," Vol. XC (Oct. 3, 1908), p. 238.

————, "Georgia's Convict Lease Law," Vol. XC (Oct., 1908), p. 295.

————, "Passing of Tom Watson," Vol. CXXXII (Oct. 11, 1922), pp. 228-229.

————, Review of Thomas E. Watson's *Napoleon*, Vol. LXXI (June 26, 1902), p. 794.

QUICK, HERBERT, "Hoke Smith and the Revolution in Georgia," *The Reader*, Vol. X (Aug., 1907), pp. 241-248.

REGIER, C. C., *The Era of the Muckrakers*. Chapel Hill, N. C., 1932.

ROBISON, DANIEL MERRITT, *Bob Taylor and the Agrarian Revolt in Tennessee*. Chapel Hill, N. C., 1935. A competent study of a milder brand of Populism.

RUTHERFORD, MILDRED, *The South in History and Literature*. Atlanta, 1906.

SCHMECKABIER, L. F., "Taxation in Georgia," Johns Hopkins University *Studies*, Vol. XVIII (Jan.–April, 1900), p. 217 *et seq.*

SCHUMAN, FREDERICK LEWIS, *American Policy Toward Russia Since 1917*. New York, 1928.

SHELDON, WILLIAM DuBOSE, *Populism in the Old Dominion*. Princeton, 1935. A sectional variation on the theme.

SIMKINS, FRANCIS B., *The Tillman Movement in South Carolina*. Durham, 1926. A good study of Populism from within the Democratic party.

SKAGGS, W. H., *The Southern Oligarchy*. New York, 1924. An arraignment of political corruption in the South.

STEPHENSON, GILBERT THOMAS, *Race Discrimination in American Law*. New York, 1910.

STEWART, ERNEST D., "The Populist Party in Indiana," *Indiana Magazine of History*, Vol. XIV (Dec., 1918), pp. 332-367; Vol. XV (March, 1919), pp. 53-74.

SWEENEY, C. P., "Bigotry in the South; Anti-Catholic Prejudice," *Nation*, Vol. CXI (Nov. 24, 1920), p. 585.

THOMPSON, C. MILDRED, *Reconstruction in Georgia, Economic, Social, Political, 1865–1872*. New York, 1915. A study by one of the Dunning school.

THOMPSON, J. HOLLAND, *From the Cotton Fields to the Cotton Mills: A Study of the Industrial Transition in North Carolina*. New York, 1906.

WADE, JOHN D., "Old Wine in New Bottles," *Virginia Quarterly Review*, Vol. XI (April, 1935), pp. 239-252. A study of agrarian recalcitrance from the Civil War to the great depression.

WELLMAN, WALTER, "Thomas E. Watson—Populist Candidate," *Review of Reviews*, Vol. XXX (Oct., 1904), pp. 419-423.

WILLIAMS, MICHAEL, *The Shadow of the Pope*. New York, 1932. An historical survey of anti-Catholicism in America.

UNPUBLISHED MONOGRAPHS

BOELL, JESSE E., "William Jennings Bryan Before 1896." Master's thesis, University of Nebraska, 1929. A little light on his early traffickings with the Populists.

BUSH, CHARLES C., "The Green Corn Rebellion." Master's thesis, University of Oklahoma, 1932. A study of draft resistance in Oklahoma.

COLLINS, JAMES F., "Thomas E. Watson: A Study of the New South." Master's thesis, New York University, 1936. Based upon limited materials.

COOPER, FLEETA, "The Triumvirate of Colquitt, Gordon, and Brown." Master's thesis, Emory University, 1931.

GRAY, SARA LOIS, "Thomas E. Watson: Leader of Georgia Populism." Master's thesis, Emory University, 1933. This work makes extensive use of state newspapers. It ends with the election of 1908.

McCOMMONS, MRS. W C., and MISS CLARA STOVALL, "History of McDuffie County, Georgia." Bound MS. in the Georgia Department of Archives and History.

RAINEY, GLENN W., "The Atlanta Race Riot of 1906." Master's thesis, Emory University, 1929. Competent work.

REDDICK, JAMIE LAWSON, "The Negro and the Populist Movement in Georgia," Master's thesis, Atlanta University, 1937.

SMITH, FLORENCE, "The Populist Movement and its Influence in North Carolina." Ph.D. dissertation, University of Chicago, 1928.

A more extensive bibliography on this subject, including secondary works of a more general nature and a list of public records and documents may be found in the Library of the University of North Carolina under the title, "The Political and Literary Career of Thomas E. Watson," a bound manuscript by this author. Two items of peculiar interest should be mentioned—"Thomas E. Watson" and "Mary Phagan," Columbia phonograph recordings of two rural ballads.

Index

Abbott, John S. C., 24, 340.
Addams, Jane, 436.
Agrarianism, ante- and post-bellum varieties, 69; versus New Departure, 82; three schools of, 124-125; and Populists, 217-219; frustration of, 330-331; of Watson, 347-351, 353-354, 402-404, 408; growth of tenancy fatal to, 404; Watson's defense of against Socialism, 406.
Agriculture, condition in South, 129-134; Watson on, 159, 208; depression of, in Georgia, 224; Northen on, in 1893, 254-255; condition of, between 1900 and 1910, 403-404.
Allen, T. S., 361-362.
Allen, William V., 297, 300-301, 315, 316, 357-358.
Alston, Robert, 107.
Altgeld, J. P., 317.
American Bimetallic League, 280, 286-287.
American Federation of Catholic Societies, 424.
American Legion, 471-473, 479.
American Plutocracy, The, Howard, 299.
American Protestant Association, 419.
Année terrible, 259.

Anti-Saloon League, 479.
Atkinson, W. Y., 254, 268.
Atlanta, "Chicago of the South," 86; as capital of New South, 116; W. D. Kelley on, 116; receives Jay Gould, 179; race riot of 1906 in, 378-379.
Augusta, Watson's boyhood in, 32; factories of, 85; "Lowell of the South," 123; election frauds in, 241-242, 269-371; "ring" of, 386.

Baker, Ray Stannard, 366.
Baker, William, 193.
Bakmeteff, Boris, 478.
Bankhead, J. H., 427.
Barnes, George T., 148-149, 156-161, 177, 232, 286.
Barrett, E. W., 199-200.
Bartram, William, 10.
Bateman, L. C., 317.
Beard, Charles A., 218.
Beecher, Henry Ward, 347, 353.
Bellamy, Edward, 139, 259, 395, 302.
Belmont, August, 255.
Benton, Thomas H., 397.
Berger, Victor, 463.
Bethany: A Story of the Old South, Watson, 353-354.
Bissell, Wilson S., 246.

503

505

Davis, Jefferson, 3, 12, 58, 113, 120.
Davis, John, 193.
Debs, Eugene V., and the Pullman strike, 261-262; Lloyd and, 278; and the Populists in 1896, 295, 297; and Bryan, 302; in the election of 1904, 362; Watson on, 365; sentenced to penitentiary, 461; Watson defends, 463; writes tribute to Watson, 486.
De France, Charles Q., 365.
De Leon, Daniel, on Watson, 407-408.
Democratic party, after Reconstruction, 54; and the "New Departure," 54, 66; and the Solid South, 67; and the Farmers' Alliance, 169, 174; Watson ridicules, 208-209; and free silver, 210; persecutes Populists, 223, 237; coerces vote of tenants and laborers, 236, 237; fraudulent methods of, 240-242; and Cleveland, 248-250; impatience with Cleveland, 253-255; John T. Graves on, 267-268; uses terror and fraud against Watson, 268-271; split over silver, 285-290; Chicago Convention of, 292-293; counter-revolution in 1904, 355; Watson returns to, 408-409.
Depew, Chauncey, 367.
Donnelly, Ignatius, 139, 202, 293, 295, 300.
Dorsey, Hugh M., 436, 437, 448-449, 470-473.
Doyle, H. S., 239-240.
Dreiser, Theodore, 367.
Driven from Sea to Sea, Post, 182-183.
Dunne, Edward F., 364.
Durham, Dr. George W., 45-46.

Ellington, C. H., 180, 196, 201, 229, 233.

Emory College, 264.
Engels, Friedrich, 406.
Erasmus, 420.
Espionage Act, 454, 457, 468-469, 476.

Fall, Secretary Albert B., 483.
Farmers' Alliance, organization of, 135-136; Negroes and, 137; emotional character of, 137-138; St. Louis Convention of, 143-144; enters Georgia politics, 147; Watson expounds principles of, 157-159; victory of, in 1890, 161-162; Grady and, 164-165; Patrick Walsh on, 167-169; Ocala Convention of, 168-169; Cincinnati Convention, 174; Watson on platform of, 178; Livingston and, 180, 185; Indianapolis Convention of, 186-187; Watson wins, to Populism, 196-198, 203; and Farmers' Union, 402-403.
Farmers' Union, 402-403, 431.
Felder, Thomas B., 427.
Felton, William H., independent leader, 68-69; Hill's attack on, 91; on Watson and Livingston, 202-203.
Field, James G., 230.
Flower, Roswell, 260.
Folk, J. W., 373, 375.
Force Bill, 222-223, 253.
Ford, Henry, 479.
Foss, Eugene, 436.
Fox, Charles, 408.
Frank, Leo M., case of, 435-449. See also *Jews*.
Free silver, Watson on, 210; in election of 1892, 229; and the Democrats, 252-256; Lloyd denounces movement for, 278-279; true place of, in Populist doctrine, 279; in West, 279-280; Watson's views on, 281-283; Democratic

509

Railroads—*Continued*
180; Watson's *The Railroad
Question*, 260; Smith attacks,
373; Watson excoriates, 377-
378; Smith's regulation of, 385;
Joseph M. Brown and, 389-391.
Randolph, John, and Watson, 476.
Reconstruction, 15-16, 53, 65, 79.
Reed, H. W., 320.
Reed, James A., 467.
Reed, Thomas B., 198, 199, 214.
Republican party, identified with
Democrats, 92; Watson charged
with endorsing, 100; tariff pol-
icy of, 209; Populist fusion with,
288, 319, 326; platform of, in
1896, 292; as "residuary lega-
tee" of Wilson, 476.
Revolution, Watson on, 337-338,
341, 478.
Revolution, The, founded, 232.
Riley, James Whitcomb, 194.
Robespierre, 338.
Rockefeller, John D., 260, 349,
369, 397.
"Roman Catholic Hierarchy, The",
Watson, 419-420.
Romilly, Samuel, 408.
Roney, H. C., 48.
Roosevelt, Theodore, on Watson
and the Populists, 305-307; Watson on, 355, 359; in campaign of
1904, 360-363; invites Watson
to White House, 363-364; Watson on trust busting of, 368; mentioned, 378, 388; entertains
Watson, 396-397; Watson urges,
to run again, 397; mentioned,
399; Watson supports, in 1912,
430; and the Colombia Treaty,
477.
Rosser, Luther, 449.
Rural free delivery, Watson and,
244-246.
Ryan, Thomas F., 367.

Sage, Russell, 260.
Seabury, Samuel A., 360, 364, 367.
Seely, F. L., 414.
Sewall, Arthur, 296, 297-300, 308,
309-317, 318-326.
Shame of the Cities, Steffens, 366.
Sherman, John, 260.
Sherman Silver Purchase Act, 252,
262.
Sidney, Algernon, 408.
Silver, see *Free silver*.
Simpson, Jerry ("Sockless"), men-
tioned, 46; Watson on, 175;
mentioned, 177; at Indianapolis,
186; and Livingston, 191; nomi-
nates Watson for Speaker, 193;
Hamlin Garland on, 194; on
Watson, 214; mentioned, 228,
283; for Bryan, 293.
Sinclair, Upton, 380.
Skinner, Charles B., 422.
Slaton, John M., seeks Watson's support, 429; and the Frank case,
439-443, 446-447.
Smith, Hoke, in 1892, 229; on Silver Democrats, 253; Watson on,
265, 266; defends Cleveland,
284; sympathizes with Watson,
315; as reformer, 373; for
Negro disfranchisement, 374;
thanks Watson for support, 375;
victory of, in 1906, 378; mentioned, 382; acknowledges indebtedness to Watson, 383; accomplishments during administration of, 384-386; loses Watson's support, 387-389; and the
race of 1908, 390-394; defeats
Brown, 410-411; Watson's threats
against, 412-414; mentioned,
433; elected, 434; enters Presidential primary, 467; vote of,
469; race for the Senate, 470-
473.
Snead, Claiborne, 77, 98-99.

512

Socialism, compared with Populism, 219; Watson charged with, 236, 240; Hearst charged with, 356; and the 1904 election, 362; Populist defections to, 404-405; Watson's articles against, 405-408; Daniel De Leon on, 407-408; Watson defends representative of, 463.

"Socialists and Socialism", Watson, 405-408.

Son of the American Revolution, Neal, 14.

South, between Reconstruction and Populism, 52-54; under the business man's rule, 65-66; inspired by Grady's message, 115f.; deluded by new hopes, 117-119; apes industrial North, 122-123; rebel tradition of, 134-135; leads Farmers' Alliance, 144; Populists in, 217-219; Watson in defense of, 348-351; breaks with National Progressivism on race question, 380.

Soviet Russia, 464, 465, 477-478, 483-484.

Spanish-American War, Watson on, 334-335, 458.

Speer, Emory, 69, 456.

Spencer, Samuel, 368, 378-379.

Stahl, John M., 244-246.

Standard Oil Company, 360, 366, 367, 477, 483.

Stanford, Leland, 183.

Steed, Epenetus Alexis, 14, 20-21, 26.

Steffens, Lincoln, 360, 366.

Stephens, Alexander H., *War Between the States*, 24; Watson's love of, 39-40; mentioned, 53; fights "New Departure", 54; and the "Triumvirate", 65; as agrarian, 69; Watson visits, 77-78; joins New Departure, 92-95; reconciliation with Hill and

Brown, 93; administration of, 103f.; pardons murderer, 107; Watson on death of, 108; resemblance to Watson, 194, 307; mentioned, 461.

Stevens, Thaddeus, 53.

Stokes, James Graham Phelps, 364.

Story, Theodosia E., 22, 32.

Story of France, The, Watson, 335-339, 341, 419-420.

Subtreasury plan, opposed by Gordon, 162, and by Walsh, 168; Watson urges adoption, 204-205.

Sumner, Charles, 53.

Taft, William H., 398, 399, 427.

Taggart, Thomas, 427.

Talleyrand, 92.

Tammany Hall, 176, 355, 427.

Tarbell, Ida M., 366.

Tariff, Watson on, 122, 128, 208; Bryan on, 208; in 1892, 229; Watson on, 282, 480.

Taubeneck, H. E., 280, 283, 289, 292.

Teller, Henry M., 292.

Tenant farmers, among Watson's family, 42-43; Watson speaks in behalf of, 107-108; Watson on condition of, 131-132; and the Populist party, 217-219; at odds with leaders, 219; Watson appeals to both races of, 221; Democrat landowners coerce vote of, 236; Watson on increase of, 403-404; growth of, fatal to populist agrarianism, 404.

Terrell, Ben, 140.

Thomson, Georgia, early history of, 14-15.

Tibbles, Thomas H., 358, 361-362, 380.

Tillett, W. F., 117.

Tillman, Benjamin, visits Watson in 1896, 325; and the nomination of Parker, 355, 358; Watson de-

514

Watson, Thomas E.—*Continued*
105; entertained by Henry Grady, 105; attacks convict lease system, 105-107; proposes relief for tenants, 107-108; on Stephens' death, 108; antagonizes Negroes, 109; attacks railroads, 110-111; on property and aesthetics, 111; disgust and resignation, 112; and Grady's New South, 114f.; influenced by the New Departure, 119; opposes Gordon, 121; for Cleveland, 122; renounces Grady, 126-128;

on exploitation of farmers, 131-133; on "apathy" of the South, 134-135; calls for rebellion, 135; and the Alliance, 139-140; and the jute trust, 140-142; enters race for Congress, 146f.; defends McGregor, 150-153; altercation with Twiggs, 153-156; race for Congress, 156-161; opposes Patrick Calhoun, 163; applies "Ocala Yardstick", 169-170; on his consecration to his task, 171; quits law practice, 171; on corrupt law, 172; on labor and history, 173; on the third party question, 174-177; appeals to labor, 178; on Gould and railroads, 179; clashes with Livingston, 180-181, 185; founds *People's Party Paper*, 181-184; at Indianapolis, 185-187; comes out as Populist, 187-189;

in Congress, 190f.; altercation with Livingston, 191-192; candidate for Speaker, 193; Hamlin Garland on, 194; on Bryan, 195-196; wins Alliance to Populism, 196-198; feud with Crisp, 198-200; represented at St. Louis Convention, 200-202; introduces Alliance bills, 203-204; urges subtreasury bill, 204-205; on

Pinkerton Detective Agency, 205-207; supports eight-hour labor law, 207; on free silver, 210; publishes *Campaign Book*, 210; the "Where was I at?" incident, 211-215;

on the struggle of 1892, 216; on the complexity of Populist ranks, 217; as landowner, 218; on the Negro and Populism, 220-222; on the condition of labor, 224-225; on Democratic perplexities, 229; "news value" of, 230; returns to Georgia, 231; campaign for reëlection, 231f.; whips defamer on train, 233; howled down at Augusta and Atlanta, 234-235; on the state election results, 237; methods used against, 238-239; protects Negro from lynching, 239-240; and the fraudulent election, 241-242; on his defeat, 242-243;

initiates rural free delivery of mails, 244-246; urges labor laws, 247; returns home, 248; on Cleveland and his views, 248-249; launches off-year campaign of 1893, 251f.; Cleveland moves against, 253; Northen's letter to Cleveland on, 254-255; results of the crusade of 1893, 256; contests Black's election, 257-258;

radical influences on, 259f.; on Emma Goldman, 260; on Debs and the Pullman strike, 261-262; on Cleveland, 262; founds *Daily Press*, 263; called "dictator" of his party, 263; nominated for Congress, 264; on Democratic schism, 265-266; adopts conciliatory tone, 268; and the election of 1894, 268-271; agrees to special election, 272; disagrees on terms of election, 273-274; loses

516

Watson, Thomas E.—*Continued*
corresponds with Bryan, 396; Roosevelt entertains at White House, 396-397; urges Roosevelt to run, 398; writes Hearst, 398; nominated Presidential candidate, 398-399; as White Supremacy candidate, 399-401; transformations in political creed of, 401-402; and the increase of tenancy, 403; growing wealth of, 403; attacks Socialism, 405-408; defends property, interest, and rent, 406; Daniel De Leon on, 407-408; takes stand for ideals of Old South, 408; returns to Democratic party, 408; and the "Golden Age", 409; effort to defeat Hardwick, 410-411; speech heckled in Atlanta, 411-412; threatens Smith, 412-414; Seely's hoax upon, 415;

on his superiority over Bryan, 416; founds press, 417; and Mrs. Lytle, 417-418; trend toward sensationalism in periodicals, 418; anti-Catholic crusade of, 418-425; profits and losses from crusade of, 425; helps organize Guardians of Liberty, 422-423; has "premonitions", 423; attempts to provoke fight with a Catholic, 423-424; Catholic reprisals against, 424; obscenity case of United States against, 424-425; campaign of, against Wilson in 1912, 426-430; dominates Georgia Democrats, 426-430; supports Roosevelt, 430;

the "following" of, 431; on Protestant foreign missions, 432; advocates flogging and lynching Negroes, 432-433; as a political boss, 433-434; in the election of 1914, 434; in the Leo Frank case, 434-449; suggests vigilante action, 439; defends Atlanta mobs, 441; and the Frank lynching, 444-445; "baffling nervous trouble" of, 444; urges revival of Ku Klux Klan, 446, and of "Gentile League", 446; and the Department of Justice, 447-448; uses Frank case to swing election of 1916, 448-449; and the Ku Klux Klan, 449-450;

on the World War, 452f.; on Wilson's administration, 451-452; urges neutrality, 452; urges intervention, 453; denounces War madness, 454; opposes conscription, 455-456; denounces militarism and War measures, 457; government suppresses papers of, 458; loses both children, 459; suffers mental collapse, 459; and the theme of frustration, 459-461; threatened with prison, 461; runs for Congress, 461-463;

attacks "'100 per cent' idiots", 464; and Wilson's foreign policy, 464; on Lenin, 464; denounces Palmer and Red-baiters, 465; defends civil liberties, 465-466; enters Presidential primary, 467; against League of Nations, 467-468; defends striking miners, 468; "amazing" vote of, 469; enters senatorial race, 470; attacks American Legion, 471-473; jailed at Buford, 472-473; elected to Senate, 473; *Nation* on victory of, 473-474; on victory of self, 474;

in the Senate, 475f.; compared with John Randolph, 476; demands release of political prisoners, 476; denounces Colombia treaty, 477; defends Soviet Russia, 477-478; on revolutionary tradition of the United States,

518